QUESTIONS DISPUTÉES D'ANCIEN TESTAMENT

Continuing Questions in Old Testament Method and Theology

BIBLIOTHECA EPHEMERIDUM THEOLOGICARUM LOVANIENSIUM

XXXIII

QUESTIONS DISPUTÉES D'ANCIEN TESTAMENT

MÉTHODE ET THÉOLOGIE

C. BREKELMANS

CONTINUING QUESTIONS
IN OLD TESTAMENT METHOD AND THEOLOGY

REVISED AND ENLARGED EDITION

BY

M. VERVENNE

J. BARR – P.A.H. DE BOER – P. BUIS – M. DAHOOD
L. DEQUEKER – E. KUTSCH – J. LÉVÊQUE – D.J. MCCARTHY
R. MARTIN-ACHARD – H.D. PREUSS – J.F.A. SAWYER

LEUVEN
UNIVERSITY PRESS

UITGEVERIJ PEETERS
LEUVEN

1989

CIP KONINKLIJKE BIBLIOTHEEK ALBERT I, BRUSSEL

ISBN 90 6186 332 5 (Leuven University Press)
D/1989/1869/35
ISBN (Uitgeverij Peeters)
D/1989/0602/55

Première édition 1974
Leuven University Press & Éditions J. Duculot
Leuven-Gembloux, 202 p.

Revised and Enlarged Edition 1989

Leuven University Press/Presses Universitaires de Louvain
Universitaire Pers Leuven
Krakenstraat 3, B–3000 Leuven-Louvain (Belgium)

AVANT-PROPOS

DE LA PREMIÈRE ÉDITION

La XXIIIe session des Journées Bibliques de Louvain (23-25 août 1972) était consacrée à des problèmes vétérotestamentaires. Environ 120 collègues ont participé à la session, dont je suis heureux de pouvoir présenter le texte des conférences et des séminaires. Le comité organisateur avait pensé qu'il pourrait être intéressant et utile d'inviter des collègues dont on connaît la diversité d'opinions sur quelques problèmes importants et actuels dans l'étude de l'Ancien Testament. Le résultat a été une confrontation des opinions de J. Barr et M. Dahood (méthode de philologie et critique textuelle), de E. Kutsch et D.J. McCarthy (l'Alliance dans l'Ancien Testament) et de H.D. Preuss et J. Lévêque (la place de la littérature sapientielle dans une théologie de l'Ancien Testament).

Le premier point a reçu un complément important dans la conférence de J.F.A. Sawyer. L'alliance a été, en fait, le centre des Journées: la confrontation de Kutsch et McCarthy s'accompagnait de deux autres conférences (de Boer, Martin-Achard) et de deux séminaires (Buis, Dequeker).

Puisque l'idée centrale de cette session était la confrontation des idées et la discussion qui en résultait, il aurait été très intéressant de publier non seulement le texte des conférences elles-mêmes mais aussi la discussion entre les deux conférenciers et l'auditoire présent. On comprendra, toutefois, qu'il est toujours très difficile de résumer une discussion vivante. Bien que ces discussions ont été l'âme de la session entière, le comité, avec beaucoup de regrets, a résolu de les omettre dans cette publication.

Il me reste de remercier tous les conférenciers qui ont accepté de venir à Louvain et qui m'ont envoyé le texte de leur conférence presque immédiatement après la fin de la session. Des circonstances imprévues ont néanmoins retardé un peu la publication. C'est ce que je regrette beaucoup.

1974 C. BREKELMANS

PREFACE TO THE SECOND EDITION

In 1972 Professor Chris Brekelmans invited scholars known to have different opinions on certain thorny problems in Old Testament studies to present their positions at the 23d session of the *Colloquium Biblicum Lovaniense*. The present book, which was well accepted, comprises the papers delivered on this occasion. They reflect the debates of that time on philological method and the Hebrew text, on the central theme of covenant and on the place of wisdom literature in the theology of the Old Testament. Since the first edition of these *Questions disputées* was out of print for many years, the Editiorial Board of the series *Bibliotheca Ephemeridum Theologicarum Lovaniensium* suggested the preparation of a revised and enlarged edition. As a matter of fact, the questions at that time turn out to be *Continuing Questions*. Today's exegetical discussions deal in a new way with biblical semantics, covenant terminology and themes, and biblical theology.

The text of the original publication is unchanged except for typographical errors. However, each contribution is supplemented with a note by the author, apart from three articles which are updated by myself. M. Dahood and D.J. McCarthy unfortunately have died, and P.A.H. de Boer could not collaborate for reasons of health.

The *Supplementary Notes* are included at the end of the book, pp. 203-222. Moreover, the present volume is supplied with a list of abbreviations, exhaustive indexes of authors and of texts, and select indexes of subjects and of words and phrases. In regard to the designation of the Ugaritic texts in the index, the *KTU* labeling is mentioned in addition to the system of reference, mostly *UT*, which was generally used not so long ago.

Leuven, 16 April 1989 Marc VERVENNE

TABLE OF CONTENTS

INDEXES

1

NORTHWEST SEMITIC TEXTS AND TEXTUAL CRITICISM OF THE HEBREW BIBLE

kî bahebel bā'
ûbaḥōšek yēlēk
ûbaḥōšek š^emô y^ekusseh

For it came from the void,
And into the darkness will it go,
And by the darkness will its name be covered (Eccles 6, 4).

In 1965 I had occasion to write : " The Ugaritic use of prepositions and particles alone sheds more light on the meaning of the text of the Old Testament than do all the Qumrân Scrolls. The simple fact that *b* and *l* both denote ' from ' in Ugaritic opens up untold possibilities for reaching the meaning of the biblical text. " [1] As was to be expected, this seemingly extravagant claim provoked a strong reaction on the part of several scholars. A. F. Rainey, for one, thinks that " Such highly subjective value judgements have no place in scholarly discussion, " [2] while J. C. Greenfield terms my claim " a totally uncalled-for remark, for we are dealing with two different types of text materials, important in two separate fields and *not* mutually exclusive. " [3] After seven years I would continue to stress home this claim because it dramatically demarcates the differences between the comparative and the traditional approaches to the study of the Hebrew text. The sharper translation and clearer understanding of hundreds of biblical verses, [4] thanks to the

1. *Ugaritic-Hebrew Philology* (Rome, 1965), 26.
2. *Ugarit-Forschungen* 3 (1971) 152.
3. *Journal of American Oriental Society* 89 (1969) 176.
4. See, for instance, J. A. Soggin, *Bibbia e Oriente* 9 (1967) 87-88, with bibliography ; J. Severino Croatto, « L'article hébreu et les particles emphatiques dans le sémitique de l'ouest », in *Archiv Orientální* 39 (1971) 389-400 ; Georg Schmuttermayr, " Ambivalenz und Aspektdifferenz : Bemerkungen zu den hebräischen Präpositionen *b*, *l* und *min*, " in *Biblische Zeitschrift*, NF 15 (1971) 29-51, with good bibliography.

application of the Ugaritic meanings and nuances of prepositions and particles, sufficiently rebut Rainey's charge that my judgment in the matter is highly subjective, and while I agree with Greenfield that Ugaritic and Qumran are important in two separate fields, we must also address ourselves to the question: "Which is more important for understanding the consonantal text of the Bible?" True scholarship demands distinctions and discrimination, obliges the constant re-evaluation of the relevance of different disciplines, in our case Ugaritic and Qumran, to the study of the biblical text. Unfortunately there are some centers of learning where neither Ugaritic nor Qumran seem to be considered important for arriving at the original sense of the text if one may judge from the reports of the courses given and the methods employed. Thus one reads in the *Annuaire 1970-1971*, Tome LXXVIII, of the *École Pratique des Hautes Études*, Ve Section, Sciences religieuses, p. 199, this description of *Introduction à l'exégèse biblique*: "Après quelques exposés traitant du texte et des versions de la Bible, qui ont permis de présenter les principaux instruments de travail, on a abordé des explications approfondies de passages difficiles et de genres variés, souvent proposés par un auditoire d'hébraïsants, et même de biblistes, avertis. Ont été expliqués: *Genèse 6/1-4, Psaume 141, Michée 1-2, Exode 3, Deutéronome 32*. Par chaque texte, on a examiné les versions, les commentaires rabbiniques, éventuellement les références qu'y font les midrashim et les Talmuds, et les divers problèmes posés à la critique moderne." No mention here of Ugaritic, indispensable, it would seem, for advancing understanding of all texts studied, save perhaps Exodus 3, and no mention of Qumran which preserves some instructive variants in Ps 141:5-10. One gathers from the above description that the accent in reality is upon the history of biblical exegesis, though the course is entitled. *Introduction à l'exégèse biblique*. The versions, the rabbinical commentaries, and the midrashim and the Talmuds, may tell us what subsequent centuries thought the biblical text meant, but we may no longer assume that that is what the original text meant to say. Ugaritic has upset that facile assumption, especially in its use of tenses, prepositions, and particles. Here I would quote the concluding paragraph of George Mendenhall's review of James Barr, *Comparative Philology and the Text of the Old Testament*: "Ideally, a solution to a difficulty in the text should be sought in uses and parallels which *antedate* the passage in question. The meaning of any word is a function of its uses in language in the past up to the point of usage in question. It is perfectly clear, then, that we have nothing but comparative material from other regions or languages when we must deal with the earliest poetry of the Pentateuch. The fact that the same root can be identified in various of the Semitic languages is all the proof we need for the fact that at some time-point in history the two traditions of language were actually in contact. Furthermore, it is just as much an aspect of the ' comparative ' method, if much later linguistic material is used for the elucidation of an earlier. The comparison across time is no more valid than a comparison across space (i.e., different dialect of West Semitic) particularly if in the latter case the phenomena being compared are contemporaneous. For the concern of religious specialists must be oriented primarily toward ' relevance ' in their own time, not what is still often regarded in religious circles today as an irrelevant or even impious curiosity about the realities of life in the past. The postbiblical interpretation of the Bible is a part of the history of the discipline, but the conclusions do not constitute evidence, any more than do fifth century patristic writings constitute historical evidence for the original intention or meaning of the New Testament writing of the first century. " [5] Earlier in Mendenhall's review we find concrete illustrations of the principles summarized in his conclusion. Thus he writes : " Though he [Barr] belabors mightily those who think Ugaritic and Akkadian might be useful in clearing up obscurities in Hebrew — which has been undeniably the case for the past generation — he nevertheless accepts solutions based upon Ethiopic, which is the most remote of all the Semitic languages both in time and place from biblical Hebrew. This is only one illustration of one of Barr's most important methodological principles : One must strain at gnats, and swallow camels. In other words, solutions of linguistic difficulties based upon evidence which comes from a time and place demonstrably closely related to a given biblical text (esp. Ugaritic) are extremely suspect, while solutions proposed by some rabbi a millennium and a half later in a social and historical context which had changed to an extent which is almost unimaginable in every way must be given preference. " [6]. Analogous to the method criticized by Mendenhall is the method pursued by R. Tournay, who in his writings constantly questions the relevance of Ugaritic because of the purported chronological gap between the Ras Shamra tablets and the Hebrew text. Thus he begins his review [7] of Nicholas J. Tromp, *Primitive Conceptions of Death and the Nether World in the Old Testament* (Rome, 1969), with the cautionary statements, « De telles comparaisons lexicographiques sont utiles et même nécessaires, pourvu qu'elles tiennent compte de l'écart chronologique qui sépare ces deux catégories de textes. Il est évident qu'un même mot a subi au cours des siècles une évolution sémantique différente en Phénicie et en Judée, comme aussi dans les autres secteurs du monde sémitique. En outre, les spécialistes d'Ugarit connaissent bien les lacunes de leur documentation et divergent beaucoup dans leurs interprétations. » He

5. *Interpretation* 25 (1971) 362.
6. *Ibid.*, 359.
7. In *Revue Biblique* 78 (1971) 292-294.

ends the review surmising : « On peut se demander si l'Égypte ne serait pas aussi indiquée qu'Ugarit (sans parler de la Mésopotamie) pour nous aider à mieux comprendre les expressions et les thèmes se rapportant en Israël à la mort et à l'au-delà. A propos de « Léviathan » (pp. 8, 62 et 164), il y a lieu de citer ici une petite incantation accadienne déchiffrée par J. van Dijk (*Or*, 38 (1969), pp. 540 ss.) « vert comme Tishpak (Dieu qui remplace Ninazu à Eshnunna), ses narines exhalent le souffle de la peste, sa bouche est une flamme, sa langue fendue est un éclair, son éclair... Le Tehom (?) « Mais, comme le suggère déjà J. van Dijk le dernier mot *li-a-wu-ti-a-am*, rappelle étrangement... Léviathan ! » and a footnote explains that Leviathan is a « Symbole très ancien de la puissance du mal, il est déjà représenté sur un cylindre de Tell Asmar (milieu du IIIe millénaire). » Having begun by putting us on our guard against the employment of the Ugaritic texts which date between 1375-1190 B.C. and are written in a dialect kindred to Biblical Hebrew, and having stressed the uncertainty of their interpretation, the Assyriologist Tournay bids us consider the relevance of an uncertain reading in Akkadian of the Ur III period and of a cylinder seal from Tell Asmar dating to circa 2500 B.C. for a better understanding of the biblical Leviathan.

While Professor Barr prefers Ethiopic, and Père Tournay favors Akkadian, J. A. Emerton of Cambridge chooses to delete the sacred text rather than admit the relevance of Ugaritic for Hebrew morphology. In 1963 I proposed [8] this translation of Prov 1,22 :

> *'ad mātay pᵉtāyîm tᵉ'ēhᵃbû petî*
> *wᵉlēṣîm lāṣôn ḥāmᵉdû lāhem*
> *ûkᵉsîlîm yiśnᵉ'û dā'at*
>
> How long will the simple love simplicity,
> And scoffers delight in scoffing,
> And fools hate knowledge ?

To uphold this version, *tᵉ'ēhᵃbû* was explained as third masculine plural with *t*- preformative, as in Ugaritic and El Amarna, and the sequence of *tᵉ'ēhᵃbû*, with *t*- preformative, and *yiśnᵉ'û*, with *y*- preformative, was compared to *UT*, 51 : V : 77-79, *tblk ǵrm mid ksp gb'm mḥmd ḫrṣ yblk udr ilqṣm*, " The mountains bring you much silver, the hills the choicest

8. *Proverbs and Northwest Semitic Philology* (Rome, 1963) 5-6.

9. " A Note on the Hebrew Text of Proverbs i.22-3, " in *Journal of Theological Studies* 19 (1968) 609-614. My proposal has, however, been accepted by A. Barucq, *Le livre des Proverbes* (Paris, 1964) 52, and by R. Lapointe, *Dialogues bibliques et dialectique interpersonnelle* (Montréal-Paris, 1971) 209, n. 11. Compare *Prov*, 6,20-22, and see P. D. Miller, Jr., in *Journal of Near Eastern Studies* 29 (1970) 129-130.

gold, the *udr* will bring you *ilṣqm*, " where the poet balances *tblk* with *yblk*. Emerton[9] rejects this analysis "not only because further evidence is desirable before a form attested centuries earlier is accepted in Proverbs but also because it would be very strange to find in the same verse two different forms of the third masculine plural of the imperfect, one with a preformative *taw* and the other with a preformative *yodh*. Second, the perfect *ḥāmᵉdû* is strange between two imperfects after *ʿad mātay*. "[10] Unwilling to admit the Northwest Semitic evidence, Emerton boxes himself into the corner of textual deletion, expelling from the text the second and third cola of the verse. But who can be comfortable with such a crude expedient ?

How may the Northwest Semitic method be described ? In his review of my *Psalms II*, F. I. Andersen describes it as follows[11] : "Dahood approaches the text as if an ancient hymnbook had been dug out of the foundations of Solomon's temple, applying to it the linguistic tools appropriate for the study of any newly discovered inscription. In Dahood's case more weight is given to evidence from Old Canaanite literature (mainly from Ugarit) than to any other data. He thus appears to ignore or slight later traditions about the text and its meaning seen in the LXX and in the vocalization of the MT. He has thus opened the way for a more systematic evaluation of the merits of these recensions. " Andersen's statement is basically correct and his observation about the attitude toward later traditions is properly nuanced by the verb "appears" [He thus appears to ignore]. Later traditions have often been examined and have usually been found wanting so far as the meaning of the original poetic text is concerned. The negative judgment passed on the ancient versions in my commentary on Psalms has found unhappy confirmation in the recently published *Le Targum de Job de la*

10. *Ibid.*, 610. First, Emerton fails to mention the presence of *tblk* and *yblk* in the same Ugaritic verse, and second he seems to be unaware of the Ugaritic-Hebrew stylistic practice of pairing *yqtl* and *qtl* verb forms ; for a list of such usages in the Psalter, see DAHOOD, *Psalms III* (Anchor Bible 17A ; Garden City, N.Y. 1970) 420-423. Emerton's failure to appreciate this usage may account for his comment on *Prov*, 3,20, *bᵉdaʿtô tᵉhômôt nibqāʿû ûšᵉḥāqîm yirʿᵃpû ṭal* : "Prov. iii 20a probably refers to the creation of channels for this water when it says that 'the depths were cleft open' since verse 19 shows that the writer has the original act of creation in mind. It is true that verse 20b describes a present truth : 'And the skies drop down the dew ; "but it is best understood of the lasting consequences of the original act" (*VTS* 15, Volume du Congrès Genève 1965 [Leiden, 1966] 122-123). Northwest Semitic philology enables us to dispense with such contorted and unconvincing exegesis ; following three *qtl* verbs, *yirʿᵃpû* is preferably rendered in the past tense : "The skies dropped down dew. " Instead of employing four *qtl* forms, the poet sought poetic variation by using the *yqtl* form, the normal verb for expressing past tense in Canaanite poetry.

11. *Journal of Biblical Literature* 88 (1969) 208.

Grotte XI de Qumrân [12]. Granting the exceptional importance of this discovery of the Targum of Job, dating perhaps to the first century B.C., for the four reasons listed by the editors (p. 8), one must sadly note that where the Hebrew text of Job is difficult for us, it was already difficult for the Aramaic translators of the first century B.C. Time and again they can be seen grappling with an incomprehensible text and producing an unconvincing version that will not lighten the burden of the modern translator of Job. For example, they reproduce the hapax legomenon phrase *kîdôdê 'ēš* in Job 41,11 by *lšny 'šh,* " tongues of fire ", where Ugaritic *kdd,* " child ", would suggest the translation " children of fire ", i.e., " sparks ", comparable to Job 5,7, *b^enê rešep,* " sparks ". [13] On the positive side, the Hebrew text it follows closely approaches that of the Massoretes, so that those who might tend to emend or transpose the *textus receptus* can find no substantive support in 11QTgJb. In other terms, we must elicit sense from the present consonantal text of Job and not expect much help from the versions or later traditions. [14] We must look for the help that the versions and later traditions cannot give in the Northwest Semitic texts of Ugarit and Phoenicia. Of course, this approach will create some tension, but this may prove healthy and stimulating. For instance, the early and vigorous opposition to the Phoenician third person singular suffix *-y* in Hebrew is now yielding to a gradual and widespread acceptance of the phenomenon in the Bible. In the past three years at least fourteen scholars have in print acknowledged the presence of this Phoenician suffix in Hebrew. [15] An example

12. Edited and translated by J. P. M. VAN DER PLOEG, O.P. and A. S. VAN DER WOUDE, with the collaboration of B. JONGELING (Leiden, Brill, 1971).

13. Cf. DAHOOD, *Mélanges E. Tisserant* (Vatican City, 1964) I, 91 ; *Biblica* 46 (1965) 327 ; C. H. GORDON, *Ugaritic Textbook,* Glossary, no. 1197 ; C. EPPING and J. T. NELIS, *Job : uit de grondtekst vertaald en uitgelegd* (De Boeken van het Oude Testament, VII. A ; Roermond, 1968) 19,179 ; W. L. HOLLADAY, *A Concise Hebrew and Aramaic Lexicon of the Old Testament* (Leiden, 1971) 156.

14. S. SEGERT concludes his article, " The Ugaritic Texts and the Textual Criticism of the Hebrew Bible, " in *Near Eastern Studies in Honor of William Foxwell Albright* (Ed. by Hans Goedicke ; Baltimore, 1971) 413-420, thus : ,, The pioneering efforts of William F. Albright and his followers demonstrate the soundness and fruitfulness of the new approach to the text of the Hebrew-Bible, using the data from Phoenician and especially Ugaritic material. The tensions between some results of the new approach and the traditional opinions are healthy and stimulating for further research along this line, which will require higher standards of learning and perceptivity, in order that it may become with every fresh attempt better documented and more creative " (p. 420). He also correctly observes that it is symptomatic of the situation in biblical studies that the present writer " attempts to go as far as possible away from the canonized tradition and criticizes the other translations, also based in principle on the Hebrew original, for paying too much attention to the traditional views expressed in the ancient versions " (p. 420).

15. To cite but three : C. VAN LEEUWEN in *Nederlands Theologisch Tijdschrift* 24

discussed some years ago [16] neatly illustrates how Ugaritic semantic usage may be combined with Phoenician morphology to elicit sense from an unexplained [17] vocable in Prov 28,23 :

môkîaḥ 'ādām	He who reproves a man
'aḥarēy (MT *'aḥaray*) *ḥēn yimṣā'*	will find with him more favor
mimmaḥalîq lāšôn	than one with a flattering tongue.

When repointed *'aḥarēy*, parsed as preposition plus Phoenician suffix *-y* and given the nuance witnessed in Ugaritic and in numerous biblical passages, [18] the verse yields a clear meaning beyond the reach of the traditional methods of Hebrew philology. The present example *'ḥry* precludes possible confusion of *y* and *w* because such an assumption must also assume *scriptio defectiva 'ḥrw* for normal *'ḥryw*.

Or again, consider Hos 11,1 :

kî na'ar yiśrā'ēl wā'ōhabēhû
ûmimmiṣrayim qārā'tî libnēy (MT *libnî*)

Traditionally rendered, " When Israel was a child, I loved him, and out of Egypt I called my son " (RSV), but when Northwest Semitic data are applied, the verse yields quite a different statement :

When Israel was a slave, I loved him,
and from Egypt I called his sons.

Ugaritic *n'r*, " child, slave " // *bn*, " son ", and the parsing of the final *-y* of *lbny* as the Phoenician suffix (LXX *tà tékna aútoû*) are the undergirding of this translation. On this new version Loren R. Fisher comments : " Here is a case where understanding via a literary parallel yields a means of access to both ' observable ' and ' actual ' facts. The *RSV* translation, ' When Israel was a child, I loved him, and out of Egypt I called my son ' obscures the ' observable ' facts of slavery and the deliverance of Israel's sons. Certainly the point about loving a slave and calling his sons is lost and hence the ' actual ' fact which the writer

(1969) 139 ; R. Lapointe, *Dialogues bibliques*, 163, n. 69 ; 285, n. 116 ; James L. Crenshaw, *Catholic Biblical Quarterly* 34 (1972) 49.

16. In *Biblica* 44 (1963) 293.

17. For a listing of some attempts to solve the enigma, consult William McKane, *Proverbs : A New Approach* (London, 1970) 631-632. On p. 256 McKane translates, " He who reproves a man *about his conduct* is more highly regarded than one who speaks smooth words. "

18. See the full study by Gregorio del Olmo Lete, « La preposición *'aḥar* / *'aḥarê* 'cum' en ugarítico y hebreo,» in *Claretianum* 10 (1970) 339-360.

is attributing to God or revealing about himself has no chance to surface." [19]

Thus the Northwest Semitic method is at a far remove from the traditional approach recently defended by William McKane who, in his attack on the comparative method, maintains that "Extraordinary solutions are unnecessary unless there are extraordinary problems in the Hebrew Bible, and no amount of philological expertise and virtuosity will compensate for a failure to understand this and to accept the discipline which it imposes." [20] But who decides what problems are ordinary and which are extraordinary? Who in the past two thousand years has ever considered Hos 11,1 an extraordinary problem? And yet it seems to benefit from the application of what in McKane's ambience must be considered an extraordinary solution. No, every single verse, above all the poetic texts, of the Hebrew Bible must be re-examined in the light of Northwest Semitic grammatical, lexical, and stylistic data. The traditional tools and textbooks, such as Gesenius-Kautzsch, Gesenius-Buhl, or Brockelmann's *Grundriss der vergleichenden Grammatik der semitischen Sprachen*, no longer suffice to solve the "ordinary" or "extraordinary" (a distinction I do not accept in this context) problems presented by the Hebrew text. But there is no need to insist on this point because comparative philological researches are steadily acquiring the proper orientation. The founding in the past three years of the journals *Ugarit-Forschungen* (1969), *Journal of Northwest Semitic Languages* (1971), and *Rivista di studi fenici* (1973), witnesses the growing importance and the increased availability of Northwest Semitic philology for biblical studies. In 1969, J. C. Greenfield [21] complained that "It is,

19. In *Ras Shamra Parallels : The Texts from Ugarit and the Hebrew* Bible (Ed. by Loren R. FISHER ; *Analecta Orientalia* 49, Rome, 1972) I, p. XX.

20. In his review of W. VAN DER WEIDEN, *Le livre des Proverbes : Notes philologiques*, in *Journal of Semitic Studies* 16 (1971) 222-236, esp. 236. McKane's negative attitude contrasts with G. R. Driver's warm endorsement of van der Weiden's study. In the *Book List of the Society for Old Testament Study* for 1971, Driver, p. 34, writes : "Many of the Ugaritic comparisons, however, are interesting and worthy of notice, as also are a number of fresh interpretations of various proverbs, some of which may well be considered in any future edition of the New English Bible (e.g. *Prov*, 7,21 ; 10,4 ; 12,27 ; 14,13 ; 16,33 ; 20,8 ; 22,8 ; 24,5 ; 25,20 ; 28,10 ; 31,29 ; 31,31). Several *obiter dicta* on obscure and difficult passage in the OT outside *Proverbs* also deserve consideration (e.g. *Jud.*, 9,9)."

21. In *Journal of American Oriental Society* 89 (1969) 174. Here Greenfield cites as an illustration my assumption that the Phoenician third person suffix *-y* is also found in Hebrew and refers to the article on this suffix in Phoenician by F. M. Cross and D. N. Freedman in *Journal of Near Eastern Studies* 10 (1951) 228-230. Greenfield stresses that the use of *-y* for "his" is not general but is to found either with nouns or verbs ending in long vowels or with singular nouns in the genitive case. It may be relevant to point out here that Prof. Freedman, an acknowledged authority on the *-y* suffix in Phoenician, fully accepts, after initial hesitation, the

rather, the virtual equation of Ugaritic, Phoenician, and Hebrew by Dahood that raises serious methodological questions. It is also the transference from one language to the other of what are, from the linguistic point of view, distinctive features of the individual languages or dialects that has brought forth opposition, " and he cited as one of his example the claim that the Phoenician third person masculine singular suffix *-y* is also found in Hebrew. But, as noted above, the opposition to the presence of this morpheme in Hebrew is gradually withering away.

On the contrary, it is the virtual equation of Ugaritic, Phoenician, and Hebrew that will give philologists a chance to reduce the thirty percent unintelligibility of, say Hosea or Job, to more modest proportions. So long as Hebraists continue to lump the Hebrew of Hosea and Job with the Hebrew of Deuteronomy, the possibilities of progress in understanding Hosea and Job remain dim. To cite Mendenhall again, " If it is true that the standard prose of biblical Hebrew derives from the Jerusalem dialect, as the general consensus holds, then it follows that the dominant language of the Hebrew Bible was not even an Israelite dialect originally, or at least it introduced considerable contrasts to an earlier linguistic situation. This may help us to understand our difficulties in dealing with the premonarchic poetry or the northern language of Hosea." [22] It seems to me, then, that we should stop producing Hebrew grammars and lexicons and undertake instead to write Northwest Semitic grammars and lexicons that will include the grammatical phenomena of Ugaritic, Phoenician, and Hebrew, and give the meaning of the words as they occur in these three Canaanite dialects.

Submitted to the method of virtually equating Ugaritic, Phoenician, and Hebrew, Job 3 reads and parses thus :

1. *ʼaḫ^{a}rê kēn pātaḥ ʼiyyôb ʼet pîhû*
   way^{e}qallēl ʼet yômô
2. *wayyaʻan ʼiyyôb wayyōʼmar*
3. *yōʼbad yôm ʼiwwāled bô*
   w^{e}hallaylāh ʼāmar hārōh (MT *hōrāh*) *gāber*
4. *hayyôm hahûʼ y^{e}hî ḥōšek*
   ʼal yidr^{e}šēhû ʼ^{e}lô^{a}h mimmāʻal
   w^{e}ʼal tôpaʻ ʻālāyw n^{e}hārāh
5. *yigʼālūhû ḥōšek w^{e}ṣalmāwet*
   tiškon ʻālāyw ʻ^{a}nānāh
   y^{e}baʻ^{a}tūhû kimrîrê yôm

presence of this *-y* suffix in Biblical Hebrew (in private correspondence carried on during the years when he edited my manuscripts on *Psalms* for the Anchor Bible.)

22. *Interpretation* 25 (1971) 360.

6. *hallaylāh hahû' yiqqāḥēhû 'ōpel*
'al yēḥad (MT *yiḥad*) *bîmê šānāh*
bemispar yerāḥîm 'al yābō'
7. *hinnēh hallaylāh hahû' yehî galmûd*
'al tābō' renānāh bô
8. *yiqqebūhû 'ōrerê yôm*
hā'atîdîm 'ōrēr liwyātān
9. *yeḥšekû kôkebê nišpô*
yeqaw le'ôr we'ayin
we'al yir'eh be'ap'appê šāḥar
10. *kî lō' sāgar daltê biṭnî*
wayyistār (MT *wayyastēr*) *'āmāl mē'ênāy*
11. *lammāh llō' meruḥam* (MT *mēreḥem*) *'āmût*
mibbeṭen yāṣā'tî we'egwā'
12. *maddûa' qiddemûnî birkāyim*
ūmah ššādayim kî 'înāq
13. *kî 'attāh šākabtî we'ešqôṭ*
yāšantî 'āz yānûaḥ lî
14. *'im melākîm weyō'aṣê 'āreṣ*
habbōnîm ḥorābôt lāmô
15. *'ô 'im śārîm zāhāb lāhem*
hamemale'îm bottêhem kāsep
16. *'ô kenēpel ṭāmûn lō' 'ehyeh*
ke'ōlelîm lō' rā'û 'ôr
17. *šām rešā'îm ḥādelû rōgez*
wešām yānûḥû yegî'ê kōaḥ
18. *yaḥad 'asîrîm ša'anānû*
lō' šāme'û qôl nōgēś
19. *qāṭōn wegādôl šām hû'*
we'ebed ḥopšî-mi 'adōnāyw (MT *ḥopšî mē'adōnāyw*)
20. *lammāh yuttan* (MT *yittēn*) *le'āmēl 'ôr*
weḥayyîm lemārê nāpeš
21. *hameḥakkîm lammāwet we'ênennû*
wayyaḥperūhûm maṭmônîm (MT *-hû mimmaṭmônîm*)
22. *haśśemēḥîm 'elê gîl*
yāśîśû kî yimṣe'û qāber
23. *legeber 'ašer darkô nistārāh*
wayyāsek 'elôah be'ōdô (MT *ba'adô*)
24. *kî lepānay* (MT *lipnê*) *laḥmî 'anḥātî tābō'*
wayyittekû kammayim ša'agōtāy
25. *kî paḥad pāḥadtî wayye'etāyēnî*
wa'ašer yāgōrtî yābō' lî
26. *lō' šālawtî welō' šāqaṭtî*
welō' nāḥtî wayyābō' rōgez

1. After this Job opened his mouth
and cursed his day.
2. Job answered and said :
3. " Perish the day I was born,
and the night that saw the conception of a man.
4. That day — let it be darkness ;
God above show no concern for it.
5. Darkness and gloom claim it,
a cloud settle upon it,
day's darkeners terrify it.
6. That night — gloom abduct it ;
let it not be seen amid the days of year,
into the number of months let it not enter.
7. Indeed that night — may it be sterile,
no joyful sound enter in.
8. Let the Sea-Cursers damn it,
those ready to stir Leviathan.
9. Its twilight stars be darkened ;
let it hope for light — but none,
let it not enjoy the pupils of the dawn,
10. because it did not shut the doors of her womb,
nor avert trouble from my eyes.
11. Why did I not die enwombed,
emerge from the belly and expire ?
12. Why did two knees receive me,
and why two breasts that I sucked ?
13. O that now I were lying down
and tranquilly asleep ;
then would I be at rest,
14. just like kings and counsellors of the earth,
who rebuilt ruins for themselves ;
15. or like princes who had gold,
who filled their houses with silver.
16. Or why wasn't I like a stillborn in the Crypt,
like foetuses that never saw the light ?
17. There the wicked cease agitation,
and there rest those wearied by wealth.
18. The Community of prisoners is at ease,
hears not the slave-driver's voice.
19. Small and great are there,
namely, slave, freedman, his master.
20. Why is light given to the tormented,
and life to the bitter of soul,

21. who yearn for Death that they be no more,
and who dig crypts for themselves ;
22. who rejoice at the arrival,
are happy when they reach the grave ;
23. to the man whose way is devious,
but whom God shields while he lives ?
24. When my bread is before me, sobbing comes upon me,
and my groans pour out like water.
25. When fear I feared, it overtook me,
and what I dreaded came upon me.
26. I have no ease and no quiet,
I rest not, and torment has arrived.

Philological and Exegetical Notes

1. *After this.* M. Pope, *Job* (Anchor Bible 15 ; Garden City, N.Y., 1965) 28, has correctly noted that in the Ugaritic texts *aḫr* similarly introduces the transition to a new episode ; e.g., *UT*, 51, III, 23 ; 2 Aqht, V, 25.

3. *The day I was born. yôm 'iwwāled bô* may be compared with *Ugaritica V*, Ch. III, text 8,24, *bym tld*, " on the day she bore " [parsing *tld* as hiphil, like Heb. *tôlîd*].

Hewing to the Canaanite poetic tradition, Job employs the imperfect form *'iwwāled* to express action in the past, and omits the pronoun as well. These grammatical observations, it may be remarked, make it difficult to endorse the common opinion that Job 3,3-10 is dependent on *Jer.* 20,14-18. For example, R. A. F. MacKenzie, *Jerome Biblical Commentary* (ed. R. Brown *et al.*) p. 512a, writes : " Verses 3,2ff. probably indicate that the author had read *Jer.* 20,14-18 ", and S. R. Driver-G. B. Gray, *Job* (ICC ; Edinburgh 1921), I, p. lxvii, contend : " It is scarcely less certain that in 3,3-10 the author of Job is dependent on *Jer.* 20,14-18, though Dillmann (p. xxxii f.) still strongly argued for the dependence of *Jer.* 20,14-18 on *Job* 3,3-10. " The corresponding passage in *Jer.* 20,14, *'ārûr hayyôm 'ašer yulladtî bô*, " Cursed the day on which I was born ", employs both the relative pronoun and the perfect form *yulladtî* to express past time. To maintain that Job is dependent on the expansionist text of Jeremiah strains credibility.

The night that saw. As in the first colon, the poet again omits the relative pronoun in *hallaylāh 'āmar*. Since *laylāh* is masculine, despite the apparently feminine ending, *'āmar* is the correct form. Compare vs. 16b, *ke'ōlelîm lō' rā'û 'ôr*, " like foetuses that never saw the light. " Ugaritic offers good instances of relative clauses without the relative pronoun in *UT*, 1 Aqht, 40-42, *'rpt tmṭr bqẓ ṭl yṭll lǵnbm*, " the clouds that rain upon the summer fruit, the dew that falls upon the grapes"; ʿnt, I, 13-15, *ks qdš ltphnh aṯt krpn ltʿn aṯrt*, "a holy cup that the woman never beheld, a beaker that Asherah never saw." One of the most disputed phrases in the chapter, the colon yields good sense when *'āmar* is taken in the Ugaritic sense "to see." Cf. also *Job* 22,29; 34,34 and 35,14. Since *'āmar*, "to see", is now widely accepted in Biblical Hebrew, a review of the evidence is here unnecessary; consult E. Ullendorff, *Ethiopia and the Bible* (Oxford, 1968) 127; E. Lipiński, *Revue Biblique* 75 (1968) 350, n. 23; W. L. Holladay, *Vetus Testamentum* 18 (1968) 485-486; M. Dahood, *Psalms* III, 60, 182-183, 297; G. del Olmo Lete, *Estudios Bíblicos* 30 (1971) 23. In a paper read at the Seventh Congress of the International Organization for the Study of the Old Testament held in Uppsala 8-12 August 1971, Rudolf Meyer of Jena stated that he would include *'āmar*, "to see", in his revision of Gesenius-Buhl *Handwörterbuch*, scheduled to appear in 1975. He cited Ps 71,10 as a convincing example of this Ugaritic nuance; see Dahood, *Psalms II*, 174, who notes that Ugaritic *amr*, "to see", permits us to dispense with de Lagarde's emendation, adopted by Gunkel, of MT *'āmᵉrû* to *'ārᵉbû*, "they lie in wait", in Ps 71,10.

Born ... conception. Parallelism with *'iwwāled* virtually rules out the LXX's understanding of *hrh* as *hᵃrēh*, *'idoù*. Cf. *UT*, 132,5, *hry wyld*; M. Held, *Eretz-Israel* 9 (1969) 78, n. 63; M. Dahood, "Ugaritic-Hebrew Parallel Pairs", in Loren R. Fisher, ed. *Ras Shamra Parallels: The Texts from Ugarit and the Hebrew Bible* (Analecta Orientalia 49; Rome, 1972), Ch. III, 170, pp. 173-174.

The conception of a man. Repointing MT *hōrāh* to infinitive absolute *hārōh* and comparing the construction *hārōh gāber* with Isa 59,4, *hārô 'āmāl*, "conceiving trouble." The recommendation of the BHK apparatus to read *zākār* for MT *gāber*, on the strength of LXX *'ársen* and *Jer.* 20,15, *zākār*, can be offset by citing *John* 16,21, "in her joy that a man *(ánthrōpos)* has been born into the world." Hence the widely-accepted translation "because a child has been born into the world," is interpretive, and the comment of R. E. Brown, *The Gospel According to John* (xiii-xxi) (Anchor Bible 29A; Garden City, N.Y., 1970) 722, that the expression is tautological, must be rejected.

4. *That day.* The biblical *casus pendens* construction has good antecedents in *UT*, 2 Aqht, VI, 35, *mt uḫryt mh yqḥ*, "Man—what will he receive as final destiny?" Cf. also *UT*, 52,39, *il aṯtm kypt*, "El—his two wives are indeed beautiful!" A. Caquot, in *Les religions du Proche-Orient asiatique* (ed. J. Chevalier; Paris, 1970) 456, construes the sentence similarly: "El! Comme les deux femmes sont belles!" The tenth-century Phoenician inscription of Aḥirom may furnish an instructive parallel in line 2: *wh' ymḥ sprh lpp šbl*, "And as for him — may his

inscription be rubbed out from beginning to end (compare *peh lāpeh*, 'from end to end') by a passerby (cf. *šebîl*, 'path')." Contrast the less plausible version by F. Rosenthal in J.B. Pritchard, *Ancient Near Eastern Texts* (3rd ed.; Princeton, 1969) 661, "and he himself wiped out! *Written by (before) ?...*"

5. *Day's darkeners.* Probably a poetic term for dark clouds, parallel to *ʿanānāh*, "a cloud." Accepting, with others, the derivation from *kmr*, "to be dark, swarthy", and comparing the formation *kimrîrê* with *sagrîr* and *ḥaklîl*, one may now cite Ugar. *amrr*, the name of a god who serves as a guide (*UT*, 51, IV, 17, *amrr kkbkb lpnm*, "Amrîr is like a star in front") and whose name would aptly stem from *amr*, "to see." Contrast Gordon, *UT*, Glossary, No. 233.

6. *Let it not be seen.* As proposed in *Gregorianum* 43 (1962) 62, and elsewhere, *yēḥad* is the Canaanite form of Jerusalemite *yēḥaz*. Cf. W. Baumgartner, *Hebräisches und aramäisches Lexikon zum Alten Testament*, 280, for citation of all texts where dialectal *ḥādāh* appears for classical *ḥāzāh*. See also J. Coppens in *VTS* IV (Volume du Congrès, Strasbourg 1956; Leiden, 1957) 99; F. F. Bruce *Journal of Semitic Studies* 5 (1960) 389; C. H. W. Brekelmans, *Ras Sjamra en het Oude Testament* (Nijmegen, 1962) 8; C. Epping-J. T. Nelis, *Job*, 20,42; A. C. M. Blommerde, *Northwest Semitic Grammar and Job* [hereafter *Job*] (Rome, 1969) 38. The parallelism between *ḥādāh*, "to see, gaze", and *bōʾ*, "to come, enter", recurs in Gen 49,6; see Dahood, *Biblica* 36 (1955) 229.

Year ... months. The parallelism between singular *šānāh*, "year", and plural *yerāḥîm*, "months", which parallelism is hapax legomenon in the Bible, has a close counterpart in *UT*, 2 Aqht, VI, 28-29, *ašsprk ʿm bʿl šnt ʿm bn il tspr yrḫm*, "I shall make you number years like Baal, like the sons of El you will number months." This rare sequence, found in Job and in Ugaritic, strengthens the identification of *yḥd* as Canaanite for *yḥz*, while the biblical juxtaposition *bemispar yerāḥîm*, "into the number of months", resembles Ugar. *tspr yrḫm*, "you will number months." Cf. also 2 Aqht, II, 43, [*ys*]*pr* [*y*]*r*[*ḫ*]*h*, "He numbers her months."

7. *Joyful sound.* The root of *renānāh* appears in the Ugaritic infinitive construct *brnk*, "when you shout for joy" (*UT*, 1001,5; compare *Job* 38,7, *beron*) and in the *yqtl* verb *arnn*, "I shall shout for joy" (1001,6).

8. *Sea-Cursers.* While adopting the interpretation of Gunkel, Pope, and others, I do not adopt their emendation of *yôm* to *yām*, since there is some biblical evidence that *yôm* may well be the Phoenician pronunciation of *yām*, "sea". Thus Dahood, *Psalms II*, 356, renders Ps. 96,2 *baśśerû miyyôm leyôm yešûʿātô*, "Proclaim from sea to sea his victory."

Cf. also Ezek 30,9b, *w^e^hāy^e^tāh ḥalḥālāh bāhem b^e^yôm miṣrayim kî hinnēh bā'āh*, " And anguish shall come upon them, upon the sea of Egypt (the Nile) indeed it has come ! " If *yôm* is here Phoenician for *yām*, " sea ", the form may have been chosen as a play on *yôm*, " day ", in the first colon of Ezek 30,9.

The conciseness and allusiveness of *Job* 3,8 precludes a clear understanding of the verse (see Pope's commentary on it), but the *New English Bible* may not be taxed with concision ; it transmutes six Hebrew words into twenty-three in English : " Cursed be it by those whose magic binds even the monster of the deep, who are ready to tame Leviathan himself with spells. "

9. *The pupils of the dawn.* A poetic term for the two planets visible at dawn, Venus and Mercury. Ugar. *'p'p(m)*, " eyes, pupils ", has led a number of scholars to realize that the traditional rendition of *'ap'appayim* by " eyelids " is inexact. See C. H. W. Brekelmans, *Bibliotheca Orientalis* 23 (1966) 308 ; H. P. Müller, *Vetus Testamentum* 21 (1971) 562 ; T. Collins, *Catholic Biblical Quarterly* 33 (1971) 36, n. 31. On Qumrânic *'p'pyh*, " her pupils " (// *'ynh*), see Dahood, *Biblica* 50 (1969) 272. If *'ap'appê* is a dual form, one may plausibly argue that first-colon *kôk^e^bê nišpô* is similarly dual, designating the two planets visible at the evening twilight. F. Vattioni, *Augustinianum* 8 (1968) 384, has correctly related the Punic personal name *'pšḥr* to biblical *'ap'appê šāḥar*, but he erroneously translated *'p'p* by *palpebra*.

10. *The doors of her womb.* The LXX renders *daltê biṭnî* by *pýlas gastròs mētròs mou*, but within the Northwest Semitic framework it is much more neatly translated " the doors of her womb ", with the suffix of *biṭnî* being parsed as third person feminine singular. A similar problem is smoothly solved in *Job* 19,17 : *rûḥî zārāh l^e^' ištî w^e^ḥannōtî libnê biṭnî*, " Foreign to my wife is my spirit, and my supplication to the sons of her womb " [Cf. *UT*, 2 Aqht, I, 17, [*w*]*yqrb b'l bḥnth*, " And Baal drew near as he pleaded. " In *rûḥî* // *ḥannōtî* may be seen the breakup of the composite phrase in *Zech* 12,10, *rû^a^ḥ ḥēn w^e^taḥnûnîm*, " a spirit of compassion and supplication ". With *daltê biṭnî* may be compared *Job* 38,8 where one finds the breakup of the composite phrase *daltê reḥem* : *wayyussak* (MT *wayyāsek*) *bidlātayim yām b^e^gîḥô mēreḥem yēṣē'*, " When the sea poured out from two doors, when it issued gushing from the womb. " Consult Blommerde, *Job*, 132-133.

Nor avert. As in Ugaritic and in Hebrew (cf. *Psalms III*, 438, with corresponding discussions), the force of the first-colon negative particle extends to the second colon.

Combining the LXX translation *apellåksen* with Northwest Semitic morphology, the Hebraist may now parse consonantal *wystr* as an infixed *-t-* form of *swr*, " to turn aside. " That numerous instances of consonantal *ystr* are preferably derived from *swr* finds dramatic confirmation in *Isa* 50,6 where lQIs[a] reads *pny lw' hsyrwty*, " I did not avert my face ", where MT offers *pānay lō' histartî*. The chiastic arrangement of Ps 69,17-18 strongly favors the infixed *-t-* analysis of consonantal *tstr* : *'ᵃnēnî yhwh kî ṭôb ḥasdekā kᵉrōb raḥᵃmekā pᵉnēh 'ēlāy wᵉ'al tstr pānekā mē'abdekā kî ṣar lî mahēr 'ᵃnēnî*, " Answer me, Yahweh, for your love is bounteous ; as befits your abundant mercy, turn your face toward me. Turn not your face from your servant ; because distress is upon me, quickly answer me. " In this A,B,B,A verbal sequence the counterpart of *pᵉnēh 'ēlāy* is *'al tstr pānekā*. Hence the root of *tstr* should be *swr*, " to turn away " rather than *str*, " to hide. " See Blommerde, *Job*, 38, and R. Lapointe, *Dialogues bibliques*, 276, on Ps 88,15. In *Job*, 9,7 ; 22,13 ; 33,16 and 37,7, *yḥtm* is probably an infixed *-t-* form of *ḥmm*, " to decree, communicate ", the root probably underlying Ugar. *tḥm*, " message, decree " ; cf. *UT*, Glossary, no. 2542.

11. *Enwombed*. My proposal in *Biblica* 44 (1963) 204-205, made both on the basis of context and in the light of the Ugaritic tendency to form denominative verbs from names of parts of the body, to read pual participle *mᵉruḥam* has been adopted by Blommerde, *Job*, 38-39, and by R. A. F. MacKenzie in *Jerome Biblical Commentary*, p. 516.

And expire. Driver-Gray, *Job*, II, 20, state that by all analogy we should expect *wā'egwā'*, but in the Northwest Semitic milieu MT *wᵉ' egwā'* may indeed be correct since the *yqtl* form normally expresses past time.

12. *Two breasts that I sucked*. *šādayim kî 'înāq* may be compared with *UT*, 128, II, 26-28, *ynq ḥlb a[ṯ]rt mṣṣ ṯd btlt ['nt]*, " Who shall suck the milk of Asherah, squeeze the breasts of virgin Anath. " Imperfect *'înāq* is another instance of past tense.

13. *O that now I were lying down*. *kî 'attāh šākabtî* most easily fits the context when interpreted as a precative expression. RSV " For then I should have lain down ", shifts the meaning of *'attāh*, " now ", to " then ". On the use of *kî* as a precative particle, see Dahood, *Psalms I*, 19.

And tranquilly asleep. Explaining *wᵉ'ešqôṭ yāšantî* as an instance of hendiadys. The parallelism *šākabtî* // *yāšantî* recalls the collocation in *UT*, Krt, 33-34, *šnt tluan wyškb*, " Sleep overcame him and he laid down ".

14. *Just like*. G. Fohrer, *Hiob*, 111, observes that *'m* " hier nicht einfach ' mit, bei ' sondern zusammengestellt mit = so gut wie ", an interpretation more readily acceptable in view of Ugar. *'m*, " like ". Cf. M. Held, *Journal of Biblical Literature* 84 (1965) 280, n. 36 ; Dahood, *Biblica* 48 (1967) 542-544, on *Job*, 29,18.

Kings ... who rebuilt. The sequence *m*ᵉ*lākîm ... habbōnîm* recalls the sequence in *UT*, 1007, 6-7, *mlk ṯġr* [*mlk*] *bny*, " the king guardian, the king builder ".

Who rebuilt ruins. Since in Ugaritic and in Hebrew *bny* can signify " to rebuild " as well as " to build ", this, the RSV version, appears preferable to that of Pope, " who built themselves ruins. " Pope, however, rightly points out (p. 31) that " the objection that kings do not usually achieve fame by rebuilding ruined sites (ICC) overlooks the fact that the Mesopotamian kings frequently boasted of their accomplishments in restoring and rebuilding ancient ruins. " One need not go so far afield for fitting parallels. The tenth-century king of Byblos YḤMLK records : *bt z bny yḥmlk mlk gbl h't ḥwy kl mplt hbtm 'l*, " The buildings which Yeḥimilk, king of Byblos, built ; he restored all the ruins of the temples " (KAI, 4,1-3). [I parse *hbtm 'l* in the same manner as Pyrgi *hkkbm 'l*, " the stars of El ", and *Num* 21,14, *hnḥlym 'rnwn*, " the wudyan of the Arnon "].

15. *Who filled their houses with silver.* For examples of the double-accusative construction in Ugaritic, see *UT*, § 13.10. J. Aistleitner, *Wörterbuch der ugaritischen Sprache*, no. 1568, finds this construction with *mla* in *UT*, 52,76, *wḥbrh mla yn*, " und er füllte sein Mass mit Wein ".

16. *Wasn't I.* *'ehyeh* is another instance of the imperfect form expressing past time.

A stillborn in the Crypt. Analyzing *nēpel ṭāmûn* as a construct chain and identifying *ṭāmûn* with the designation for the netherworld in *Job* 40,13, *ṭomnēm ba'ᵃpar* (MT *be'āpār*) *yāḥad p*ᵉ*nêhem ḥ*ᵃ*bōš baṭṭāmûn*, " Hide them in the slime of the Community, bind their faces in the Crypt " [This literal rendition of *p*ᵉ*nêhem ḥ*ᵃ*bōš* reveals the custom mentioned in *John* 11,44 ; 20,7]. The same vocable probably recurs in *Job* 20,26, *kol ḥōšek ṭāmûn liṣpûnāyw*, " All the darkness of the Crypt is for his treasured ones. " In our verse, the poet depicts the creation of the human body in the netherworld, an image documented and discussed in *Psalms III*, 295. *Job* 1,21 is especially pertinent to our present purpose ; cf. also *Job* 30,23. That *ṭāmûn* designates a place follows from vs. 17 where *šām*, " there ", needs an antecedent ; the same argument will be used in vss. 18-19 where the antecedent of vs. 19 *šām* is identified in vs. 18, *yaḥad*, " Community ". That the dark Crypt and the Community are congenial concepts is confirmed by *UT*, 137,20, *tk ġr ll 'm pḫr m'd*, " to the mountain of Night, toward the gathering of the Assembly ".

Foetuses. Customarily rendered " infants ", *'ōl*ᵉ*lîm* seems here to bear the nuance of Aram.-Syriac *'ûlāh*, " foetus, child ". Compare also *Isa* 49,15, where *'ûlāh* may signify " her foetus ".

That never saw. Another example of a relative clause without the relative pronoun, a form of ellipsis well documented in Ugaritic ; see the comment on vs. 3b.

17. *There. šām* looks back to *ṭāmûn,* " the Crypt ".

Cease. Employing the verb *ḥādᵉlû,* the poet sounds the theme of *ḥādel* " Cessation ", a designation of Sheol in *Isa* 38,11, studied by the writer in *Biblica* 52 (1971) 215-16.

Agitation. rōgez, recurring in vs. 26, is well attested in the Phoenician inscriptions ; cf. C. F. Jean-J. Hoftijzer, *Dictionnaire des inscriptions sémitiques de l'ouest,* 274.

Those wearied by wealth. Being hapax legomenon, *yᵉgîʿê kōᵃḥ* must be explained by the context. Since in *Job,* 24,6 ; 36,6 ; 36,17 ; *Isa,* 53,9, *rᵉšāʿîm* " the wicked, " bears the connotation " rich, " one would be warranted to attach to *kōᵃḥ* the connotation manifested in *Job,* 6,22 ; 36,19 ; and *Prov.,* 5,10 ; cf. Gesenius-Buhl, *Handwörterbuch,* 340b.

18. *The Community.* Traditionally rendered " together, " *yaḥad* provides the necessary antecedent of *šām,* " there, " in vs. 19. The appearance of *yḥd,* " community, " in Ugaritic and its frequency in Qumrân (cf. A. Steiner, *Biblische Zeitschrift* 15 [1971] 9) lead one to suspect that in many biblical texts this purported adverb functions better as a substantive. Hitherto, Hebrew lexicons recognize the substantive only in *Deut,* 33,5 and *I Chron.,* 12,18. For the present purpose, *Job,* 40,13, translated above in connection with vs. 16, is most instructive in that it balances *yaḥad,* " Community " and *ṭāmûn,* " the Crypt, " the two terms used here to describe Sheol. Cf. also *Job,* 34,15, *yigwaʿ kol bāśār yāḥad wᵉʾādām ʿal ʿāpār yāšûb,* " All flesh shall expire in the Community, and man shall return to the Slime, " where the poet splits the composite phrase of *Job,* 40,13, *ʿᵃpar yāḥad,* " the slime of the Community ", and puts the components in parallel cola. In *Biblica* 53 (1972) the present writer proposes to find this meaning in *Job,* 38,7. That Sheol was pictured as an assembly of shades is not difficult to establish ; compare *Job,* 30,23 where it is termed *bêt môʿēd,* " the house of meeting, " and *Prov.,* 5,14 ; 21,16 ; 26,26 where *qāhāl,* " Assembly, " describes the netherworld, as argued by W. van der Weiden, *Le Livre des Proverbes : Notes philologiques* (Rome, 1970) 56, 144-145. See also the explanation of Ugar. *rpum* proposed by H. L. Ginsberg, *The Legend of King Keret* (New Haven, 1946) 41.

Of prisoners. Dahood, *Psalms II,* 305 ; *Psalms III,* 319, examines some texts comparing Sheol to a prison. The motif was also known in Phoenicia as appears from Eshmunazor, 21-22, *lm ysgrnm ʾlnm hqdšm ʾl,* " Lest these holy gods imprison (namely, in the nether dungeon) them. " Cf. *Isa,* 19,4 ; Dahood, *Biblica* 50 (1969) 341-342 ; J. Teixidor, *Syria* 48 (1971) 475.

19. *Namely, slave, freedman, his master.* I adopt the reading and translation proposed by Blommerde, *Job,* 39. In this version both the categories mentioned in the first colon — *qāṭôn wᵉgādôl* — receive

explicit mention in the second colon. One may point out here that the collocation of *'ebed,* " slave, " and vs. 17, *'ᵃsîrîm,* " prisoners, " reflects the Canaanite parallelism attested in *UT,* 137,36-37 ; see Dahood in *Ras Shamra Parallels,* Ch. II, 403, pp. 286-287.

20. *Is given.* Those who retain the MT active pointing *yittēn* insert in their translations " he " or " God " as the subject and seek to explain the omission of the subject as due partly to reverence and partly to reluctance to make charges against God. A limping explanation that is upset by the explicit mention of God in the next verse. Job was not noted for shyness when talking to or about God. Since there is massive evidence that the Massoretes were unfamiliar with the qal passive, a strong case can be made for the qal passive vocalization *yuttan,* with the ancient versions. Cf. *Job,* 37,10 where *yuttan* must again be read for MT *yittēn.*

The collocation in our verse of *yuttan* and *ḥayyim* evokes the famous command in *UT,* 2 Aqht, VI, 27, *irš ḥym watnk,* " Ask for life and I will give it to you. "

Light... and life. Placing *'ôr* in the first colon and *ḥayyîm* in the second, the poet breaks up the composite phrase *'ôr ḥayyîm* of *Job,* 33,30. The subtle use of this poetic device in Ugaritic has stimulated study of this stylistic phenomenon in Hebrew poetry. Here one may briefly note that *Job,* 17,13-14, which balance *yᵉṣû'ay,* " my couch, " and *rimmāh,* " worm, " require a new reading and grammatical analysis of *Isa,* 14,11, *yuṣṣa' rimmāh,* where a masculine verb is predicated of a feminine subject. Grammar and style are better served by the reading *yᵉṣūᵃ' rimmāh,* " a couch of worms " ; thus each colon contains a nominal sentence : " Beneath you a couch of worms, and maggots your blanket. "

21. *Death.* Taking *māwet* in a local sense, as in *Job,* 28,22 ; 30,23 ; 38,17, etc. ; cf. Brown-Driver-Briggs, *Lexicon,* 560b.

That they be no more. *'ênennû,* sometimes emended to *'ayin,* may be analyzed into *'nn* plus plural ending *-û.* Ugaritic witnesses both *in* and *inn,* with afformative *nun.*

Who dig... for themselves. The suffix of *yaḥpᵉrūhûm* is parsed as *dativus commodi* ; compare the same idea expressed by prepositional *lāmô* in vs. 14, *habbōnîm ḥᵒrābôt lāmô,* " who rebuilt ruins for themselves. " Though *-hēm* would be the expected vocalization, *-hûm* may be allowed to stand in view of singular *hû'* and Arab. *hum.*

Since the Massoretic purchase on dative suffixes was very tenuous, one can readily account for the false division of consonants. A similar misunderstanding is widely admitted in *Job,* 15,18, *wᵉlō' kiḥᵃdûm 'ᵃbôtām,* " and which their fathers did not conceal from them. " The Ugaritic employment of datival suffixes has opened a new chapter in biblical research on this grammatical and stylistic phenomenon ; as a consequence, the translation of numerous biblical verses has been sharpened and their parsing rendered more precise.

Crypts. This seems etymologically the best rendition of *maṭmôn*, from *ṭāman*, " to hide, " since Greek *kryptein* means just this. The description sounds much like *Isa*, 22,16, ,, that you have hewn here a tomb for yourself, you who hew a tomb on the height. "

22. *The arrival*. Much-disputed *gîl* (vocalization uncertain) may tentatively be related to Ugar. *gly*, " to reach, arrive. " On *gly* in *Ruth*, 3,7, see Dahood, *Biblica* 43 (1962) 224 ; M. J. Mulder, *Ugarit-Forschungen* 2 (1970) 365. Parallelism with *ye'ᵉtāyw*, " they come, " in *Job*, 30,14 permits the claim that the hapax legomenon *hitgalgālû* derives from *gly* (compare *gly* / /*ba*, " to come " in *UT*, 49, I, 6-7) and not from *gll*, " to roll. "

They reach. Ugar. *mṣa* /*mǵy*, " to reach " (see especially M. Held, in M. Ben-Horin, ed., *Studies and Essays in Honor of Abraham A. Neuman* (Leiden, 1962) 289, n. 1) furnishes a philological undergirding for the New American Bible's (or CCD ; New York, 1970) version, " and are glad when they reach the grave, " which was scarcely in the mind of the translators who elsewhere evince innocence of matters Ugaritic. In J. L. McKenzie, ed., *The Bible in Current Catholic Thought* : *Gruenthaner Memorial Volume* (New York, 1962) 57, the present writer has studied *timṣā'* in *Job*, 11,7 in the light of Ugaritic usage. See also S. Iwry, *Textus* 5 (1966) 36-39 ; and Dahood, *Psalms III*, 146, on Ps. 116,3.

23. *The man*. In *geber*, following upon the heels of vs. 22 *qāber*, there may be a deliberate wordplay ; cf. Ugar. *ṯigt*, " roar, " but also written *ṯiqt* in a doublet.

Is devious. Fohrer's comment on his own translation of *darkô nistārāh*, " dem sein Weg verborgen ist, " illustrates the semantic leaps one must make if one does not exploit Northwest Semitic : " Das heisst, der sich verirrt hat " (*Hiob*, 112). Precisely the meaning postulated by Fohrer emerges when *nistārāh* gets parsed as the infixed *-t-* form of *sûr*, as in vs. 10. Parallelism with the verb of motion *ya'ᵃbôr* favors the same analysis in *Isa*, 40,27b, *nistᵉrāh darkî mēyhwh ûmē'ᵉlōhay mišpāṭî ya 'ᵃbôr*, "My way is removed from Yahweh, and my cause has passed from my God's notice. " Note the parallelism of *sûr* and *'ābar* in Eccles 11,10, *wᵉhāsēr ka'as millibbekā wᵉha'ᵃbēr rā'āh mibbᵉśārekā*, " so remove anguish from your mind, and banish pain from your body. "

Whom. As in *Job*, 29,12, the *wāw* is construed as the relative *wāw* ; cf. Dahood, *Psalms I*, 18, on Ps. 3,4, and *Psalms II*, 183, on Ps. 72,12.

Shields while he lives. Repointing the hapax legomenon phrase *wayyāsek ba'ᵃdô* to *wayyāsek bᵉ'ōdô*. Of course, the interpretation of this phrase depends on the construction put upon the first colon. The root *skk*, " to shield, screen, " is attested in *Job*, 40,22 and predicated of God in Ps.

140,8 and elsewhere, while the confusion between *ba'ᵃdî* and *bᵉ'ōdî* can be seen in Ps. 3,4 and 138,8 ; cf. also *Jer.*, 11,14 and Dahood, *Psalms III*, 282. For the thought of the two cola, compare *Job*, 21,7-17.

24. *My bread is before me.* The phrase *lᵉpānay laḥmî* bears comparison with *UT*, 127,48-49, *lpnk ltšlḥm ytm*, " Before you, you do not feed the fatherless. "

Before me. A step toward the clearer understanding of the unexplained first colon may be taken when *lipnê* is repointed *lᵉpānay*.

Sobbing comes upon me. Literally " my sobbing comes ", but the genitive suffix of *'anḥātî* may have dative force. Cf. *Job* 35,4 ; Joüon, *Grammaire*, § 129h, and *Zeph* 3,10, *yôbīlûn minḥātî*, " They shall bring me tribute ", where the genitive suffix of *minḥātî* really fulfils a dative function with *yôbīlûn*. See the discussion by L. Sabottka, *Zephanja : Versuch einer Neuübersetzung mit philologischem Kommentar* (Rome, 1972) 122.

Sobbing... my groans. Both *'anḥātî* and *ša'ᵃgōtāy* have counterparts in Ugar. *anḫ* and *ṯigt /ṯiqt*, respectively.

My groans pour out like water. A number of scholars have correctly compared *yittᵉkû kammayim ša'ᵃgōtāy* to *UT*, Krt, 28-29, *tntkn udm'th km ṯqlm arṣh*, " His tears are poured out like shekels toward the ground ". (The simile " like shekels " reveals the commercial character of Canaanite civilization). In the *Journal of Northwest Semitic Languages* 2 (1972) 40, F. C. Fensham makes the further point, " It is, however, noteworthy that both in Ugaritic and Hebrew *ntk* can also be used in G or Qal to denote ' pouring out ', viz. in I Aqht 82 *ytk* with *dm['h]* as subject and *Job* 3,24. This remarkable agreement between Ugaritic and Hebrew in the actual usage of a construction must be noted. "

The lack of gender agreement between *yittᵉkû* and *ša'ᵃgōtāy* may well be explained by the intervention of *kammayim* between the verb and the subject. This phenomenon, biblically well attested (e.g., I *Sam*, 2,4 ; *Job*, 16,22 ; 22,9 ; *Prov.*, 1,16 ; 2,10 ; GK, *Grammatik*, § 145 p.) seems to occur in *UT*, 125,103, *uḫštk lbky 'tq*, " Or will your happiness turn into tears, " where we have *'tq* for an expected *'tqt*. Though *'tq* might be an infinitive absolute, this explication appears less probable.

25. *It overtook me.* *wayye'ᵉtāyānî* is triply interesting, consisting of the *waw apodoseos*, a verb preserving the original third radical *-y* and followed by the dative suffix. The syntax of the first colon seems to be identical with that of *Hos*, 11,1, *kî na'ar yiśrā'ēl wā'ōhᵃbēhû*, " When Israel was a slave, I loved him, " and enjoys an instructive analogue in *UT*, Krt, 31, *bm bkyh wyšn*, " While he cried, he fell asleep. " Cf. also Fensham in *Journal of Northwest Semitic Languages* 2 (1972) 39, and Blommerde, *Job*, 28, who cites *Job*, 10,7 ; 15,17 ; 41,3. Consequently we must reject the opinion of Georg Beer, *Der Text des Buches Hiob* (Marburg,

1897) 22. " Das *w* (of *wy' tyny*) ist vielleicht mit GPV zu streichen, doch vgl. 4.5. "

The preservation of the original *-y* in *y'tyny* (cf. Ugar. *tity*) assumes particular significance because in the next verse *šlwty* preserves the original third radical *-w*, as in Ugar. *ašlw* " I shall take my ease. " Perhaps only here in the Bible does one encounter in successive verses two weak verbs preserving the original third radical.

Overtook me... upon me. The parallelism between the dative suffix of *wayye'etāyēnî* and the prepositional phrase is a phenomenon characterizing the style of *Job* ; cf. 6,4 ; 15,17 ; 20,22 ; 29,16 ; 32,14 ; 33,5,33 ; 40,30 ; 41,20-21. The appreciation of this stylistic practice may occasionally prove decisive for the translation of a passage. For example, *Job*, 29,16, *'āb 'ānōkî lā'ebyônîm werîb lō' yāda'tî 'eḥqerēhû*, " A father was I to the needy, and the cause of one I did not know, I investigated for him. " Often parsed as the resumptive suffix of *rîb*, *-hû* of *'eḥqerēhû* is preferably construed as the dative of advantage, balancing the preposition *la* of the preceding three cola. The poet achieved variety by employing a dative suffix in the final of four parallel cola.

Canaanite antecedents for this usage may be seen in *UT*, 125,25-26, *bn al tbkn al tdm ly*, " My son, weep not for me, mourn not for me, " where datival suffix of *tbkn* is balanced by prepositional *ly*, and in ʿnt, III, 17-18, *rgm iṯ ly wargmk*, " I have a word and I will speak it to you. " Cf. *Job*, 15,17, *'aḥawwekā šema' lî* " I will explain it to you, listen to me ", and *UT*, 2 Aqht, VI, 34-35.

Came. yābō' is yet another instance of the *yqtl* form stating past time.

26. *I have no ease.* The one *lamedh waw* verb in Hebrew with the *waw* preserved in qal (Driver-Gray, *Job*, II, 22 ; GK, *Grammatik*, § 75b) is witnessed in *UT*, Krt, 149, *ašlw*.

I rest. Well attested in Ugaritic, *nāḥtî* occurs also in El Amarna 147,56 as *nu-uḫ-ti*.

In summary, *Job*, 3 exhibits the following Northwest Semitic features :

Phonetics : 6, *yēḥad* for *yēḥaz*
8, *yôm* for *yām*

Morphology : 10, *biṭnî* for *biṭnāh*
10,23, *yistār*, infixed *-t-* form
20, *yuttan*, qal passive
21, *'êynennû*, with afformative *-n*
25, *ye'etāyēnî*, preservation of third radical *yod*.
26, *šālawtî*, preservation of third radical *waw*.

Syntax : 3,16, elliptical relative clauses
15, double accusative construction

21, *yaḥp^{e}rūhûm*, dative suffix
24, *'anḥātî*, genitive suffix with dative function
25, *ye'^{e}tāyēnî*, dative suffix

yqtl expressing past tense :
3, *'iwwāled*
10, *'āmût, 'egwā'*
12, *'înāq*
16, *'ehyeh*
25, *yābō'*

Vocabulary : 3, *'āmar*, " to see "
9, *'ap'appê*, " pupils "
11, *m^{e}ruḥam*, " enwombed "
14,15, *'im*, " just like "
18, *yaḥad*, " community "
22, *gîl*, " arrival "
yimṣ^{e}'û, " they reach "

Style : 10, double-duty negative
19, *ḥopšî-mi*, enclitic *mi*
20, *'ôr* // *ḥayyîm*, breakup of composite phrase
22-23, wordplay on *qāber-geber*
24b, simile
25, dative suffix // prepositional phrase.

Four Texts from Isaiah

Northwest Semitic philology proves equally relevant for the translation and grammatical analysis of Isaiah. The following passages have been chosen to illustrate the sharp conflict between the comparative and the text-critical methods ; the discovery of 1QIs^{a} at Qumrân enables the Hebraist to assess directly the understanding of Hebrew poetry in Judea in the second-first centuries B. C. and indirectly the LXX's comprehension of the sacred text.

Isa 14,30-31 *w^{e}rā'û b^{e}kôray* (MT *b^{e}kôrê*) *dallîm*
w^{e}'ebyônîm lābeṭaḥ yirbāṣû
w^{e}hēmattî bārā'āb šoršēk
ū^{e}še'ērîtēk yah^{a}rōg
hêlîlî ša'ar za'^{a}qî 'îr
nāmôg p^{e}lešet kullēk
kî miṣṣāpôn 'āšān bā'
w^{e}'ên bôdēd b^{e}mô'ādāyw

And the poor will pasture in my hollows,
and the needy will in safety lie down ;
but I will kill your offspring with hunger,
and your remnant I will utterly slay.
Wail, O gate, cry out, O city,
melt, O Philistia, all of you,
for from the north smoke is coming,
and none will escape his hordes.

30. *In my hollows*. If we assume complete A,B,C / /C',B',A' chiasmus, consonantal *bkwry* should be a prepositional phrase balancing *lābeṭaḥ*, " in safety. " Analyzed into *b*ᵉ and *kwry*, whose long *ô* may reflect the Phoenician *â* > *ô* sound shift, the phrase designates a place matching the preposition of manner in the second colon. The substantive *kar*, " hollow ", occurs in *Isa* 30,23 and elsewhere in the Bible ; for recent discussions, see J. S. Kselman, *Catholic Biblical Quarterly* 32 (1970) 579-581, and L. Sabottka, *Zephanja*, 78-79. The spelling *kwr* here suggests derivation from *mediae waw* root ; the lexicons often relate *kar*, " hollow ", to *kārāh*, " to burrow ".

Your offspring. Ugar. *šrš*, " offspring, scion " (/ /*bn*, " son "), supplies the nuance that makes *šoršēk* an apt object of *w*ᵉ*hēmattî bārā'āb*, " but I will kill with hunger. " *The New English Bible* offers a kind of conflate translation, " the offspring of your roots I will kill by starvation, " a version obviated by Ugar, *šrš*.

I will utterly slay. For MT *yah*ᵃ*rōg*, lQIsᵃ reads first person *'hrwg*. Is this alteration necessary ? Within the Northwest Semitic ambience, consonantal *yhrg* can neatly be explained as a yiphil infinitive absolute (with elative force) continuing the action of the main verb, just as in vs. 31 the niphal infinitive absolute *nāmôg* is a stylistic surrogate for the preceding imperatives. That Qumrân did not appreciate the yiphil conjugation is further evidenced by *Isa* 63,16, *kî 'abrāhām lō' y*ᵉ*dā'ānû w*ᵉ*yiśrā'ēl lō' yakkîrānû*, " though Abraham does not know us or Israel recognize us. " Here lQIsᵃ reads hiphil *hkyrnw*, showing that it did not understand the Phoenician yiphil causative. As pointed out by C. H. Gordon, *Jahrbuch für kleinasiatische Forschung* 2 (1951) 50, the form is yiphil perfect and not imperfect both because of the parallelism with *y*ᵉ*dā'ānû* and because of the suffix *-ānî* in *yakkîrānî*. It should also be noted that in *Isa* 37,19, the MT infinitive absolute *w*ᵉ*nātôn* is read as a finite verb *wytnw*, an inferior reading in my opinion.

Melt. Though König (*Lehrgebäude*, p. 473) and Franz Delitzsch (*Commentar über das Buch Jesaja* ; 4th ed. Leipzig, 1889, 473) in the last century parsed *nāmôg* as the niphal infinitive absolute (cf. *Isa*, 59,13 *nāsôg*) continuing the feminine imperatives *hêlîlî* and *za'*ᵃ*qî*, the more recent lexicons such as Gesenius-Buhl, Koehler-Baumgartner analyze it as niphal masculine perfect. But this appears highly improbable since *pᵉlešet* is feminine. The Ugaritic-Phoenician penchant for infinitives absolute and the presence of other Ugaritic-Phoenician elements in these verses, suggest that Zorell, *Lexicon Hebraicum*, 416a, is correct when, with König and Delitzsch, analyzing *nāmôg* as niphal infinitive absolute.

Escape his hordes. The phrase *bôdēd bᵉmô'ādāyw* (1QIsᵃ reads *mwdd bmwd'yw*) continues to lend itself to varying versions, but modern philology makes it possible to uphold the Vulgate rendition *non est qui effugiet agmen ejus*. Being parallel to *min* of *miṣṣāpôn*, *bᵉ* of *bᵉmō'ādāyw* probably has separative force. Combined with Sir. 12,9, *wbr'tw gm ry' bwdd*, "But in his misfortune even a friend withdraws," this observation leads to the literal translation of *wᵉ'ên bôdēd bᵉmō'ādāyw*, "and there will be none withdrawing from his hordes." Cf. Arab. *badda*, "to cause to withdraw."

Isa 30,27 *hinnēh šēm yhwh bā' mimmerḥāq*
bō'ēr 'appô wᵉkābēd maśśī'āh (MT *wᵉkōbed maśśō'āh*)
śᵉpātāyw mālᵉ'û za'am
ûlᵉšônô kᵉ'ēš 'ōkelet

Behold Yahweh's name coming from afar,
burning are his nostrils and his liver fuming;
his lips are full of anger,
and his tongue is like a devouring fire.

The disputed words *kbd mś'h* yield vivid sense with the recognition of the chiastic order in *bō'ēr 'appô wᵉkābēd maśśī'āh* and that the poet is enumerating the different parts of the body. That Yahweh too should have a liver is suggested by the Ugaritic tablets which ascribe livers to El and Anath. E.g., *UT*, 75, I, 12-13, *il yẓḥq bm lb wygmḏ bm kbd*, "El laughed from his heart and guffawed from his liver." The nuance "fuming" of the hiphil feminine participle (*kābēd* is feminine; see Dahood, *Ugarit-Forschungen* 1[1969]23) is suggested both by the chiastic parallelism with *bō'ēr* and by *maś'ēt*, ("smoke-)signal," in *Judg*, 20, 40; *Jer* 6,1, and Lachish *mś't*. Cf. also Ps. 18,9, *'ālāh 'āšān bᵉ'appô wᵉ'ēš mippîw tō'kēl*, "Smoke rose from his nostrils, and fire from his mouth devoured." Thus Ugaritic mythology helps us recover a motif that was lost in the traditional transmission of the text.

Isa, 33,2-3 *yhwh ḥonnēnû*
lᵉkā qiwwînû
hᵉyēh zᵉrō'ā-mi (MT *zᵉrō'ām*) *labbᵉqārîm*
'ap yᵉšû'ātēnû bᵉ'ēt ṣārāh
miqqôl hāmôn nādᵉdû 'ammîm
mērômᵉtekā (MT *mērômᵉmūtekā*) *nāpᵉṣû gôyim*

Yahweh, have mercy on us,
to you we call.
Be our arm every morning,
also our victory in time of siege.
At the voice of your army, may peoples flee,
at the sound of your soldiers, may nations be scattered !

The suspiciously long sequence *mrwmmtk*, read by 1QIs[a] as *mdmmtk*, yields sense and parallelism when divided to read *mērôm m^e^tekā*, " at the sound of your soldiers. " The verse thus scans parallelistically into an A,B,C,D / /A',B',C',D' sequence : *qôl* matches *rôm* and recalls the phrase *rm tph*, " the sound /roll of his drum " in Ugaritic and *qôl rām* in *Deut* 27,14 ; cf. also *Hab* 3,10, *qôlô rôm*, " his loud voice. " In other terms, *qôl* / /*rôm* illustrates the breakup of a composite phrase. In *hāmôn* / / *m^e^tekā*, the former shares the suffix of the former, an interlocking device that tightly links the cola. Cf. *Isa* 5,13, which collocates *metê*, " men of, " and *h^a^mônô*, " his throng. " Since the metaphor in our verse is military (cf. vs. 2), *hāmôn* assumes the well-attested meaning " army " (e.g. *Isa* 13,4 ; 29,5) and *m^e^tekā* bears the sense found in *Isa* 3,25, " your soldiers (*m^e^tayik*) will fall by the sword and your warriors (*g^e^bûrātēk* abstract for concrete) in battle. " The alliterative perfects *nād^e^dû* and *nāp^e^ṣû* parse as precatives, stylistically balancing the two imperatives of vs. 2, *ḥonnēnû* and *h^e^yēh*.

Isa 47,1 *r^e^dî ûš^e^bî 'al 'āpār*
b^e^tûlat bat bābel
š^e^bî lā'āreṣ 'ên kissē'
bat kaśdîm

Come down and sit upon the dust,
virgin daughter Babylon !
Sit upon the ground without a throne,
daughter of the Chaldaeans !

This verse affords an instructive opportunity to match Northwest Semitic philology against Qumrân and against the LXX. For MT *š^e^bî lā'āreṣ* 1QIs[a] reads *šby 'l h'rṣ*, while the LXX omits *'ên kissē'*. *UT*, 67, VI, 11-14 may be cited to validate MT on both counts : *yrd lksi yṯb lhdm wl hdm yṯb larṣ*, " He [El] came down from the throne, sat upon the footstool ; and from the footstool he sat upon the ground. " Here the Canaanite poet describes the ritual followed by El when he learns about the death of Baal. The Ugar. phrase *yṯb larṣ* equals *š^e^bî lā'āreṣ* and the mention of the throne precludes its omission by the LXX, which was evidently unfamiliar with the mourning ritual involved. What is more, the use of the same verb with two different prepositions, *š*e*bî ʿal ʿāpār* and *š*e*bî lāʾāreṣ*, is widely attested in Hebrew poetry (e.g., *Isa*, 43,7 ; 46,13) and has Canaanite antecedents in *UT*, 51, II, 32-33 ; III, 14-16 ; VIII, 5-6 ; 137,19-20, etc.

M. Dahood

See *Supplementary note*, p. 205.

2

PHILOLOGY AND EXEGESIS

SOME GENERAL REMARKS, WITH ILLUSTRATIONS FROM JOB

I do not propose to repeat here the arguments of my book *Comparative Philology and the Text of the Old Testament* (1968). What I shall do is the following: First, I shall make some remarks about the discussion in general, taking into account some points made by reviewers. [1] Secondly, since this is the introduction to a joint discussion with Professor Dahood, I shall say something about his position in particular. Thirdly, since he and I have agreed on a common text for discussion, I shall refer to some examples from Job 3. Fourthly, I shall try to say something about the philosophy of the matter and place this debate about biblical Hebrew within the wider framework of the general modern discussion of language and semantics.

Since the reception of the book has been generally favourable and encouraging, and since the ensuing discussion has given me little reason to change my mind about major points, it may be good to start with one or two questions of general aim and emphasis in the work as a whole. The first such points are taken up in Father Dahood's detailed review. [2]

The first question is about the scope of the investigation. Dahood remarks, and quite rightly, that my study is devoted mainly to lexical elements, such as nouns and verbs, for which new meanings have been

1. The fuller reviews of *Comparative Philology* (title thus abbreviated) so far include: F. I. ANDERSEN, *JBL* 88 (1969) 345 f.; J. BLAU, *Kiryat Sepher* 44 (1968-1969) 223-5; F. PÉREZ CASTRO, *Sefarad* 28 (1968) 321-326; M. J. DAHOOD, "Comparative Philology Yesterday and Today," *Biblica* 50 (1969) 70-79; T. N. D. METTINGER, *Svensk Teologisk Kvartalskrift* 45 (1970) 129-133; W. L. MORAN, *CBQ* 31 (1969) 239-243; E. ULLENDORFF, *BSOAS* 32 (1969) 143-148; S. D. WALTERS, *JAOS* 89 (1969) 777-781; P. WERNBERG-MØLLER, *JThS* 20 (1969), 558-562. Citations of these scholars by name in the following will refer to these reviews. I do not take as serious comment the wild ranting of G. E. MENDENHALL in *Interpretation* 25 (1971), 358-362, although points of interest are occasionally touched upon by him.

2. I would like to acknowledge the generally pleasant tone of Father Dahood's review; some points where he becomes more scornful, and where this scorn may be misplaced, will be mentioned in the course of this article.

identified in modern times ; it says much less about pronouns, suffixes, particles, and grammatical categories such as tenses. He thinks that if one writes about " philology " one has to include full treatments of comparative phonetics, syntax, etc. I recognize that there is a valid point here, and that Dahood's own work contains a great deal that consists not of new *lexical* identifications but rather of interpretations of suffixes and the like. But there is no issue of principle here. I was not writing a full treatise on comparative philology, but a study of one type of operation which is an *application* of comparative philology to the biblical text. Within the total impact of this operation, it is the lexical examples which seem to have the most striking and drastic effect. Questions of suffixes, tenses and the like are commonly much more marginal ; it is the lexical instances which have made the question critical for our generation. Dahood's own work would be very different in its impact if it offered no new lexical identifications but only new interpretations of suffixes, syntactical elements, prosodies and so on. In any case, I did make it clear in the book that non-lexical instances did occur, and discussed a few of them. [3] If it had been my aim to discuss not the general impact of this kind of applied philology, but Dahood's work in particular, the proportions might have had to be different ; but this was not my intention.

In itself then there is no real issue here, but it leads on to something which may perhaps be a real issue, namely Dahood's distinction between " the traditional philological approach and the new method and criteria introduced by Northwest Semitic discoveries of the past forty years. " [4] Dahood seems to imply three things : firstly, that the older scholars worked almost only by lexical means — the point discussed in the last paragraph ; secondly, that any faults which existed in the older method have been left behind by the newer ; thirdly, that the discussion in my book was out of due time, since the situation described was one now left far behind. [5]

Of these latter two points, neither seems to me to have substance. As for timeliness, although the method under discussion is not a new one, its cumulative effect has quite suddenly become very much greater, both through the amount of material published and through the particular fact that so much has been made public in the form of popular Bible

3. *Comparative Philology*, pp. 30-33. The remarks about enclitic *mem* have excited some comment ; a " perverse attack ", says Andersen. Perverse perhaps, but not an attack : I do not in fact express any opinion of my own about the existence of enclitic *mem* in Hebrew, but only about the character of certain arguments offered.

4. Dahood, p. 71.

5. Dahood, pp. 71, 79 and *passim* ; also the title of his review, " Comparative Philology Yesterday and Today ".

translations. [6] As for quality, I do not share the view that the " new method and criteria ", if we are to judge by Dahood's own publications and those of his pupils, stand at a higher level than the work of an older generation such as Tur-Sinai, Driver and Winton Thomas. On the contrary, that work of older scholars has seemed to me to have a much better and more responsible character, and it is for this reason that most of the examples I studied in the book were taken from this group. Though in the end I came to regard many of them as unconvincing, the study of them was a real intellectual stimulus ; few of them were just obviously wrong, and only a careful analysis of the sources enabled one to form a judgement. The study of them was of real value. That Dahood should look down on this work of an older generation as deficient, and that it should often be simply ignored or disregarded in works inspired or guided by him, [7] is very difficult to understand. It is true that my study paid proportionately more attention to the work of older scholars, and that it cited less of Dahood's suggestions than it might have done ; but a main reason for this, I must in frankness say, is that if I had cited more of the latter I would have felt liable to the charge of picking out quite obviously fantastic suggestions in order to bring ridicule on the method as a whole. The fact that this accusation was indeed made [8] confirms that I was right in being sensitive to the possibility of it. In fact, in my selection of examples for discussion I leant over backwards to avoid, wherever possible, the citation of suggestions which were obviously worthless, which did not teach some useful lessons through the study of them, or which might seem designed simply to bring the method into ridicule. [9]

Thus, if my book gives less attention to the work of Professor Dahood than some would expect, this does not have its cause in any special hostility towards his work. [10] On the contrary, I have no consciousness of ascribing to his suggestions any value different from that which is ascribed to them by the vast majority of Old Testament scholars. This is a powerful fact which has to be faced by Dahood — not because majority opinion determines what is true, but because the final court of appeal for so many of his suggestions lies not in Ugaritic or in Phoenician, but *within the Hebrew text of the Bible itself* ; the final criterion is their alleged concinnity, their alleged improvement of sense, in the

6. On this see further below, pp. 59 f.

7. Cf. for instance W. McKane's remarks in his review of W. A. van der Weiden, *Le Livre des Proverbes*, in *JSS* 16 (1971) 222-236, especially pp. 232-234.

8. Andersen, p. 345.

9. Plenty of such suggestions, however, can be cited ; cf. below, pp. 45 ff.

10. Andersen, *ibid.*, uses the phrase " ill-concealed hostility towards the work of Fr. Mitchell Dahood. "

Hebrew Bible, and it is of this that Old Testament scholars are the proper judges. If scholars are sceptical of Dahood's suggestions, as I believe the great majority of them are, this is not to be attributed to any opposition to the use of Ugaritic or any distrust of " the Northwest Semitic method, " but to their experience of the way in which these suggestions have been made and supported : their experience of wildness in the use of evidence, extreme bad taste in respect of that which constitutes a probable understanding of the text, obsessive attachment to the discovery of a Ugaritizing solution at any price, absence of proper justification, [11] and exaggeration of the difficulty of the present text and /or meaning in order at all costs to secure a new understanding, said to be based on Phoenician or Ugaritic. [12] For — and this must be emphasized — the logically decisive step in operations like those of Dahood, and in the process of evaluating them, often lies not in the Phoenician or Ugaritic facts but in the fitness of the proposed interpretation for its context within the Hebrew biblical text. These points will be illustrated below.

There is however one particular point about Dahood's approach which I had not sufficiently taken into account in the writing of my book, and which to me seems even more unclear now than it was then : is Dahood's method really intended to be a comparative approach at all ? I have devoted my investigation to those explanations of Hebrew where meanings are derived from the meanings of forms in a *cognate* language, i.e. a language related but different. Dahood's position, at least sometimes, seems to be rather that Ugaritic *is* Hebrew and Hebrew *is* Ugaritic ; the two are the same language in somewhat different temporal and local manifestations. [13] His method then is not really comparative, in the

11. See recently for instance C. J. Labuschagne's review of A. C. M. BLOMMERDE's *Northwest Semitic Grammar and Job*, in *Ugarit-Forschungen* 3 (1971) 373-374.

12. On all these points McKane's remarks in the review quoted seem to me to be right in themselves and also to express what is held by the central current of scholarship. For a view which stands at the absolutely opposite extreme from Dahood's, cf. J. F. A. Sawyer's remarks on the generally lucid, intelligible and meaningful character of the Masoretic Text, *Semantics in Biblical Research* (1972), p. 14.

13. It is, of course, perfectly conceivable that Ugaritic and Hebrew should be " the same language " in this sense ; and if this is so, then of course it is so. Dahood's work can be represented as an exploration of the hypothesis that this is so ; but the exploration is carried out in such a way as to override as far as is possible all the evidence that might indicate that it is not so. His presentation of evidence is not designed to assist discussion of the question *whether* Ugaritic is thus related to Hebrew *or not* ; it does not leave such questions open. Any real comparative discussion is difficult, since there is very little in Ugaritic of which Dahood will grant, even for the purpose of discussion, that it does not exist in Hebrew, and vice versa. This is, incidentally, one reason why I published a comparative table of Syriac and Hebrew verbs rather than one of Ugaritic and Hebrew (cf. MORAN, *op. cit.*,

sense in which I have used the word, but consists of *internal* elucidation within the unitary Ugaritic-Canaanite-Hebrew world. The demonstration of this unitary (though diversified) linguistic (and also cultural) *mélange* is Dahood's real interest in the matter. When he contrasts his method with that of the older scholars, it is at least possible that he is trying to say that their method was really a comparative one, working with languages which are recognized to be cognate but different, while his is a non-comparative one, working with internal relations which at most are only dialectal.

If this is indeed Dahood's intention, then two things follow : firstly, I failed to give proper attention to this (reasonably enough, since Dahood himself does not make it clear) ; and secondly my arguments do not deal, and were not intended to deal, with that segment of his work which is intended to be not comparative but internal in its method. But, on the other hand, even if Dahood's work with Canaanite languages is not comparative but internal, there is no doubt that he in fact shifts the whole time back and forward between comparative and internal operations, and that the comparative segment of his work is affected by, and subject to, my arguments just as before.

This brings us back conveniently to a point of principle, namely that the validity of comparative philology as a discipline is not at all in question, at least from my side. It is the logic of comparative philology that is taken for granted, with only slight modifications, throughout my investigation ; and if solutions are found to be deficient it is because comparative philological method, when properly examined, shows that there is evidence against them. My purpose was to state properly the methods required by comparative philology, so that readers might be better able to judge whether suggestions, allegedly thrown up through the use of this method, were in fact validated by it. The notion, pursued in Wernberg-Møller's review, that I want to " dismiss " comparative philological method or to erect a " new edifice " to take its place, has very little to do with my purpose. [14]

Our subject here however is not comparative philology itself but a sort of applied comparative philology. The basic work of comparative

p. 241) : under the present circumstances, one would not have an adequate agreed basis for the setting up of the latter table.

14. See WERNBERG-MØLLER, p. 559. His picture (especially on pp. 560 and 562 of his review) of my ideas about the relation between philology and linguistics is wildly remote from my actual opinions and often attributes to me the opposite of what I think ; many of his notions are quite expressly excluded by clear statements of mine. Cf. also my " The Ancient Semitic Languages — the Conflict between Philology and Linguistics ", *Transactions of the Philological Society*, 1968, 37-55 ; also, in general, my paper " Hebrew Lexicography ", to be published in the proceedings of the Florence Colloquium on Semitic Lexicography, held at Easter 1972.

philology is, let us say, to establish a picture of the Semitic languages and their interrelations through the joint use of data from the various branches of the family. This basic philological work provides the fundamental logic for the task which we are discussing. But what we are talking about is not itself comparative philology in that sense : rather, it is an *applied* and *heuristic* operation, dependent on (or at worst parasitic upon) comparative philology. It is an operation which appears to use the insights of comparative philology but can very easily override them. Those whose prime interest has been to reconstruct a hitherto unknown stage of Hebrew or its prehistoric relations with Ugaritic have not necessarily observed the proper needs and rules of comparative philology (or historical linguistics, as it might be better called) ; and the principles of that discipline need to be reasserted and to be protected against being pushed aside in the impetus of the rush to identify and to reconstruct. Several sections of my book were intended to do just that ; one instance is the treatment of the phonological correspondences. [15]

One of the aspects of comparative philology which needs to be emphasized is the need for each language to be seen and understood for itself. The study of Semitic languages was long damaged by the enslavement of each one to the ancillary service of explaining the text of the Bible — Arabic was a principal case in point. The present interest in Ugaritic is something which in itself should be approved and supported in every possible way. But the frenetic desire to exploit its resources as a means of explaining the Hebrew Bible threatens to hold Ugaritic study within the same framework of slavery to *sacra philologia* from which other

15. F. I. ANDERSEN, *op. cit.*, p. 345 f., regards this as a falling back on neogrammarian dogma. No " dogma " is involved. If there are correspondences other than those which have been recognized as normal, then of course there are, and that is all there is to it. Andersen must be willing to use his terms very loosely if he classes the linguists cited on p. 83 n. of *Comparative Philology* as " neo-grammarians ". I make it entirely clear in the book, pp. 83 f., that there is a difference between accepting the existence of such abnormalities and taking them as a *basis* for identification where *ex hypothesi* the semantic component is the quantity to be discovered. Cf. also *Transactions of the Philological Society*, *ibid.*, pp. 48 f.

Meanwhile DAHOOD, *op. cit.*, p. 75 waxes scornful over the discovery of *nbš* for *npš* in a Hebrew ostracon. The scribe, he says, mocks my warning on this matter. What is mocked is Dahood's ability to understand an argument. Though the empirical finding of *nbš* had not occurred when my text was written, the entire argument was written in order to provide for this sort of possibility, and only factual details, but nothing in the structure of the argument, require to be altered. From another side, cf. the comments of Mettinger, p. 130b. Dahood's argument becomes totally unintelligible to me when he alleges with some heat that I, " hamstrung by textbook theories " (what textbook ?), " cannot bring myself to admit " that pairs like *lbš* and *lpš*, *nbš* and *npš* " are non-phonemic variations. " I never supposed they were anything else.

Semitic language studies, such as Arabic or Akkadian studies, have been liberated. While Akkadian studies have long established their freedom from a status ancillary to biblical study, Ugaritic studies still suffer damage from the *Entdeckerfreude* of those who have exploited them for the elucidation of the Old Testament. I would set it forth as a good principle : if you want to know something reliable about Ugaritic, ask an Ugaritologist who is interested in looking at the material for itself, and not at the material as a quarry from which new quick identifications of Hebrew meanings can be dug. The position I take, far from seeking to ignore or diminish the importance of Ugaritic, is interested in the valuation of Ugaritic as a quantity in itself. The haste to establish the maximum possible equation between Ugaritic and Hebrew can be criticized not only for creating Hebrew in the image of Ugaritic but also for creating Ugaritic in the image of Hebrew.

The same is true of Phoenician, and an example from it (actually from Punic, but this makes no difference) will illustrate some of the points which have been made above. Dahood complains that I do not discuss any Phoenician form ; [16] let us see what happens when we do discuss one.

One of the words identified by Dahood is a Hebrew noun *māgān* "suzerain, sovereign". It is discussed on p. XXXVII of the Introduction to his *Psalms I*, and more fully on p. 16, with reference to Ps. 3,4. He translates this as :

> But you, O Yahweh, are my Suzerain as long as I live...

This involves, of course, a departure from the traditional understanding of Hebrew *magen* as "shield". Thereafter the same suggestion is repeated several times : at Ps. 7,11 ("My Suzerain is the Most High God" ; see note on p. 45, there qualified with "perhaps") ; at 18,31 (note on p. 114), 47,10 (pp. 286f.), 59,12 (but here the understanding "shield" is retained by Dahood, with only the possibility of "suzerain", see *Psalms II*, p. 72), 84,10,12 (*ibid.*, pp. 282f., with note alleging that this rendering demolishes the interpretation of "the anointed" in *The Jerusalem Bible*). All of these go back to the same starting point, the notes on pp. XXXVII and 16f. On p. XXXVII we hear that the reading as *māgān* is "based on the Punic name for 'emperor', *māgōn*" ; and on p. 17 we read the following remarkable assertion :

16. DAHOOD, p. 71. Dahood's assertion is entirely incorrect in point of fact ; he seems to have counted only the five mentioned under "Phoenician" in my index, which refer to general statements about that language ; actual words discussed are entered in the index of examples, and cf. also under "Canaanite". Some Phoenician instances discussed, such as *št'* on pp. 180, 294 etc., are among the suggestions treated most favourably.

> In Punic the Carthaginian generals are given the title *māgōn*, which Latin inscriptions reproduce by *imperator*, " suzerain ", or *dux* ; see Louis Maurin, « Himilcon le Magonide. Crises et mutations à Carthage au début du IVe siècle avant J.-C. », *Semitica* 12 (1962) 5-43.

Let us then look at the article of Maurin, from which such drastic effects upon the Hebrew Bible have been derived. The article concerns an important family who are known as the Magonids, so known because they are descended from one whose name was Magon — the normal usage, of course, for noun formations in *-id*. The genealogy is set out by Maurin on p. 13. Magon is the first name, the descendants have equally familiar names like Hasdrubal, Hamilcar, Hannibal. [17] In about the fifth century, as Maurin puts it, the known members of this family " seem to have been regularly invested with the generalate at Carthage. " (p. 13).

The passage upon which Dahood appears to be relying (for there is no other in the article which is to his purpose) is on p. 16 :

> Les titres des Magonides se retrouvent eux aussi de Malchus à la fin du IVe siècle. Les textes latins emploient avec constance ceux d'*imperator* ou de *dux* pour qualifier les généraux carthaginois, et une seule fois le mot « dictatures » est utilisé par Justin à propos d'Hasdrubal, le fils de Magon.

Maurin then goes on to discuss the titles used in Greek texts, where for instance Diodorus often distinguishes between the title of king and that of general. This last is the point that Maurin is discussing. The question is whether a man, whose name might be Hasdrubal or Hannibal, has the title (and office) of king, or that of general. With this question in mind Maurin considers the name Malchus. Does this word mean " king " and function as a title, or is it just the personal name of the man involved ? Maurin thinks it is the latter :

> Le nom de Malchus ne représente pas forcément le titre royal lui-même, comme on le croit ordinairement, mais il peut en être un composé ; d'ailleurs les transcriptions antiques de ce nom sont variables ; on pourrait peut-être le comparer avec le nom de Magon, qui se rattacherait à une racine signifiant « protecteur », et qui n'est pas un titre. [18]

17. The persons concerned are well known and are fully described in any standard history.

18. MAURIN, *op. cit.*, p. 16, n. 2 ; I have omitted the references to other literature which are included in parentheses.

In fact one sees that everything said about Punic *magon* by Dahood is wrong. The word is a personal name, and not a title. Carthaginian generals were not given *magon* as a title ; either it was their personal name before they became general, or it was not. Latin *imperator* or *dux* is not a reproduction of *magon*, but a designation of the office of general held by people with names like Hannibal or Hasdrubal, who happened to belong to the family of the Magonids. The passage has nothing to do with a reproduction of Punic words in Latin inscriptions ; it is a matter of terms used by Latin (or Greek) historians to designate the office held by certain Carthaginian leaders. The idea that *magon* is a title, or that it is " the Punic name for ' emperor ' ", is not only not supported, but is expressly ruled out as self-evidently untrue, by the source quoted by Dahood in favour of his interpretation. [19]

In fact the sense of the name Magon is well known : it comes from a very common word meaning " give ", perhaps " offer, deliver ". This occurs in Hebrew but is rather rare. In Punic on the other hand it is very common. The overwhelmingly probable meaning of the name Magon is " he has given (a son) ". [20] It belongs to the same common type as the Hebrew name Nathan. Far from being rendered by Latin and other bilingual inscriptions as " emperor " (!), it is " rendered " simply as the name Magon, and very numerous examples can be found.

Thus Dahood's entire construction of a sense " suzerain " for *m-g-n* in Hebrew lacks any basis in Phoenician-Punic evidence, and is contradicted by the sources to which Dahood appeals. This is not a matter of evidence in existence, which might be interpreted one way or another : the entire construction built up by Dahood, and repeated at several places in the Psalter, rests on mere misunderstandings and misconstructions. It looks as if some one has misinterpreted material registered on a card index ; and this of course can happen to anyone, and is nothing to worry about. But there is a more serious side to the matter : considering the extremely high frequency of the name Magon in Punic texts

19. The only mistake in Maurin (whom I take to be a classicist rather than a Semitist) is that he renders Magon as *protecteur*, implying the root *g-n-n* " protect ", present in the familiar Hebrew *magen* " shield ". This does not make any difference for our purpose : he rightly takes it as obvious that the familiar personal name Magon is a personal name and not a title, and argues from this that the term Malchus is also a personal name, i.e. that it does not imply that its bearer was called *king*. On Magon, Maurin refers to the article of J. G. Février, " Paralipomena Punica ", *Cahiers de Byrsa* 6 (1956) 13-27, see p. 21 ; but this makes no difference to our question : Février is simply discussing whether a writing apparently *mgnm* should be read as the name Magonam or as a noun " protector ", with the reading *mgnn*.

20. For instance, Donner-Röllig, *KAI* ii. p. 67 : " Er hat (einen Sohn) geschenkt ". For an instance of the rendering of this name as the same name in another language, cf. the Numidian text of *KAI* no. 101, and the Latin forms as exemplified in *KAI* ii. p. 67.

and the plentiful opportunity given to students to observe its usage, I find it impossible to understand how a misconstruction such as this could have been believed and accepted by anyone actually at home in the study of Punic texts. So perhaps we may hope to hear less from Professor Dahood about the ignorance and non-appreciation of Ugaritic and Phoenician on the part of those who do not share his approach.

To sum up, this instance illustrates how the study of the cognate sources (in this case Punic) is damaged and corrupted by the zeal to make them into material for a novel understanding of the Hebrew Bible. For surely no one can suppose that this whole construction of *magon* as meaning " suzerain " and acting as a title for Carthaginian generals would ever have arisen out of the Punic sources studied for themselves. It is the presence of the sequence *m-g-n* in Hebrew, and it alone, which initiated the whole operation. Yet in Hebrew itself there is no support for it, since the idea that God is shield fits perfectly well in all the instances concerned.

The instance illustrates also the method of numerical accumulation which is so prominent in Dahood's work : the suggestion, once made, is repeated again and again, and when one asks for the justification of any single example one is told that numerous other examples of the same thing have been detected. In this case all the examples are equally nugatory, the basis for all of them being nil.

Here we see a contrast with the majority of the examples discussed in my book, in which something is to be learned from the analysis of the example even if it turns out to be unconvincing. By contrast, examples like the *magan* just discussed contribute nothing ; they teach no new lessons in philology, and nothing is learned from the analysis of them. The process of analysis can only be negative. Unhappily, it can be repeated over many instances.

As I have said, the final decision in many cases rests with the taste of the scholar dealing with Hebrew, rather than with Ugaritic or other cognate evidence. Dahood, for example, thinks it impossible to take Ps. 58,11 as " he washes his feet in the blood of the wicked ". [21] According to him, one cannot wash one's feet in blood ; " no clear visual image emerges " from it. Well, I am delighted to leave it to the judgement of Old Testament scholars. But Dahood goes on : " One schooled in Ugaritic " would have known that it meant not washing *in* blood, but washing *from* blood : thus " he will wash his feet of the blood of the wicked ".

So let us look at the Ugaritic text CTA 3, ii. 34 (Gordon ʿnt, II, 34), one of those which Dahood cites. The text as a whole seems to me to be interpretable as follows. Firstly, ʿAnat's slaughter has its climax in her

21. DAHOOD, p. 77.

wading in blood (thus lines 13-14, repeated more or less in 27-28). This slaughter goes on until she is satisfied (line 29). Now (lines 31 f.) something is poured into a bowl, apparently *dm* " blood ". After this it goes straight on to say that 'Anat washed her hands *bdm ḏmr*. It seems natural to suppose that this is a ceremonial washing in blood. There follows a scene with some movement of furniture ; and after this, line 38, 'Anat draws water and washes. It is at least feasible that there are two washings here, one in blood and one in water with dew, and the lack of repetition of phraseology supports the view that these are different (contrast the double reporting, in similar words, of her earlier wading in blood, above). I do not insist that this interpretation is right, but it seems entirely reasonable ; and in any case the view that 'Anat washes *in* the blood of *ḏmr* in this passage is no novelty of mine, but can be found in a number of experienced workers on Ugaritic, [22] though the contrary view (that she washed her hands *from* blood) is also found. We may hope therefore to hear rather less from Professor Dahood about what will be thought by those " schooled in Ugaritic ". [23]

It is of course absurd that one should have to appeal to a Ugaritic text on such a matter, and I do not in fact so appeal ; I simply point out that the Ugaritic evidence itself is very likely a good deal more ambivalent than Dahood supposes. Another such point may be added : in so far as I understand Dahood's objection to the idea of washing one's feet in blood, he seems to mean that " wash " means " cleanse " ; blood however is not a cleansing medium but a dirty substance, so that you wash not *in* blood, but *to get rid of* blood. If this is intended, it is a crassly literalist point of view, ignoring both the metaphorical nature of the Psalms passage, which by no means maintains that blood is a good substance for washing the feet, and also the familiar religious conceptions of blood as a cleansing agent and of the shedding of blood as a form of retribution. But, apart from these obvious points, the semantics of *raḥaṣ* do not necessarily imply *cleansing*, in the sense of removing a dirty object ; they may imply soaking, splashing, bespattering. This can be seen in Hebrew (*Song of Songs* 5,12 : " splashed by the milky water ", NEB ; *Job* 29,6) ; it applies in Ugaritic (if 'Anat " washes " in blood, it does not imply that she uses blood to cleanse away

22. Cf. C. H. GORDON, *Ugaritic Literature* (1949) ; p. 18 : " She washes her hands in the blood of soldiery " ; G. R. DRIVER, CML, p. 85 : " washed... her hand(s) in the blood of the guards " ; recently A. S. KAPELRUD, *The Violent Goddess* (Oslo, 1969), p. 50 : " She washed her hands in the blood of soldiers " ; and not least W. F. ALBRIGHT, *HUCA* 23 (1950-51) 20,38: "with whose blood she washed her hands".

23. On the point at issue in all this, i.e. the recognition of *b* meaning " from ", my position has the welcome agreement of W. L. MORAN, pp. 239 f. — he being doubtless also unschooled in Ugaritic.

some other matter, but that she wets or splashes herself in blood), and in Akkadian, e.g. :

> " [Just as] this chariot with its base-board
> is spattered [*ra-aḫ-ṣa-tú-u-ni*] [with blood] ; just so, [in battle with]
> your [enemy], may they spatter your chariots
> with your own [blood]. " [24]

These examples must suffice as illustrations of some of the problems one must feel about Dahood's work ; but it certainly does not exhaust them. I leave aside such matters as Dahood's attitude to the consonantal text, which to me seems to be a compound of a traditional religious-superstitious reverence for the signs on paper on one hand, and the pragmatic necessities of his own method on the other. I leave aside his mode of semantic discussion, which commonly seems to me to work from the semantics of the *English* words used in his renderings, rather than from the Hebrew or the Ugaritic. These and many other issues must be left aside here. Basically, my idea of language is entirely different from his, and also my idea of what constitutes care in the handling of philological evidence. Some further general points will be added later in this article. The following remarks about some words in *Job*, 3 are not of a very controversial character : their main purpose is to illustrate the complexity of strata with which we have to deal in the analysis of a Hebrew text, and the unlikeliness that simple philological parallels will prove to be in themselves decisive.

First of all let us look at the well-known case of the word *ṣalmawet*, which occurs in *Job* 3,5. [25] As everyone knows, the older tradition took this as " the shadow of death " ; but more recent scholarly tradition has taken a different turn, holding that it is a word *ṣalmut* (or *-ot*) of the root *ṣ-l-m*, with the sense " obscurity, darkness ". This has now come to be so completely accepted that some works have ceased to mention that the older tradition of meaning ever existed. This is surprising, for even in modern times there has been a current of very significant opinion in favour of the older understanding. Th. Nöldeke, after all — and whose opinion could be more weighty in a matter like this ? — wrote in 1896 a short article [26] defending both the traditional pronunciation and the sense " shadow of death ". He pointed out, though he cautiously refrained from pressing the point, that an early-Islamic poem included the

24. *Iraq* 20 (1958) 75, line 612-615 (D. J. Wiseman). I am grateful to my colleague M. E. J. Richardson for very helpful discussion of these questions.

25. Cf. also J. F. A. Sawyer in *JSS* 17 (1972) 257 ff. (review of Holladay's dictionary), and his *Semantics in Biblical Research* (1972), pp. 14, 40, 90.

26. *ZAW* 17 (1897) 183-187.

phrase *ẓill al-mawt*, with the sense of " thick shadow " [27] — in this case not unpleasant gloom but refreshing shade of trees; he denied the existence in Hebrew and Aramaic of the root *ṣ-l-m* " dark ". The reading as *ṣalmawet* was again defended by J. Hehn in an article in 1918, which carried farther the line developed by Nöldeke; [28] and the arguments of Hehn proved sufficiently strong to convince Bauer and Leander, whose detailed grammar records their judgement in his favour. [29] Certainly not all of the arguments of Nöldeke and of Hehn could stand unchanged today; [30] some of the terms in which the question was discussed in the ninteenth century might seem out of date by now; but, in spite of modifications which would have to be made, the weight of opinion, especially with Nöldeke's judgement involved, is still imposing, and it is surprising that these opinions seem to have been very much neglected. [31]

It is not my purpose here, however, to argue that the older tradition is " right " and that the word should indeed be read as *ṣalmawet* and understood as " the shadow of death ". My purpose is rather to show the importance of this tradition for the understanding of the word, and thus to show that the philological facts, even if *ṣalmut* is the right reading and " darkness " the " right " meaning, cannot short-circuit the complicated task of unravelling the tradition of understanding.

Even if we accept that " darkness " is the right meaning, this can hardly be the end of the matter. The understanding as " the shadow of death " is very old: out of the 18 or so cases in the Hebrew, about 10 or 11 are rendered with σκιὰ θανάτου in Greek. These include not only some in the Writings, such as in Job itself and in the Psalms, but also two in the Major Prophets (*Isa* 9,1 and *Jer* 13,16). Since, on quite other grounds, Job may be a somewhat late book, at least in its final form, no very great distance in time may separate its completion from

27. *Ibid.*, p. 184; the source is Yāqūt 4, 566, 21. Nöldeke refrained from pressing the point because he thought that the Arabic phraseology might have undergone indirect influence from the Old Testament. Some counter-arguments against Nöldeke's general position were offered by S. R. Driver (*Job*, ICC, part ii, pp. 18f.), but they scarcely constitute a refutation, as Dhorme (*Job*, p. 27) thought.

28. In *Orientalistische Studien, Fritz Hommel zum 60. Geburtstage... dargebracht* (Leipzig, 2 vols., 1917 and 1918 = Mitteilungen der Vorderasiatisch-aegyptischen Gesellschaft, 21 & 22 (1916 and 1917), vol. ii, pp. 79-90.

29. *Historische Grammatik*, § 61*uι*, p. 506.

30. My own studies in Hebr. *ṣelem* « image » (*BJRL* 51 (1968-9) 18 and 21) led to conclusions about this word which differed from Nöldeke's arguments: I doubt its connection with an Arabic *ṣ-l-m* " cut off " — a suggestion made by him only hesitatingly in any case; and I give hesitant favour to the derivation from *ṣ-l-m* " dark " of the two instances in the Psalms (39,7; 73,20), so that I do not share his confidence that the root *ṣ-l-m* with the sense " dark " did not exist in Hebrew and Aramaic at all.

31. Hehn's article was published during the war and is somewhat inaccessible.

the Septuagintal interpretation of this word. It is thus quite possible that the sense " the shadow of death " was already understood by the final redactor of the canonical text of Job, or was known to him and influenced his thinking, even if it was not intended by the earliest composer of ch. 3.

This in turn only leads us to further questions. As we have seen, it is usual to say that the word should be read as *ṣalmut*, with the abstract noun-ending *-ut*. But is it really probable that the tradition took a word which had previously always been pronounced as *ṣalmut* and altered its pronunciation to *ṣalmawet*, purely in order to support a midrashic-etymological explanation, and without any justification whatever in the current phonetics of the word ? This seems to me unparalleled in what we know of the transmission of the text. Midrashic-etymological explanations were of course many, but were not generally accompanied by a systematic change of the pronunciation of words for the sake of conformity to the explanation. The case of names including heathen divinities or apparent obscenities is a different matter from such a change of pronunciation, if the original form was *ṣalmut*. One reason, therefore, against the modern explanation of *ṣalmawet* is that it makes the phenomenon into something quite isolated and peculiar.

It may be apposite to mention here some places where the generally accepted sense " darkness " does not fit very well ; some of these were already mentioned by Nöldeke or Hehn. (a) In *Job* 38,17 the parallel is with *mawet* " death ". Hehn maintained that " darkness " was impossible here. Even if this is going too far, the sense " shadow of death " seems a strong contender. Note also that *ṣalmawet* is in this case a *place*, a place with doors (or door-keepers — so NEB with its " the door-keepers of the place of darkness "). (b) In *Ps.* 44,20 there seems to be a parallel between " in the place of *tannim* " (probably to be read, or understood, as referring to the *tannin* or dragon) and *b^eṣalmawet*. " You have covered us with darkness " seems rather lame and thin after a previous half-verse which talks of crushing " in the place of dragons ". It is perhaps because of this consideration that NEB renders with :

> Yet thou hast crushed us as the sea-serpent was crushed
> and covered us with the darkness of death

— in other words, the recognition of *death* as a semantic element in the sentence gives it a proper balance. [32]

32. It is possible, however, that NEB presumed a textual error and read the text as *ṣalmut mawet*. The corruption would be easily explained as haplography ; but there is no other example, so far as I know, of such a collocation.

(c) In *Jer* 2,6 our word occurs in the description of the desert, parallel with terms suggesting its quality of waste and dryness. " Darkness " does not fit well here, at least if one takes it in the more natural sense, and this would seem best in view of the other terms in the passage, which are used in very normal ways. That " darkness " is difficult here seems to have been felt by the NEB translators, who for MT *b*e-*'ereṣ ṣiyya w*e*ṣalmawet* write : " a country barren and ill-omened ". I do not know precisely what philological evidence was taken into consideration in rendering " ill-omened ".

I do not wish to claim too much for these examples ; but it is only right that they should be set alongside the well-known cases where *ṣalmawet* stands in parallel with words for " darkness " like *ḥošek* or in opposition to words for " light " such as *'or*.

Two further aspects seems worthy of attention. One is the investigation of locutions in which a pattern like " the *x* of God " is taken to mean " a very great *x* ". Professor D. Winton Thomas in an article on " Unusual Ways of expressing the Superlative in Hebrew " devoted several pages to combinations with *mut* and *mawet*. [33] He did not there mention, however, the case of *ṣalmawet*.

In 1962 Professor Winton Thomas published a full study of our word, in which he resumed some of the early arguments and brought to bear also the force of his own studies in *mut/mawet* as an expression for the " superlative ". [34] He also concluded in favour of the sense literally " shadow of death ", but in effect " deep, thick darkness ", and in favour of the form *ṣalmawet*. The case of this word is a curious one, in that the majority opinion in modern times has certainly been in favour of the form *ṣalmut* and the sense " darkness " (root *ṣ-l-m*), but among scholars who have devoted full independent studies to the word the trend has been in the opposite direction.

He provided some further discussion in another article in 1968. [35] Meanwhile S. Rin had published a note on " The *mwt* of Grandeur ", which widened the subject by making reference to the deity Mot and the work of Cassuto. [36] These contributions appear to give some support to the idea that *ṣalmawet*, if analysed as " shadow " plus " death ", nevertheless might — in some cases at any rate — have had a sense like

33. *VT* 3 (1953) 209-224, especially pp. 219-222. Quite incidentally, it seems a little unfortunate that this construction has come to be categorized as a mode of " expressing the superlative " — this is hardly what is meant.

34. In *JSS* 7 (1962) 191-200. I developed the arguments of this present paper independently of Winton Thomas's article, which might have made this section superfluous ; in any case my position is not quite the same as his, and I develop the facts in a different way.

35. *VT* 18 (1968) 120-124, especially pp. 122 f.

36. *VT* 9 (1959) 324 f.

" very deep shadow ", independently of any referential component specifying death. If this were so, then the understanding as " the shadow of death ", as represented for instance in the LXX renderings, would be no more than a literal representation of the original idiomatic phrase. Such a representation leaves it uncertain how far the total sense of the idiom was still appreciated, or how far on the other hand that total sense had now been replaced by the sum of the independent senses of the two component parts. The questions then remaining would be : (a) why the vowel of the first element is *a*, instead of the *e* customary in the free form of the construct *ṣel* " the shadow of... " and (b) why the whole idiom was written as one word, without word division. Neither of these is a very serious difficulty. [37]

Another relevant consideration, which can hardly be ignored even if it is not clear in what direction it leads, is that *ṣalmawet* has a certain similarity to a personal or place name. There are in Hebrew at least two comparable forms, and these are both proper names: *ḥᵃṣarmawet* "Hadramaut ", and *ʿazmawet* " Azmaveth " or (spelling of NEB) " Azmoth ". This latter is the name of several persons in early Israelite history ; there was also a place called Beth-azmaveth. There is good reason to suppose that these names were compounds including the divine name Mot. [38] It is a reasonable surmise that *ṣalmawet* could have had some association with this type of name. (a) This would account for the " compound " word form and the anomaly of the vowel *a* ; phenomena of this kind are frequent in names. (b) The root *ṣ-l-l* with the sense " shelter " is of course common in Semitic names ; cf. e.g. Tallqvist, *Assyrian Personal Names*, p. 303b, and in Hebrew the familiar Bezaleel (and very likely Zelophehad). [39] (c) In this case the analysis of the term into " the shadow of death " would be not only a linguistic process but also part of the demythologizing, so to speak, of a name associated with an alien deity and the " shelter " given by him — the deity becomes ordinary human death, the shelter becomes shadow. [40]

37. The argument sometimes made against the form *ṣalmawet*, namely that " compounds of this kind do not exist in Hebrew ", is a weak one ; for no more is necessarily involved than a *graphic* peculiarity, i.e. the writing of the entire phrase without a word-dividing space. But cf. also another aspect, to be mentioned below.

38. On Hadramaut see already G. R. DRIVER in *PEQ* 1945, pp. 13f. ; on Azmaveth, see CASSUTO, *Ha-elah ʿAnat* (Jerusalem, 1953), pp. 28f., 47ff.

39. Cf. NOTH, *Die israelitischen Personennamen*, p. 152 ; Noth seems wrong in rejecting a connection between *ṣ-l-l* and the name Zelophehad ; a sense like " may the deity (*paḥad*) shelter, protect " would seem very probable ; cf. NOTH, p. 256, no. 1204.

40. I merely mention, for the sake of the information, the pair of apparent names *ġlmt* and *ẓlmt* in CTA 4, vii, 54 f. (p. 30), Gordon *UT* 51, VII, 54. These may be relevant but I am not sure how. *ẓl* " shadow " is well established in Ugaritic,

That there was a place with the name *ṣalmawet* cannot, of course, be demonstrated. We have already noted, however, that the word does occur in spatial contexts on some occasions. One piece of possible support lies in the similarity between " the valley of *ṣalmawet* " in Ps. 23,4 and " the vale of the *baka'* " in Ps. 84,7. It is commonly held, and with quite good reason, that this latter was the name of a particular real place. But, whatever the " original " meaning of the name, it is very probable that from an early date it was understood to have the suggestion of " Vale of Weeping ", and this provides the universality required for use in the Psalm context. This understanding therefore, though found for example in the LXX with its ἐν τῇ κοιλάδι τοῦ κλαυθμῶνος, is probably already intended in the Hebrew text of the Psalm. In general, it is likely that the Ps. 23 passage has played a central part in spreading the " shadow of death " understanding of our term.

I do not claim to have solved the problem with these considerations, but only to have shown that it is a more complicated one than is generally supposed, and one in which several different levels of explanation can be and must be held together in the mind at one time. It is at least possible that the total history involves : (a) forms from a root *ṣ-l-m* " dark " ; (b) an idiom where " shadow " plus " death " meant " deep shadow " ; (c) a name of the type " may Mot give protection ". The eventual standardization of " shadow of death " would then be not an artificial invention, but a universalization over the entire usage of that which had earlier belonged only to a part. The phonetic form preserved in MT is not an artificial invention but has real foundations in the history of the term.

The case is an example, then, of the complexity of the strata of tradition and understanding with which we have to deal in the analysis of a Hebrew text, and the improbability that simple philological parallels will prove to be in themselves decisive. In particular, philological information from cognate languages is something that is to be taken into account, but does not in itself provide a decision ; and the provision of a " correct translation " cannot be a correct representation of the dimensions of the tradition.

From the same verse we can speak more briefly about another illustration, MT *kimᵉrire yom*. It has long been customary to identify here a word " darkness " from a root *k-m-r* (Syriac *kmir* " gloomy, sad ; black, dark ") [41] and this of course would make good sense ; but is it what the poet wrote ? There is evidence in early post-biblical Hebrew

but *ẓlm* " darkness " is not ; this may be relevant to the question whether it ever existed in Hebrew.

41. The Hebrew dictionaries tend to give an impression that the sense " black " is basic in Syriac. My impression is that the sense " be sad " (of personal emotion)

which points in another direction. Sir. 11, 4 has *'l tqls bmryry ywm,* and in the Qumran Hodayot and Pesharim we have several phrases like *wnpšy bmryry ywm.* [42] Perhaps it would be hasty to conclude with Mansoor on this evidence that the text in Job *must* be read as " as the bitterness of the day " ; it would still be possible that the Sirach and Qumran texts are restorations or restitutions, formed within late Hebrew on the basis of the MT in Job. [43] Nevertheless the probability lies with Mansoor's position : even if the root *k-m-r* appears to make better sense, and even if it " lay behind " an early stage of the Job poem, which is itself unlikely, it is likely that the final stage of the Hebrew intended the phrase to be understood as *k* plus *m-r-r.* [44] There is, in fact, very little trace of *k-m-r* in a sense like " gloomy, dark " anywhere in Hebrew, either before Job or after. May *k-m-r* in this sense be an isolated development of Syriac ? [45]

Our next instance concerns the importance of parallelisms and word-pairs, whether traditional or otherwise. At *Job* 3,8 it is an easy suggestion, and one commonly adopted, that instead of MT *yom* we should read *yam* " sea ", giving the parallelism of sea /Leviathan. If we do this, we may be tempted to go a step farther and make the verbs parallel also : having *'-r-r* " curse " as the first, we may go on and say that the second is cognate with Ethiopic *tä'ayyärä,* giving a sense " revile ". [46] Parallelism in the verbs is achieved also by the NEB rendering [47] :

> Cursed be it by those whose magic binds even the monster of the deep,
> who are ready to tame Leviathan himself with spells.

We shall concentrate, however, on the question of parallelism in the nouns, and bring the verbs in only incidentally.

We recognise the intrinsic probability of a connection between Leviathan and the sea ; since Leviathan was a sea-monster, that can go without saying. It does not decide however what the poet of Job was

is much more central than that of colour ; for the colour *black* Syriac uses primarily other words, especially the root *'km.*

42. See M. Mansoor, *VTS* 9 (1963) 316 f. The Qumran readings support for Sirach the reading as cited above, as against the variant *kmryry* (= MT in Job). The citation *bmryry,* above, is the form as given by Mansoor ; for our present purpose it makes no difference if it is read as *bmrwry.*

43. On such formations, see my discussion in *Comparative Philology,* pp. 227ff.

44. For the syntax, cf. perhaps *kimᵉribe kohen,* Hos. 4,4.

45. Akkadian *kamāru* is " heap up ", and not " overshadow, darken ", as is said by Dhorme, *Job,* p. 27 ; Ethiopic *kəmr* is also " heap ".

46. This is example no. 242 in my *Comparative Philology* ; cf. text on p. 125.

47. I do not know on what evidence NEB based the rendering with " to tame with spells " ; surely hardly Arabic *ta'wīdh, 'ūdha* " charm, spell, amulet ".

saying. In his context the basic subject matter is a day or a night, the day of Job's begetting or of his birth, his " day " (3,1). In verse 7 he is still talking about this same thing, about a " night ". In verse 9 also we are still dealing with features of this day — its twilight, its unsuccessful longing for light, its relation to the twilight or dawn. The probability then is that the MT is right with its *yom* : the poet is talking about the " day-cursers ", and there is nothing about the sea in the passage. [48] A traditional parallelism between sea and Leviathan is so likely that it hardly needs to be proved, and one need not doubt its presence in the " background " here ; but in the actual poem as produced, this relationship has now become otiose. Because the poet is concerned with *day*, he now has a significant poetical connection between *'or^{e}re* and the waiting for light, *'or*, in the next line ; it may perhaps have elements of ambiguity, suggesting both " those who curse " and " those who give light ". As for *'orer*, it is most probably the familiar Hebrew with the sense " stir up ". The primary need of the exegete is not to " identify " the mythological background, in the sense of stating exactly what pre-existing myth is presupposed ; what is more important is the myth as it is reconstituted by the poet for his own purposes. There are, he hints, powers that can or may or do curse the day, just as there are powers that give light ; these powers can also give trouble by stirring up Leviathan, a bad-tempered monster who is opposed to the cosmic order. The pre-Israelite background is interesting information, but is not more than ancillary to the explanation of the passage.

* * *

I would like to conclude with some remarks of a more philosophical character, if one may call it so : some remarks which take the discussion of Hebrew philology, the use of Ugaritic, etc., and bring it into relation with the other main problem which has concerned me, the discussion of biblical semantics. When my book on semantics was published, one of the main criticisms made against it was that it belonged to an extreme current of empiricism or positivism. [49] In itself, of course, such a remark

48. I do not feel quite certain about this view ; one could of course go the opposite way and say that these considerations are the reason why the tradition altered an original *yam* into *yom*. If " sea " is correct, then the verse introduces ideas and images which are quite extraneous to the remaining structure of the chapter. This, and the fact that the reading as *yam* is an extremely facile surface emendation, seem to tip the scales in favour of the position I state above.

49. On this see my *Biblical Words for Time* (2nd edition, London, 1969), pp. 194-207, " The Philosophical Background ". One reviewer, there quoted (p. 194 n.), identified " an extreme positivist and formalist attitude, which detests any introduction of philosophical content. "

is nothing to worry about : the giving of names such as empiricism and positivism does not constitute argument. But, I ask myself : supposing that there is some real issue here, and supposing that there are really empiricist or over-empiricist, positivist or over-positivist, attitudes to be found in the treatment of biblical language, then among whom are they to be found ? The direction in which I can see such viewpoints lies among the scholars whose work I investigated in the book on *Comparative Philology*. It is among them that I, as I view the matter, see the out-working of a fairly extreme empirical positivism. I would not admit that empiricism and positivism are in themselves in any way terms of re-proach ; but it is here, among the Drivers and the Dahoods of scholar-ship working on the detailed biblical text, that I find not just an empi-ricism or positivism but an almost entirely *uncritical* and *unanalytical* empiricism and positivism. And I do not use these terms as mere labels, but will explain the characteristics which I have in mind : the concen-tration on a *method* which has simple, obvious and practical outlines ; the emphasis on details in black and white, which details form the units of demonstration in the method ; the almost complete absence of critical and thoughtful analysis of the basis of the method ; an alienation from the sophisticated discussion of ideas, of entities such as theologies ; the use of purely pragmatic criteria in argument ; and, because no properly argued foundation is provided, the corroboration of each detail and its function not by any theoretical foundation but by the mere addition of yet more details of the same kind and on the same level [50] — a principle which at its worst deteriorates into that of validation through claims to multiple success.

Out of all this I shall pick one or two special cases for further mention. It is hardly disputable that the scholars who have been most productive with philological suggestions, who have produced not just a few but hundreds or even thousands, have at the same time been people rather alienated from the main currents of exegesis. Form criticism, for instan-ce, which is one of the major modern approaches to biblical literature, seems to have passed them by. Not only this, but even fundamental literary criticism seems often to have passed them by ; some of the points at which philological explanations have been offered were diffi-culties requiring new interpretations only if widely accepted literary-critical solutions were ignored. I shall illustrate this from only one instance, a case which I mentioned in *Comparative Philology*, without however touching on this aspect of it. [51] At *Num.* 16,1 the text begins with *wayyiqqaḥ qoraḥ*, at first sight apparently " and Korah took " —

50. Cf. the contrast I make between a logic dominated by discovery and a logic dominated by analysis, *Transactions of the Philological Society*, *ibid.*, p. 54.

51. *Comparative Philology*, pp. 17f.

but there is no object ; and hence the suggestion that this is a completely other verb, meaning " was insolent, was defiant, rebelled ". The NEB, I notice, has " Now Korah... challenged the authority of Moses ", which I take to be the same interpretation in a more generalized form. This is a place, however, where traditional literary criticism had already provided an alternative explanation, by suggesting that two different sources were compounded. In one source, let us say, Korah " took " the " men " who appear as the fourth word in verse 2 ; some others out of the long list of names, now in verse 1, form the subject of the other verb " and they arose " at the beginning of verse 2. Thus we have two sources :

(a) And Korah took men of the children of Israel (P?)
(b) Dathan and Abiram, etc., arose before Moses (JE?)

I do not say that this analysis is necessarily correct ; [52] but if it is even taken into consideration as a possibility, the case for finding a difficulty in the present text with the sense " and he took " is likely to disappear. In my distinction of two modes of dealing with a difficult text, the textual through emendation and the philological through new identification of meaning on the basis of a cognate language, I should have added for some cases the source-critical, as here.

Something similar can be said on the level of theological exegesis. Proponents of the philological identification from cognate sources seem often to suppose that the provision of a right translation of the words constitutes more or less a complete exegesis ; on the other hand, the handling of the ideas and the theologies of the texts is often wild and irresponsible. It ranges from a kind of reductionism, which seeks to diminish as far as possible the theological dimensions of the text — a tendency very visible in the work of Driver — at the one end, to a blind traditionalism, at the other end, which discovers in the Psalms traditional beliefs like that in immortality, in defiance of all that has been learned through patient study in the religion and theology of the Old Testament. In Dahood's case it seems likely that the values and terms of a highly traditional Christian theology are attached to the Hebrew-Ugaritic cultural-religious *mélange* which accompanies in his eyes the linguistic indistinguishability of the two.

The aspect of translation has already been mentioned, and must be further stressed. It is unfortunate that many of the philological suggestions now being mooted have been aired for the first time, or almost

52. It seems to have the support of S. R. DRIVER, *Introduction to the Literature of the Old Testament* (1891), p. 59 ; more recently, R. PFEIFFER, *Introduction* (1941), pp. 171, 189.

the first time, in translations ; and not only in translations but in translations intended for the general public and as such magnified by the full publicity of modern advertising. The work of translation is not in my judgement at all a good way of making these suggestions available for discussion. It is of course only right that the general public should have made available to it the results of the latest scholarly opinion. But it is only in our generation that for the first time interpretations of a quite novel and drastic type have been made known to the general public *before* they were known to — and, still more, before they were accepted by — scholarly opinion. With the publication of the Old Testament of the NEB it has become something of a sport among scholars to try to work out the basis upon which some of the renderings have been produced. Even those who have studied hundreds of modern philological suggestions can be left open-mouthed, wondering how the translators obtained from the Hebrew what they did. Just to cite one case, at a well-known place in *Zech.*, 3,2 the phrase *ha-boḥer birušalayim* has been detached from God and attached to Satan, so that it is no longer God who " chooses Jerusalem " but Satan who " is venting his spite on Jerusalem ". Thus NEB prints : " The LORD rebuke you, Satan, the LORD rebuke you who are venting your spite on Jerusalem. " Only by pure luck had I happened to come across the suggestion on which this was presumably based [53] — the identification of a *b-ḥ-r*, different from the familiar word " choose ", and related to Arabic words " to steam " and the like ; this new word is found in no less than seven places in the Old Testament.

My own belief is that translations, at least such as are supposed to be a considered interpretation, presented to the public, can and should be produced only *after* a full consideration by the world of scholarship, and only after a full process of exegesis, including literary-critical, form-critical, *redaktionsgeschichtlich* and theological consideration.

To return then to the general philosophy of the study of biblical language, I believe that the position I have taken in the two main discussions, though often classed as an extreme and negative one in the first impression made, is in fact a moderate one. As I see it, the positions investigated in *Semantics* and in *Comparative Philology* are the two opposed extreme positions in the study of biblical language : in very rough terms, one was idealist, the other positivist, if such terms have meaning. To sum up the case about comparative philology, there is nothing wrong with the *method* of using cognate languages in order to derive novel senses for Hebrew words ; but of all the products said to have been derived from this method in the last decades, only a small proportion are satisfactory. Those who think this judgement too negative

53. DRIVER, in *Mélanges Marcel Cohen* (1970), pp. 236f. See my remarks in *JSS* 17 (1972) 133.

have a simple course open to them : they can print the list of such suggestions which they personally consider to have been established beyond doubt. The judgement which I passed upon the products of this method in my book, though subject to some modification in proportions, is, I believe, in its basic structure a right and fair one ; and, far from taking any extreme position, I believe that in making this judgement I have spoken for the central current of Old Testament scholarship, in which I have confidence.

J. Barr

See *Supplementary note*, p. 209.

3

THE "ORIGINAL MEANING OF THE TEXT" AND OTHER LEGITIMATE SUBJECTS FOR SEMANTIC DESCRIPTION

An assumption which dominated the study of the Old Testament for a very long time was that " the original meaning of the text " was virtually the only legitimate subject for intellectually respectable scientific research. The reasons for this narrow attitude to the history of tradition were partly archaeological, one suspects, and partly religious. On the one hand, there was the wealth of new archaeological data that swamped the field of biblical research and encouraged the overoptimistic view that now we would be able to find out what really happened and what the biblical authors originally meant ; while on the other hand, there was a Protestant view that many ecclesiastical abuses and theological errors were due to misinterpretations or mistranslations of scripture, and that the hope of the church lay in getting back to the original meaning of the text. [1]

This assumption that the nearer we can get back to what was in the original author's mind, the nearer we are to authenticity or truth, however, has in recent years been frequently called into question. Examples of this refreshing trend would include a new interest in the final form of the text, papers on " the age of the Chronicler " and the psalm-headings, studies of Qumran variants and the ancient versions, not just for their relevance to textual criticism, but as pieces of literature in their own right [2]. The omission of the psalm-headings from the New English Bible, because, among other things, they are not " original ", was a throwback to a former less enlightened age, and widespread disapproval of NEB's decision on this question is a measure of contempo-

1. See B. S. Childs, *Biblical Theology in Crisis* (Philadelphia, 1970), especially pp. 139-147, for a recent discussion of this subject.

2. Cf. M. Noth, *Exodus* (London, 1962), p. 18 (*ATD* 5 (Göttingen, 1959), p. 8) ; P. R. Ackroyd, *The Age of the Chronicler* (Suppl. to *Colloquium* (the Australian and New Zealand Theological Review) 1970) ; F. F. Bruce, " The earliest Old Testament interpretation " (*OTS* 17 (1972), 37-52) ; S. Jellicoe, *The Septuagint and Modern Study* (Oxford, 1968) pp. 352f.

rary interest in all levels of biblical tradition, not just the earliest [3]. The semanticist in these permissive days, whether he is a translator, commentator, theologian or lexicographer, can freeze the cumulative process of biblical tradition wherever he likes, and describe the meaning of the text in 10th century B.C. Jerusalem or 6th century B.C. Babylon or 3rd century B.C. Alexandria or 1st century A.D. Palestine, according to his own individual interests or skills. The essential thing is that he makes it clear at the outset exactly what he is doing [4].

Before the pendulum swings too far in this direction and it becomes fashionable to argue that it does not really matter what " the original meaning of the text " was, and that in many cases we will probably never know and there are often more interesting levels at which to describe the meaning of the biblical text, the " original meaning " is likely to remain a fairly important concept in Old Testament studies and one which it was thought might be worth while examining. The conclusions turned out to be for the most part predictable, but in reaching them some discussion of semantic method was necessary which it was hoped might not be out of place at this conference.

The first point to make is that the meaning of a text is just as objective a part of our data as its grammatical or literary form, so that in order to reconstruct the original meaning of a text, certain scientific procedures must be employed, corresponding to, but different from, the methods of textual and literary criticism [5]. Out of the semantic methods available at present, I am not thinking primarily of comparative philology, about which we have probably heard at least as much as we would wish. It is basically a clumsy instrument whose value in our field is mainly restricted to giving very general clues to the meaning of obscure or unknown words and phrases. Translation is another rough-and-ready method of semantic description : it is, for example, of great practical value to be able to describe דָּבָר as " meaning *word* in some contexts and *thing* in others " [6]. But it is more likely that the semantic spread of דָּבָר is wider than either *word* or *thing*, even if in some varieties of Hebrew (e.g. Job and Modern Hebrew) its spread is limited by the co-presence

3. *The New English Bible* (Library Edition, Oxford & Cambridge, 1970), p. XVIII. BRUCE (*op. cit.*, p. 44, note (2)) discusses the meaning of " original " in this context.

4. On this subject, see most recently the present author's *Semantics in Biblical Research* (London, 1972), especially pp. 4-16, 112-114.

5. Cf. *op. cit.*, chapters III and IV ; J. LYONS, *Introduction to Theoretical Linguistics* (Cambridge, 1968), chapters 9 and 10.

6. Cf. J. BARR, *The Semantics of Biblical Language* (Oxford, 1961), p. 133.

of the Aramaic loanword מִלָּה [7]. An example of the " monolingual " approach to semantic description, still a novelty in biblical research, would be the description of הוֹשִׁיעַ as closer to עָזַר than to הִצִּיל in not being so frequently followed by the preposition מִן־ but distinguished from עָזַר in being restricted almost exclusively to religious contexts and in becoming unproductive in post-biblical and Modern Hebrew [8].

Neither comparative philology nor translation is nearly subtle enough to describe the meaning of common Hebrew terms in any detail, or to detect overtones and associations which they may have in certain contexts. Was צֶלֶם in *Genesis* 1,26f selected by the author because it had fewer idolatrous associations than its synonyms ? Did Isaiah choose הֶאֱמִין in two passages because of the " stability-overtones " of its root א-מ-ן ? Comparative philology is little help here and translation obscures the very information we want. But possible answers to this type of question may be found in an examination of the semantic fields in which the terms occur, and there is no doubt that here we have a valuable semantic technique which is going to provide new information, even at this late date, on the meaning of biblical Hebrew [9]. An interesting observation on the meaning of *Job*, 19,25-27 (" I know that my redeemer liveth... ") emerged from a similar study : no less than seven items from the associative field of Hebrew terms for the resurrection of the dead occur in these three short verses [10]. In discussing the goal of biblical semantics it is this kind of much more subtle information that we are aiming at, not only at explanations of the more obscure hapax legomena and textual corruptions.

From these few comments on the meaning of " meaning ", we come now to the " original meaning ". The term is used in two entirely different senses in our dictionaries and commentaries, one of which has been so universally criticized in recent years that fortunately it is slowly becoming obsolete. I refer, of course, to the use of original in an etymological sense : the original meaning of תַּחְבֻּלוֹת, for example, derived

7. מִלָּה is much more frequent in Job. (34x) than דָּבָר ; and in Modern Hebrew דָּבָר can hardly ever be translated " word " except in fossilized expressions.

8. *Semantics in Biblical Research*, pp. 102-105.

9. Cf. J. Barr, " The Image of God in the Book of Genesis — A study of terminology " (*BJRL* 51 (1968), 11-26) ; Sawyer, " Root-meanings in Hebrew " (*JSS* 12 (1967) 43-46) ; *id.*, *Semantics in Biblical Research*, pp. 28-59.

10. Sawyer, " Hebrew Words for the Resurrection of the Dead ", (*VT* 23 (1973) 218-234).

from its root ח-ב-ל, was "probably 'rope-pulling, i.e. steering'" [11]. Evidence that this word was in fact associated with חֶבֶל "a rope" or רַב הַחֹבֵל "a ship's captain" comes from the septuagint translation of the term (κυβέρνησις), and also from the rabbinic literature, so that McKane's recent translation of *Proverbs* 1,5b has some justification: "and a perceptive man learns the ropes" [12]. But without such contextual evidence, the "original meaning" of a term can never be reliably derived from its etymology. Using the contextual criteria on which semantics ultimately depends, all that "original" in this etymological sense can refer to, is the meaning of a term as it was used in Proto-Semitic which may be entirely different from its use in Biblical Hebrew. In dictionaries, pride of place as still unfortunately usually given to the origins of every Hebrew word, and an "original" (or "literal" or "strict" or "actual") meaning as derived from the customary, interesting, but usually quite unnecessary tour of the entire semitic language-family, still figures prominently in recent publications [13]. It is illuminating to see how the absence of this elaborate etymological machinery produces different definitions of some terms in Holladay's English translation of Koehler-Baumgartner (e.g. יְרַקְרַק, כֵּן) [14].

Much more productive is the use of the term "original" in a contextual sense: the original meaning of the text is the meaning which it had in its original context. Here biblical scholarship and modern semantic theory converge [15]. There are two main types of argument concerning the original meaning of a text: one based on its literary context (style, genre, *Gattung*, and the like), the other on its non-verbal, or situational context (social and political circumstances, the religious atmosphere,

11. BROWN, DRIVER & BRIGGS, *A Hebrew and English Lexicon on the Old Testament* (Oxford, 1959), p. 287.

12. *Proverbs* (London, 1970), p. 211; cf. M. JASTROW, *A Dictionary of the Targumim, etc.* (New York, 1950), vol. II, p. 1660a.

13. E. g. E. JONES, *Proverbs and Ecclesiastes* (London, 1961), p. 197 (תַּחְבֻּלוֹת); N. H. SNAITH, *Leviticus and Numbers* (London & Edinburgh, 1967), pp. 29 (קָרְבָּן), 95 (נֶתֶק); J. GRAY, *Joshua, Judges and Ruth* (London & Edinburgh, 1967), pp. 89 (עֵמֶק), 112 (קָצִין), 417 (גֹּרֶן); H. RINGGREN, *Israelite Religion* (London, 1966), p. 243 (שְׁאוֹל).

14. W. L. HOLLADAY, *A Concise Hebrew and Aramaic Lexicon of the Old Testament* (Leiden, 1971).

15. Cf. R. LAPOINTE, « La valeur linguistique du Sitz im Leben » (*Biblica* 52 (1971), 469-487); and the present author's "Context of Situation and Sitz im Leben" (*Proc. of University of Newcastle upon Tyne Philosophical Society* 1 (1967), pp. 137-147).

or *Zeitgeist* at a particular time). The modern argument, for example, that the Hebrew word for " immortality " אַל־מָוֶת in *Proverbs*, 12,28 is not original is based on factors both in its literary context and in its non-verbal or situational context. It is argued that immortality is not an original concern of the opposition between life and death in this type of Israelite sentence literature [16]. In other words, if it could be proved that the verse in question did not belong to this literary type or was in some ways exceptional, the argument would collapse. The situational argument is similar (אַל־מָוֶת cannot be original because the concept of life after death is late) [17], and would be invalid if it could be proved that in its original context there were people who believed in life after death. In another recent commentary the argument that בְּאַחֲרִית הַיָּמִים in *Isai*, 2,2 " originally refers to a moment within history " depends on the statement that " the later Jewish conception of the absolute end of the present world era... is alien to the characteristic thinking of the Old Testament " [18].

Such arguments are linguistically unexceptionable, and it is the absence of this type of contextual information that tends to undermine a good many attempts to discover the " original meaning of the text ". Dahood's well-known work on the Psalms and Proverbs is a case in point [19]. In the context of ancient North West Semitic religious belief and practice, as documented in the Ugaritic literature, no doubt some of the language from which Old Testament Hebrew is derived did refer to life after death or immortality, as he argues. But there is evidence that in ancient Israel, this area of religious belief was not very fully or explicitly developed. It might also be argued that associations with Canaanite religious beliefs were actually avoided. Admittedly arguments such as these are not unassailable : for example, it could be that Psalms and Proverbs reflect beliefs which it was the concern of the official establishment to suppress. But whatever the situation in which this literature was produced, it has to be investigated, and it is this type of investigation which seems to be missing in Dahood's otherwise attractive arguments. The same problem arises here as in the " etymologizing " referred to above.

There is however, another level at which we can examine the original meaning of the text, and one which might incidentally support some of

16. R. Tournay, « Relectures bibliques concernant la vie future et l'angelologie » (*RB* 69 (1962) 498) ; McKane, *op. cit.*, p. 451.

17. *Loc. cit.* ; Jones, *op. cit.*, p. 126.

18. O. Kaiser, *Isaiah 1-12* (London, 1972), *ad. loc.* (*ATD* 17 (Göttingen, 1963), *ad. loc.*).

19. M. Dahood, *Biblica* 41 (1960) 176-181 ; *Psalms 1-50* (New York 1965), *passim*.

Dahood's conclusions on the meaning of certain passages, although not his methods. The original meaning of the final form of the text is, to coin a phrase, no less original than the original meaning of its separate units. This may appear almost too obvious to mention, and yet there is a curious inconsistency in this area of biblical research. While it is widely agreed nowadays that the final texture is as important and legitimate a subject for scientific research as its separate threads [20], there are very few attempts at defining words like חַיִּים and מָוֶת as they were used in the *Sitz im Leben* of the final form of the text. At the phonological and grammatical levels of linguistic description, it is also generally agreed that Biblical Hebrew has developed quite a long way from the language actually spoken in ancient Israel [21], and yet at the semantic level Biblical Hebrew is almost universally discussed and described in terms of its usage in an ancient Israel. Probably the masoretes sometimes succeeded in preserving ancient elements, but the language of the Hebrew Bibles which we still use as the basis for exegesis and theology is certainly not identical with the language of its original authors, either phonologically or grammatically, and yet, semantically, in terms of its context and the associations or overtones which it has, we continue to treat it as if it was. The numerous homonyms discovered in modern times, and critically examined by Barr, are glaring examples of this tendency to study the final form of the text at the phonological and grammatical levels, but at the semantic level to attempt to get back to what it meant at an earlier stage [22].

A widely accepted linguistic classification envisages three periods in the history of the Hebrew language: (1) an Early Period down to about the fourth century B.C., when Hebrew was increasingly replaced by Aramaic and Greek as the first language of the Jews, (2) a Middle Period covering Mishnaic and Mediaeval Hebrew as well as the latest parts of the Hebrew Bible, and (3) the Modern Period [23]. One interesting implication of this division is that most, if not all Biblical Hebrew belongs, not only on phonological and grammatical criteria, but presumably also on semantic criteria, to the Middle Period. On literary criteria, too, a good many books of the Bible must be said to have reached their final form in the Middle Period. If this is so, then anyone who professes an interest in studying the final form of the text of, let

20. See above.

21. See most recently C. Rabin, "Hebrew" in *Current Trends in Linguistics*, vol. 6, ed. T. A. Sebeok (The Hague & Paris, 1970), pp. 304-308 (bibliography).

22. J. Barr, *Comparative Philology and the Text of the Old Testament* (Oxford, 1968), pp. 134-155.

23. Rabin, *op. cit.*, pp. 316-339 (bibliography) and paper referred to in note 10 above.

us say, the Book of Isaiah, must reckon, as Bernhard Duhm did so brilliantly 80 years ago, with theological and religious developments in Jewish communities during the last three or four centuries before Christ. One would also have to reckon with Hebrew usage throughout the Middle Period, because diversities in the Hebrew language as between the beginning of this period and the end are probably not so great as diversities between the Early Period and the Middle Period.

I should like to end with one example. One of the religious or theological developments of the last few centuries before Christ was the emergence and elaboration of a belief in life after death. It is very hard to accept that this belief appeared suddenly, like Athene fully armed from the head of Zeus, in the Maccabaean Period, as some have implied [24]. The scantiness of our written evidence for such a belief before that time is probably due to official attempts to suppress it ; but at the same time it would be hard to prove that all the writers and scholars who produced the Book of Isaiah or the Book of Psalms during this period were as conservative in their attitude to these beliefs as, for example, the author of Ecclesiasticus. Indeed a study of the associations and overtones of many of the words and phrases that are used during the Middle Period in references to and descriptions of the resurrection of the dead, suggests that as soon as passages like *Ps.* 1,5, *Ps.* 17,15 and *Isa,* 53,8-12 reached their final form, they could hardly be understood except in an eschatological sense in a context where life after death was a live issue, whatever the original author had intended and whatever the official hierarchy at the time demanded [25]. Père Tournay called such passages like these "relectures bibliques", but argued that they are nonetheless legitimate and important subjects for study [26]. I wonder whether we might not go a little farther and suggest that this was the original meaning of the text, in the sense that these passages did not reach their final form until a period when belief in life after death and resurrection from the dead was popular and well-established, if controversial. The original meaning of these passages in their final form cannot be properly described without reference to their original context in the fourth or third centuries before Christ.

It might be objected that this somewhat arbitrary, however legitimate procedure, is going to reduce the Old Testament to the product of a particular Jewish sect at a particular, in many respects undistinguished

24. E.g. O. S. RANKIN, *Israel's Wisdom Literature* (Edinburgh, 1936), pp. 218f ; J. A. MONTGOMERY, *The Book of Daniel* (Edinburgh, 1927), p. 471 ; H. H. ROWLEY, *The Faith of Israel* (London, 1956), p. 168 ; N. W. PORTEOUS, *Daniel* (London, 1965), p. 171f (*ATD* 23 (1962), pp. 143f).

25. See paper referred to in Note 10 above.

26. *Op. cit.*, pp. 504f.

time. I think there are three answers to this objection. (1) This would be only part of Old Testament studies, going on at the same time as semantic description at other levels, including the earliest. (2) The interpretations of Pharisaic Judaism may have found in some texts rather less than the original author intended, but such interpretations do not always coincide with the original meaning of the final form of the text as is being envisaged at the moment. It appears that *Isai*, 53,11 מֵעֲמַל נַפְשׁוֹ יִרְאֶה יִשְׂבָּע ... "after his suffering he will see and be satisfied..." originally described the resurrection of the servant from his grave among the wicked. This emerges from a comparison of the passage with two other passages in the same book where the resurrection of the dead is described in more detail (26,19; 66,24), and parallels in *Ps.*, 17,15 and *Dan.*, 12,3 [27]. The original reference, however, seems to have been played down by later Jewish commentators, perhaps partly because of the strong Christian associations with which *Isaiah*, 53 was imbued from the first century A.D. on [28].

(3) Of course it is an arbitrary choice of context and meaning, but so is any other choice, and in favour of this one is the fact that it means we can turn our attention for a moment way from the quest for Israel's earliest origins which takes up so much of our university and college curricula, and focus for a time on a period when the last chapter of Old Testament Theology was written and the religion from which both Judaism and Christianity very soon emerged had begun to take on its final shape.

J. F. A. SAWYER

See *Supplementary note*, p. 210.

27. A connexion between the second half of this verse and *Dan.* 12,3, the resurrection-passage *par excellence* in the Old Testament, was recognized by B. DUHM, *Das Buch Jesaia*[3] (Göttingen, 1914), p. 375; and also in most commentaries on Daniel (e.g. MONTGOMERY, *op. cit.*, p. 472; PORTEOUS, *loc. cit.*). On *Isa.*, 26,19 and 66,24 see paper referred to in Note 10 above.

28. 7 verses of the "Fourth Servant Song" are quoted a total of 9 times in the New Testament: cf. *Matt.* 8,17; *Mark* 15,28; *Luke* 22,37; *John* 12,38; *Acts* 8,32f; *Romans* 10,16; 15,21; *I Peter* 2,22,24.

4

GOTTES ZUSPRUCH UND ANSPRUCH

b^erît IN DER ALTTESTAMENTLICHEN THEOLOGIE

Unser heutiger Studientag ist dem Thema „Bund" gewidmet — oder sagen wir lieber vorsichtig: dem Thema *b^erît*. In der Tat — wir sind seit langem gewöhnt, das hebräische Wort *b^erît* mit „Bund", „verbond", „alliance", „covenant" wiederzugeben. Unter der Voraussetzung, daß diese Übersetzung richtig ist, daß sie die Meinung des hebräischen Wortes zutreffend wiedergibt, liegt die besondere Bedeutung dieses Begriffes auf der Hand; denn dann bezeichnet und beschreibt *b^erît* das Verhältnis zwischen Jahwe und Israel, zwischen Gott und Mensch. Es ist allerdings die Frage, ob das hebräische *b^erît* wirklich „Bund" meint. Die Frage nach der Bedeutung von *b^erît*, heute neu gestellt, spielt bereits in der Geschichte des berühmten Wörterbuches von Wilhelm Gesenius eine Rolle. Ein zweimaliger Wechsel der Auffassung tritt hier zu Tage. Gesenius selbst war in seinem Thesaurus [1] von der Bedeutung „foedus" für *b^erît* ausgegangen, registrierte daneben aber auch den Sinn der „conditio huius foederis": einerseits das „promissum Dei", andererseits die „praecepta Dei ab Israële servanda i.e. lex divina". Dieses Verständnis von *b^erît* hat sich zunächst auch in seinem Handwörterbuch durchgehalten, bis von der 8. Auflage an F. Mühlau und W. Volck davon abgegangen sind [2]. Nach Mühlau und Volck war die Grundbedeutung von *b^erît* nicht „Bund", sondern „Entscheidung, Bestimmung, Festsetzung", und zwar mit den Nuancierungen: „*a*) eine Bestimmung des Gesetzes, durch welche etwas angeordnet wird... *b*) eine Bestimmung der Verheissung, durch welche jemandem etwas zugewendet wird... *c*) eine Bestimmung, welche jemand sich selbst auferlegt, indem er sich einem Andren gegenüber zu einer Leistung verpflichtet, dah. Gelöbniss". Von dem Ausgangspunkt „Entscheidung, Bestimmung, Festsetzung" aus kann man auch eine

1. *Thesaurus philologicus criticus linguae Hebraeae et Chaldaeae Veteris Testamenti*, I, [2]1835, S. 238f.

2. W. Gesenius, *Hebräisches und chaldäisches Handwörterbuch über das Alte Testament*, 8. Auflage, neu bearbeitet von F. Mühlau und W. Volck, 1878.

Bedeutungsentwicklung zu „Bund" hinführen. Dieser Sinn liegt bei *b^e^rît* dann vor, wenn und sofern „eine Festsetzung und Bestimmung ein gegenseitiges Verhältnis und Verhalten ordnet"[3]. Im Gegensatz zu (Mühlau-) Volck ist dann F. Buhl bereits bei der ersten von ihm vorgenommenen Neubearbeitung des Handwörterbuchs von Gesenius zu „Bund" als Grundbedeutung von *b^e^rît* zurückgekehrt[4]; und diese Auffassung hat sich in der Folgezeit so stark durchgesetzt, daß auch L. Koehler[5] und W. Baumgartner[6] — mit nur 4 Ausnahmen[7] — die Bedeutungen „Abmachung", „Vereinbarung", „Bund", für den theologischen Bereich „Bund zwischen Gott und Menschen" geben. Demgegenüber ist die Auffassung von (Mühlau-) Volck bald ganz aus der wissenschaftlichen Diskussion verschwunden — wie neuere Arbeiten[8] zeigen: sehr zu Unrecht.

Hier soll uns vornehmlich die Frage beschäftigen, welche Bedeutung *b^e^rît im theologischen Bereich,* d.h. für das Gegenüber von Gott und Mensch gehabt hat. Dazu gehen wir — in Beschränkung auf die wichtigsten alttestamentlichen Aussagen — aus von den in dieser Form üblichen deutschen Begriffen „Abrahambund", „Sinaibund" und „Davidbund". In einem I. Abschnitt geben wir einen kurzen Uberblick über Meinungen und Ergebnisse einschlägiger Untersuchungen, entwikkeln in einem II. Abschnitt an charakteristischen Beispielen die tatsächliche Bedeutung von *b^e^rît* und stellen von hier aus in einem III.

3. A.a.O. S. 132. — Diese Deutung von *b^e^rît* geht zurück auf Volcks Lehrer J. Chr. K. von Hofmann; vgl. dessen Buch: *Weissagung und Erfüllung im alten und neuen Testamente.* I, 1841, S. 138.

4. W. GESENIUS, *Hebräisches und aramäisches Handwörterbuch über das Alte Testament,* bearbeitet von F. Buhl, [12] 1895, S. 122.

5. L. KOEHLER-W. BAUMGARTNER, *Lexicon in Veteris Testamenti libros,* 1953, S. 150-152.

6. *Hebräisches und aramäisches Lexikon zum Alten Testament* von L. KOEHLER† und W. BAUMGARTNER, 3. Auflage, neu bearbeitet von W. Baumgartner, I. Lfg., 1967, S. 150-152.

7. *Am.,* 1,9 *b^e^rît 'aḥîm* „Pflicht gegen Brüder", *2Sam.* 23,5 *śam b^e^rît 'ôlam* „Gott gibt e(ine) immer gültige Zusage", *Num.,* 25,13 *b^e^rît k^e^hunnăt 'ôlam* „Recht auf dauerndes Priestertum", *1Sam.,* 18,3 „Blutsbrüderschaft".

8. E. KUTSCH, *Gesetz und Gnade. Probleme des alttestamentlichen Bundesbegriffs, ZAW* 79 (1967) 18-35; ders., *Der Begriff* b^e^rît *in vordeuteronomischer Zeit* (*Das ferne und nahe Wort.* Festschrift für Leonhard ROST [BZAW 105], 1967, S. 133-143); ders., *Von* b^e^rît *zu „Bund", KuD* 14 (1968) 159-182; ders., *Sehen und Bestimmen. Die Etymologie von* b^e^rît (*Archäologie und Altes Testament.* Festschrift für Kurt GALLING, 1970, S. 165-178); ders., *Verheißung und Gesetz. Untersuchungen zum sogenannten „Bund" im Alten Testament* (BZAW 131), 1973; L. PERLITT, *Bundestheologie im Alten Testament* (WMANT 36), 1969; auch: G. FOHRER, *Altes Testament — „Amphiktyonie" und „Bund"?* (Studien zur alttestamentlichen Theologie und Geschichte (1949-1966) (BZAW 115), 1969, S. 84-119, sowie N. LOHFINK, *Die Landverheißung als Eid* (SBS 28), 1967.

Abschnitt dar, was das Alte Testament zu den Themen „Abraham-*bᵉrit*", „Sinai-*bᵉrît*" und „David-*bᵉrît*" de facto sagt. Zum Schluß fassen wir das Ergebnis kurz zusammen (IV).

I

1. Wenn in älterer Literatur vom „Bund" gehandelt wird, dann ist damit in erster Linie das Verhältnis zwischen Jahwe und Israel gemeint. Dieses Verhältnis ist — das ist die Meinung — am Sinai, während des Aufenthaltes des Volkes am Gottesberg, in einem von Jahwe initiierten Akt hergestellt worden. Deshalb bezeichnet man diesen „Bund" als „Sinaibund". Dieser „steht als rocher de bronce am Anfang der Geschichte des Gottesvolkes; er ist ihr Grund, auf dem sie sich erhebt, den sie nie aufgegeben hat"[9]. Entsprechend dem deutschen Begriff „Bund" ist das Verhältnis zwischen Gott und Volk als durch gegenseitige Rechte und Pflichten bestimmt gedacht[10], wobei diese Rechte und Pflichten unterschiedlich definiert werden. So ist — um hier als Beispiel L. Köhler[11] zu zitieren — „die durch Mose offenbarte Abmachung, der sogenannte Sinaibund zwischen Jahwe und Israel, dadurch gekennzeichnet, ... daß Jahwe Israel als sein Volk beschützt, das ist Jahwes Teil an Pflichten und Israels Teil an Rechten, und daß Israel Jahwe verehrt und ihm Gehorsam leistet, das ist Israels Teil an Pflichten und Jahwes Teil an Rechten." Nun berichtet das Alte Testament neben dem sog. „Sinaibund" auch noch von anderen sog. „Bünden", die ebenfalls von Jahwe ausgehen und an denen — nach der üblichen Auffassung — Jahwe als „Partner" beteiligt ist. Zum Teil liegen sie — folgt man der zeitlichen Ordnung der alttestamentlichen Darstellung — *vor* dem „Sinaibund": so der „Noahbund" (*Gen.*, 9,8-17) und der „Abrahambund" (*Gen.*, 15,18; 17)[12]; jünger als der „Sinaibund" ist der „Davidbund". Von diesen „Bünden" spielt der „Bund mit Noah" insofern eine besondere Rolle, als er nicht auf das Volk Israel zielt, sondern auf die ganze Menschheit; deshalb klammern wir ihn im Folgenden auch weithin aus. So bleiben neben dem „Sinaibund" der „Abrahambund" und der „Davidbund". Von diesen drei steht der „Abrahambund" dem „Sinaibund" insofern näher als der „Davidbund", als er mit dem Stammvater des Volkes Israel „geschlossen" worden ist und deshalb sich auch auf das Volk selbst auswirken konnte und mußte, während

9. O. PROCKSCH, *Theologie des Alten Testaments*, 1950, S. 521.
10. Vgl. zu dieser Bestimmung: J. PEDERSEN, *Der Eid bei den Semiten*, 1914, S. 33 f.
11. *Theologie des Alten Testaments*, ³1953 (⁴1966), S. 52.
12. Von dem „Bund" mit Levi (*Mal.*, 2,4f.8; *Jer.*, 33,21b vgl. 18.22) bzw. mit Pinehas (*Num.*, 25,12f.; vgl. *Neh.*, 13,29) sei hier abgesehen.

demgegenüber der „Davidbund" der Daviddynastie, also nur einem begrenzten Personenkreis aus dem Gottesvolk, galt.

2. Suchen wir festzustellen, wie man sich das Verhältnis von „*Sinaibund" und „Abrahambund*" gedacht hat, so stoßen wir auf recht unterschiedliche Auskünfte. Nach Procksch [13] hat der Jahwist den Abrahambund dem Sinaibund „vorgeordnet" und damit „eine richtige Erweiterung des Bundesgedankens vorgenommen". Für Procksch besteht darin Übereinstimmung zwischen beiden „Bünden", daß allein Jahwe „Bundesstifter" ist, und daß sowohl Abraham wie Israel „als reiner Empfänger" in den „Bund" eintreten [14]. Ähnlich ist nach J. Hempel [15] mit dem „Abrahambund" die am Sinai haftende Bundesvorstellung in die Patriarchenzeit „hineingetragen" worden, während H. Ringgren [16] den „Abrahambund" als eine Rückverlegung des „Sinaibundes" in die Zeit der Erzväter versteht. E. Sellin [17] sieht die beiden „Bünde" in der Weise auf einer Ebene liegen, daß der „Abrahambund", weil auf ihn in jüngeren Texten Bezug genommen wird, in nachexilischer Zeit „den Sinaibund geradezu verdrängt zu haben scheint" [18]. Und nach W. Eichrodt [19] waren für die Männer der deuteronomischen Reform Abrahambund und Sinaibund „zwei aufeinander angelegte Ereignisse, die als Vorstufe und Erfüllung begriffen werden". Zu diesen beiden „Bundschlüssen" ist dann nach Eichrodt „als Dritter in der Reihe" noch der Bund vom Lande Moab hinzugetreten [20].

In diesen und zahlreichen weiteren Aussagen werden mit Hilfe des Begriffes „Bund" das, was man „Abrahambund", und das, was man „Sinaibund" nennt, auf ein und dieselbe Ebene gebracht. Eine schärfere Differenzierung zwischen den beiden Größen findet sich in dem Aufsatz: „*Sinaibund und Abrahambund*" von W. Zimmerli [21]. Zimmerli erkennt, daß es sich bei dem „Abrahambund" um einen „reinen Verheißungsbund Jahwes mit den Vätern" handelt [22], während der „Sinaibund"

13. A.a.O., S. 522.
14. A.a.O., S. 522.
15. Artikel „*Bund im Alten Testament*" (RGG² I, 1927, Sp. 1360-1362), Sp. 1361.
16. *Israelitische Religion*, 1963, S. 106.
17. *Theologie des Alten Testaments*, 1933.
18. A.a.O. S. 95 unter Hinweis auf *Gen.*, 28,3f.; 35,11f.; 48,3f.; *Lev.*, 20,34; *Num.*, 33,53; *Dtn.*, 29,12 bzw. *Neh.*, 9,8.15.23; *Ps.*, 105,9.
19. *Theologie des Alten Testaments*, I, ⁵1957, S. 21.
20. Hier folgt Eichrodt der Darstellung von R. Kraetzschmar, *Die Bundesvorstellung im Alten Testament in ihrer geschichtlichen Entwickelung*, 1896, S.137f.: „Eine fortlaufende Linie führt von dem Väterbunde zum Horeb- und Moabbunde hin."
21. *ThZ* 16 (1960) 268-280 = *Gottes Offenbarung. Gesammelte Aufsätze*, 1963, S. 205-216.
22. A.a.O., S. 277 = S. 214.

als Kern die Mitteilung des göttlichen Willens in Form einer „ Rechtsproklamation, der eine Ausführung über Segen und Fluch folgte ", hatte [23]. „ Im Zeugnis vom Bund Jahwes mit Abraham kennt schon die alte Tradition Israels eine wesentlich anders strukturierte Bundesaussage, die nicht [wie der Sinaibund] von den hetitischen Vasallitätsverträgen her zu beleuchten ist und der die Rechtsproklamation und die vom Menschen unter Anhörung der Aussagen von Segen und Fluch übernommene Bundesverpflichtung ... fehlt " [24]. Gegenüber dem Begriff des „ Verheißungsbundes " würde sich für den „ Sinaibund " der des „ Gesetzesbundes " nahelegen [25]. Hier ist ein wesentlicher Unterschied zwischen dem sog. „ Abrahambund " und dem sog. „ Sinaibund " herausgearbeitet. In ähnlicher Weise stellt D. R. Hillers [26] fest, daß „ Abrahambund " und „ Sinaibund " nur den Namen „ Bund " gemeinsam haben, daß aber die Rollen der „ Bundes "-Partner sehr verschieden sind [27].

3. In stärkerem Maße hat sich in den letzten 25 Jahren das Interesse dem Nebeneinander bzw. Gegenüber von „ *Sinaibund* " *und* „ *Davidbund* " zugewandt. Der Grund dafür ist darin zu sehen, daß diese beiden „ Bünde " nicht so einfach miteinander in Beziehung zu setzen waren wie Sinaibund und Abrahambund. Zwar konnte noch Procksch das Verhältnis von Sinaibund und Davidbund dahingehend bestimmen, daß der „ Davidbund " als „ Sonderbund " „ innerhalb des Gottesbundes zwischen Jahwe und Israel " stand [28]. Demgegenüber aber bemüht sich L. Rost in dem ersten dem Thema „ *Sinaibund und Davidsbund* " gewidmeten Aufsatz [29] um eine geschichtliche Differenzierung. Den Inhalt der beiden „ Bünde " unterscheidet Rost so, daß Jahwe in dem „ Sinaibund " seine Verbundenheit mit seinem Volk Israel zugesagt — vgl. die sog. „ Bundesformel " : „ Ich will euer Gott sein, und ihr sollt mein Volk sein " —, in dem „ Davidbund " aber den dauernden Bestand der Dynastie garantiert habe [30]. Nach Salomos Tod habe das Nordreich, Israel, durch die Wahl dieses Namens den Sinaibund für sich bean-

23. A.a.O., S. 278 = S. 214.
24. Zimmerli a.a.O., S. 279 = S. 215.
25. Zimmerli selbst gebraucht ihn nicht. — Daß zum „ Sinaibund " wesentlich die Mitteilung des fordernden Gotteswillens gehört, hat Zimmerli ein Jahrzehnt später erneut und eindringlich unterstrichen (*Erwägungen zum „ Bund ". Die Aussagen über die Jahwe-*bᵉrît *in Ex., 19-34* (*Wort — Gebot — Glaube.* Beiträge zur Theologie des Alten Testaments, Walther Eichrodt zum 80. Geburtstag, 1970, S. 171-190).
26. *Covenant : The History of a Biblical Idea,* Baltimore 1969.
27. A.a.O. S. 103.
28. A.a.O. (Anm. 9) S. 529.
29. *ThLZ* 72 (1947) 129-134.
30. A.a.O., 129.

sprucht, während das Südreich, Juda, sich an den Davidbund hielt. Durch Josia wurde dann auf der Grundlage des Deuteronomiums der am Sinai geschlossene Bund nunmehr auch für das Südreich, für Juda, erneuert. Dadurch sind beide Ideenkreise, der im Sinaibund und der im Davidbund verkörperte, an *einem* Ort zusammengebracht, wodurch ihre Verschmelzung in nachexilischer Zeit vorbereitet wurde [31].

Andererseits findet Rosts Schüler M. Sekine, daß der Prophet Jeremia seit der Unheilsansage über den König Jojaqim in *Jer.*, 36,30 die Idee des Davidbundes nicht mehr festgehalten, dafür aber den Sinaibund in den Mittelpunkt seiner Weissagung gerückt habe, wie die in die letzte Zeit der Wirksamkeit des Propheten anzusetzende Ankündigung eines ,, neuen Bundes " nach Analogie des Sinaibundes in 31,31ff. erkennen lasse [32].

Wieder anders verbindet A. H. J. Gunneweg [33] die Frage nach dem Verhältnis von Sinaibund und Davidbund mit der ,, umfassenderen Frage nach dem Verhältnis von Amphiktyonie und Staat " [34]. Neben die ältere in der Amphiktyonie beheimatete Tradition vom Sinaibund tritt in dem von David und seiner Dynastie beherrschten Staat die Davidbundtradition als Ausdruck des Versuchs, ,, die Notwendigkeit einer zentralen Führung den älteren Überlieferungen der Amphiktyonie einzugliedern " [35]. Beide Traditionen werden miteinander verknüpft, wenn in der wiederholt zu begehenden Feier der Ladeüberführung nach *2Sam.*, 6 [36] ,, der Davidide, der hier die Funktion des Hüters der Lade, die Aufgabe also eines amphiktyonischen Beamten, des Nasi, antritt, *als König* in die Tradition der Amphiktyonie eingeordnet wird " [37].

31. Gegenüber dieser wenigstens zeitweisen Zuteilung der beiden ,, Bünde " auf die beiden israelitischen Staaten gibt M. Noth zu bedenken, ,, daß innerhalb der gesamtisraelitischen Tradition die an die dem Davidshause gegebenen Zusagen geknüpften Erwartungen, wo immer sie überhaupt im Kreise der israelitischen Stämme aufgenommen wurden, sich in das altüberlieferte Verhältnis Gott-Volk als ein besonderes und mehr und mehr vor allem in die Zukunft weisendes Element einfügten " (*Gott, König, Volk im Alten Testament*, ZThK 47 (1950) 157-191 = Gesammelte Studien zum Alten Testmant, 1957, S. 188-229, S. 188 = 224f).

32. *Davidsbund und Sinaibund bei Jeremia*, *VT* 9 (1959) 47-57.

33. *Sinaibund und Davidsbund*, *VT* 10 (1960) 335-341.

34. A.a.O., S. 338.

35. A.a.O., S. 339.

36. Allerdings handelt es sich — entgegen der von S. Mowinckel, *Psalmenstudien II. Das Thronbesteigungsfest Jahwäs und der Ursprung der Eschatologie*, 1922 (= 1961), S. 109ff., und zahlreichen anderen vertretenen Auffassung — in den Darstellungen von *2Sam.*, 6,1-19 und *1Kön.*, 8,1-8 nicht um Widerspiegelungen einer alljährlich, etwa am Neujahrsfest, begangenen Feier, sondern um die Berichte über zwei verschiedene Ladeüberführungen : 1. nach der Davidstadt, 2. von der Davidstadt in den nördlich davon errichteten Tempel.

37. A.a.O., S. 340.

In zweifacher Hinsicht erhielt die Diskussion um das Verhältnis zwischen „ Sinaibund " und „ Davidbund " weitere Anregungen : durch die Frage, welche Rolle die beiden Traditionen im Kult gespielt haben, und durch den Vergleich alttestamentlicher Texte mit dem Formular altorientalischer Vasallenverträge.

Nach H.-J. Kraus sind beide Traditionen dadurch miteinander in Beziehung gesetzt worden, daß sie „ gemeinsam während des Laubhüttenfestes gefeiert " wurden [38]. Das große Herbstfest war — darin folgt Kraus Mowinckel [39] und G. v. Rad [40] — der „ Sitz im Leben " der Überlieferung vom Sinaibund. In der Zeit nach David kam in dem von Kraus vermuteten „ königlichen Zionsfest " am ersten Tag des Laubhüttenfestes in der Feier der Erwählung Davids und des Zion der Davidbund hinzu. Wenn in der Folgezeit nach alttestamentlichen Berichten wiederholt durch Kultusreformen (sogenannte) Erneuerungen des Sinaibundes herbeigeführt wurden — so durch die Könige Asa (*1Kön.*, 15,9ff.), Joas (bzw. den Oberpriester Jojada ; *2Kön.* 11,13ff.), vor allem durch Josia (*2Kön.*, 23,4ff.) —, so zeigt das nach Kraus, daß der Sinaibund zeitweise hinter dem Davidbund zurückgetreten war und deshalb durch die Neuverpflichtung des Volkes auf die amphiktyonischen Grundlagen wieder aktualisiert werden mußte [41].

So wie man unter anderen „ Bundschlüssen " den „ Sinaibund " als Vasallenvertrag und den Aufbau der Sinaiperikope von dem Formular der altorientalischen Suzeränitätsverträge her hat erklären wollen [42], so hat R. de Vaux versucht, auch den „ Davidbund " mit jenen Verträgen in Verbindung zu bringen [43]. Allerdings geht de Vaux dabei nicht direkt von dem Formular aus, sondern stellt eine Reihe von Entsprechungen in dem Verhältnis Davids zu Jahwe und dem eines Vasallen zu seinem Oberherrn fest : Einsetzung über das Volk durch Jahwe bzw. den Oberherren, Bezeichnung als „ Knecht ", Garantie des Schutzes, Abhängigkeit des Bestehens des Vertrages von der Vasallentreue, Urkunde mit den Vertragsbestimmungen (zum Alten Testament vgl. die Überreichung der *'edût* an den neuen König nach *2Kön.*, 11,12).

38. *Die Königsherrschaft Gottes im Alten Testament* (BHTh 13), 1951, S. 46 Anm. 3.

39. A.a.O.

40. *Das formgeschichtliche Problem des Hexateuchs* (BWANT IV, 26), 1938 = *Gesammelte Studien zum Alten Testament*, 1958, S. 9-86.

41. H.-J. Kraus, *Gottesdienst in Israel*, 1954, S. 77ff. ; ²1962, S. 222ff. — Zu der mit diesen und weiteren Stellen verknüpften These von der „ Bundeserneuerung " vgl. E. Kutsch, *„ Bund " und Fest* (*ThQ* 150, 1970, S. 299-320), bes. S. 309ff. ; ders., *Verheißung und Gesetz*, S. 161ff.

42. Vgl. vor allem K. Baltzer, *Das Bundesformular* (WMANT 4), 1960 (²1964).

43. *Le roi d'Israël, vassal de Yahvé* (*Mélanges Eugène Tisserant*. I, 1964, S. 119 /bis 133), bes. S. 124ff.

Auf Grund dieser Entsprechungen hat de Vaux auch den Davidbund als Vasallenvertrag bestimmen wollen [44].

Wie Zimmerli den Unterschied zwischen ,, Sinaibund " und ,, Abrahambund ", so hat R. E. Clements [45] den Unterschied zwischen ,, Sinaibund " und ,, Davidbund " schärfer erkannt. Er versteht den Sinaibund als ,, a law covenant ", demgegenüber den Davidbund als ,, a promissory covenant " [46] — und hat mit dieser Differenzierung wiederum einen wesentlichen Gesichtspunkt erfaßt.

4. Wenden wir uns nun noch dem Nebeneinander von *,, Abrahambund " und ,, Davidbund "* zu. Deren Verhältnis zueinander ist das eigentliche Interesse der genannten Untersuchung von Clements. Die Unterscheidung zwischen den Bezeichnungen ,, law covenant " (für den Sinaibund) und ,, promissory covenant " (für den Davidbund) führt ihn zu der Frage, wo — gegenüber der altisraelitischen Tradition vom Sinaibund als einem ,, Gesetzesbund " — die Wurzel der Vorstellung von einem ,, Verheißungsbund " zu suchen sei. Er findet sie in der alten Tradition vom Abrahambund : Auch der Abrahambund war ein ,, promissory covenant ". David wie die Tradition vom Abrahambund waren in derselben Stadt, in Hebron, beheimatet. Nach Errichtung des davidischen Königtums in Jerusalem ist — nach Clements — auch die Überlieferung von dem Abrahambund in die neue Hauptstadt übertragen worden, und hier konnte die Vorstellung von einem Bund Jahwes mit David an die vom Abrahambund anknüpfen.

Offenbar unabhängig von Clements sieht auch Hillers [47] das Moment der Verheißung sowohl beim Abrahambund als auch beim Davidbund. Dem Patriarchen wird im Abrahambund der Besitz des Landes, dem David im Davidbund die dauernde Herrschaft seiner Dynastie verheißen. Dominierend bleibt aber auch für Hillers der Begriff ,, Bund ". Die Vorstellung vom ,, Bund " ist ihm auch dort gegeben, wo das Stichwort *b^{e}rît* fehlt, etwa bei den Propheten des 8. Jhs. [48].

Wir schließen hier unseren Überblick ab. Den genannten Arbeiten — wie auch den sonstigen Untersuchungen der letzten Jahrzehnte zum Thema — ist gemeinsam, daß sie von der Übersetzung ,, Bund " für das hebraïsche Wort *b^{e}rît* ausgehen. Einige dieser Untersuchungen reden vom ,, Bund " zwischen Gott und dem Volk bzw. zwischen Gott und

44. Vgl. dazu auch D. J. McCarthy, *Der Gottesbund im Alten Testament. Ein Bericht über die Forschung der letzten Jahre* (SBS 13), 1966, S. 74f. ; ders., *The Old Testament Covenant. Survey of current Opinions*, 1972, S. 50f.

45. *Abraham and David. Gen., 15 and its Meaning for Israelite Tradition* (Studies in Biblical Theology II, 5), 1967.

46. A.a.O., S. 53.

47. A.a.O. (Anm. 26), S. 119.

48. A.a.O., S. 120ff.

einem einzelnen Menschen auch da, wo der Begriff *b^e^rît* im Hebräischen nicht vorkommt. Besonders fällt ins Gewicht, daß zahlreiche Autoren es unterlassen, nach dem speziellen Inhalt von „Abrahambund", „Sinaibund" und „Davidbund" zu fragen. Bevor wir auf dieses Problem eingehen, fragen wir, welchen Sinn das hebräische Wort *b^e^rît* tatsächlich hat.

II

Die Bedeutung von *b^e^rît* sei hier an drei Beispielen aufgezeigt: an *Gen.*, 15,18; *Ez.*, 17,13-14 und *1Kön.*, 5,26.

1. In *Gen.*, 15,18 lesen wir: „An diesem Tag schnitt Jahwe mit Abraham eine *b^e^rît* folgendermaßen: Deiner Nachkommenschaft gebe ich dieses Land vom ‚Bach' [49] Ägyptens bis zum großen Strom, dem Euphratstrom." Der Inhalt der *b^e^rît*, die hier Jahwe mit Abraham „schneidet", d.h. „festsetzt" [50], findet in der Jahwerede Ausdruck: Es ist die Zusage des Landes zwischen dem Bach Ägyptens und dem Euphrat, die Jahwe dem Abraham für dessen Nachkommenschaft gibt. Subjekt der *b^e^rît* ist — allein — Jahwe; er ist es, der die *b^e^rît* „festsetzt". Er — Jahwe — setzt für sich eine Verpflichtung fest. Abraham auf der anderen Seite ist nur der Empfänger der *b^e^rît*. Würde *b^e^rît* „Bund" bedeuten, dann wäre zu erwarten, daß auch Abraham seinerseits eine Verpflichtung gegenüber Jahwe übernähme. Aber von einer solchen Verpflichtung Abrahams sagt der Text kein Wort. Das ist im Prinzip schon früher erkannt worden [51]; nur hat man zu Unrecht an der Übersetzung „Bund" für *b^e^rît* festgehalten. Die Meinung, daß Jahwe einseitig eine Selbstverpflichtung eingeht, wird noch unterstrichen durch die Darstellung, daß Jahwe — und nur Jahwe allein — den Ritus einer bedingten Selbstverfluchung vollzieht, indem er — der Text sagt dafür: „ein rauchender Ofen und eine Feuerfackel" — zwischen den Hälften eines zerschnittenen Tieres [52] hindurchgeht [53]. Gegen diese Deutung von *b^e^rît* als einer einseitigen Selbstverpflichtung

49. Zum Text vgl. BHK und BHS.

50. Zu der Bedeutung „festsetzen" für das Verbum *krt*, vornehmlich in der Wendung *karăt b^e^rît*, vgl. KUTSCH, *Verheißung und Gesetz*, S. 41ff.

51. Aus der oben angeführten Literatur vgl. Zimmerli a.a.O. (Anm. 21) S. 277 (= S. 208); Clements a.a.O. (Anm. 45), S. 21f.; Hillers a.a.O. (Anm. 26) S. 119.

52. Der Text nennt jetzt drei Tiere: eine Jungkuh, eine Ziege, einen Widder; dazu zwei — unzerteilte! — Vögel. Überlieferungsgeschichtlich primär handelt es sich aber nur um ein Tier wie auch bei der Parallele in *Jer.*, 34,18. Vgl. dazu S. E. LOEWENSTAMM, *Zur Traditionsgeschichte des Bundes zwischen den Stücken*, *VT* 18 (1968) 500-506; KUTSCH, *Verheißung und Gesetz*, S. 42ff.

53. Zur Bedeutung dieses Ritus vgl. Kutsch a.a.O., S. 45f. bei und mit Anmerkung 25-29.

kann man nicht anführen, daß nach dem hebräischen Wortlaut Jahwe die *b^erît* ,, mit " — *'et* — Abraham festgesetzt habe. Wohl bedeutet *'et* — wie auch *'im* — zunächst ,, mit ", ,, bei ", z.B. *2Sam.*, 16,17b : ,, Warum gehst du nicht mit deinem Gefährten *'ät-re'äka* ? " Aber beide Präpositionen können auch (von dieser Grundbedeutung aus) in einem speziellen Sinn gebraucht werden ; so z.B. *Sach.*, 7,9 : ,, Übt Gemeinschaftstreue und Erbarmen *'îs 'ät-'aḥîw* ! " *'et* bedeutet hier nicht ,, (zusammen) mit ", sondern ,, an ", ,, zugunsten von " : ,, Übt Treue... jeder an seinem Bruder ! " [54] Ebenso meint *ḥäsd^eka 'ät-re'äka* in *2Sam.*, 16,17a ,, deine Treue an deinem Gefährten [55] ; vgl. weiter *hêṭîb 'im Gen.*, 32,10 und *'aśā ṭôb 'im Ps.*, 119,65 ,, Gutes tun an, zugunsten von ", *'aśā rā' 'im Gen.*, 31,29 ,, Böses tun an " und andere derartige Belege. Dementsprechend bedeutet *karăṯ b^erît 'et* in *Gen.*, 15,18 ,, eine Selbstverpflichtung festsetzen zugunsten von ".

2. In *Ez.*, 17,13-14 wird festgestellt, wie Zedekia als Vasall des babylonischen Herrschers Nebukadnezar König von Juda geworden ist :

> ,, (13) Er (der Babylonier) nahm (einen) aus königlichem Samen, und er setzte mit ihm eine *b^erît* fest und ließ ihn in einen Fluch eintreten, und er nahm die Vornehmen des Landes, (14) damit das Königtum niedrig sei, ohne sich zu erheben, daß es seine (des Nebukadnezar) *b^erît* bewahre, damit es Bestand habe. "

Nebukadnezar, als Sieger auf dem Plan, hat an Stelle des nach Babel verschleppten Jojakin (*2Kön.*, 24,15) dessen Enkel Matthanja als König in Jerusalem eingesetzt und ihm zum Zeichen seiner Abhängigkeit einen neuen Namen, Zedekia, gegeben (*2Kön.*, 24,17) [56]. Er, der Babylonier, ist Subjekt der in *Ez.*, 17,13f. genannten *b^erît*, er setzt diese dem Zedekia fest (V.13aβ) ; er läßt weiter diesen ,, in einen Fluch eintreten " (V.13bα). Nur der Judäer steht also unter einem Fluch. Allein Zedekia ist es auch, der eine Verpflichtung, eben die ihm von dem Nebukadnezar auferlegte Verpflichtung übernimmt : Er (bzw. das Königtum) muß die *b^erît* des Nebukadnezar ,, bewahren " (V.14b) ; er ist es, der dann den ihm auferlegten Fluch verachtet und die *b^erît* des Babyloniers ,, bricht " (V.16aβγ. 18a.19a). Abgesehen davon, daß man ein solches Vasallenverhältnis zwischen Zedekia und Nebukadnezar nicht als ,, Bund " bezeichnen kann — *b^erît* bezeichnet hier gar nicht jenes Verhältnis, sondern nur die Verpflichtung, die der Babylonier dem

54. Cf. (Th. H. Robinson-) F. HORST, *Die Zwölf Kleinen Propheten* (HAT I, 14), ²1954 (= ³1964), S. 240.

55. *ḥäsäd 'et* bedeutet nicht ,, Gemeinschaft mit ", gegen Baumgartner a.a.O. (Anm. 6) S. 97b.

56. Ebenso war zuvor der Pharao Necho mit Jojaqim verfahren : *2Kön.*, 23,34.

Judäer auferlegt hat und die jener befolgen muß. Hier ist *b^e^rît* nicht „ Selbstverpflichtung ", sondern „ Fremdverpflichtung ".

3. In *1Kön.*, 5,26 heißt es nach der Feststellung, daß zwischen Hiram, dem König von Tyrus, und Salomo „ *šalôm* " war : „ Und die beiden setzten eine *b^e^rît* fest. " Beide Herrscher erscheinen hier als Subjekt von *b^e^rît*. Nach dem Kontext ist deutlich, daß jeder von beiden gegenüber dem anderen Verpflichtungen übernommen hat (vgl. *1Kön.*, 5,22-25). Hier liegt also *b^e^rît* als gegenseitige Verpflichtung vor. Solcher hier und an einigen wenigen weiteren Stellen zu beobachtender Sprachgebrauch hat dazu geführt, daß *b^e^rît* als „ Bund ", „ Vertrag " o.ä. verstanden worden ist.

Diese drei Beispiele machen deutlich, daß — entsprechend der Sicht von Volck — die Grundbedeutung von *b^e^rît* nicht „ Bund " ist, sondern die „ Verpflichtung ", die „ Bestimmung ". Im Einzelfall kann es sich um Selbstverpflichtung (oder Zusage), um Fremdverpflichtung und um gegenseitige Verpflichtung handeln. Allerdings begegnet die dritte Möglichkeit — *b^e^rît* als gegenseitige Verpflichtung — nur im profanen Bereich, nicht aber im theologischen, d.h. für das Gegenüber von Gott und Mensch.

4. Das hier aufgezeigte Ergebnis ist in zweifacher Hinsicht zu unterbauen : durch die neben *b^e^rît* stehenden Parallelbegriffe und durch die Wiedergabe von *b^e^rît* durch die alten Ubersetzungen.

a) Dort, wo *b^e^rît* die Selbstverpflichtung meint, kann das Substantiv in Parallele stehen zu *š^e^bu'ā* „ Eid, Schwur " (*Ps.*, 105,9 = *1Chr.*, 16,16 ; vgl. auch *nišbă' b^e^rît* „ eine *b^e^rît* schwören " *Dtn.*, 4,31 ; 8,18 neben *nišba' š^e^bu'ā* „ einen Eid schwören " *Num.*, 30,3 ; *Jos.*, 9,20). Und von der Seite, die bei dem „ *b^e^rît*-Festsetzen " eine Selbstverpflichtung übernimmt, kann es gleichzeitig heißen, daß sie „ schwört " (*Ps.*, 89,4 ; vgl. *Jos.*, 9,15b mit V.15a, *1Sam.*, 20,17 mit 18,3, *Esr.*, 10,5 mit V.3). Wo dagegen *b^e^rît* die Verpflichtung eines anderen bezeichnet, finden sich parallel dazu andere Substantive, die diesem Charakter entsprechen : *tôrā* „ Weisung " (*Hos.*, 8,1 ; *Ps.*, 78,10), *ḥuqqîm* und *ḥuqqôt* „ Satzungen " (*2Kön.*, 17,15 ; *Ps.*, 50,16 bzw. *1Kön.*, 11,11) u.a. Und wo das Subjekt der *b^e^rît* einen anderen verpflichtet, da schwört es nicht selbst, sondern „ läßt jenen schwören " (*2Kön.*, 11,4). Schließlich gibt es bei der gegenseitigen *b^e^rît* insofern eine Parallele, als es hier heißen kann, daß „ beide (einander) schwören " (vgl. *1Sam.*, 20,42 mit 23,18, *Gen.*, 21,31b mit V.32a).

b) Daß *b^e^rît* im Alten Testament nicht als „ Bund " verstanden worden ist, bestätigen die Versionen. Das Aramäische der Targume gibt (bei nur drei Ausnahmen) *b^e^rît* mit *q^e^jam* wieder, das (nicht „ Bund ", sondern) die „ Aufstellung ", die „ Bestimmung " meint (vgl. *qijjem* bzw. *qăjjem*). Daß mit *q^{e}jam* die volle Breite des Bedeutungsfeldes von *b^{e}rît* erfaßt ist, kann man daran ersehen, daß *q^{e}jam* außer für *b^{e}rît* einerseits auch für hebr. *š^{e}bû'ā* „ Eid, Schwur " (z.B. *Num.*, 30,3 ; *Dtn.*, 7,8) oder für *nedär* „ Gelübde " (z.B. *Gen.*, 28,20 ; 31,13), andererseits aber auch für *ḥoq* „ Satzung " (z.B. *Ex.*, 18,16.20 ; *Ps.*, 99,7) [57] stehen kann. — Die LXX setzt für *b^{e}rît* bei ± 267 (von insgesamt 287) Belegen διαθήκη im Sinne von „ Setzung ", „ Bestimmung " ; sie läßt allerdings bei diesem Wort, das sonst zumeist die „ letztwillige Verfügung " bezeichnet, das Moment des „ Letztwilligen " außer Betracht [58]. Erst die jüngeren Übersetzungen von Aquila, Symmachus und Theodotion geben — in unterschiedlichem Umfang — *b^{e}rît* mit συνθήκη wieder — und bereiten damit die Übersetzung „ Bund " für *b^{e}rît* vor [59].

III

Wir haben gesehen : *b^{e}rît* bedeutet nicht „ Bund ", sondern die „ Verpflichtung ", die „ Bestimmung ". Von dieser Basis aus fragen wir nun nach dem, was man „ Abraham-*b^{e}rît* ", „ Sinai-*b^{e}rît* " und „ David-*b^{e}rît* " nennen kann, präzise : was in jedem Fall *b^{e}rît* genau bedeutet und was der Inhalt der jeweiligen *b^{e}rît* ist.

1. Wir beginnen mit der *Abraham-b^{e}rît*. Der älteste Beleg für eine *b^{e}rît* Jahwes mit Abraham ist *Gen.*, 15,18. Wie wir schon festgestellt haben, meint *b^{e}rît* hier die Selbstverpflichtung Jahwes, seine Zusage an den Erzvater. Inhalt dieser Zusage ist die Gabe des Landes an die Nachkommen Abrahams. Dieser Text wird meist dem Jahwisten zugesprochen [60] ; nach N. Lohfink [61] hat der Jahwist den Text von *Gen.*, 15 bereits vorgefunden und in sein Werk eingearbeitet. Diesen zeitlichen Ansetzungen widerraten vornehmlich zwei Beobachtungen : erstens bringt *Gen.*, 15 für J nichts Neues und ist also dort ganz entbehrlich [62] ; zum andern unterscheidet sich die Abgrenzung des verheißenen Landes nach *Gen.*, 15,18 — „ vom ‚ Bach ' Ägyptens bis zum großen Strom, dem Euphratstrom " — stark von der jahwistischen, die mit der Bezeichnung „ alles Land, das du hier (d.h. vom Heiligtum Bethel aus) siehst " in *Gen.*, 13,14f. keinesfalls mehr als den Bereich „ von Dan bis Beerseba " (vgl. *Ri.*, 20,1 ; *1Sam.*, 3,20 ; *2Sam.*, 3,10 u.ö.), wahrscheinlich aber nur

57. Vgl. auch bibl.-aram. *q^{e}jam* „ Verordnung " *Dan.*, 6,8.16.

58. Derselbe Sprachgebrauch ist auch bei Aristophanes, *Aves* 440f., zu beobachten ; vgl. dazu Kutsch, *Verheißung und Gesetz*, S. 178 Anm. 12.

59. Vgl. dazu Kutsch a.a.O. S. 181 ff.

60. Vgl. z.B. O. Eißfeldt, *Hexateuch-Synopse*, 1922, S. 24* ; M. Noth, *Überlieferungsgeschichte des Pentateuch*, 1948, S. 29.

61. A. a. O. (Anm. 8), S. 84.

62. Perlitt a.a.O. (Anm. 8) S. 75ff. ; Kutsch a.a.O. S. 67 bei und mit Anm. 88.

das Gebirge Ephraim und das Gebirge Juda umreißt. Die Umschreibung von *Gen.*, 15,18bβ läßt eher an die Zeit der Bemühungen des Königs Josia, das Davidreich wiederherzustellen, denken, was eine Ansetzung in die Zeit zwischen 625 und 609 bedeutet [63].

Nach *Gen.*, 15,18 begegnet die Landzusage als *b^{e}rît* an Abraham — an Abraham allein, nicht an die drei Erzväter insgesamt — nur noch zweimal im Alten Testament : in *Gen.*, 17,8 und in *Neh.*, 9,8. Das Kapitel *Gen.*, 17 bietet innerhalb der Priesterschrift insofern einen Schwerpunkt, als hier das Thema von Gottes *b^{e}rît* an Abraham breit ausgestaltet ist. Über *Gen.*, 15,18 und die dortige Aussage hinaus hat hier göttliche *b^{e}rît* drei verschiedene Inhalte. Die Landgabe als Gegenstand einer göttlichen *b^{e}rît* ist hier in V.8a unmittelbar verbunden mit einer weiteren Zusage in V.7.8b : Gott, dem Abraham nach V.1bα als El Šaddaj erschienen, spricht :

> ,, (7) Ich richte meine *b^{e}rît* auf zwischen mir und zwischen dir und zwischen deinem Samen nach dir nach ihren Geschlechtern als ewige *b^{e}rît*, daß ich dir und deinen Nachkommen nach dir Gott sein werde. (8) Ich gebe dir und seinen Nachkommen nach dir das Land deiner Schutzbürgerschaft, das ganze Land Kanaan, zu ewigem Besitz ; und ich werde ihnen Gott sein. "

Als Inhalt der göttlichen *b^{e}rît* ist zunächst V.7b anzusehen : ,, Daß ich dir und deinen Nachkommen nach dir Gott sein werde. " Diese Ankündigung ist in V.8b noch einmal aufgenommen : ,, Ich werde ihnen Gott sein. " Der Inhalt dieser *b^{e}rît* entspricht dem ersten Teil der üblicherweise — wenn auch zu Unrecht — so genannten ,, Bundesformel ", die in knappster Abstraktion vollständig lauten würde : ,, Jahwe — Israels Gott, Israel — Jahwes Volk " [64]. Daß Jahwe dem Abraham und seinen Nachkommen Gott sein will, ist für die Empfänger der *b^{e}rît*, für diejenigen, denen der Inhalt der *b^{e}rît* zugute kommt, heilvolles Geschehen. Das findet seine Bestätigung in dem Zwischenstück in V.8a in der Ankündigung, Gott werde, wiederum Abraham und seinen Nachkommen nach ihm, ,, das ganze Land Kanaan zu ewigem Besitz geben ". Der Sachverhalt, daß einerseits nach *Gen.*, 15,18 der Inhalt der *b^{e}rît* Jahwes an Abraham die Landgabe ist, daß andererseits aber auch die Priesterschrift in *Ex.*, 6,4f. auf die Landgabe als *b^{e}rît* zurückgreift,

63. Vgl. dazu Kutsch a.a.O. S. 67 ff.

64. Vgl. dazu R. Smend, *Die Bundesformel* (ThSt 68), 1963. — Da *b^{e}rît*, insbesondere im theologischen Bereich, nicht ,, Bund " bedeutet, andererseits aber auch nirgends das Verhältnis zwischen Jahwe und Israel bezeichnet, sollte man die Bezeichnung ,, Bundesformel " durch ,, Zugehörigkeitsformel " ersetzen ; vgl. Kutsch a.a.O. S. 146-149.

macht es wahrscheinlich, daß auch die Verheißung der Landgabe in *Gen.*, 17,8a noch als Bestandteil der *b^e^rît* von V.7a gedacht ist [65].

Nun tritt in *Gen.*, 17 noch ein weiterer Inhalt von *b^e^rît* hinzu : die Vermehrung Abrahams zu einem großen Volk. Diese Mehrungs-*b^e^rît* erscheint jetzt in zweifacher Gestalt : in V. 2 + 6 und in V.3-5, wobei die letztere wohl sekundär in den zwischen V.2 und 6 bestehenden Zusammenhang eingearbeitet worden ist [66].

In allen drei Fällen — bei der Ankündigung der Landgabe, des Gottseins zugunsten Israels und der Mehrung — ist *b^e^rît* verstanden als die von Gott gegebene Zusage. Gott verpflichtet sich selbst dem Abraham gegenüber zur Leistung der genannten Heilsgaben. Wenn *b^e^rît* ,, Bund " bedeuten würde, dann würde man auch eine Angabe über eine Verpflichtung erwarten, deren Erfüllung dem Abraham obläge. Eine Verpflichtung Abrahams liegt tatsächtlich in V.9-14 vor in dem Beschneidungsgebot, und man hat denn auch darin ,, die logische Fortsetzung einer der vorhergegangenen Bundesaussagen " sehen wollen [67], zumal nun auch dieses Gebot als *b^e^rît* bezeichnet ist (V.9-11.14). Indes widerspricht einem solchen Verständnis der Text selbst. Die Gottesrede an Abraham, die in V.1b begonnen hatte und die die verschiedenen *b^e^rît* als Zusagen Gottes enthalten hatte, ist mit V.8 zu Ende gegangen. Mit V.9 setzt, mit den Worten : ,, Und Gott sprach zu Abraham " eine neue Gottesrede ein. Dadurch wird das Folgende deutlich von dem Vorhergehenden abgehoben und damit auch die im Folgenden behandelte *b^e^rît* gegenüber der dreifachen *b^e^rît* in V.2-8. Der Neueinsatz wird aber auch noch unterstrichen durch die Einleitung zu dem eigentlichen Beschneidungsgebot von V.10b-14 in V.10a : ,, Dies ist meine *b^e^rît*, die ihr bewahren sollt zwischen mir und zwischen euch. " [68] Hier wird nicht an die vorher genannte *b^e^rît* angeknüpft — hier geht es um eine neue, eine andere *b^e^rît*. Daß diese *b^e^rît* auch anders geartet ist, das zeigt ihr Inhalt : Es ist ein Gebot, das Abraham — bzw. die Israeliten — zu halten haben. *b^e^rît* meint hier die Verpflichtung, die Gott diesen auferlegt hat, d.h. Fremd-

65. Vgl. G.v. RAD, *Das erste Buch Mose, Genesis* (ATD 2-4), 1972, S. 109.
66. Cf. KUTSCH a.a.O. S. 57.
67. So v. RAD a.a.O. S. 170.
68. Der Text von *Gen.*, 17,9-14 ist insofern uneinheitlich, als die Jahwerede sich teils an einen einzelnen, teils an eine Mehrzahl von Personen wendet. Offenbar ist in v. 10-14 eine Beschneidungsordnung für die Israeliten aufgenommen, die ihrerseits bereits in die Form einer Jahwerede gekleidet war. Deren Text liegt in V.10aα. b.11.12a.13b (und 14) vor, wo eine Mehrzahl von Personen angeredet ist. Die Anrede an eine Einzelperson in V.10aβ.12a.13a setzt den Kontext der an Abraham gerichteten Jahwerede voraus. Bei der Übernahme der Beschneidungsordnung hat der Verfasser des Kontextes diese durch den Text von V.10aβ.12b.13a erweitert und so seiner Darstellung (V.10aβ) und seiner besonderen Intention (V.12b.13a) angepaßt.

verpflichtung. Nicht ist dagegen *b^e^rît* gebraucht gewissermaßen als „Dachbegriff", der sowohl die *b^e^rît* mit unterschiedlichen Verheißungsinhalten als auch die *b^e^rît* als das Gebot umfaßt. Mit anderen Worten : *b^e^rît* bedeutet auch in *Gen.*, 17 nicht „Bund".

Der dritte Beleg für eine Abraham-*b^e^rît* im Alten Testament, *Neh.*, 9,7f., lautet :

> (7) Jahwe, du bist der Gott, der den Abraham erwählt, ihn aus Ur in Chaldäa herausgeführt und seinen Namen Abraham genannt hat. (8) Du hast sein Herz treu vor dir befunden und mit ihm die *b^e^rît* festgesetzt, das Land der Kanaanäer, der Hethiter, der Amoriter und der Perissiter und der Jebusiter und der Girgasiter zu geben — zu geben seinem Samen.

Wenn hier die Umbenennung Abrahams aus *Gen.*, 17,3-5 erwähnt ist, dann ist die Kenntnis des Kap. *Gen.*, 17 vorausgesetzt. Die dem Abraham gewährte *b^e^rît* hat aber allein die Landgabe zum Inhalt. Damit sowie mit der Aufzählung kanaanäischer Völker als Vorbesitzer des Landes — wenn auch mit Unterschieden hinsichtlich Zahl und Namen — folgt *Neh.*, 9,8 dem Text von *Gen.*, 15,18-21.

Wo sonst die Landgabe als Inhalt der Jahwe-*b^e^rît* erscheint, gilt sie als an die drei Erzväter ergangen : so in *Ex.*, 6,4f. (danach wohl auch in 2,24, beide P) ; *Lev.*, 26,42, besonders in *Ps.*, 105,8-11 = *1Chr.*, 16,15-18, wahrscheinlich auch in *Dtn.*, 4,31 ; 7,12 ; 8,18.

Dreierlei Inhalt von an Abraham (bzw. an die Erzväter) ergangener *b^e^rît* nennt also das Alte Testament : daß Gott ihm/ihnen und ihren Nachkommen das Land Kanaan geben werde, daß er sie zahlreich machen werde und daß er ihnen Gott sein werde. Nun zeigt es sich, daß diese drei *b^e^rît*-Inhalte in anderen altestamentlichen Texten auch sowohl durch das einfache göttliche Wort verheißen als auch durch einen göttlichen Schwur zugesagt werden. Die Landzusage durch einfaches Wort findet sich z.B. in *Gen.*, 12,7 (J) : „Jahwe erschien Abram und sprach : Deinem Samen werde ich dieses Land geben", weiter in *Gen.*, 13,14f.17 ; 24,7 ; 28,13 (J) u.ö. Als Schwur ist sie ausgedrückt z.B. in *Gen.*, 24,7 ; 26,3 (beides Zusatz zu J) ; 50,24 (E) ; *Dtn.*, 1,8.35 u.ö. — Die Vermehrung der Nachkommen ist in Form des einfachen Wortes verheißen z.B. in *Gen.*, 12,2 (J) : „Ich (Jahwe) werde dich zu einem großen Volk machen", in *Gen.*, 26,24 (J) ; 26,4 (Zusatz zu J) ; 22,17 (R^{Je}) ; 28,3 ; 48,4 (P) ; *Ex.*, 32,13 (deuteronomistisch). Als Eid qualifiziert erscheint die Mehrungszusage in *Gen.*, 22,17 (R^{Je}) ; *Ex.*, 32,13 ; *Dtn.*, 13,18. — Schließlich wird auch das Gott-Sein durch das einfache Wort verheißen ; allerdings ist hier diese Ankündigung nicht an die Erzväter, sondern an ihre Nachkommen, die Israeliten, gerichtet ; so *Ez.*, 34,24 : „Ich, Jahwe, werde ihnen Gott sein... ; ich, Jahwe, habe es gesagt "; *Ex.*, 29,45 (P); *Lev.*, 11,45; *Dtn.*, 29,12aβ u.ö. Zugeschworen ist das Gott-Sein den drei Erzvätern in *Dtn.*, 29,12: „Damit er dich heute zum Volk bestelle und er dir Gott werde, wie er dir gesagt und wie er deinen Vätern Abraham, Isaak und Jakob geschworen hat ".

Daraus, daß ein und derselbe Verheißungsinhalt einmal als einfaches Wort, dann als Eid, Schwur und ebenso auch als *b^e^rît* bezeichnet werden kann, ergeben sich folgende Schlüsse:

1) Wenn *b^e^rît* auf einer Ebene liegt mit Eid und einfachem Wort, dann bestätigt das, daß *b^e^rît* nicht „Bund " bedeutet, sondern (in solchem Zusammenhang) eine besondere Art der Zusage: die (feierliche) Selbstverpflichtung zur Gewährung des Zugesagten.

2) Bei der Land- und der Mehrungszusage zeigt sich, daß die einfache Zusage durch das Wort am frühesten begegnet: im Werk des Jahwisten *Gen.*, 12,7.2. Zeitlich folgt die Form der Verheißung als Eid: für die Landzusage in *Gen.*, 50,24 E; *Dtn.*, 1,8.35 u.ö. im Deuteronomium und in den wohl vom Deuteronomium abhängigen Zusätzen zu J in *Gen.*, 26,3 und in 24,7, für die Mehrungszusage bei R^{Je} in *Gen.*, 22,17, im Deuteronomium und in *Ex.*, 32,13. Erst als jüngste Stufe werden Landzusage und Mehrungszusage als *b^e^rît* bezeichnet (*Gen.*, 15,18 (wohl letztes Viertel des 7. Jh.s); *Dtn.*, 4,31; 7,12; 8,18; *Gen.*, 17,8; *Ex.*, 2,24; 6,4f. P; *Lev.*, 26,42; *Ps.*, 105,8-11 = *1Chr.*, 16,15-18 bzw. *Gen.*, 17,2 + 6.3-5 P). Daneben ist die Zusage Jahwes an Abraham und seine Nachkommen bzw. an Israel, ihnen Gott sein zu wollen, kaum vor dem 6.Jh. anzusetzen und also an sich schon jung (*Ez.*, 34,24 u.a.), so daß hier die Formen des Eides (*Dtn.*, 29,12b) und der *b^e^rît* (*Gen.*, 17,7b.8b) zeitlich nicht wesentlich später als die einfache Ankündigung liegen. So erscheint hier *b^e^rît* als letzte und wohl gewichtigste Form der Zusage. Es ist sicher kein Zufall, daß dieser Begriff gerade in der Zeit der Restauration unter Josia sowie in der Notzeit des Exils und danach verwendet worden ist. Hatte schon eine frühere Zeit der göttlichen Zusage durch die Form des Eides erhöhtes und vielleicht erneutes Gewicht verliehen, so führt diese Zeit zu einer weiteren Betonung der Zusage durch den Begriff der *b^e^rît*, durch den nun die Gewißheit der göttlichen Verheißung verstärkt werden konnte und sollte.

Was man in der Vergangenheit als „Abrahambund " bezeichnet hat, ist also nichts anderes als eine besondere Form der göttlichen Verheißung an den Erzvater. Zimmerli etwa hat das durchaus richtig gesehen; nur ist in dem Terminus „Verheißungsbund " der Wortteil „Bund " wegzulassen.

2. Entsprechend ist auch die *David-b^e^rît* eine besonders gewichtige Form der Verheißung Jahwes an David. Den Inhalt dieser *b^e^rît* formuliert knapp *Ps.*, 89,4f.:

(4) Ich habe meinem Erwählten eine *b^e^rît* festgesetzt,
habe meinem Knecht David geschworen :
(5) Für immer setze ich deine Nachkommenschaft ein,
baue für alle Geschlechter deinen Thron.

Der Text selbst setzt *b^e^rît* und Eid mit einander in Parallele. Der Inhalt von beiden ist nichts anderes als das, was nach *2Sam.*, 7,16 und anderen Belegen Gegenstand der einfachen Zusage Jahwes an David war : die Garantie der Dynastie und des Thrones. Eine Überhöhung tritt hier insofern noch ein, als diese Verheißung in *2Sam.*, 23,5 sogar als eine *b^e^rît 'ôlam*, eine ewig gültige Zusage bezeichnet ist.

Ebenso ist im übrigen die *Noah-b^e^rît* in *Gen.*, 9,8-17 (P) inhaltlich dasselbe wie die Verheißung Jahwes von *Gen.*, 8,21 (J), keine Sintflut mehr über die Erde zu bringen — die in *Jes.*, 54,9 wiederum als ,, Schwur " firmiert ist.

3. Wer nun nach dem gewohnten Schema diesen beiden, Abraham-*b^e^rît* und David-*b^e^rît*, eine Sinai-*b^e^rît* gegenüberstellen will, gerät in Schwierigkeiten. Nach einer solchen wird man hauptsächlich die Sinai-Perikope, also *Ex.*, 19-34, befragen. Das Substantiv *b^e^rît* begegnet hier 10 mal : 19,5 ; 23,32 ; 24,7.8 ; 31,16 ; 34,10.12.15.27.28. Von diesen fallen für unsere Frage 23,32 ; 34,12.15 sofort aus, weil hier *b^e^rît* im zwischenmenschlichen Bereich gebraucht ist und die Lebens- oder Bleibezusage der Israeliten an die kanaanäische Vorbevölkerung meint. In 34,10 ist *b^e^rît* die Zusage Jahwes, unerhörte Wunder zu tun, wobei nicht einmal ein Gegenüber genannt ist [69]. Demgegenüber ist in 31,16 (P^s) lediglich das Sabbatgebot als *b^e^rît 'ôlam* bezeichnet ; das ist nicht ein ,, Sabbat-Bund ", sondern die ,, immerwährende Verpflichtung " [70] für Israel, den Sabbat zu feiern. In 19,3b-8 kündigt Jahwe den Israeliten an, sie werden sein Eigentumsvolk sein, wenn sie auf seine Stimme hören und seine *b^e^rît* bewahren. Wenn das Bewahren der göttlichen *b^e^rît* die Vorbedingung für das (neue) Verhältnis zwischen Jahwe und dem Volk Israel ist, dann kann mit der *b^e^rît* nicht das Verhältnis selbst gemeint sein. In Parallele zu ,, auf meine Stimme hören " kann ,, meine *b^e^rît* bewahren " nur die Einhaltung von Jahwes ,, Verpflichtung " bedeuten.

Ist hier nur allgemein von ,, Verpflichtung " die Rede, so geben nun die übrigen vier Belege — *Ex.*, 24,7.8 und 34,27.28 — Anhalt für eine — zweifache — *b^e^rît*, die man — da sie am Sinai mitgeteilt wird — als ,, Sinai-*b^e^rît* " bezeichnen kann. Nach 24,7, hat Mose den Israeliten

69. Erst die LXX hat ,, dir " ergänzt. — Vgl. dazu KUTSCH, *Verheißung und Gesetz*, S. 77f.

70. So richtig z.B. die Zürcher Bibel.

aus einer „Rolle der *b^e^rît*" vorgelesen und das Volk mit Opferblut besprengt, das er „Blut der *b^e^rît*" nennt; und nach 34,28 hat Mose „Worte der *b^e^rît*" aufgeschrieben, Worte — so V.27 —, auf Grund deren Jahwe mit ihm und mit Israel eine *b^e^rît* festgesetzt hat. Die „Worte der *b^e^rît*" in 34,28 — ebenso in *Dtn.*, 28,69; 29,8; *2Kön.*, 23,3 — sind dasselbe wie die „Worte der *tôrā*" in *Dtn.*, 17,19 und 8mal in Dtn; *Jos.*, 8,34; *2Kön.*, 23,24, wie der parallele Gebrauch der beiden Wendungen in *2Kön.*, 23,3 bzw. 24 beweist. Und ebenso ist „Rolle der *b^e^rît*" in *Ex.*, 24,7 — und *2Kön.*, 23,21 — dasselbe wie die „Rolle der *tôrā*" in *Dtn.*, 31,26; *Jos.*, 1,8. Hier ist *b^e^rît* gleichbedeutend mit *tôrā* „Weisung", „Gesetz", *b^e^rît* meint hier also wie in 19,5 die von Jahwe dem Volk auferlegte Verpflichtung. Die „Worte Jahwes" (24,4), die die Israeliten befolgen sollen, sind deshalb „Worte der *b^e^rît*", „Worte der Verpflichtung", weil Jahwe auf ihrer Grundlage „mit" ihnen, d.h. zu ihren Lasten, eine *b^e^rît*, eine Verpflichtung festgesetzt hat (24,8b; 34,27b). Gemeint sind mit diesen „Worten" in 24,7 das sog. „Bundesbuch" in 20,22-23,19, in 34,27f. die in 34,11-26 zusammengestellten Bestimmungen [71].

Ein besonderes Problem bietet noch *Ex.*, 24,8: die Besprengung „des Volkes" mit einem Teil des Blutes von Opfertieren und dessen Bezeichnung als *dăm hăbb^e^rît* „Blut der *b^e^rît*". In der neueren Forschung sieht man in der Handlung von 24,8aβ häufig den zweiten Teil eines Ritus, dessen erster Teil die Sprengung der anderen Hälfte des Opferblutes an den Altar, der dabei Gott repräsentiert, ist; dieser Ritus markierte im ganzen einen „Bundesschluß", bei dem beide „Bundespartner" durch das „Bundesblut" miteinander verbunden werden. Aber diese Erklärung basiert mehr auf dem Zwang der Gleichung „*b^e^rît* = Bund" als auf der Aussage des Textes. Daß das Blut der Opfertiere an den Altar gesprengt wird, entspricht den sonst im Alten Testament bekannten Opfervorschriften: *Lev.*, 1,5.11; 9,12; *2Kön.*, 16,15; *Ez.*, 43,18 für Brandopfer, *Lev.*, 3,2.8.13; 9,18; 17,6; *2Kön.*, 16,13 für *š^e^lamîm*-Opfer. Nach 24,6-8 wird nun ein Teil dieses Blutes für einen besonderen zusätzlichen Ritus verwendet. Was die Besprengung des anwesenden Volkes mit dem Opferblut bedeutet, veranschaulicht ein Text bei Aischylos, „Sieben gegen Theben" (Z. 42-48). Die sieben Führer des argivischen Heeres schwören, die Stadt, Theben, zu zerstören; dabei tauchen sie ihre Hände in das Blut eines als Eidopfer geschlachteten Stieres. Hier wie in *Ex.*, 24,8 begleitet die Applizierung von Opferblut den Akt einer Verpflichtung. Der Ritus ist in beiden Fällen als Fluchhandlung gedacht: So wie das Blut des Opfertieres vergossen wurde, soll das Blut derjenigen, die mit dem Tierblut in Berührung kamen, vergossen werden, wenn sie ihren Eid — so die Argiver — bzw. ihre

71. Zu *Ex.*, 24,7f.; 34,27f. vgl. KUTSCH a.a.O. S. 80ff.

Verpflichtung — so die Israeliten — brechen. Dabei ist in *Ex.*, 24,8 stillschweigend vorausgesetzt, was der griechische Text in Z.47f. ausdrücklich sagt :

> Sie wollten Kadmos' Feste tilgen mit Gewalt,
> Oder, sterbend selbst, mit Blut begießen unser Land.

Wenn in *Ex.*, 24,8 das Blut der Opfertiere im Blick auf die Handlung, bei der es verwendet wird, als ,, Blut der *b^e^rît* " bezeichnet ist, dann bedeutet diese Wendung völlig sachgemäß ,, Blut der Verpflichtung ".

Nirgends in der Sinai-Perikope meint also *b^e^rît* ,, Bund " oder bezeichnet das Wort das Verhältnis zwischen Jahwe und Israel. Mit Hilfe des Wortes *b^e^rît* ist demnach in *Ex.*, 19-34 die Vorstellung von einem ,, Sinaibund ", d.h. von einem am Sinai zustande gekommenen Bund zwischen Jahwe und Israel, nicht zu belegen. Aber auch die Annahme, das Mahl, das nach *Ex.*, 24,9-11 Mose und seine Begleiter auf dem Gottesberg nach der Gottesschau eingenommen haben, sei ein ,, Bundesmahl " gewesen, kann allein die These von einem ,, Sinaibund " nicht tragen. Von einer Sinai-*b^e^rît* dagegen kann man insofern sprechen, als damit die *b^e^rît* gemeint ist, die ,, Verpflichtung ", die Jahwe den Israeliten am Sinai ,, festgesetzt " hat (*Ex.*, 24,8b ; 34,27b). Gegenstand dieser Verpflichtung ist nach der einen Vorstellung — *Ex.*, 24,7f. — der Text des sog. ,, Bundesbuches ", nach der anderen — *Ex.*, 34,27f. — die Sammlung von Bestimmungen in 34,11-26. Die Mitteilung des Gotteswillens ist wohl immer mit der Überlieferung vom Sinai verbunden gewesen. Die Rede von der *b^e^rît* als der Verpflichtung des Volkes auf die ,, Worte der *b^e^rît*, der Verpflichtung " (*Ex.*, 24,7f. ; 34,27f.) dagegen ist kaum in vordeuteronomische Zeit anzusetzen ; die älteren Quellenschriften des Jahwisten und des Elohisten kennen sie noch nicht [72].

IV

Wir fragen nun noch einmal nach dem Verhältnis von Abraham-*b^e^rît*, David-*b^e^rît* und Sinai-*b^e^rît*, wobei wir berücksichtigen, daß ihre Inhalte schon in älterer Zeit vorlagen, in der die Bezeichnung ,, *b^e^rît* " noch nicht üblich war. Abraham-*b^e^rît* und David-*b^e^rît* stimmen insofern überein, als bei beiden *b^e^rît* die göttliche Zusage meint. Inhaltlich dagegen sind sie ganz verschieden. Die Zusage an Abraham, vom letzten Viertel des 7. Jh.s an als *b^e^rît* bezeichnet, zielt auf die Geschichte des Volkes Israel bis hin zu ihrer Erfüllung in der Inbesitznahme des Landes

72. Neben diese *b^e^rît* vom Sinai-Horeb tritt nach deuteronomistischer Vorstellung die *b^e^rît* vom Lande Moab, d.h. die dort erfolgte Verpflichtung der Israeliten auf das Deuteronomium ; vgl. *Dtn.*, 28,69 und dazu KUTSCH a.a.O. S. 138 ff.

Kanaan und der zahlenmäßigen Größe des Volkes. (Von der Bedeutung, die diese Zusagen, vor allem auch die Verheißung, daß Jahwe Israels Gott sein will, für die spätere Zeit gewonnen haben, wollen wir hier absehen.) Die Zusage an David gilt nicht dem Volk, sondern der Dynastie Davids. Deshalb hat sie auch allein für das Südreich, für Juda, Relevanz gehabt; als *b*^{e}*rît* galt sie erst von der letzten Königszeit an (*Ps.*, 89,4. 29.35.40).

Gegenüber diesen beiden ist die Sinai-*b*^{e}*rît* Verpflichtung des Volkes; als Inhalt hat sie nicht Verheißung, sondern Gebot, Gesetz. Diese zentrale Differenz schließt aus, daß etwa die Abraham-*b*^{e}*rît* irgendwie aus der Sinai-*b*^{e}*rît* hervorgegangen ist — oder umgekehrt —, wie man immer wieder angenommen hat [73]. Zimmerli und Hillers waren auf dem richtigen Wege, haben aber noch das Stichwort „Bund“ beibehalten. Auch Sinai-*b*^{e}*rît* und David-*b*^{e}*rît* sind wie in der Bedeutung — Verpflichtung Israels gegenüber der Selbstverpflichtung Jahwes —, so auch dem Inhalt nach radikal verschieden [74]. Die Verpflichtung Israels auf das Gesetz hat in jeder Hinsicht einen anderen „Sitz im Leben“ als die Zusage von Dynastie und Thron [75]. Hier hat Clements Richtiges gesehen, ohne daß er die Konsequenz gezogen hat, den Begriff „Bund“ aufzugeben.

Abraham-*b*^{e}*rît* und David-*b*^{e}*rît* enthalten Gottes *Zuspruch*, die Sinai-*b*^{e}*rît* Gottes *Anspruch* an den Menschen. Abraham-*b*^{e}*rît* und David-*b*^{e}*rît* sind Ausdruck der göttlichen *Gnade*, die Sinai-*b*^{e}*rît* ist Verpflichtung auf Gottes *Gesetz* [76].

E. KUTSCH

See *Supplementary note*, p. 213.

73. S. oben S. 74.

74. Dies zu Rost, Sekine, Gunneweg.

75. Gegen Kraus und de Vaux.

76. In dem sog. „Sinaibund“ einen „Gnadenbund“ (vgl. z.B. Eichrodt a.a.O. [Anm. 19] S. 25: „Gottes herablassende Gnade in der Bundschließung beim Auszug aus Ägypten“), in dem Sinaiereignis „die Geburtsstunde des alttestamentlichen Heils“ (W. Eichrodt, *Bund und Gesetz* [*Gottes Wort und Gottes Land.* Festschrift für Hans-Wilhelm Hertzberg zum 70. Geburtstag, 1965, S. 30-49], S. 45) zu sehen, wurde dadurch ermöglicht, daß man mit Hilfe des unkritisch verwendeten Begriffes „Bund“ die Vorstellung von der Gnadengabe Gottes, die in der Abraham-*b*^{e}*rît* vorliegt, auf das Sinaiereignis übertragen hat.

5

COVENANT-RELATIONSHIPS

Covenant [1] was a public thing. As something designed to regulate relations among men, it had to be. It was a point of reference, a reminder of obligations, and a norm to which to appeal in the face of wrongs. A thing like this will normally have a relatively fixed formula. Society establishes fixed ways of making contracts and the like so that they may be accessible to all to whom they pertain. One needs to know exactly what to do to make one validly, and what to look for in order to judge whether someone has fulfilled his obligations. [2] Further, making a covenant was a secular activity. To be sure, it was not without a religious aspect (what part of ancient life was not ?) because it involved an oath and so the gods. However, it can properly be called secular because it was directly concerned with relations among men and not with things of the gods such as the cult. It was, then, as something known from secular experience and as something with a well-defined profile that covenant came to be applied to the religious purpose of describing and explaining the relation between Israel and Yahweh.

If we wish to understand the basic meaning and especially the connotations, the " feel " of covenant, we should look for descriptions of its basic secular form. And it would be desirable to give special attention to any texts which reveal something of the formal structure which

1. " Covenant " is used here for *b^e^rît* although this translation (or its German equivalent, *Bund*) has been questioned for putting too much emphasis on relational ideas when *b^e^rît* means essentially "obligation": See E. Kutsch, *Gesetz und Gnade. Probleme des alttestamentlichen Bundesbegriffs, ZAW* 79 (1967) 18-35; "*Der Begriff* bryt *in vordeuteronomischer Zeit* ", *Rost Festschrift*, (BZAW 105), Berlin, 1967, 133-143 ; " *Von* bryt *zu "Bund"*", *Kerygma und Dogma* 14 (1968) 159-182 ; THAT I, cols. 339-352. However, I believe that " covenant " remains the best translation and retain it here. For discussion see D. J. McCarthy, S.J., " B^e^rît *and Covenant in the Deuteronomistic History* ", *VTSuppl.* 23. Leiden, 1972, 74-75.

2. Because it was stylized, publically known, and enforcable, covenant may properly be called a legal matter. Thus I am extending the use of " legal " beyond what G. M. Tucker allows in his demonstration that covenant was not formally a contract according to the categories of ancient law (*Covenant Forms and Contract Forms, VT* 15 (1965) 487-503). However, this is to restrict the legal to a particular aspect of law (largely that concerned with property), when, in fact, it is something much broader than this.

covenant-making as a public activity must have had. In fact, there is evidence which meets these requirements in the reports of covenant-making scattered through Genesis and the Deuteronomistic History. They give a unified picture of an activity with settled elements and procedure which are presented as understood by the actors in the process and intelligible to the authors' intended audience. And surely these were things current in the society which produced them, not peculiar to some coterie, because they appear in traditions from various parts of that society. We can supplement this picture from the passing references to covenant-making which occur in the deuteronomistic material and the prophets. However, in part because they deal *ex professo* with covenant-making and in part because they give a convincing picture of a complete and ordered activity, it is the reports which must guide our understanding of the other material. For example, a passing reference to covenant will usually ignore the negotiations which the reports show to have been a regular feature of covenant-making.

It is the purpose of this paper to examine some of these reports in detail and then see what this examination reveals about covenant in general. The first part will concentrate on the reports of covenant-making in Genesis, since I have already studied the complex and important material from the Deuteronomistic History elsewhere. [3] In the second part devoted to some of the problems about covenant which recur in recent literature we will use the results of the analysis of all the material.

I. The Reports in Genesis

As the text of Genesis now stands there are three full reports of covenant-making : *Gen.*, 21,22-34 ; 26,23-33 ; and 31,25-32,3. However, consideration of the sources behind these texts reveals that they contain elements of several more reports so that the extent of our evidence is appreciably increased. Thus, in *Gen.*, 21 we have a J form of the story, verses 25-26,28-30,32-34, and an E form, verses 22-24,27,31. [4] *Gen.*, 26,23-33 is all J, but *Gen.*, 31,25-32,3 is again composite. This latter text,

3. See *VTSuppl.* 21 (1972) 55-75.

4. The assignment to J and E follows Gunkel with the agreement of many commentators. G. von Rad, ATD 2/5 believes that there are two E traditions here. This seems less likely, but even if it were true it would leave us with two reports of covenant-making. M. NOTH, *A History of Pentateuchal Traditions*, N.J., 1972, 35, n. 131, thinks that there is an E tradition glossed from *Gen.*, 26,15ff., but this does not really do justice to the completeness of the two descriptions of the covenant-making.

however, is a difficult case for source analysis, and its problems demand more extended notice.

There clearly are different parallel traditions of the covenant between Jacob and Laban, but how are they to be divided from one another, and to what sources are the various parallel accounts to be assigned ? The only clear connections within the passage are between the stone-heap (*gāl*) in 31,46 and 51-52, and the only really exclusive doublets are the meals which occur at different points in the proceedings (31,46 and 54). Beyond this the possibilities multiply. Are the three monument-signs, the stone-heap, the pillar (*maṣṣēbâ*), and the watchtower (*miṣpâ*) marks of three traditions ? Or are we to identify the pillar and the watchtower on the basis of the assonance of the Hebrew names as Gunkel suggests in his Genesis commentary ? This is plausible but not demonstrative. Or are we to take the word *miṣpâ* as a proper name for the stone-heap ? Then, what part of the report uses Elohim and what Yahweh ? Are we to keep Yahweh with the MT in verse 49, or read Elohim with the LXX ?

These are some of the more obvious alternatives which the text poses for the analyst. In themselves and especially in combination with one another and with other data they open the way to a bewildering variety of possibilities in the reconstruction of sources. [5] Discretion is surely indicated. But perhaps with care we can reach some conclusions which, though they must remain incomplete, allow us to build on something more than mere hypothesis. For this it helps to keep in mind that the problem here is not to reconstruct the historical order among the texts but simply to discern whatever different clues to the nature of covenant we can. In this line, we can at least be sure that the doublets and inconsistencies demonstrate the existence of several independent reports of the Jacob-Laban covenant. Moreover, no matter how one selects verses as belonging to sources or what sources he attributes them to, the reconstructions produce at least two similar pictures of covenant-making. There are always negotiations and the construction of a monument-sign which occasions a formulation of terms. It is unsatisfactory not

5. There is no agreement among the commentators : e.g., in the verses which principally concern us Gunkel divides 44,46,48.51-53a (J) and 45.49-50.53b-54 (E) ; Procksch 45.49-50.51b.53b-54 (J) and 44.46-48.51a.52-53a (E) ; Wellhausen 46.48a. 50a (J) and 45.51-54 (E). This is not divergence, it is contradiction ! I find Gunkel's analysis convincing, but one can hardly say that it has been demonstrated to be true. Basing an argument on a particular analysis in a case like this is to restrict oneself to hypothesis. However, it is not necessary to do this when one is not dealing with history of tradition or of sources. Here we clearly have multiple data relevant to covenant-making, and we will find that these data have a common structure and content. This evidence is independent of detailed assignment to sources.

to be able to go beyond this to a sure, simple reconstruction of sources, but it is all the more striking that amid so much obscurity and confusion a repeated pattern does occur. *Gen.*, 31,25-32,3, then, offers multiple evidence, wherever it may have come from, for a structure in reports of covenant-making. With our other Genesis texts it makes a total of at least five originally separate reports of covenant-making available to us.

In these five reports certain formal elements, means of expression, topics, and structural relations among the parts of the process, recur. To look first at this last element, we find that the larger structure of the report of covenant-making is clear and simple. Once the parties have been brought together there are negotiations. That is, some kind of give-and-take aimed at clarifying the situation is introduced. Then there is an action which is itself a sign or which at least produces a sign related to the covenant. In most instances this relation appears in the fact that the terms, which are always stated, are formulated as an explanation of the meaning of the sign. Finally, the report concludes with a notice that a covenant has been made.

This is the over-all structure. It is so organized that one can call it stylized, and the same can be said for many details within it. The negotiations involve an explicit challenge and a response. This can take the form of a question. [6] Or there can be a protest. [7] Or there can be an imperative or cohortative : " Swear, " or " Let us make a covenant ! " or the like. [8] This is functional stylization. It poses a problem, clarifies its solution, and brings out what is involved for the several parties to the covenant. It would appear that covenant-making, or at least the literary representation of covenant-making, which after all is what concerns us, followed an established procedure with a recognized syntax which covered the presentation of the negotiations as part of the whole process. This appears too in the comparative formulations used in the negotiations reported in *Gen.*, 21,23 and 26,28 : as you received good from us, so be good to us. This usage also occurs in ancient legal forms related to covenant. The treaties call for loyalty in similar terms, and the same thing recurs in royal decrees, documents from the same mold as the treaties. [9] Not only is the language of covenant-making stylized, then, but the stylization reflects firmly established legal traditions of the ancient near eastern world.

6. *Gen.*, 26,27 ; 31,26-44 where two sources are combined, each of which makes extensive use of questions.

7. *Gen.*, 21,25. Note the technical legal expression *hôkîah*.

8. *Gen.*, 21,23 ; 26,28 ; 31,44.

9. For example, from outside Israel see A. GOETZE, *Kizzuwatna*, New Haven, 1939, 27-30 : a royal decree establishing a priesthood and tying it to the king.

Another regular feature connected with the negotiations reported in our texts is the role of the sign. In 21,28 (J) the gift of some ewes occasions an explanation in which the terms of the covenant are given an exact formulation. In *Gen.*, 31 we have two and perhaps three signs in the stone-heap, the pillar, and the watchtower, which may or may not have been originally identified with one of the other signs. In any event, the important thing here is that the signs receive an explanation which constitutes the formal statement of the terms of the covenant : in one case, a guarantee of the rights of Laban's daughters as Jacob's wives, in the other, a border guarantee. This seems to establish the role of a visible sign in covenant-making. It helps us to interpret less clear cases. In *Gen.*, 21,27 (E) there is a gift of cattle, the function of which is not explained. In the light of the other examples surely this feature of the report must be interpreted as a relic of a functional sign in the story of the covenant. If a sign was thus normal in covenant-making as reported in Genesis, this would explain the occurence of a formal meal in several of our texts : 26,30 ; 31,46 ; and 31,54. Like the gift the meal was a recognized sign of covenant, and we may see the meals in the Genesis reports as elements integral to the covenant-making process. [10]

The last element in the reports of covenant-making proper is the final notice that " they made a covenant " or that " he/they swore " [11]. This obviously has a formal function. It concludes the report, and after it the action goes on to other things. In itself it serves to affirm and record the fact that a covenant has been completed. It sums up the result of the action. It seems doubtful that in addition to this it is intended to present a separate action or at least a separate element in the total action. It is not as though something in addition to the negotiations, the sign and the rest were required. Thus, the J section of *Gen.*, 21 clearly implies that the setting apart of the gift-sign settles things. The gift lambs are themselves the surety that Abraham has the right to the well, and their acceptance is Abimelek's acknowledgment of this right. There is no need for an added ceremony, and the concluding notice stands as a summary for the whole. Now, as we have seen, all the reports have some kind of sign, a material thing or an action. That is, they contain an element strictly parallel to the functional sign in 21,27-30. In this text this is what constitutes the covenant, and the concluding notice is a formal element. One would assume the same in the parallel

10. On the function of gifts etc. in ancient near eastern law dealing with agreements see M. WEINFELD, *Deuteronomy and the Deuteronomic History*. Oxford, 1972, 102 (with references). On the covenant meal see D. J. McCARTHY, S.J., *Three Covenants in Genesis*, *CBQ*, 26 (1964) 184-185 ; W. McCREE, *The Covenant Meal in the OT*, *JBL* 45 (1926), 120-128.

11. *Gen.*, 21,27 (E) ; 21,32 (J) ; 26,31 ; 31,53b.

cases. The notice of covenant-making, then, would be a statement affirming the validity of the transaction, a usage not without its parallels.[12]

Finally, some notes about vocabulary. The notices of covenant-making alternate *krt b^erît* and *nšb'*. Nor is the equivalence of *krt b^erît* and taking an oath merely a matter of parallels in different texts which might reflect usage in different traditions or the like rather than real synonyms. In both *Gen.*, 26,28-31 and 31,44-53 a proposal to *krt b^erît* is concluded by the statement that an *oath* was taken. [13] That is, an explicit demand for "cutting a covenant" is satisfied by an oath. However, oath and covenant are not to be treated as simply identical. In *Gen.*, 26,28 we have "oath" (*'ālâ*) and *b^erît* used together to describe the thing that Abimelek seeks from Isaac. This is a hendiadys which is paralleled in other ancient near eastern languages. "Oath and tie" together designate a treaty by combining its two chief features. They are different features of the whole, even though now one, now the other can stand for the whole or for one another (cf. *Deut.*, 29,12-27 for examples), and they should not simply be identified. Covenant implies oath; it is not simply an oath. [14]

There is a last feature of these reports of covenant-making which needs attention from a formal point of view. They are among other things name etiologies. They are not this in the sense of being stories made up to explain a name. The stories are too complete and too important and too independent of any particular name for that. The naming seems rather a mnemonic device for the sake of the story rather than the story's being for the sake of the name. One is reminded of the possibility that monuments, shrines and material "witnesses," may have been used to recall important events like significant covenants involving a clan or tribe. [15] In any case, the naming element does tie the covenants in two of our reports to a shrine important in the patriarchal traditions. Nor is this connection peculiar to the texts which involve monuments. There are other links in these reports between covenant-making and holy places. *Gen.*, 21 ends with a notice of Abraham's stay at Beersheba centered on the planting of a (sacred) tree and the naming of the place *yahweh 'ēl 'ôlām*. In *Gen.*, 26 the covenant report is preceded by a notice of Isaac's stay at Beersheba. This notice turns about a theophany, a

12. Note the function of the affirmation in sacrificial law: G. von Rad, *Old Testament Theology* I, New York, 1962, 260-262.

13. This, of course, may be true only of the final redacted text, depending on how one assigns 31,44 and 53b to sources, but it remains true that the combination stands in the text.

14. See H. Brichto, *The Problem of "Curse" in the Hebrew Bible.* (JBL Monograph 13), Philadelphia, 1963, 30-31; G. M. Tucker, *VT* 15 (1965) 487-503.

15. See D. J. McCarthy, S.J., *CBQ* 26 (1964) 186, with references to Albright and Vincent.

shrine foundation, and a naming. In *Gen.*, 32 the E narrative continues from chapter 31 with a "theophany" (actually, *mal'aekê 'ĕlohîm* are involved, but formally this is a theophany), and a naming. This is not placed at the same locality where the covenant was made as is done in the other examples, but nevertheless both in E and in our final text it constitutes the immediate literary context of the covenant-making. It seems, then, that the tendency was to associate the covenant reports with sacral places and events. Why ? For one thing, there is the fact that the priests were concerned with traditional law, necessarily so in an undifferentiated society. [16] This probably was especially true in the case of covenant law because covenant, made by oath and under divine protection, involved the divine. A connection with sacred places, then, is natural. And this too connects with the larger near eastern tradition for it is well known that the treaty documents were kept in sanctuaries where, in fact, treaties may often have been made. [17]

The formal characteristics of the reports of covenant-making reveal a number of things. Their uniformity and the precision of their language confirm the hypothesis that covenant-making, a public activity, would conform to a settled pattern. This reflects a setting in society, a legal tradition which made it clear that a covenant obligation had been created by dictating a procedure suited to the purpose and known to be such. There are, in fact, explicit ties to such a tradition. The use of a sign, the comparative formulation of terms, the hendiadys "oath and tie", and the association with a sacred place, are all elements paralleled in ancient legal tradition, specifically that which appears most often in the treaties. This is not to claim that our texts are formally treaties, but merely to note the fact that they belong to a tradition which came to expression in one way in the covenants and in an analogous way in the treaties. Making a covenant was a complex thing rooted in a firm setting. The determination of the whole significance of covenant must take into account the connotations which all this gives the word.

This should have something to say to the problems which are raised in contemporary discussions of covenant. One thing leaps to the eye. In our texts covenant-making is always tied to negotiations. This seems

16. See the traditions of priestly responsibility for the Torah and especially *Deut.*, 17,8-13 where even the "secularizing" deuteronomist allots an important judicial role to the priests.

17. This may have been more than mere custom and convenience of storage. Was there some feeling that there was an intrinsic connection between certain covenants and the numinous ? This would appear in the desire to share the blessings of the divinely favored person, the succesful party, be he patriarch or Great King. For this desire see *Gen.*, 21,22 and 31,42 (E) and 26,28 (J) (see on this G. von Rad, ATD 2/5 at *Gen.*, 21,22) and *I Sam.*, 20,15 (Jonathan and David) and *2 Sam.*, 3,18 and 5,2 (David and Israel).

to rule out any idea that covenant is one-sided in the sense that it is simply imposed by one party without any consideration of the other. The point of the negotiations is to arrive at some kind of agreement, something acceptable in some way to both parties. Of course, negotiations arrive at a compromise, something not completely the wish of either party, but it is still something acceptable relative to other possibilities. Indeed, even when a report of negotiations is a pure formality, when there is not real give and take, it is significant that the formality is required. It is felt that something of the sort is necessarily tied to covenant.

Another striking thing is the way all the negotiations reported presuppose a relationship which already exists. Thus, the negotiations concern *ḥesed* (21,23) and *šalôm* (26,29). These are relational things, and they already exist between the parties in fact. The problem is to define them and to assure their continuation. This is emphasized by the use of comparatives in speaking of these things. Abimelek wants *ḥesed* and *šalôm* to obtain from the patriarch to himself just as they already obtain from him to the patriarch. Clearly the dealings take place in a context of relationships which already exist. The same thing is true in other cases, though they are expressed differently. Abraham asserts that he has rights to the well at Beersheba which Abimelek is already bound to respect, and Abimelek accepts this existing fact. Again, the negotiations in *Gen.*, 31 seek recognition of rights that already exist and are to be respected, rights of marriage, of fatherhood, of property. The point is not to create a connection but to define and confirm one.

And what of the content of the terms at which the negotiations arrive ? Do they affect only one party ? Are they unilateral, or can they be bilateral ? In some cases they are clearly unilateral. Abimelek is to respect Abraham's rights to the well at Beersheba without a return being demanded from Abraham, and Jacob's power over his wives, Laban's daughters, is restricted without his receiving anything explicit in return. Other examples are not really so clear. Abraham is asked to swear *ḥesed* and Isaac *šalôm* to Abimelek. Abimelek makes no explicit commitment. The direct object of the covenants, then, seems to be to tie one party to the other without a return. But this is hardly the whole story. There is surely an obligation on the second party, though this is implied in the situation, not stated. The patriarchs are to treat Abimelek as he them. This comparative formulation surely means that the patriarchal obligations were in fact conditional. If Abimelek's good conduct should cease, the basis of their obligation would fail. This means that the obligation here is really mutual. The last example, the border pact between Jacob and Laban, is explicitly bilateral in its terms. So far as our examples go, then, a covenant may be unilateral or bilateral. Whether it is one or the other is not determined by the simple fact that there is a covenant but by the particular nature of a given covenant. However, the more or less hidden mutuality in two of our examples emphasizes a further point. One must always consider the social context. Covenant was made within a well-defined framework of social usage, and this means that some things did not need to be made explicit. The implications of things like relational expressions and comparative formulations must be remembered. But there is especially the fact that the whole process of setting up a covenant took place within the framework of established relationships. Though the concern may be to emphasize the role of one only of the parties to the covenant so that his obligations are brought to the fore, this is always against the background of the total, multi-sided relationship which is not denied nor abrogated.

Another question often asked about covenant concerns the agent who makes a covenant. Who is represented as the author of a covenant ? Is it the work of one party imposed on or accepted for another ? This question is commonly asked in terms of inferior and superior. Can any party, stronger or weaker, greater or less, take the first steps ? In these Genesis texts it is not easy to decide who is thought of as the superior party, though it seems to me clear enough that the tradition would always have maintained the superiority of the patriarch. [18] But in regard to one aspect of agency, namely the question : who initiates covenant-making as a whole, this need not be determined since any party can make the beginning. In 21,22 (E) Abimelek opens the proceedings, but in the J parallel, 21,25, Abraham does so. In 26,26 Abimelek makes the first move, though Isaac is actually represented as speaking first. In 31,26 Laban seeks out Jacob as Abimelek had Isaac, but then he goes on to speak first as well. Thus we need not decide whether the patriarch or his partner is held to be the superior. The tradition allows either party to begin things. It is indifferent who begins covenant-making, and this observation corresponds to the indications of the reports of covenant-making in the Deuteronomistic History. [19]

But there is another way in which one may ask about the agent in covenant-making. Perhaps anyone can ask for a covenant. But who is actually said to make a covenant when all is said and done ? In fact, in three of the four notices of covenant-making which occur in our Genesis reports both parties are said to " cut " the covenant or to swear. What is notable here is the lack of correlation between this fact and the direction of apparent obligation. That is, the terms may seem unilateral, binding only Abimelek or Abraham or Isaac, as the case may be, but still the making of the covenant is said to depend on both. Both are responsible for the covenant. In such circumstances one cannot speak of a merely

18. See D.J. McCarthy, S.J., *CBQ* 26 (1964) 183-184.
19. *VTSuppl.* 23 (1972) 73-74.

unilateral covenant simply because the terms are one-sided. As long as the covenant is made by both parties it depends on the will of each. It is not imposed but accepted. Of course, this fact may simply confirm our earlier observation that the covenants involved are really bilateral even though the terms are apparently unilateral. The notice of covenant-making may simply make explicit the reality behind the situation, the responsibility of all parties.

However, this exactness in the usage is not confirmed by the last example. The pact between Jacob and Laban is, of course, a complicated literary problem. Given the uncertainty about source divisions, it is hazardous to affirm too strongly what terms were originally tied to the notice that Jacob took an oath (31,53b) which serves as the notice of covenant-making. I am inclined to think that this is to be coupled with the unilateral marriage pact in verse 50 and assigned to E. However, this is subject to argument, and for present purposes it is not necessary to insist on it. The point is that in the final redacted text this notice is coupled with a summons to a mutual covenant-making action (31,44: " Let *us* make a covenant ") and with bilateral terms in verses 51-52. That is to say, it was perfectly possible for the compiler to describe a covenant involving two-sided obligations as the work of only one of the parties. He may have done this for reasons not directly connected with the concept of covenant, e.g., as many commentators suggest, to magnify Jacob's role. The point is that he could do this without its being too incongruous in a procedure which had a well-established contour. No doubt it was easier to do this because this concluding notice is largely a formal element. Perhaps too the urge to retain the maximum from the sources helped override formal exactness. In any event, the ability to do this at all points to a certain freedom in covenant-making (or in describing it, which for us who must deal only with the descriptions comes to the same thing) which warns us against being too apodictic in asserting what covenant could and could not involve. And we will find that this freedom exists in the deuteronomistic material as well.

II. Summary

It may be helpful to draw together some central points which we have discovered about covenant-making. At the same time I shall note how these relate to the results of the study of the Deuteronomistic History. [20] First some elements characteristically associated with it will be listed.

---

20. Detailed summaries of these results will be found in *VTSuppl.* 23 (1972) 71-73, II.A-F.

1. Negotiations

Challenge and response, a give and take involving both sides, is part of all the covenant-making reported in Genesis. This is true of all the reports in the Deuteronomistic History but one. [21] We may conclude that mutual activity aimed at producing some meeting of minds was an ordinary part of the covenant-making process.

2. Terms

A. *Formulation of terms*

The Genesis reports all show the negotiations arriving at a precise formulation of terms. This is not unexpected in an established legal procedure. In view of this, it is interesting that the deuteronomistic material sometimes leaves the terms without explicit definition. They are left to be understood from the negotiations or the social context. One might imagine at first that the deuteronomistic reports reflect less concern with legal niceties. However, notice the matter of these reports. They deal with vassal subjection, relations between a hero and his *comitatus*, or the covenant between the king and the people. These are situations where social usage provides a definition of the relationship so fixed and clear that it need not be expressed in full in a report of the transaction. Of course, this conforms to the evidence for the force of social usage already found in Genesis.

B. *Unilateral or bilateral ?*

In Genesis the explicit terms are more often unilateral. Once in the sources (31,51) they are bilateral. In two of the texts as they now stand the combination of the sources has turned apparently unilateral covenants into explicitly bilateral ones. Clearly covenant in itself allows either unilateral or bilateral terms. This is evident when we add the data from

21. The force of social usage and the danger of ignoring it when discussing covenant may be illustrated from another text outside the reports of covenant-making. *Deut.*, 7,2 which forbids making covenant with Canaanites (*lo'-tikrot lahem bᵉrît*). This has been taken to mean "grant (i.e., unilaterally) no covenant." However, the subject matter of the covenant in question is connubium (an important matter often dealt with along recognized lines in ancient pacts ; cf. C. H. W. Brekelmans, *OTS* 10 (1954) 223), and this was no one-sided thing. It implied negotiations and mutual concessions as in *Gen.*, 34 (and note the implications of mutual influence even in *Deut.*, 7,3-4). We must not forget a recognized context like this simply because it is not mentioned in a passing allusion to covenant made for purposes other than describing a covenant.

the deuteronomistic texts, for there the terms are the opposite of the apparent terms of the Genesis examples : normally bilateral.

3. Relationships

Covenant-making occurs when a relationship already exists. The point is to define and affirm the connection. This is the case in all the examples in Genesis ; it is usually so in the deuteronomistic examples as well.

4. Social usage

The fact of relationship is based on accepted usage. For example, good treatment of a specific kind calls for a specific kind of return. The force of social usage is even clearer in the Deuteronomistic History. Some aspects of covenant relationships were so well known that they could be assumed without needing explicit statement (see 2. A above).

5. Variety of agent

In Genesis the act of making the covenant is usually attributed to both parties. In the Deuteronomistic History there is no uniformity and there are no apparent rules. The fact of making a covenant is regularly affirmed, but this is attributed now to one, then to the several parties to the covenant without apparent concern for other circumstances.

In conclusion we may note that this has a good deal to say to the problems which are raised in contemporary discussions of covenant. It is fair to say that these center on the nature and direction of the covenant relationship. It is a one-sided thing, or is it mutual ? Or, even if it should be indifferently unilateral or bilateral in itself, can it be one or the other at the will of one of the parties to covenant-making, and ideally should it be so ? Or should both parties be concerned ? Or should we ask about relationship at all ? Does our translation, " covenant " (or *alliance* or *Bund*), mislead us by implying something of agreement, of mutuality, while *b^erît* actually looks in another direction ? Then there are questions, perhaps less exercised but nonetheless real. Is *b^erît* properly the action which establishes a lasting relation and not the relation ? Or is *b^erît* merely more or less a synonym for " oath ? " [22] Such are the

22. For the discussion of these matters see E. Kutsch cited in n. 1 on the translation of *b^erît* ; J. Begrich, *Berit. Ein Beitrag zur Erfassung einer alttestamentlichen Denkform, ZAW* 60 (1944) 1-11, on covenant as grant ; A. Jepsen, *Berith. Ein Beitrag sur Theologie der Exilzeit, Rudolph Festschrift,* Tübingen, 1961, 161-179, on

questions. They approach covenant from the point of view of the act, the circumstances and the effect of the act, and the agent. We can respond according to these categories.

Covenant (*b^e^rît*) can indeed be equated with the act of taking an oath, but it denotes and connotes a good deal more than merely taking an oath. As a totality involving an action, a thing done or made, it regularly implicates all the parties involved in it. This is clear in the negotiations which aim at defining some aspect of a relationship or relationships which include all the parties and which already exist. That is, it does not create a connection but presupposes one. Thus it is understood only as something between parties, as part of a complex relation which involves all. This can usually be seen in the terms which no matter how expressed really implicate all parties. Covenant is made within a framework of relations which it fixes in a recognized form. Moreover, however terms may be phrased, the several parties are said to have "made (cut) a covenant" or to have "sworn," that is, covenant depends on the wills of all involved. Again, this is confirmed in the negotiations : anyone may begin this first step toward covenant, but the others must respond.

Covenant-making, then, is a complex action, and so is its result. As an amalgam of negotiations, of relationships specified, of signs relating to all parties, covenant cannot be reduced to any one element in the whole nor to any aspect of its total meaning, however important that aspect may be in a given case. It is not simply the act, nor the obligation on one party which results from the act, nor anything else so simple. One will expect it to involve all parties both as a relationship and as an act. It cannot usually come about unless all join in making it, and it means nothing unless all are somehow involved in it, even tied by it. No doubt this can be changed in a particular case, but this is its basic character, and it is doubtful whether these connotations are usually lost in any context or even whether they can be lost completely in a very special context.

D. J. McCarthy

See *Supplementary note*, p. 214.

covenant as act ; N. Lohfink, *Die Landesverheissung als Eid*, (Stuttgarter Bibelstudien 28.) Stuttgart, 1967, on covenant as oath.

6

QUELQUES REMARQUES SUR L'ARC DANS LA NUÉE

(GENÈSE 9,8-17)

Le déluge dont seul Noé fut sauvé avec les êtres vivants qui l'accompagnaient dans l'arche est, suivant le rédacteur du récit, un châtiment dû à la corruption des hommes. « La terre se corrompit à la face d'Elohim et la terre fut remplie de violence ».

Elohim décide donc la fin de toute chair. L'introduction à ce qui est nommé en 6,9 « l'histoire de Noé », *tôledôt nōaḥ*, énonce cette explication théologique avec encore plus de netteté : « Yahvé vit que la malice de l'homme sur la terre était grande et que tout l'objet des pensées de son cœur n'était toujours que le mal. Yahvé se repentit d'avoir fait l'homme sur la terre et il s'irrita en son cœur.... Mais Noé trouva grâce aux yeux de Yahvé ». (*Genèse* 6,5-6.8) [1].

Dans le passage intitulé «histoire de Noé», 6,9ss., Elohim révèle à Noé sa résolution de détruire toute chair, verset 13. Il est cependant manifeste dès le début qu'elle ne le concerne pas, car Noé est une exception parmi les hommes, un homme juste, parfait parmi ses contemporains, qui marchait en compagnie d'Elohim, comme il dit au verset 9. L'expression *hithallēk 'et* se trouve dans *Genèse* 5,22, « Hénoch marcha en compagnie de l'Elohim », et dans l'histoire de David où elle s'applique aux relations intimes que David et ses gens entretiennent avec les bergers de Nabal, *1 Samuel* 25,15.

Elohim donna donc des instructions à son familier Noé pour qu'il construisit l'arche, grâce à laquelle il se sauverait et assurerait aussi l'avenir de sa famille et des autres vivants sur la terre, car « toute ce qui est sur la terre expirera », (v. 17).

Cette prédiction et ces instructions ne sont pas une « grâce » car elle est en harmonie avec les relations intimes avec Elohim. En ces jours Elohim ne fait pas sa *bĕrît* avec Noé, mais il maintient son pacte avec son

1. Traduction de DHORME dans *La Bible*. Pléiade, Paris, 1956.

intime ami. En effet, on lit dans *Genèse* 6,18 non pas *kārat bĕrît*, mais la forme hiphil de *qûm*, *hēqîm bĕrît*, à comparer avec l'emploi qui est fait de ce verbe entre autres en *1 Samuel* 13,14, dans ces mots que Samuel dit à Saül : « et maintenant, ta royauté ne tiendra pas ». En divers endroits, on lit la forme *hēqîm* avec le sens de tenir : tenir sa promesse, rester fidèle à son serment, *Gen.* 26,3, *Jér.* 11,5 etc. Ainsi donc, Elohim maintient sa relation avec Noé et, en conséquence, lui donne des instructions pour la construction de l'arche.

Cette « histoire de Noé » ne fournit qu'une seule indication sur la nature de la *bĕrit*, les mots du verset 9 qui déclarent que Noé marchait en compagnie d'Elohim. C'est du fait que Noé était un homme juste, parfait, *ṣaddîq tāmîm*, que découlaient ces relations intimes. En conséquence, la *bĕrît* entre Elohim et Noé n'est nullement, à mon avis, quelque chose de nouveau, mais le maintien d'une relation existante. La traduction de *Genèse* 6,18 par 'établir' ou 'conclure une alliance' me paraît fautive.

L'histoire de Noé et de l'arche s'achève en *Genèse* 8,18 et 19. Noé exécute alors l'ordre intimé par Elohim de quitter l'arche. Dans la présentation qui nous est faite du récit, vient ensuite la scène du sacrifice de Noé sur l'autel bâti à Yahvé. Il est notable qu'en ce passage qui, à plus d'un égard, rappelle l'introduction yahviste à l'histoire de Noé, à savoir *Genèse* 6,5-8, l'explication théologique du déluge, châtiment de la corruption humaine, a disparu. Yahvé se fait cette réflexion, constate — littéralement ' dit en son cœur ', comme le texte le porte — que le mal est demeuré. Le déluge n'a donc pas répondu au but de dieu. Les causes pour lesquelles Yahvé « se repentit d'avoir fait l'homme » (6,6) n'ont pas été supprimées. Yahvé accepte l'échec et se résigne au fait que *jēṣer lēb hā'ādām ra'*, que l'objet du cœur de l'homme soit le mal (8,21). Il déclare : « Je ne recommencerai plus à frapper tout vivant comme je l'ai fait » (8,21). Au lieu d'une proposition théologique suit maintenant une conclusion philosophique, comme Dhorme l'a bien montré en sa note sur le verset 22 : ' La nature a ses lois qui sont définies par la succession régulière des saisons, des travaux et des jours, comme dans le poème d'Hésiode ' [2].

> « Tous les jours que la terre durera
> Semailles et moissons, froid et chaud,
> Été et hiver, jour et nuit,
> Point ne cesseront. » (*Gen.* 8,22)

Je n'éprouve aucune difficulté à parler, en ce cas, de philosophie, à condition toutefois de ne pas oublier que cette philosophie de la nature

2. *La Bible*, t. I, p. 27.

ou des lois de la nature, est fondée sur un sentiment religieux de la nature, pour parler comme Kristensen — ' een godsdienstig natuurgevoel ' [3].

Nous ne rendons pas justice à la foi, et certainement pas à celle des époques primitives de la Bible, lorsque nous la rattachons seulement à des intuitions morales, même si nous déclarons que ces intuitions sont ressenties par le croyant comme venant de son dieu. Nous nous fermons même l'accès à la foi de l'ancien Israël, si nous prenons pour règle de sa croyance les conceptions morales sur le dieu et sur ' le peuple élu ' des siècles plus récents et d'un temps où un groupe de Juifs menacés de disparition interpréta les mythes en fonction de son existence et de son avenir national.

Le début du chapitre suivant, *Gen.* 9, caractérise en quelques lignes la vie sur la terre. Les hommes, c'est-à-dire les descendants de Noé, dominent les animaux et se nourrissent de plantes et d'animaux. Ils ne peuvent manger de la chair avec son âme, c'est-à-dire avec son sang. S'ils versent le sang d'un homme, ce meurtre sera sanctionné par la mort du meurtrier.

Cette sorte de description cadre avec ce qui a été dit à la fin de l'histoire de Noé et de l'arche, 8,15-17 : « Elohim parla à Noé en disant : Sors de l'arche, toi et ta femme, tes fils, etc. avec toi, tous les animaux... Qu'ils foisonnent sur la terre, qu'ils fructifient et se multiplient sur la terre », 9,1 ; et 9,7 : « Quant à vous, fructifiez et multipliez-vous, foisonnez sur la terre, et soyez nombreux en elle ». (La Septante lit : ayez autorité sur elle ; suivie par Dhorme). Mais ultérieurement, il n'est plus fait mention de l'histoire de Noé, sauf lorsque le texte parle des hommes comme de « Noé et ses fils ».

Par contre, les versets 8 à 17 du même chapitre sont nettement rattachés au récit du déluge. Les êtres vivants sur la terre, désignés au verset 12 par l'expression : « Les générations à jamais », reprennent les mots « Noé et ses fils avec lui » du verset 8 et les mots « avec tout animal qui est avec vous » du verset 10.

Toutefois, l'idée dominante du passage, sur laquelle je désire faire quelques observations, est la promesse qu'Elohim fera en sorte que sa *bĕrît* soit effective: il tiendra sa *bĕrît*. Il semble que le rédacteur fasse ici allusion à la promesse faite par Elohim à Noé au début du récit sur le déluge, en 6,18 : « Je tiendrai ma *berît* etc. ». On retrouve un emploi des mêmes termes : *hĕqîm 'et-bĕrîtî'et.* Comparer 6,18 et 9,9.11 et aussi 17.

Il n'est pas parlé ici d'un fait nouveau. Soit dit en passant, il en va de même, me semble-t-il, pour la circoncision, au chapitre 17, et le sabbat, en *Exode* 26,13-17 ; ce ne sont pas des institutions nouvelles.

3. W. B. KRISTENSEN, e.a. dans *The meaning of religion*, The Hague 1960. Voir General index s.v. " religious sense of nature ".

Nouvelle est l'interprétation des faits ; ils comportent maintenant une signification et une obligation imposées par Elohim. Dans les prescriptions sur le sabbat, il pourrait cependant y avoir une systématisation en ce que le repos est prescrit tous les sept jours, systématisation qui est probablement d'origine sacerdotale.

Par contre, en *Osée* 2,20, il s'agit bien d'une réalité nouvelle : « Je conclurai — littéralement couperai — pour eux une *bĕrît* en ce jour-là avec la bête sauvage, l'oiseau des cieux, le reptile du sol ; l'arc, l'épée, la guerre, je les briserai loin du pays et je les ferai dormir en sécurité » (je permettrai aux gens de dormir en sécurité, Dhorme).

Comme il fallait s'y attendre, Osée emploie en ce cas les mots *kārat bĕrît* puisqu'il annonce un nouveau type de relation, un comportement nouveau de la part de Yahvé. Semblablement — entre autres — Yahvé et Abram, *bajjôm hahu'*, *Gen.* 15,18 ; Laban et Jacob, *Gen.* 31,44 ; et en Jérémie, lorsqu'il est parlé expressis verbis d'une *bĕrît ḥadāšā*, on trouve les mots *kārat bĕrît*.

En notre péricope (*Genèse* 9,8-17) nous devrions donc renoncer à traduire ‚ établir ' ou ‚ conclure mon pacte ' et opter pour la traduction : ‚ tenir, ou maintenir ma *bĕrît* [4]. Le pronom possessif, *bĕrîti*, ma *bĕrît*, confirme la thèse du maintien d'une relation existante. La conséquence de ce maintien est exprimée clairement au verset 11 : « qu'il n'y ait plus de déluge pour détruire la terre », mots à comparer avec ce qui est dit au verset 15, un des doublets de notre péricope, « qu'il n'y ait plus d'eaux pour un déluge pour détruire toute chair ». Mais la question se pose aussi de savoir si ce passage comporte des éléments qui permettent d'en déduire la signification précise de l'expression *bĕrîti*.

Dans ce qui est nommé ‘ l'histoire de Noé ', la *bĕrît* indique une relation intime entre Elohim et Noé, *'îš ṣaddîq tāmîm*. Cependant, bien que les hommes soient regardés dans notre péricope comme la descendance de Noé, ils n'en sont point pour autant déclarés « justes et parfaits » ! Si Elohim maintient sa *bĕrît*, la raison doit donc, dans notre péricope, être ailleurs. Si je vois bien, la *bĕrît* d'Elohim avec les hommes et les animaux est ici une *bĕrît* d'Elohim avec la terre, en parallélisme avec le thème de *Genèse* 8,22 : la nature a ses lois.

On sait que divers interprètes du passage s'efforcent d'en tirer une conception morale de la divinité, à partir de la restriction alimentaire : « Vous ne mangerez point la chair avec son sang » et de la déclaration : « qui répand le sang de l'homme, son sang sera répandu ». Ainsi seraient indiquées les conditions auxquelles l'homme devrait satisfaire pour appartenir à la *bĕrît* d'Elohim. Mais il n'existe, en fait, dans notre passage, aucun mot ou allusion qui renferme une telle idée. Le signe de la *bĕrît*,

4. Voir E. König, *Die Genesis eingeleitet, übersetzt und erklärt*, Gütersloh [2.3]1925, p. 386 : " einen Bund aufrecht erhalten ".

l'arc-en-ciel, n'est nullement lié à une obligation imposée à l'homme et a fortiori aux animaux. C'est, à mon avis, un non-sens que d'établir un rapport entre l'interdiction de manger de la chair avec son sang, plus celle de tuer l'homme, et la *bĕrît* de cette péricope.

La *bĕrît* de notre péricope indique, en réalité, une relation entre Elohim et la terre, ou plus précisément, la vie sur la terre. L'effet de cette relation est une protection de la vie sur la terre : aucun cataclysme — *mabbûl* — n'anéantira plus jamais la vie sur la terre, savoir la vie animale et humaine. Mais nous ne sommes pas informés clairement sur le caractère propre de cette relation. Est mentionné seulement un phénomène naturel qui est le signe, *'ôt*, de la *bĕrît* d'Elohim avec la terre, savoir « mon arc dans la nuée ». Si nous pourrions nettement déterminer la signification de l'arc dans la nuée, nous y gagnerions une idée plus précise de ce que signifie *bĕrît* dans notre péricope.

Avant de faire quelques remarques sur l'arc-en-ciel, portons notre attention un moment sur le verbe *zākar*. Le verbe s'y trouve deux fois avec le mot *bĕrît* comme complément, à savoir aux versets 15 et 16. ' Rappeler ' me paraît fournir un sens plus juste que , se souvenir ' employé par Dhorme et de Vaux [5]. *Zākar* signifie : faire présent, effectif ; je me permets de renvoyer à mon étude *Gedenken und Gedächtnis in der Welt des Alten Testaments* [6]. L'emploi de *zākar* est une indication supplémentaire qu'il ne s'agit nullement là d'une nouvelle *bĕrît*, mais du maintien d'un rapport déjà existant [7].

Le signe de la *bĕrît* est l'arc-en-ciel. Puisque le maintien de la *bĕrît* signifie l'exclusion de tout nouveau déluge, ce à quoi il est fait nettement allusion, il s'ensuit normalement que le signe de cette *bĕrît* soit regardé comme un message de salut. Le commentaire habituel sur ce texte fait l'observation suivante que je cite d'après de Vaux, dans *La Bible de Jérusalem* : « L'alliance noachique, dont le signe est l'arc-en-ciel, s'étend à toute la création ; l'alliance avec Abraham, dont le signe sera la circoncision, n'intéresse que les descendants du patriarche, *Genèse* 17 ; sous Moïse, elle se limitera au seul Israël avec, en contre-partie, l'obéissance à la loi (*Exode* 19,5; 24,7-8) et notamment l'observation du sabbat (*Exode* 31,16-17) ».

Si nous considérons les autres signes, *'ôtôt*, ce qui en différentie « mon arc » apparaît aussitôt. L'humanité et les animaux forment, dans notre péricope, un ensemble aussi vaste que le monde ; quant au signe de cette *bĕrît*, il est complètement hors de la portée des hommes.

5. *La Sainte Bible* (« la Bible de Jérusalem »), Paris 1956.

6. Stuttgart, 1962.

7. Voir encore le texte illustratif de *Deutéronome* 8,18 : « Rappelles-toi de Yahvé ton dieu, car c'est lui qui t'a donné cette force — afin de maintenir sa *bĕrît*, jurée à tes pères, comme aujourd'hui ». Cf. *Gedenken und Gedächtnis*, p. 37.

L'Ancien Testament n'a pas de mot propre pour désigner l'arc-en-ciel. Il emploie le mot *qešet* pour désigner une arme, celle du tireur à l'arc, du chasseur. On m'a appris que l'accadien n'a pas non plus de terme propre pour désigner l'arc-en-ciel. La langue arabe possède un terme qui désigne l'arc-en-ciel, présage du temps [8]. On y connaît les proverbes suivants : ' arc-en-ciel au matin : voyage sans inquiétude ; arc-en-ciel au soir : recherche un creux bien chaud '. ' Arc-en-ciel d'Orient en Occident : sommeille en chemin ; arc-en-ciel du Midi au Nord : détache le bœuf de la charrue (il va pleuvoir) '.

En dehors de notre péricope, l'arc, *qešet*, désignant l'arc-en-ciel, se trouve au premier chapitre d'Ezechiel. La gloire de dieu se manifeste dans une apparition éblouissante : « comme la vision de l'arc qui se forme dans la nuée un jour de pluie, telle était la vision de la clarté environnante : c'était la vision de l'image de la gloire — *kābôd* — de Yahvé » (*Ez.* 1,28.) Le Siracide emploie le mot *qešet* d'une manière semblable : en 43,12 et 13, il est regardé comme une des merveilles de la création ; en 50,8 il est une image de la gloire multicolore du grand prêtre Simon.

Les mots d'Ezechiel *bĕjôm haggešem*, rendus par le Père Auvray « les jours de pluie » [9], par le professeur Zimmerli « am Regentage » [10] ne se rencontrent pas ailleurs dans l'ancien Testament. Il est évident que l'arc-en-ciel suppose un temps pluvieux. Et ceci nous fournit la raison pour laquelle il est si peu parlé de l'arc-en-ciel dans la littérature du Proche-Orient. L'arc-en-ciel est effectivement assez rare en Palestine [11]. La Palestine possède moins que nos régions les conditions nécessaires à la formation de l'arc-en-ciel. Elle se trouve, en effet, à 20 degrés de latitude plus au sud. Il y a donc une vingtaine de degrés de différence dans la hauteur du soleil par rapport à nos régions. Ainsi, les circonstances atmosphériques comme la situation géographique expliquent que l'arc-en-ciel soit relativement rare dans le Proche-Orient.

L'arc, les flèches et l'épée sont les marques distinctives de la guerre. Je cite à nouveau *Osée* 2,20 : « Et je conclurai pour eux un pacte, en ce jour-là, avec la bête sauvage, l'oiseau des cieux, le reptile au sol ; l'arc, l'épée, la guerre, je les briserai loin du pays et je les ferai dormir en sécurité ». Ce texte est à rapprocher de la prophétie de Gog en *Ezechiel* 39,3ss. : « Je briserai ton arc dans ta main gauche et je ferai tomber les

8. *qos quzaḥ*, voir G. DALMAN, *Arbeit und Sitte* I, 2, Gütersloh, 1928, p. 647, et la littérature citée à cet endroit.

9. *La Sainte Bible*, 1957.

10. W. ZIMMERLI, *Ezechiel* I, 1969, p. 30.

11. Les pluies sont relativement rares ; elles n'ont lieu qu'en début ou en fin d'année, *hā'ēt gešāmîm* (*Esr.* 10,13). Il pleut dans cette période souvent un jour entier, mais il y a aussi de fortes ondées tandis que le soleil n'apparaît qu'avant où après ces pluies.

flèches de ta main droite. Tu tomberas sur les montagnes d'Israël... ». Et au verset 9 : « Alors les habitants des villes d'Israël sortiront : ils feront un feu, ils l'alimenteront avec les armes, le petit et le grand bouclier, l'arc et les flèches, le javelot et la lance... ». Comparer le bouclier de Saül dans l'élégie de *2 Sam.* 1 ; l'épée de Goliath avec quoi le Philistin était décapité, dans le temple de Nob, *1 Sam.* 21. Les armes du vaincu sont brisées et brûlées : celles des vainqueurs honorées.

Lorsqu'Elohim met son arc dans le ciel, c'est d'un arc bandé qu'il s'agit, non de l'arc détendu et mis de côté, signe de la fin du combat. Ceux qui voient un signe de paix dans l'arc apparaissant dans la nuée, à savoir la fin du châtiment d'Elohim par le déluge, sont amenés à cette conclusion par l'interprétation théologique du déluge qui se lit dans l'introduction yahviste du récit (Genèse, 6,5-8) et leur manière de voir semble être corrobée par les mots qui, dans notre péricope, suivent le maintien par Elohim de sa *bĕrît* « pour qu'il n'y ait plus d'eaux pour un nouveau déluge pour détruire toute chair», 9,15.

Cette interprétation est fréquente depuis Wellhausen. Mais elle semble, à mon avis, perdre de vue le fait que l'arc n'est pas remisé, détendu, mais est montré au contraire comme un arc bandé. Elohim montre son arc bandé, assurément comme un signe de combat, non contre les hommes et la vie sur la terre, mais contre une puissance menaçante pour cette vie, celle des hommes et des animaux. Le combat d'Elohim signifie qu'il maintient sa *bĕrît* avec la terre, plus précisément avec la vie existant sur la terre.

Il se pourrait bien qu'il y ait un sens à une différentiation que nous pouvons constater dans le texte, tel qu'il nous est transmis. Nous lisons, en effet, au verset 8 : *wajjōmer 'ᵉlōhîm 'el-nōăḥ wĕ'el-bānāw 'ittô* et au verset 17 : *wajjōmer 'ᵉlōhîm 'el-nōăḥ* mais au verset 12 nous ne lisons plus que les mots : *wajjōmer 'ᵉlōhîm* sans que Noé soit mentionné. Il n'y a là qu'une hypothèse, je le reconnais, mais qui a l'avantage de mieux rendre compte de l'image de l'arc, si l'on admet, comme il est vraisemblable, que le passage central de cette péricope se trouve aux versets 12, 13 et 16.

Il aura existé un ancien mythe décrivant un combat entre Elohim et une puissance adverse, un combat analogue à celui de Baʿal et Môt mais non identique, qui, à l'époque des pluies, a été décidé en faveur d'Elohim. Elohim est le dieu de la vie sur la terre, celles des humains et des animaux. Lorsqu'il montre son arc, c'est le signe qu'il maintient sa *bĕrît*. Il se porte garant de la vie des hommes et des animaux qui s'est trouvée en péril. Du contexte, on peut conclure que l'ennemi d'Elohim n'est pas une puissance comme Môt, le dieu de la sécheresse, mais une puissance comme Yâm, l'inondation, le déluge, *mabbûl*. La victoire doit être remportée à nouveau chaque année.

Au temps des pluies, le croyant fait l'expérience d'une puissance qui détrempe la terre, remplit les citernes, alimente les sources : c'est le dieu qui apporte la vie. Mais il fait aussi l'expérience d'un autre aspect, une puissance qui inonde et ravage. C'est le dieu qui anéantit. Le croyant se confie dans le dieu qui maintient sa *bĕrît* avec la terre et il nourrit sa foi par le récit, le mythe, qui fait voir dans l'arc-en-ciel un signe de ce dieu. « Et Elohim dit : Je mets mon arc dans la nuée et il sera le signe de pacte entre moi et la terre. » (*Gen.*, 9,12.13).

Il me paraît en outre possible que le verset 16 ait gardé quelques mots de l'ancien mythe. Le texte lit : *wĕhajtā haqqešet be'ānān urĕ'îtîhā lizkōr bĕrît 'ôlām bēn '^{e}lōhîm ubēn ⟨kol bāśār '^{a}šer 'al⟩ hā'āreṣ*. En effet, si l'on prend Elohim, l'Elohim qui a mis son arc dans la nuée, comme sujet de la forme verbale *urĕ'îtîhā*, ainsi que le suggère le texte actuel, la phrase devient étrange : « l'arc sera dans la nuée et je (Elohim) le verrai pour me rappeler la *bĕrît* entre Elohim et tout animal vivant en toute chair, qui est sur la terre ». La Septante traduit au lieu de « entre Elohim »: *entre moi* et est suivie par plusieurs interprètes, entre autres par SPEISER, sans qu'il avertisse qu'il s'écarte ici du texte hébreu [12].

Eerdmans voyait dans ce verset une trace de polythéisme, puisque le sujet du verbe est autre que Elohim [13]. En fait, si une partie du verset 16 provient de l'ancien mythe où Elohim maintient sa *bĕrît*, mais où d'autres puissances entrent aussi en jeu, le sujet de la forme « je le verrai » pourrait être la puissance qui, à la vue de l'arc-en-ciel, reconnaît — *zākar* — le pacte entre Elohim et la terre.

De plus, l'absence de pronom possessif au terme *berît*, alors qu'Elohim parle au verset 13 de « mon arc », s'expliquerait mieux ainsi ; c'est l'autre puissance qui parle de l'arc-en-ciel. Quant aux versets 14 et 15, ils paraissent dépendre de l'ancien mythe. La difficulté du sujet pour le verbe *rā'ā* y est éliminée. On lit le passif : *wĕnir'^{a}tā*.

J'ai conscience de corroborer l'hypothèse d'un ancien mythe israélite, si je pouvais rapporter un tel mythe accadien, ou plutôt ugaritien. Dans ce cas il faudrait remarquer que « Israël » a usé le mythe sans croire à sa réalité, comme une expression poétique. De cette manière on affaiblit les textes mythologiques de la Bible, n'est-ce pas ? Il n'est pas nécessaire de dire que je n'ai pas de confiance en cette pratique car le mythe supposé dans notre péricope n'a pas de pareil dans la littérature de l'ancien Proche-Orient, à ma connaissance. Plus important, je crois, seraient des traces d'un mythe semblable à celui que je suppose, dans les textes de la Bible même.

Possiblement l'Ancien Textament nous a gardé la mémoire du mythe ou d'une idée semblable dans quelques lignes du livre de Job et dans les Psaumes. Yahvé donne l'ordre à la mer

12. E. A. SPEISER, *Genesis*, Anchor Bible, 1964.
13. B. D. EERDMANS, *Alttestamentliche Studien* I, Giessen, 1908, p. 29.

« jusqu'ici tu viendras et ne continueras point
ici se brisera l'orgueil de tes flots » (*Job.*, 38,11) [14].

L'expression *gĕ'ut hayyām* se trouve aussi dans *Deutéronome* 33,26 ; Ps. 46,4 et Ps. 89,10 [15]. Ps. 89,10 lit :

« c'est toi — Yahvé, 'elohe Seba'ot — qui domines l'orgueil de la mer ».

Si l'hypothèse qu'il reste des traces d'un ancien mythe dans la péricope *Genèse* 9,8 à 17 se situe dans une bonne voie d'interprétation, il devient alors évident que l'amalgame de cet ancien mythe avec le récit de Noé est secondaire. La question se pose alors de savoir pourquoi le rédacteur n'a-t-il pas complètement éliminé ce vieux mythe. Je n'y vois qu'une seule réponse. Manifestement, la foi suscitée par l'étrange phénomène de l'arc-en-ciel était si fortement ancrée jusque dans les milieux pour lesquels écrivait le rédacteur, qu'il n'a pas pu le passer sous silence.

Par l'introduction de ce mythe dans la présentation des récits sur Noé le pacte d'Elohim avec la terre s'identifie avec le pacte entre Elohim et Noé. Deux significations dissemblables du terme *bĕrît* sont égalisées. Ainsi s'établit un lien entre l'ancienne et la nouvelle foi, et le vieux dieu israélite est assimilé au dieu d'un cercle juif, toujours plus restreint, qui aboutit à ce qui est, suivant l'écrivain sacerdotal, le véritable « Israël », le « peuple élu du dieu unique ».

Le terme *bĕrît* n'a certainement pas eu la même signification tout au long des siècles. Dans l'ancien mythe, que je suppose intégré dans notre péricope, la notion de *bĕrît* peut être définie comme une relation entre Elohim et la terre, relation maintenue par dieu, grâce à laquelle la vie continue d'exister sur la terre et dont le croyant voit le signe dans l'arc-en-ciel [16]. L'arc-en-ciel est la manifestation multicolore du dieu

14. Traduction de Dhorme, *o.c.*

15. M. Dahood, Anchor Bible, *Psalms*, 1966, rend avec « le dos de la mer ».

16. Quoiqu'il n'aît pas été le but de cette étude à discuter les sens du terme *bĕrît*, une description puisse expliquer ici l'expression « relation entre Elohim et la terre » et l'expression usée plus haut, « relation intime entre Elohim et l'homme ». *bĕrît* signifie, je crois, la relation entre deux parties de quoi l'une est plus forte que l'autre. On peut observer que cette relation est unilatérale, un décret, une ordonnance. Le décret règle les obligations du vassal. Le décret divin établit et garantit les lois de la nature. L'ordonnance de dieu avec son peuple ou avec son serviteur signifie aussi toujours des obligations imposées par le dieu. Mais la relation peut être aussi bilatérale, avec des obligations pour les deux parties. On peut traduire cette relation avec pacte. Les pactes sont régulièrement assurés avec des actes religieux, comme des sacrifices et des serments. Les obligations et les conditions pour le pacte sont en premier lieu à remplir par la partie faible. Mais la partie plus

vainqueur qui arrête net les forces de destruction. Au contraire, dans la présentation du rédacteur sacerdotal, la *bĕrît* n'est plus qu'une garantie de la persistance de la vie humaine sur la terre, parce qu'il faut qu'existe « le peuple élu ».

P. A. H. DE BOER

See *Supplementary note*, p. 216.

forte s'oblige aussi aux certaines obligations. Dans la relation intime avec dieu le croyant a aussi le courage de compter sur des obligations à remplir par son dieu. On trouve des exemples de cette croyance audacieuse dans l'intercession, voir mon étude *De voorbede in het Oude Testament*, Leiden, 1943.

7

NOAH AND ISRAEL

THE EVERLASTING DIVINE COVENANT WITH MANKIND

Very little attention has been paid by biblical scholars, at least during the last decades, to the everlasting covenant with all mankind, which is mentioned in the bible along with the covenants with Israel, i.e. the Sinai-covenant and the covenant with the forefathers [1].

Obviously, the covenant with Noah is not considered to belong to saving history, which is thought to start with the patriarchs, i.e. with the election of Israel. World history from Adam to Babel is seen as a prelude without any special meaning in the structure of saving history. Gerhard von Rad is correct when he says that, by means of the covenant theology, the entire mass of the Hexateuchal traditions is arranged beneath a threefold arch of prophecy and fulfilment : the patriarchs, the descendants of the patriarchs and Israel. [2] But, strangely enough, the covenant with Noah is not included in that structure.

Scholars usually stress the fact that the covenant with Noah is proper to the Priestly document (*Gen.*, 9,1-17). It is not mentioned by the Yahwist (comp. *Gen.*, 8,20-22). The Priestly tradition changed the structure of the canonical saving history, according to these scholars, by anticipating twice the theme of the covenant. First, P would have applied to the covenant with the forefathers some of the very characteristics of the Sinai-covenant. Then, the idea itself of a covenant was applied to the divine promises to Noah. [3]

1. In G. von Rad, *Old Testament Theology* (Edinburgh, 1962), for example, there is no special heading, neither is there a special paragraph on the covenant with Noah. Very typical is J. Plastaras, *Creation and covenant* (Contemporary college theology series ; Biblical theology section), Milwaukee, 1968. The author moves immediately from ' Sin enters Creation (Gen., 3,1ff) ' to ' Abraham the Man of Faith '.

On the history of the Noah-exegesis in the biblical and *early* post-biblical jewish and christian materials, see Jack P. Lewis, *A Study of the Interpretation of Noah and the Flood in Jewish and Christian Literature*, Leiden, 1968.

2. G. von Rad, *op. cit.* Vol. I, pp. 129-135 : The Time-Division of the Canonical Saving History by means of the Covenant Theology.

3. G. von Rad, *loc. cit.*, p. 134-135. See W. Zimmerli, *Sinaibund und Abrahambund. Ein Beitrag zum Verständnis der Priesterschrift*, in *ThZ* 16 (1960) 266-288.

A thorough-going analysis of the Priestly covenant theology has not yet been undertaken, at least as far as we know. Moreover, scholars seem to favour the 'canonical' saving histories of the Yahwist and Elohist. The Priestly theology is taken as a 'transformation' (eine Umgestaltung), which could be taken to imply that it was unauthentic, not original. [4]

In this paper we should like to call attention to the specific structural meaning of the Noah-covenant in biblical theology. W. Eichrodt correctly represented the relationship between the covenant with Noah and the covenant with Abraham as that between two concentric circles. According to W. Eichrodt, the covenant with Abraham is established only within the dimension of the covenant with Noah, which obliges all mankind [5]. We will demonstrate that the Noah-covenant is not a preliminary stage in the history of mankind. The covenant with Noah is the background to the situational and theological context of the divine covenant with Israel. Israel's covenant is a typical example of what the bible believes is the basic relationship between God and mankind.

A further purpose of this paper is to point out that the Priestly document did not innovate by calling the guarantees given to Noah a divine covenant, i.e. by putting the covenant with mankind in the same context as the covenant God made with Israel. We are convinced that the Yahwist understood the relationship between Israel and humanity in the same sense, although, in the Flood narrative, he did not use any technical covenantal terminology. What the Priestly document did, was to emphasize over and again the basic theological insights of 'the canonical saving history' by means of a consistent theological terminology. We shall point out that the Priestly document did the same in relation to the Sinai-covenant and the covenant with the forefathers.

4. For example L. PERLITT, *Bundestheologie im Alten Testament* (WMANT 36), Neukirchen, 1969, p. 6 : " Die spätere Umgestaltung der dt Bundestheologie durch die Priesterschrift bleibt weitgehend ausserhalb der Betrachtung ". On the other hand we note the serious attempt to explain the transformation, made by W. ZIMMERLI, *art. cit.*

5. " Das Verhältnis Gottes zu den Menschen hat sich gleichsam " in zwei konzentrischen Kreisen " verwirklicht (so Procksch, Genesis [2]518), nämlich dem Noah-Bund für die ganze Menschheit und dem Abrahamsbund für Israel allein " (W. EICHRODT, *Theologie des Alten Testaments*, 5. Aufl. Göttingen 1957, p. 24. ,, Nicht nur die Israeliten, sondern auch die Heiden stehen in einer gottgegebenen Lebensordnung drin, die ihre Beziehungen zu Gott regelt : Erst innerhalb des Noahbundes, der alle Menschen verpflichtet, wird der Abrahamsbund aufgerichtet " (*Ibidem*, p. 278).

The covenant with the forefathers in the Priestly document

According to G. von Rad, whose opinion is followed by many scholars, the content of the covenant with Abraham is larger in scope in the Priestly document than in the older traditions. In the Priestly document it contains three promises, instead of the two traditional promises : the promise that he would possess the land and the promise that he would become a people. The Priestly document adds the promise " I will be your God " (*Gen.*, 17,7b.8b.19b LXX). That promise of an exceptional relationship to God is said to be a prelude to the revelation at Sinai, because it anticipates the second term of the characteristic formula proper to the Sinai-tradition : " You are to be my people — I will be your God " (*Ex.*, 6,7) [6].

We agree that the promise " I will be your God — You are to be my people " is typical of the Priestly document, as it is of the Deuteronomist and of the prophets Jeremiah, Baruch, Ezekiel and Zechariah [7]. But the formula reflects older formulas in covenant theology, which are to be found in the promises to the patriarchs. The basic structure of the formula ' I will be your God — You are to be my people ' is the same as the theological structure of the older formulas : " I am with you " or " I am the God of your fathers — so I am with you ". See *Gen.*, 26,24(J). " I am the God of... " means in this context : I bound myself to your father, I was his God, he belonged to me. So I am connected with you, fear not, you belong to me. The formula expresses that ' special relationship to God ', which is proper neither to the Sinai-covenant, nor to the Priestly presentation of the patriarchal covenant. Further examples in the patriarchal stories can be given. See *Gen.*, 28,13.15(J) [8] or in a developed form *Ex.*, 3,16(J).

6. G. von Rad, *op. cit.* Vol. I, p. 134-135. Especially G. von Rad, *Verheissenes Land und Jahwes Land im Hexateuch* (1943), in *Gesammelte Studien zum AT*, 3. Aufl. München, 1965, p. 91 : " Wenn die Priesterschrift den Verheissungsinhalten noch ein , ich will euer Gott sein ' hinzufügt (*Gen.*, 17,7b.8b.19b LXX ; *Ex.* 6,7), so liegt die Vermutung einer Rückprojection aus der Sinaitradition sehr nahe ".
Thus M. Noth, *Die Ueberlieferungsgeschichte des Pentateuch*, 3. Aufl. Stuttgart 1966, p. 260 n. 631 and p. 263. W. Zimmerli, *art. cit.*, p. 266-288.

7. *Ex.* 6,7a ; *Lev.*, 26,12 ; *Dt.*, 29,12 (probably Dtr) ; 2 *Sam.*, 7,24 ; *Jer.*, 7,23 ; 11,4 ; 13,11 ; 24,7 ; 30,22 ; 31,1.33 ; 32,28 ; *Bar.*, 2,35 ; *Ez.*, 11,20 ; 14,11 ; 36,28 ; 37,23.27 ; *Zech.*, 8,8.

8. Compare the Laban-story *Gen.*, 31,42a : " If the God of my father, the God of Abraham and the Fear of Isaac, had not been with me... ". This literal translation of *hyh ly* appears to correspond better with the structure we are dealing with, than for example the new Dutch translation (Katholieke Bijbelstichting Nederland 1966) : " Als hij mij niet had *bijgestaan* " (to assist, to help).

The Elohist also knows the structure. See *Gen.*, 31,5 ; *Gen.*, 46,3-4. Or in a more developed form : *Gen.*, 48,15. Finally *Ex.*, 3,6.9-15, which is commonly attributed to E [9]. The text shows the structure twice. First vv. 6 and 12 : " I am the God of your forefathers, the God of Abraham, the God of Isaac, the God of Jacob " (v. 6) — " I am with you " (v. 12) [10]. Then, in the much debated vv. 13 and 14 : " The God of their forefathers has sent me to them... " (v. 13) — " I am : I am (with you) " (v. 14) [11].

Thus : the divine promise given to Abraham in the Priestly document : " I will be your God — I will be God to your descendants " (*Gen.*, 17,7-8), does not change, nor does it develop the original content of the patriarchal promises as they appear in the older sources. The promise corresponds with the traditionally repeated affirmation : I am with you, because I am the God of your father. The Priestly document reaffirms the promise in strictly theological formulas, as : " I will adopt you as my people, and I will become your Lord ", or " You shall know that I, the Lord, am your God " (*Ex.*, 6,7b ; 29,46). The so called exceptional relationship to God is, from the beginning, a characteristic of covenantal theology.

We mentioned this feature of the Priestly document, in reaction to the tendency to characterize the Priestly tradition as an energetic innovation of covenantal theology succeeding the disaster of the exile. For instance, we do not agree with the opinion of many scholars, represented e.g. by W. Zimmerli, that P was in reaction to the Law-covenant at Sinai, and that for that reason he stressed the Grace-covenant with the forefathers [12]. We do not agree because this opinion presupposes the opposition between Law and Grace which is in fact not biblical in its origin [13]. Furthermore, the exegetical argument for saying that P transferred to the patriarchal covenant the most characteristic feature of the Sinai-covenant, is inappropriate, as we have demonstrated.

9. Compare A. Besters, *L'expression ' Fils d'Israël ' en Ex., I-XIV*, in *RB* 74 (1967) 326ff. : « L'attribution de 3,9-15 à E ne s'impose en aucune manière ; il s'agit plutôt d'éléments J remaniés ultérieurement par P » (p. 326-327).

10. Again in the new Dutch translation *kî-'èhyèh* *ᶜimmaka* = ik zal u bijstaan.

11. Taking into account the meaning of the verb *hyh* in the advanced structure we prefer this translation (or : I am who Is with you) to the evasive : ' I AM ; that is who I am ' proposed by others (New English Bible).

12. W. Zimmerli, *art. cit.*, p. 279 : " Der Sinaibund in seiner alten Gestalt ist P als Grundlage des Gottesverhältnisses fraglich geworden. So wird die ganze Begründung des Bundesstandes in den Abrahambund zurückverlegt, der schon nach den alten Quellen ein reiner Gnadenbund gewesen ist. "

13. Comp. E. Kutsch *Gesetz und Gnade*, in *ZAW* 79 (1967), 18-35.

Primeval history and salvation history

If the priestly rendering of the Abraham-covenant (*Gen.*, 17,7-8) is not a transposition of the themes proper to the covenant at Sinai, what then of Noah ? Did the Priestly document transfer to Noah the features of salvation history ? And if so, what is the significance of that transfer ?

In order to solve the problem, we must investigate in a general way the relationship between primeval history and salvation history, both in the Yahwist and in the Priestly traditions. This will enable us to discover the theological meaning of the Noah story in the Yahwist strand. Then we can investigate whether the meaning was changed by P.

It is a widely held opinion about primeval history that it is the history of a first period in human history, i.e. the history of mankind before the election of Israel. With the election of Israel, primeval history definitively came to an end. A new, i.e. another period in human history began, which can properly be called 'salvation history'. Primeval history was nothing but a 'prehistory', a painful prelude to the history of Israel.

With Cl. Westermann in the Introduction of his Commentary on Genesis, we should like to stress the one-sidedness of this view. [14] The mistake is simply that one did not distinguish between the two literary forms, primeval history (*Gen.*, 1-11) and salvation history (*Gen.*, 12ss.) They differ too much in form to be simply placed one after the other in a chronological arrangement.

Gen., 1-11 belong to the mythological genre. From Gen., 12 on, the genre is different, it becomes historiography, even when the narratives are mixed up with sagas. Cl. Westermann states as a principle that the attitude of the bible towards myth is positive rather than negative or apologetic. Biblical belief was able to make a synthesis between myth and the Yahwistic belief. [15] Westermann agrees with the general understanding of myth proposed by the Italian scholar Rafaele Pettazzoni. [16]

14. Cl. Westermann, Genesis (BKAT 1), Neukirchen, 1966, p. 89-97 : § 4 *Zur theologischen Bedeutung der Urgeschichte.*

15. Cl. Westermann, *op. cit.*, p. 27 : " Wir müssen heute fragen, ob diese apologetisch wertende Einstellung den biblischen Texten wirklich gemäss ist. Es ist vielmehr ernsthaft zu fragen, ob es nicht eine positive Bedeutung für unser heutiges Verstehen dieser Texte haben könnte, dass das biblische Wort in dieser besonderen Aussage nich primär anderen entgegen, sondern mit anderen zusammen steht. "

16. Cl. Westermann, *op. cit.*, p. 28ff. R. Pettazzoni, *Myths of Beginnings and Creation-Myths*, in idem, *Essays on the History of Religions*, Leiden, 1954, p. 24-36.

According to Pettazzoni "the proper worth of myth consists in the necessary and sufficient justification which it gives to whatever is most essential to human life and to society, by relating it to a primordial act of foundation recorded by the myth " [17]. Further : " The existence of mankind depends in some sort on the myth which tells of the appearance of the first man on earth, for the recital of that myth has the power to establish and ensure the continuity of human life. The recital of the myth of the origin of the world makes real and guarantees the stability and duration of the universe ". [18] Myth has a positive value in human life, even in religion. To consider myth as a lie, as the counterpart of true history is simplistic ; it contradicts both the results of biblical exegesis and the recent discoveries of mythology [19].

The form-critical definition of Gunkel, " Myths are stories about Gods. They are to be distinguished from sagas where the active persons are human " [20] appears to be too narrow. We would prefer the broader definition of myth which is current now among Old Testament scholars, represented, for instance, by James Barr : " Myth is a totality first of all because mythological thinking is striving for a total world view, for an interpretation or meaning of all that is significant. Mythology is not a peripheral manifestation, not a luxury, but a serious attempt at integration of reality and experience, considerably more serious than what we loosely call today one's " philosophy of life ". Its goal is a totality of what is significant to man's needs, material, intellectual and

17. R. PETTAZZONI, *op. cit.*, p. 26.

18. R. PETTAZZONI, *ibidem.*

19. G. VAN DER LEEUW, *Die Bedeutung der Mythen*, in *Festschrift Alfr. Bertholet zum 80. Geburtstag*, Tübingen, 1950, p. 287-293. J. HEMPEL, *Glaube, Mythos und Geschichte im Alten Testament*, in *ZAW* 64 (1953) 110ff. B. S. CHILDS, *Myth and Reality in the Old Testament* London, 1960. J. BARR, *The Meaning of ' Mythology ' in Relation to the O.T.*, in *VT* 9 (1959) 1-10. J. SLØK, *Mythos und Mythologie. I : Mythos begrifflich und religionspsychologisch*, in *RGG*, 3. Aufl., B.IV, Tübingen, 1960, 1263-1268. P. BARTHEL, *Interprétation du langage mythique et théologie biblique. Étude de quelques étapes de l'évolution du problème de l'interprétation des représentations d'origine et de structure mythiques de la foi chrétienne*, Leiden, 1963. I. GOLDZIHER, *Mythology among the Hebrews and its historical development*, 1967. A. OHLER, *Mythologische Elemente im AT. Eine motivgeschichtliche Untersuchung*, Düsseldorf, 1969. Th. H. GASTER, *Myth, legend and custom in the O.T.*, New York, 1969. J. F. PRIEST, *Myth and Dream in Hebrew Scripture*, in J. CAMPBELL (ed.), *Myths, Dreams and Religion*, New York 1970, 48-67. W. PANNENBERG, *Christentum und Mythos. Späthorizonte des Mythos in biblischer und christlicher Ueberlieferung*, Gütersloh, 1972. E. LEACH, *Lévi-Strauss in the Garden of Eden. An Examination of some recent developments in the analysis of myth*, in E. NELSON-T. HAYES (eds.), *Claude Lévi-Strauss : the Anthropologist as Hero*, Cambridge-London, 1970, 47-60. J. SCHREINER, *Mythos und Altes Testament*, in *Bibel und Leben* 12 (1971), 141-153. W. PANNENBERG, *Christentum und Mythos*, Tübingen, 1972.

20. H. GUNKEL, *Genesis*, Göttingen, 1917, XIV.

religious. It has then its aspects which correspond to science, to logic and to faith, and it would be wrong to see myth as a distorted substitute for any of these " [21].

If there is any need for a short definition, which is more ' functional ' than form-critical, we would propose the following : " Myth is a story or a narrative-cycle which grounds and gives meaning to the totality of man's existence by relating it in a fundamental way with the totality of the universe, i.e. by relating it to the perfection of the primeval times or with the fullness of the end of times ". Myths always talk about the fundamental origins, and (or) the completed end. We might refer to the well known correspondence of " Urzeit und Endzeit " [22]. It's not by accident that myths are to be found in the Bible, especially in the primeval history *Gen.*, 1-11 and in the apocalyptic literature.

A historical fact is, as the Germans say, ' einmalig '. It happens but once, even when the consequences are far reaching, or even when " history repeats itself ". ' Facts ' related in a myth are never ' einmalig '.

21. J. BARR, *op. cit.*, p. 3.

22. " Die Apokalyptik ist in die Zukunft profiziertes Urgeschehen, wie das Gunkel in ' Schöpfung und Chaos in Urzeit und Endzeit ' ausgeführt hat. Das bedeutet aber-und das ist bisher noch nicht genügend beachtet worden- : die Apokalyptik ist ihrem Kern und ihrer ursprünglichen Intention nach nicht der ' Heilsgeschichte ', sondern der Urgeschichte, insbesondere der Schöpfungs- und Flutgeschichte zugeordnet " (Cl. WESTERMANN, *op. cit.*, p. 70). The correspondence of " Urzeit und Endzeit " may be explained by the idea that the course of time is not a constant progression but a cyclical (the periodicity of the course of wordly events). Thus f. ex. R. BULTMANN, *History and Eschatology*, Edinburgh, 1957, p. 23-24. See however W. PANNENBERG, *op. cit.*, p. 57-58 : " Bei genauerem Zusehen zeigt sich jedoch dass in den eschatologischen Texten der jüdischen und urchristlichen Literatur zwar eine *Entsprechung* der Endzeit zur Urzeit zum Ausdruck kommt, also nicht einfach ein ' lineares ' Verständnis des geschichtlichen Fortgangs, aber auch *keine Gleichheit*, keine Rückkehr zum Anfang. Vielmehr handelt es sich um diejenige Entsprechung, die seit langem unter dem Stichwort Typologie diskutiert wird. " About the definition of myth see W. PANNENBERG, *op. cit.*, p. 13-19 : " In der philosophischen und theologischen Diskussion über Mythos und Entmythologisierung findet der religionswissenschaftliche Begriff des Mythos gemeinhin nicht die ihm gebührende Beachtung. Man arbeitet weiter mit Begriffen von Mythos als Symbol, als poetischer Schöpfung oder als primitiver Naturerklärung, die aus früheren, durch die moderne Religionswissenschaft überholten Epochen der Mythenforschung stammen. Dadurch entsteht nicht nur terminologische Verwirrung. " The fact must be stressed that R. BULTMANN handles an old philosophical definition of myth, which goes back to Chr. G. HEYNE : " Bultmann fasste den Mythos als eine , Vorstellungsweise ' auf, die ihren Ausdruck besonders in einem ' mythischen Weltbild ' gefunden habe, das für den heutigen, durch wissenschaftliches Denken geprägten Menschen ' vergangen ' sei... " (p. 13). " Bultmann hat also den von Heyne stammenden Begriff des Mythischen aufgegriffen als Gegenbegriff zu seinem eigenen Verständnis der Wirklichkeit Gottes. " (p. 16).

Mythological facts represent the most fundamental and almost permanent experiences of humanity, in the form of a primordial or eschatological event.

The Myth is not directed towards an intellectual need, which might be satisfied by the discovery of a primary cause.

' Primordial acts ' satisfy a vital need, ' *eine Lebensbedürfnis* ', looking for an ideological foundation capable of grounding the existence of man and of the universe [23].

Israel shares the basic sense of the myth with the Ancient Near East. But there is more. The genre of myth was integrated by Israel into its own life. It was adapted to the genre of historiography which is more common in the bible. Properly speaking, the genre of the myth is non-historical. Or better : if we are to speak about time in mythology, it is *sui generis* [24]. In the bible, however, the myth functions only between the framework of history [25]. Israel is related to the primordial events, not only by the ritual celebration of myths, but also, and more specifically, by a historical development. The primordial events of the traditional myths became in the bible a primeval history : ' vom Urgeschehen zur Urgeschichte '. [26]

In the bible, the intimate relation between primeval history and salvation history is most clear at the transition from ch. 11 to ch. 12 in Genesis. Chapter 12, the beginning of the Abraham-saga, belongs mainly to the J stratum [27]. We agree with G. von Rad that the section 12,1-9 is a transitional paragraph, proper to the collector of the older patriarchal traditions. That collector is the Yahwist himself [28]. From the structural analysis of the section, esp. vv. 1-4a, proposed by H.W. Wolff [29], one concludes that, according to the Yahwist, both the promise

23. Comp. R. PETTAZZONI, *op. cit.*, p. 28-29.

24. " Der Mythos transzendiert die Grenzen der Geschichte ; die Geschehnisse, von denen er berichtet, liegen jenseits der realen Zeit, in der die Geschichte eines Volkes sich entfaltet hat. Der Mythos hat seine eigene Zeit, die mythische Vorzeit oder Endzeit " (J. SLØK, *art. cit.*, 1263).

25. " It will probably be agreed that the importance of history in the Israelite mind was the greatest factor in enforcing the differences from the mythological environment. It is thus perhaps possible to say that the central position in Israelite thought is occupied by history rather than myth, and that such survivals of myth as exist are controlled by the historical sense " (J. BARR, *art. cit.*, p. 8).

26. " In der biblischen Urgeschichte ist das Urgeschehen zu einer Geschichte geworden " (Cl. WESTERMANN, *op. cit.*, p. 89).

27. 12,4b-5 = P.

28. G. VON RAD, *Genesis. A commentary* (The Old Testament Library), London, 1966, p. 160.

29. H. W. WOLFF, *Das Kerygma des Jahwisten*, in *Ev. Th.* 24 (1964) 73-98. English translation : *The Kerygma of the Yahwist*, in *Interpretation* 20 (1966)

of the land and the promise to become a great nation are subsumed into the final and solemn promise : " all the families of the earth shall be blessed in you " (v. 3c) [30]. In particular this last promise appears to be a response to the preceeding primeval history, and shows how salvation history and primeval history belong together.

The promise to become a great nation comes after the note of the Yahwist at the end of ch. 11 : " Sarai was barren ; she had no child ". This is the context of the promise. The promise of the land also has its situational context in ch. 11 : the wandering nomadic tribe Terach (11,28-30). It is thus quite normal to also seek the situational context of the blessing of Abraham and all the families on earth in ch. 11 in the story of the tower of Babel and the confusion of language. The election and blessing of Abraham is the only answer to the scattering of mankind abroad over the face of the earth ' after ' its revolt while building the tower of Babel. The word ' curse ' is missing in ch. 11, we agree. So the blessing is not a direct response to a curse. But the curse is expressed in other words. The wandering of Abraham's forefather Terach is the result of the ' preceding ' scattering of mankind. And the blessing of Abraham, which is a new starting point for the blessing of mankind, consists specifically in the gift of a fixed home. Also the promise ' I will make your name great ' (12,2b), understood as a divine initiative, appears to be in answer to the proud attempts of humanity at Babel :

131-158. The structure is as follows (with a few corrections in regard to H. W. Wolff) :

v. 1a Go from your land... (imperative)

* consecutive clauses in the imperfect-cohortative form (= promises)
  — to the land which I will show you (1b)
  — I will make you a great people (2a)
  — I will bless you and make your name great (2b)

Be a blessing (2c = imperative !)

  — I will bless those who bless you (3a) but whoever despises you, him will I curse (3b)

* consecutive clause with the consecutive perfect (= conclusion) :
  — So, then, all the families of the earth can gain a blessing in you (3c).

v. 4a And so Abram set out... (the order is carried out).

30. The translation of the verse advocated by other scholars : " All the families on earth will pray to be blessed as you are blessed " does not weaken our thesis. From the structural point of view the verse remains a conclusion, which is a response to the curse laid upon humanity ' after ' the building of the tower. We put ' after ' between quotation marks, because there is much more than a simple chronological succession between the tower of Babel and the election of Abraham.

" let us make a name for ourselves, lest we be scattered abroad upon the face of the whole earth " (11,4) [31].

Making the bridge between *Gen.*, 12 and 11, the entire structural relationship between primeval history and salvation history becomes clear, for the moment at least, at the level of the J-stratum. There is, indeed, no decisive difference between the function of the story of the tower and the function of the Flood-narrative in primeval history. The narratives of the biblical primeval history must be considered as parallel myths. The stories of Paradise and of the Fall, the story of Cain and Abel, the Flood, and the story of the Tower of Babel, cannot be considered as the succeeding stages of an historical development; although they are, especially in the P-level, combined by means of the genealogies and a strict chronology. What we are saying about the relationship between the election of Abraham and the story of the tower, can thus be repeated, in general, for the relationship between salvation history and primeval history, and, in particular, for the relationship between the election of Israel and the Flood-narrative.

According to Rolf Rendtorff the end of the Yahwistic primeval history is to be found in *Gen.*, 8,21, after the Flood-narrative. There, the curse, which lays upon mankind and which is the characteristic of primeval history in the J-stratum, is removed: " I will never again curse the ground because of man " [32]. In a second paper on the same topic, R. Rendtorff nuanced his thesis by admitting that *Gen.*, 12,1-4a is in the line of 8,21. [33] After the Flood, Yahwe removed his curse from the earth, but the real history of blessing begins with the election of Abraham, i.e. with the beginning of salvation history [34].

Rendtorff has clearly seen that the divine guarantees given to Noah (*Gen.*, 8,21), correspond with the election of Abraham and with the blessing of mankind in *Gen.*, 12,1-4a. We do not agree, however, with the general characterization of the Yahwistic primeval history as a

31. The three promises, summarized in the transitional paragraph 12,1-4a: the land, the posterity and to be a blessing for humanity, are extended by the Yahwist in the three following narratives: *Gen.*, 15 (= the land); 18,1-15 (the posterity) 18,16-19,29 (Abraham a mediator of blessing for the people of Sodom).

32. R. Rendtorff, *Genesis* 8,21 *und die Urgeschichte des Jahwisten*, in *Kerygma und Dogma* 7 (1961), 69-78.

33. R. Rendtorff, *Hermeneutische Probleme der biblischen Urgeschichte*, in *Festschrift für Fr. Smend zum* 70. *Geburtstag*, Berlin 1963, 19-29. Comp. O. H. Steck, *Genesis* 12,1-3 *und die Urgeschichte des Jahwisten*, in H. W. Wolff (ed.), *Probleme biblischer Theologie. G. von Rad zum* 70. *Geburtstag*, München 1971, 525-554.

34. " Hier beginnt nun erst wirklich die Geschichte des Segens: in der Erwählung Abrahams als Anfang der ' Heilsgeschichte ' Gottes mit Israel " (R. Rendtorff, *Hermeneutische Probleme...*, p. 21).

history of curse, opposed to salvation history as a history of blessing [35]. Primeval history is characterized by a constant variation, or better, by a permanent tension between sin and grace. After the Fall, there is the short, but structurally very important promise : " I will put enmity between you and the woman " (3,15). Later, the murderer Cain obtains a special divine mark on his head, so that anyone meeting him should not kill him (4,15). And after the Flood there is the divine promise : " no more... " (8,21-22). Also after the story of the tower there must be a positive answer. It is required by the internal dynamics of the whole primeval history : it is the final response of salvation history.

G. von Rad advocates the idea that the election of Abraham *Gen.*, 12,1-4a is the key to the understanding of primeval history. It is only in this way that the theological significance of that universal ' preface ' to saving history becomes understandable [36]. The idea is correct for two reasons. First : Without the election of Abraham the existential questions put forth by the biblical myths of primeval history remain unanswered. They end with an unacceptable disaster : the scattering of mankind all over the face of the earth. Furthermore : in Israel's history, the primeval myths of humanity become concrete, since they are interpreted in the saving history of a specific people. Conversely, we can say that primeval history is the key to the understanding of Israel's salvation. The answer to the question : ' why was Abraham, the father of Israel, elected ? ' is to be found only in the history of mankind, as it is described in the primeval history : Abraham was called to become a blessing for all the peoples on earth. As long as the primeval and universal dimension of *Gen.*, 1-11 is not taken into account, Israel's salvation history will seem outrageous.

Noah and Israel —
God's everlasting covenant with mankind

Taking into account the structural relationship between primeval history and salvation history as we have described it, what are the relationships between the divine covenant with Israel and the covenant with Noah ?

35. " Für den Jahwisten ist also die Urgeschichte die Geschichte des Unheils und des Fluches. Sie endet mit der Katastrophe der Sintflut und ist damit endgültig abgeschlossen. Die Geschichte Gottes mit der Welt beginnt noch einmal ganz neu, und sie steht nun unter dem entgegengesetzten Vorzeichen des Segens " (R. Rendtoff, *ibidem*, p. 22).

36. G. von Rad, *Genesis*, p. 150.

The Yahwist does not use the term 'covenant' (*b*ᵉ*rît*) in referring to the divine guarantees given to Noah. One can ask however if he did not see any theological and structural relation between the guarantees given to all mankind in Noah and the covenantal promises made to the patriarchs and Israel ?

We noted the structural parallelism between *Gen.*, 8,21-22 and 12,1-4a in the J stratum : the removal of the curse, which was guaranteed to Noah, has a concrete form in the blessings given to all mankind by the election of Abraham. We know that in dogmatics, the guarantees given to Noah and the promises of the Israelite covenant are often opposed to one another as nature and grace, i.e. the order of creation on the one hand, the history of salvation on the other. The biblical stories of primeval history, however, have to do with grace. There is no separation of nature and grace in the bible. Creation is not simply the causative act of the very beginning of existence. Creation is also the protection of human existence against the continual threat to life constituted by evil, that means : creation is salvation. And if the Flood is considered by the bible to be a punishment for sin, the rescue of humanity from the Flood must be an act of salvation, must be grace. There can thus be a theological correspondence between the guarantees given to Noah and the covenantal promises for Israel.

The preservation of humanity, that is : the everlasting bond between mankind and the earth as the dwelling-place of men, is guaranteed by God by a solemn word of self-affirmation : " When Yahweh smelt the soothing odour, he said within himself : Never again will I curse the ground because of man... " (*Gen.*, 8,21). Did the Yahwist make any connection with the solemn engagements of Yahweh in favour of the patriarchs and Israel ? We think so. The sacrifice offered by Noah corresponds in the J-stratum with the sacrifices and ritual acts of the patriarchs each time after the solemn divine promises of land and posterity. We do not claim that the sacrifice of Noah is a 'covenantal sacrifice' in the style of *Ex.*, 24,5-6. The only thing we wish to stress is the structural correspondence within the J-stratum, with the ritual acts of Abraham building an altar to Yahweh at Shechem after the solemn promise 'I give this land to your descendants' (*Gen.*, 12,7) ; Abraham building an altar near the terebinths of Mamre, after the repetition of the same promise at Hebron (*Gen.*, 13,14-18). Furthermore, the correspondence with Isaac, building an altar at Beersheba after the confirmation of the promises, given to his father Abraham (*Gen.*, 26,23-25). Finally, the ritual act of Jacob, erecting a sacred pillar in Bethel after the Lord said : " I am the Lord, the God of your father Abraham and the God of Isaac. This land on which you are lying I will give to you and your descendants" (*Gen.*, 28,13-16.18) [37]. In each case, beginning with Noah and continuing in the history of Israel, the divine promise refers to the bond, the existential link between the man and his dwelling-place, the earth. The divine promises given to the patriarchs — especially the promise of the land — are a concrete and specific form of the everlasting guarantees given to all mankind. The 'covenantal' promises given to the forefathers of Israel are relevant, theologically speaking, only in the context of the preservation-solemny confirmed by God-of human life on earth.

The further question we have to answer is : did the Priestly tradition change the biblical belief which we have just described, when the divine guarantees given to all mankind are called a covenant ?

In the J-stratum, the link between primeval history and salvation history was made by the transitional paragraph *Gen.*, 12,1-4a. The P-stratum does not have any similar theological reflection on the relationship between the two histories. But the link is made, precisely by the redactional processes of the genealogies and the biblical chronology : *Gen.*, 17,1 is connected with the P-verses in ch. 11 : vv. 10-27 and 31-32 (the genealogy of Sem). The Priestly document confirmed and stressed the traditional relation between primeval history and saving history, by the use of a consistent terminology. Two typical themes, which were used by the tradition in the histories of the patriarchs and Israel, are applied now to primeval history, as a final confirmation of the traditional link between the history of Israel and the history of mankind. In the J-stratum the idea of blessing, although intimately related with primeval history, was restricted to the promises given to the patriarchs (*Gen.*, 12,2-3 ; 24,1). P extends the terminology and uses the word 'blessing' in the creation-narrative and in the Flood story (*Gen.*, 1,22.28 ; 2,3 ; 5,2 ; 9,1) [38].

The same is true for *b^{e}rît*. Very probably, the word was used for the covenants with the forefathers and with Israel by the tradition before P. P applies the term to the divine guarantees given to Noah : *Gen.*, 6,18 ; 9,9.12.

37. Taking into account the structural correspondence with the previously mentioned texts, verse 18 (and vv. 10-11) must be Yahwistic. According to O. EISSFELDT's *Hexateuch-Synopse* they are E.

38. In the patriarchal stories of P : *Gen.*, 17,16-20. According to R. RENDTORFF, P in so doing changed the structure of salvation history : "Für den Jahwisten begann die eigentliche 'Heilsgeschichte', auf die sich sein ganzes theologisches Interesse richtete, mit der Erwählung Abrahams, und das heisst mit dem Anfang der Geschichte Israels... In der Priesterschrift hingegen beginnt die theologisch gewichtige Geschichte nach der Flut mit Noah... Es ist deutlich, dass die Priesterschrift den Rahmen des göttlichen Geschichtshandelns wesentlich weiter gezogen hat als der Jahwist" (*art. cit.*, p. 24).

In a paper addressed to the present Biblical Conference at Louvain 1972 [39], E. Kutsch noted, in this respect, a very interesting evolution in terminology. J refers to the guarantees given to Noah as a divine word : " and the Lord *said* within himself " (*Gen.*, 8,21). According to *Isaiah*, 54,9 God *swore* the same guarantees : " These days recall for me the days of Noah : as I swore that the waters of Noah's flood should never again pour over the earth ". This is the terminology of the Elohist and the Deuteronomist [40]. The Priestly tradition uses the word *b^erît*.

The evolution in terminology which we indicated appears to favour the translation of *b^erît* proposed by Prof. Kutsch. The original meaning of *b^erît* is not properly a relation or a covenant between two parties, rather it is the decision or the pledge (*die Verpflichtung*) of one party in favour of the other [41]. If we accept both the evolution of the terminology as proposed by E. Kutsch and his translation of the term *b^erît*, the parallelism we argue between the Priestly and the Yahwist account of the solemn guarantees which were given to Noah are most clear. Moreover, the correspondence of the Noah-covenant and the Israelite-covenant becomes fully acceptable. The covenant with Noah is the theological and situational context of the covenant God made with Israel and her forefathers. Israel was able to read the history of mankind in her own salvation history.

A final remark concerns an observation made by Prof. P. de Boer at this same Biblical Conference in Louvain [42]. It deals with the relation between creation and the covenant with Noah. P. de Boer proposed the following translation of *Gen.*, 6,18 (*wah^aqimotî 'èt b^erîtî 'itak*) and 9,9 (*wa'^anî hin^enî meqîm 'èt-b^erîtî 'itkèm*) : " I will *maintain my covenant* with you ". He refuted the current translation : " With you I will *make a covenant* " — We agree with the proposal, although we would prefer, for the moment, the terms ' pledge ' or ' commitment ' to ' covenant '. The undertaking to which the word *b^erîtî* (with possessive pronoun !) in *Gen.*, 6,18 and 9,9 refers is the divine guarantee which is embodied in

39. *Gottes Zuspruch und Anspruch. B^erît in der alttestamentlichen Theologie* (see pp. 71-90). Vgl. E. Kutsch, *Gesetz und Gnade* (n. 13); Idem, *Von B^erît zum 'Bund'*, in *KuD* 14 (1968), 159-182.

40. *Gen.*, 22,16 ; 24,7 ; 26,3b ; 50,24. *Dt.*, 6,18.23 ; 8,1.18 ; 9,5 ; 10,11 ; 11,8-9. 18-21 ; 26,3.15 ; 29,12 ; 28,11 ; 31,7.20.

41. In Dutch we could say : een *verbintenis* aangaan tegenover iemand ; men heeft zich tegenover iemand *verbonden*. " *B^erît* meint-mindestens von Hause aus-die (gesprochene) Zusage, Verpflichtung und nicht ein ' Verhältnis ' zwischen zwei Partnerns. Wo *b^erît* in dieser Weise verstanden ist als göttliche Zusage, als Verheissung, Selbstverpflichtung, tritt Gott dem Menschen entgegen mit seinem heilvollen, hilfreichen Handeln, mit seine Treue ; *b^erît* ist hier Ausdruck seiner *Gnade* " (E. Kutsch, *Gesetz und Gnade*, 28-29).

42. *Quelques remarques sur l'arc dans la nuée* (Genèse 9,8-17) (see pp. 105-114).

creation (*der Schöpfungsbund*). Not only the so called covenant with Noah, but the entire concept of creation (the preservation of life by God) must be taken into account as the only theological context of the covenant (i.e. the commitment) God made in favour of Israel.

L. Dequeker

See *Supplementary note*, p. 217.

8

COMMENT AU SEPTIÈME SIÈCLE ENVISAGEAIT-ON L'AVENIR DE L'ALLIANCE?

ÉTUDE DE LV. 26,3-45[1]

I. Analyse au niveau de l'expression verbale

Il faut noter tout d'abord que le texte se présente comme un discours adressé par YHWH aux Israélites à qui Il dit « vous ». Ce système *je/vous* existe jusqu'au v. 36 où apparaît le système *je/ils* (36aβ-37a et 39aβ-45) alternant avec le précédent.

Il n'est pas possible d'étudier ici tous les procédés de composition tels que parallélismes poétiques et allitérations, nombreux dans ce morceau. Mais il faut signaler au moins la manière dont l'auteur bâtit des chaines de parfaits invertis terminées par un imparfait. Le procédé est bien visible en 5-6.7-10.12 et plus encore en 3-4.28-29.32-33.42 où on a successivement le même verbe au parfait inverti puis à l'imparfait. On peut penser que ces imparfaits indiquent des fins de paragraphes ou de sections.

Ce qui nous retiendra surtout ici, ce sont les mots ou groupes de mots qui indiquent la structuration du texte. On remarque immédiatement en 3 et 15 deux conditionnelles qui ont en commun un certain nombre de mots : *'im beḥuqotay... ʿaśah miṣwotay* ; mais elles s'opposent par les verbes qui commandent ces expressions. On peut noter aussi en 11 et 30 une même expression : *w^{e}gaʿalah* (ou : *tig^{e}ʿal naf^{e}ši 'et^{e}kem* (la racine *gʿl* revient encore en 15.43 et 44 dans des expressions assez différentes). Cette expression semble être un signal annonçant une fin de section. On peut déjà reconnaître dans le texte deux sections : la première commence en 3 et se termine après 11, certainement au v. 13 ; la seconde commence en 15 et se termine après le v. 30 ; on pourrait voir la fin de cette section au v. 33 où se termine une chaîne de parfaits invertis.

1. La base de cette étude est l'ouvrage de R. KILIAN, *Literarkritische und formgeschichtliche Untersuchung des Heiligkeitsgesetzes*, Bonn, 1963, spécialement les pp. 148-163. Mais la démarche suivie ici est différente.

34 et 35 où manquent les verbes à la première personne, seraient à considérer comme une parenthèse, un développement accessoire [2].

Et c'est au v. 36, avec le passage de *vous* à *ils*, qu'on peut faire commencer la troisième section. Si les vv. 36-45 semblent à première vue former un bloc assez incohérent, plein de répétitions, une étude plus attentive montre qu'en réalité on a affaire à une section bien charpentée par une série de parallélismes successifs ou emboités :

(36) *w^{e}hanniš^{e}arim bakem...*
ḥereb ... w^{e}'en rodef
(37) *ḥereb w^{e}rodef 'ain*
(39) *w^{e}hanniš^{e}'arim bakem*
(39) *yimmaqu ba'aonam... w^{e}'af ba'^{a}onot avotam yimmaqu*
(40) *w^{e}hit^{e}wadu ' et- 'aonam* *w^{e}'at-'^{a}on avotam*
(41) *'az yir^{e}ṣu 'et-'^{a}onam*
(42) *w^{e}zakarti 'et-b^{e}riti ...*
(43) *w^{e}hem yir^{e}ṣu 'et- '^{a}onam... ga'alah naf^{e}šam*
(44) *lo' ga'al^{e}tim*
(45) *w^{e}zakarti lahem b^{e}rit...*

Les trois sections étant ainsi délimitées, on peut encore chercher si elles sont liées entre elles. La fin de la troisième renvoie aux vv. 12.13 et 15 qui forment la charnière entre la première et la deuxième (43b et 44 renvoient à 15 et 45 à 12.13) ; mais aucun lien n'est marqué entre la deuxième et la troisième. Au contraire, la première et la deuxième sont construites parallèlement comme on l'a déjà noté (3|| 15 — 11 || 30 plus beaucoup de termes communs aux deux sections). La liaison entre ces deux sections est marquée par d'autres parallélismes entre la fin de la première et le début de la seconde : *tig^{e}'al nefeš* en 11 et 15 — *b^{e}riti* en 9 et 15.

Il faut mentionner enfin la structure la plus apparente de ce texte : une série de conditionnelles commençant par *'im lo tišm^{e}'u* ou par *'im tel^{e}ku qeri*. Ce système comprend les vv. 14.18.21.23-24.27-28 ; on doit encore y rattacher les vv. 40b.44a qui ont la forme d'une relative, mais qui contiennent les mêmes expressions caractéristiques. Il s'agit d'un système cohérent comprenant à chaque fois une protase et une apodose, sauf en 14 où il n'y a que la protase et en 40b. Entre les cinq protases et la relative de 40b se répartissent quatre *lo tišm^{e}'u* et quatre *tel^{e}ku qeri* (les deux derniers ont *b^{e}qeri*). Les quatre apodoses forment un système encore plus construit :

18. *yasaf^{e}ti l^{e}yass^{e}rah* *šeba 'al ḥaṭṭotēkem*
21. *yasaf^{e}ti... makkah* *šeba k^{e}ḥaṭṭotēkem*

2. Cf. KILIAN, *op. cit.*, p. 156.

24.	*w^ehalak^eti... b^eqeri... w^ehikketi...*	*šeba ʿal ḥaṭṭotēkem*
28.	*w^ehalak^eti baḥamat-qeri w^eyissar^eti*	*šeba ʿal ḥaṭṭotēkem*

Cette structure n'explique pas l'ensemble du morceau puisqu'elle n'en recouvre qu'une partie. Elle se superpose à la structure mise en évidence plus haut. Ce n'est pas une sous-structure qui charpenterait la deuxième partie, mais une structure sur-imposée à la deuxième et à la troisième. On remarque en effet que la protase du v. 14 fait double emploi avec celle du v. 15 ; de même 40b.41a s'intègre mal à son contexte, comme peuvent en témoigner tous les traducteurs à qui ces versets donnent bien du fil à retordre.

II. Analyse au niveau des significations

Au niveau des idées exprimées, on peut mener l'analyse suivant différents thèmes. On n'en utilisera ici que trois, qui s'imposent dès l'abord.

A. Thème des sanctions

De ce point de vue le texte se divise évidemment en deux parties qui s'opposent : récompenses promises au peuple s'il accepte les volontés du Seigneur (3-13), punitions dont on le menace en cas de refus. Cette deuxième section se prolonge jusqu'au v. 39 et peut-être même jusqu'en 41a si l'on pense que les verbes se rapportent au futur.

Il est possible de comparer les deux listes de sanctions :

récompenses : — pluies assurant de bonnes récoltes, élimination des bêtes dangereuses et des ennemis, multiplication du peuple, réalisation de l'alliance, habitation de Dieu —.

punitions : maladies, mauvaises récoltes, défaite — sécheresse, envoi de bêtes dangereuses qui font diminuer la population, invasion, blocus des villes fortes, destruction des sanctuaires — dévastation du pays, déportation, insécurité et mort en exil.

Les deux séries entre tirets se correspondent à peu près, sauf que la réalisation de l'alliance n'a pas de contrepartie dans les punitions. On remarque aussi que la liste de punitions est plus longue, mais on sait que c'est un procédé habituel dans des textes de ce genre. Il est plus important de remarquer que les récompenses sont exposées sans autre motivation que la conditionnelle du v. 3, alors que la liste de punitions est surchargée de motivations (spécialement par la série de conditionnelles étudiée à la page précédente). Il y a donc une nette dissymétrie entre les deux listes (également au niveau lexical), beaucoup plus visible que la symétrie fondamentale qu'on peut tout de même observer entre elles et que fait attendre la similitude des formules d'introduction (3 et 15).

Si on réduit le texte à ses idées essentielles (par rapport au thème des sanctions), on voit que la révélation à Israël des volontés de YHWH ouvre une alternative : le peuple peut accepter ou refuser. Son choix déclenche un des termes d'une autre alternative posée en même temps : sécurité, vie, réussite ou bien : agressions, mort, échec. Le lien entre les deux alternatives est un mécanisme de sanctions : entre obéissance et bonheur, il n'y a qu'un lien externe : l'attitude du peuple invite YHWH à agir dans un sens ou dans l'autre ; mais la récompense n'est pas une conséquence nécessaire et inévitable de l'obéissance.

Si le peuple choisit la deuxième possibilité et subit les châtiments prévus, on voit alors apparaître une autre dimension du problème. Comme le soulignent les vv. 42-45, au moment où le peuple est sur le point de disparaître, on voit qu'une réalité subsiste : l'alliance. Elle existait précédemment puisque YHWH peut se la rappeler ; elle n'a pas été touchée par le refus du peuple. Elle se réalisait dans les récompenses (v. 9) mais elle se distingue d'elles ; c'est ce que met en lumière le refus et la punition, puisqu'à ce moment elle subsiste seule.

La structure fondamentale du texte semble donc être l'opposition entre l'alliance, réalité durable et non-conditionnée, et le complexe commandements et sanctions, qui dépend entièrement des choix du peuple. Si au départ les deux réalités semblent coïncider, la disparition de la deuxième rend évidente la différence.

B. Thème du péché

Il est beaucoup question de péché dans tout ce texte à partir du v. 14. Il s'agit essentiellement d'un refus d'obéissance aux ordres du Seigneur, en soulignant l'aspect d'opposition personnelle qu'implique ce refus ; c'est surtout marqué dans la série 14.18.21 etc. La punition est également présentée comme une réaction personnelle et délibérée de YHWH qui retourne à Israël son attitude d'opposition, qui venge son alliance (25).

Ces vérités élémentaires de théologie biblique semblent avoir été peu évidentes pour les destinataires du texte, puisque l'auteur prend le soin de les inculquer avec une insistance presque lassante. Il le fait d'abord par la série de conditionnelles (18.21.23 etc.) qui décrivent une sorte d'escalade dans le refus et la punition ; ensuite par diverses expressions comme : « l'épée qui venge l'alliance » (25), « ils dépériront à cause de leur faute » (39) et spécialement la formule de parité de 15.16 : « si vous rejetez mes lois... au point de ne pas *faire* mes volontés... voici ce que moi, je *ferai* ».

Les vv. 40-42 montrent quel était le but de la longue suite de punitions décrite à partir du v. 16 : c'est la prise de conscience du péché. Car les malheurs qui s'abattent sur le peuple risquent toujours d'être interprétés comme autre chose que des sanctions. Ils doivent être multipliés jusqu'à ce que le peuple comprenne qu'il s'agit de punitions, répondant à des péchés qui doivent être reconnus. C'est seulement à ce moment-là que YHWH pourra se rappeler l'alliance ; ce qui revient à dire que celle-ci ne peut pas se réaliser sans une prise de conscience du péché de la part du peuple.

On peut préciser davantage quelles sont les fausses interprétations des malheurs que l'auteur veut écarter. La première serait d'y voir un signe d'absence de Dieu, d'abandon. On serait d'autant plus tenté de la faire que la présence de Dieu au milieu de son peuple figure en bonne place au milieu des récompenses (11.12). Or, rien dans la section punitions ne parle de l'abolir. Seules seront supprimées les médiations liturgiques (31) de cette présence. Dans cette phase punitive, YHWH est présent partout, c'est Lui qui agit d'un bout à l'autre (noter le nombre impressionnant de verbes à la première personne). Cette présence ne cesse même pas quand le peuple est chassé de son sol ; il retrouve encore son Dieu dans les pays ennemis non seulement pour achever une punition qui n'a pas encore atteint son but, mais aussi pour révéler une alliance et un amour qui continuent là-bas aussi bien que sur la terre d'Israël.

Une autre erreur serait de voir dans les malheurs du peuple un signe que Dieu a violé son alliance. Le contraire est affirmé fortement au v. 44. C'est exprimé aussi de façon indirecte. Alors que les récompenses sont expliquées comme une réalisation de l'alliance (9), sa suppression ne figure pas parmi les punitions comme on pourrait s'y attendre. YHWH n'a pas oublié son alliance ; c'est Israël qui l'a violée (15) et cela justifie ses malheurs.

C. Thème de la terre

Sans vouloir faire une étude exhaustive, on peut noter rapidement de quelle façon est présentée la terre d'Israël dans ce morceau. Si elle est un moyen de production (4.19.20.32 la présentent sous cet aspect), elle est surtout le lieu de la sécurité et de la paix (5.6 et indirectement 36 et 37). C'est une réalité autonome qui a ses droits (Israël les a méconnus), qui a des devoirs entre Dieu (34.35) et dont YHWH se souvient spécialement.

Par rapport à ce thème le v. 36 marque une nette coupure. Jusque-là tout se passait sur le sol d'Israël ; à partir de là il est question des pays ennemis. Le fait que cette coupure soit bien marquée au niveau des expressions verbales, prouve que pour l'auteur ce thème de la terre est important. On doit noter qu'il n'y a pas trois parties par rapport à ce thème ; il n'y a pas d'autre lieu prévu après les pays ennemis, il n'est pas explicitement question d'un retour au pays d'Israël. C'est en exil que s'achève la purification et que YHWH se souvient de son alliance. Seule la fin du v. 42 : « je me souviendrai du pays » pourrait faire penser à l'espoir d'un retour.

III. L'alliance

Le terme *b^erit* qu'on traduit — faute de mieux — par *alliance* se rencontre huit fois dans ce chapitre, toujours en position de complément direct. C'est donc des verbes qui le commandent qu'il faut faire l'inventaire :

v. 9 : le verbe est *haqim.* = mettre debout, ce qui permet au moins deux traductions. On peut comprendre : maintenir l'alliance, avec cette nuance que l'alliance ne se maintient que si elle continue à produire ses effets. On a ce sens par exemple en *Dt* 8,18 (et sans doute en *Gn.* 17,21) où *b^erit* désigne la promesse aux patriarches. Mais on peut comprendre aussi : instaurer l'alliance, ce qui revient à « s'engager solennellement » ; c'est le cas en *Gn.* 9,9 et 17,6-7. Bien qu'il y ait beaucoup de points communs entre le v. 9 et *Gn.* 17,6, on peut difficilement adopter le deuxième sens ; car cela amènerait à dire que la fidélité aux commandements est récompensée par l'octroi d'une alliance.

v. 15 : le verbe est *hafer* qui signifie habituellement : violer l'alliance en refusant ses exigences (*Jr.* 31,32 ; *Ez.* 16,59 ; 44,7 ; *Dt.* 31,16.20 etc.).

v. 25 : *n^eqam b^erit,* venger l'alliance ne figure pas ailleurs dans la Bible pas plus que dans des textes diplomatiques ou historiques. Cette expression implique que la *b^erit* est touchée par les refus du peuple.

v. 42 et 45 : le verbe est *zakar,* se rappeler. Dans *Ex.* 2,24 ; *Gn.* 9,15 ; *Ez.* 16,60 on voit que YHWH se rappelle son alliance quand Il en tire de nouvelles conséquences, par exemple en libérant son peuple (*Ex.* 2,24) ou en le restaurant (*Ez.* 16,60). *Ex.* 2,24 pourrait aider à comprendre le v. 45 et inviterait à le traduire ainsi : « je me souviendrai de l'alliance avec les prédécesseurs au nom de laquelle je les ai fait sortir d'Égypte... pour être leur Dieu ». « Prédécesseurs » désignerait alors Abraham à qui effectivement YHWH avait promis qu'Il serait le Dieu de sa descendance (*Gn.* 17,7). Mais c'est loin d'être évident ; le seul autre cas où *rišonim* soit employé comme substantif est *Dt.* 19,14 où il s'agit des contemporains de Josué et non des patriarches.

v. 44 : on a encore *hafer b*^{e}*rit*, mais cette fois c'est pour dire que YHWH n'a pas trahi son alliance (cf. *Jg.* 2,1) ce qui peut se dire avec tous les sens du mot *b*^{e}*rit*.

Il paraît difficile de donner à *b*^{e}*rit* le même sens dans les huit cas. On ne peut donc faire une synthèse de ces versets qu'en privilégiant certains emplois au détriment des autres. Voici deux exemples de synthèse possibles :

1° *B*^{e}*rit* désigne essentiellement la promesse faite à Abraham telle qu'elle est décrite en *Gn.* 17. Elle comportait la multiplication du peuple (v. 9 cf. *Gn.* 17,6) dont YHWH deviendrait le Dieu (v. 12 et 45, cf. *Gn.* 17,7) et à qui il donnerait un pays ; ce dernier élément n'est pas mentionné dans le chapitre 26 (il l'est en 25,38) mais on y parle beaucoup du pays. C'est par la libération d'Égypte que le deuxième élément de la promesse a été réalisé (v. 45). La bénédiction permanente d'Israël, conditionnée par son obéissance, est la réalisation actuelle de cette *b*^{e}*rit* (v. 9), mais d'autres sont possibles (v. 44). Dans cette hypothèse, il faut supposer pour les vv. 15 et 25 une autre signification de *b*^{e}*rit*, indépendante du sens principal.

2° Désignées par le même mot *b*^{e}*rit*, il y a plusieurs alliances. Il y en a eu une pour chaque patriarche, comme l'indique le v. 42 (cette idée n'apparaît pas ailleurs). Il y en a eu une autre pour Israël sortant d'Égypte (v. 45 si on le traduit : « l'alliance avec les prédécesseurs que j'ai fait sortir d'Égypte... ») dont le v. 12 nous donne la définition : « je serai votre Dieu et vous serez mon peuple ». Cette alliance, dont le maintien est l'essentiel des récompenses promises, dépend donc de l'attitude du peuple ; elle peut être violée (15), abolie. Dans cette hypothèse, la difficulté vient du v. 44 : de quelle *b*^{e}*rit* est-il question ? S'agit-il d'une alliance plus générale englobant toutes les autres (cf. la première hypothèse) ? ou de l'alliance avec les patriarches qui retrouve son actualité quand l'autre a disparu ? ou de l'alliance conclue avec Israël, qui revit après sa disparition ? Il est difficile de trancher. Dans tous les cas, on retrouverait ici, à l'intérieur même de la notion d'alliance l'opposition entre non-conditionné et conditionné, qui est une des structures fondamentales du texte.

Cette deuxième hypothèse laisserait donc supposer que *b*^{e}*rit* recouvre en partie ce que les théologiens appellent « alliance bilatérale » [3]. Cette

3. Parmi les nombreuses études sur ce sujet, on peut signaler : K. BALTZER *Das Bundesformular*, Neukirchen, 1960 ; D. MCCARTHY, *Der Gottesbund im Alten Testament* (SBS 13), Stuttgart, 1967 ; P. BUIS, *Le Deutéronome*, Paris, 1969, pp. 195-206.

conception de l'alliance, exprimée à l'aide d'un schéma inspiré des traités, insiste sur l'aspect réciprocité ; elle fait de l'alliance une réalité fragile, toujours menacée par les infidélités du peuple. On peut se demander si cette conception largement répandue dans la Bible (mais très rarement sous le nom de *b^{e}rit*) ne figurerait pas dans le texte étudié.

On s'aperçoit que c'est le cas, si on cherche les tenants et aboutissants des premiers mots du texte : « mes lois et mes commandements » (v. 3). Cette expression n'a de sens que si ces lois ont déjà été présentées. Nous sommes ainsi renvoyés aux chapitres précédents de la loi de sainteté où on trouve non seulement l'exposé, mais aussi la motivation des prescriptions. Celle-ci revêt diverses formes, mais la formule qui a le plus de chances de provenir du même auteur que le ch. 26 est : « c'est moi YHWH votre Dieu » [4]. C'est à ce titre que YHWH impose sa volonté aux Israélites. Mais la question rebondit : pourquoi est-Il le Dieu d'Israël? La réponse est donnée en 26,45 et 22,33 : « (c'est moi) qui vous ai fait sortir du pays d'Égypte pour être votre Dieu, c'est moi YHWH ».

On reconnaît là la logique de l'alliance bilatérale ; on aurait même de quoi reconstituer le schéma classique inspiré des traités avec des phrases de la loi de sainteté :

titulature : « c'est moi YHWH » (22,33 ; 26,45 etc.).

rappel historique : « qui vous ai fait sortir d'Égypte, pour vous donner le pays de Canaan » (25,38) ou « pour être votre Dieu » (22,33 ; 26,45) [5].

définition de l'alliance : « pour vous je serai Dieu et, pour moi, vous serez mon peuple » (26,12).

exigences de l'alliance : la loi de sainteté jusqu'à 26,2.

sanctions : notre texte.

Il semble possible de dire que l'auteur de la loi de sainteté connaît l'alliance bilatérale et son formulaire, mais qu'il désarticule systématiquement le schéma classique. Même le paragraphe des sanctions qui est habituellement le plus structuré, perd sa rigueur formelle et sa symétrie. On a l'impression que l'auteur veut présenter cette alliance comme une réalité en pleine décomposition, peut-être même déjà disparue. L'intérêt qu'il porte à ce qui se passera après l'application des sanctions, ne fait que renforcer cette impression.

4. Cf. KILIAN, *op. cit.*, p. 169.

5. On pourrait noter aussi la formule d'*Ex.* 29,46 : « qui les ai fait sortir du pays d'Égypte pour habiter au milieu d'eux » qui éclaire bien le v. 11. On sort des limites de la Loi de sainteté proprement dite, mais on sait qu'un certain nombre de fragments d'*Ex.*, *Lv.* et *Nb.* semblent devoir lui être rattachés.

IV. Situation historique

Les diverses observations faites au cours de cette étude permettent d'esquisser une histoire du texte. La troisième section (36-45) paraît être la partie la plus récente du chapitre. Sa mise en place a entraîné un remaniement des deux premières sections, spécialement l'adjonction de la série de conditionnelles (14.18 etc.) ; pour cette série, on peut même se demander si elle n'a pas été ajoutée après la mise en place de la troisième section (ce qui expliquerait un peu les difficultés des vv. 40.41), mais cette hypothèse ne s'impose pas absolument [6].

Dans sa première forme le texte ne devait comprendre que les deux premières sections, la seconde sans ses surcharges ; il servait de conclusion à la Loi de sainteté, comme *Dt.* 28 pour le code deutéronomiste.

La datation de ces deux étapes de rédaction est sans doute plus facile que pour le reste de la Loi de sainteté. La majorité des auteurs pense que la troisième section, et donc la rédaction finale, ne peut être située qu'aux environs de 587 : la manière dont l'auteur parle de l'exil fait penser que c'est une réalité très proche, sinon déjà présente. Mais la façon dont il décrit la dévastation du pays — totalement vidé de ses habitants et laissé en friche pour de longues années (33-36a.43) — contredit si évidemment la réalité historique (telle que l'atteste Jérémie par exemple) qu'il n'est pas vraisemblable que le texte ait été écrit après 587. Il faut le placer un peu avant, tout comme *Jr.* 31 et *Dt.* 30,1-10. Ces trois textes représentent trois essais pour décrire l'avenir meilleur qu'on espère connaître au-delà de la catastrophe imminente ; de ces essais *Lv.* 26 est certainement le plus timide, mais c'est aussi celui qui ouvre le plus grand nombre de possibilités.

La première étape de la rédaction est plus difficile à fixer. Si on admet la thèse de Smend, selon laquelle la formule d'alliance du v. 12 date de la réforme de Josias [7], on doit placer cette première rédaction après 621. Sinon, on peut envisager une date plus haute. De toute façon, on doit supposer une date plus haute pour une bonne partie du texte, dans la mesure où il s'inspire d'une tradition liturgique orale ou écrite qui est utilisée indépendamment par Ezéchiel [8]. Il est possible de définir le Sitz im Leben de cette tradition, mais pas celui du texte de *Lv.* 26. Dès sa

6. Ce qui est plus probablement postérieur à la mise en place de la troisième section, c'est le développement sur les années sabbatiques (vv. 34.35.43a).

7. R. Smend, *Die Bundesformel*, Zürich 1963.

8. C'est la thèse développée par H. G. Reventlow dans *Wächter über Israel*, Berlin, 1962. On peut contester la reconstitution que fait cet auteur de la tradition liturgique ; mais l'existence de cette tradition n'est pas remise en cause pour autant.

première étape, le texte apparaît comme une œuvre littéraire destinée à la lecture privée ou en cercle restreint ; une destination liturgique ou juridique est peu vraisemblable.

On voit par ces quelques notations quelle contribution originale et pleine de possibilités *Lv.* 26 apporte à ce vaste mouvement de recherche qui s'est développé à la veille de l'exil. Toute une génération s'est employée à scruter l'avenir de cette alliance dont on achevait tout juste de découvrir les richesses au moment où les événements annonçaient sa remise en question.

P. Buis

See *Supplementary note*, p. 217.

9

QUELQUES REMARQUES SUR LA NOUVELLE ALLIANCE CHEZ JÉRÉMIE

(Jérémie 31,31-34)

Deux observations s'imposent au début de cet exposé, l'une concerne l'emploi du mot alliance pour rendre le terme hébreu *b^e^rit*, et l'autre le choix de la péricope de Jér. 31,31-34 pour les quelques réflexions que je vais vous présenter.

Si je continue à parler d'alliance, bien que je sache que cette traduction de *b^e^rit* est aujourd'hui contestée, surtout depuis les nombreux et importants travaux du professeur E. Kutsch [1], c'est parce que je ne suis pas encore convaincu qu'il nous faille abandonner ce vocable au profit d'une expression qui serait meilleure.

Je me demande d'abord si dans le cas de *b^e^rit* comme dans maints autres cas — par exemple à propos de *ḥesed* ou de *ṣedaqah* — il existe un terme équivalent en français, en anglais ou en allemand, capable de rendre la richesse sémantique et les nuances du mot hébreu, ou si nous ne devons pas admettre que toute traduction sera toujours plus ou moins approximative et conventionnelle. Il s'agit de choisir une expression qui se rapproche le plus possible de son modèle hébreu, tout en demeurant conscient de la distance qui subsiste entre le vocabulaire que nous employons et celui que nous lisons dans le texte de l'Ancien Testament.

Sans doute le professeur E. Kutsch a-t-il entièrement raison quand il proteste contre l'emploi univoque des mots alliance, Covenant ou Bund, qui risque de favoriser des interprétations doctrinales erronées qui ne tiennent pas compte de la variété des significations que peut revêtir le terme hébreu, ni de sa dimension diachronique. La question se pose alors de savoir dans quelle mesure il faut traduire le même vocable de l'Ancien Testament par un même terme emprunté à nos langues occi-

1. On trouvera un résumé des travaux de E. Kutsch dans le *Theologisches Wörterbuch zum Alten Testament*, I, 1971 (*b^e^rît* Verpflichtung, col. 339-352) et dans un récent volume de la collection *BZAW131* (1972), Verheissung und Gesetz.

dentales ou ne pas hésiter à adopter des expressions différentes et même divergentes selon les contextes où nous rencontrons le mot hébreu. Nous ne pouvons pas donner de réponse a priori à cette question, chaque cas doit être examiné pour lui-même.

En ce qui concerne *b^e^rit*, E. Kutsch a remarquablement mis en lumière deux aspects au moins de ce terme, en particulier dans le langage théologique : *b^e^rit* s'identifie en effet tantôt avec la promesse que Yahvé fait à son peuple, tantôt avec les exigences qu'il impose à Israël ; on peut parler à son propos de Zuspruch ou d'Anspruch et être ainsi amené à adopter deux traductions distinctes du même vocable hébreu. Mais n'est-il pas frappant de constater que l'Ancien Testament utilise *b^e^rit* pour désigner deux réalités apparemment si diverses ? Cela ne signifie-t-il pas qu'au niveau de la tradition vétérotestamentaire, l'opposition entre les deux aspects de la relation entre Dieu et les siens n'est pas absolue et que l'un d'entre eux n'exclut pas l'autre ? Autrement dit nous aurions affaire avec le mot *b^e^rit* à une ellipse à deux foyers, dont les éléments constitutifs relevés par E. Kutsch (promesse et exigences) peuvent être attestés différemment selon les textes sans en être jamais complètement absents. Le mot alliance ne conviendrait-il donc pas pour exprimer les rapports, divers au cours des siècles, qui ont réuni Dieu et l'humanité, où, comme dans le lien conjugal, chacun des partenaires a dû être de quelque façon le répondant de l'autre?

Enfin on nous propose de traduire *b^e^rit* par Verpflichtung ou encore par Bestimmung, donc par obligation, engagement ou disposition. Mais la notion d'engagement est-elle totalement étrangère à celle d'alliance ? L'une ne conduit-elle pas à l'autre, la seconde ne suppose-t-elle pas la première ? L'engagement me semble créer un lien entre celui qui le prend et celui envers lequel il est pris, que le mot alliance pourrait exprimer à juste titre.

Ces remarques visent à justifier mon hésitation à renoncer à la traduction usuelle de *b^e^rit*, bien que je sois conscient du danger qu'il y a à mettre dans ce terme d'alliance un contenu qui ne correspondrait pas aux intentions des écrivains de l'Ancien Testament et je remercie le professeur E. Kutsch des mises en garde qu'il nous adresse à cet égard.

* * *

Si j'ai choisi de traiter de la nouvelle alliance chez Jérémie dans le cadre de notre rencontre, c'est en particulier pour rendre hommage à celui qui a fondé et animé pendant de longues années les Journées bibliques, et qui, de 1927 à 1967, a honoré la chaire de l'Ancien Testament de l'Université dont nous sommes aujourd'hui les hôtes, Mgr J. Coppens.

Puisse ce travail être un modeste écho de l'hommage mérité qui lui a été rendu lors de la 18e session des Journées bibliques en 1967 [2], puisqu'il reprend un sujet que Mgr J. Coppens a lui-même abordé il y a près de 10 ans dans un article dont nous allons reparler.

Je n'ai pas besoin d'insister sur l'importance du passage de Jérémie qui nous retient maintenant ; il a joué un rôle dans la communauté de Qumrân comme l'indique en particulier le Document de Damas ; plusieurs textes du Nouveau Testament s'y réfèrent, ainsi notamment Hébr. 8,1ss., 2 Cor. 3,4ss. et certaines versions du récit de la Cène (Luc 22,20 ; 1 Cor. 11,25) ; il peut enfin, comme je l'écrivais en 1962, éclairer une réflexion théologique portant d'une part sur la relation entre les deux Testaments et de l'autre sur les rapports entre Israël et l'Église. Encore faut-il que toute élaboration doctrinale sur ces points tienne compte du fait que les relectures néotestamentaires de Jér. 31,31-34 ne se situent pas dans le simple prolongement de la déclaration prophétique ; elles supposent un autre milieu et des problèmes nouveaux, donc une certaine distance par rapport à la vision originale de la nouvelle alliance, comme un article tout récent de L. Dequeker vient de le rappeler [3].

Il nous faut en premier lieu essayer de comprendre notre texte pour lui-même sans faire intervenir des interférences doctrinales et même les écrits apostoliques, ce qui est moins aisé qu'il ne le semble. Je rappellerai d'abord comment trois auteurs ont lu récemment cette péricope du livre de Jérémie, puis, dans une deuxième partie, je tenterai de présenter une vue synthtétique de Jér. 31,31-34, et enfin je tâcherai de situer le thème de l'alliance dans les perspectives d'avenir des trois prophètes du début de l'époque exilique, soit Jérémie, Ezéchiel et le Second Isaïe.

J'ai choisi parmi les études de ces dernières années, celles de Mgr J. Coppens, dans The Catholic Biblical Quarterly, 1963, du P. P. Buis, dans Vetus Testamentum, 1968, et enfin du professeur S. Herrmann dans « Die prophetischen Heilserwartungen im Alten Testament », 1965 [4]. Sans doute d'autres travaux pourraient être cités [5], mais ceux

2. Cf. à ce sujet l'ouvrage collectif : « De Mari à Qumrân. L'Ancien Testament. Son milieu. Ses Écrits. Ses relectures juives », Hommage à Mgr J. Coppens. (*Bibliotheca Ephemeridum Theologicarum Lovaniensium*, 24, 1969.)

3. Dans un article qui m'a été remis aux Journées bibliques et qui a paru en néerlandais, avec un résumé en anglais, sous le titre : « Het Nieuwe Verbond bij Jeremia, bij Paulus en in de Brief aan de Hebreeën », *Bijdragen*, 33 (1972), 234-261.

4. Mgr J. Coppens, « La nouvelle alliance en Jér. 31,31-34», *The Catholic Biblical Quarterly*, 25 (1963), 12-21 ; P. Buis, « La nouvelle alliance», *Vetus Testamentum* 18 (1968), 1-15 ; S. Herrmann, « Die prophetischen Heilserwartungen im Alten Testament », (*BWANT*, Fünfte Folge, V), 1965, notamment pp. 179-185 et 195-204.

5. Pour des études antérieures, cf. en particulier avec l'étude de J. Coppens, une bibliographie dans R. Martin-Achard, La nouvelle alliance selon Jérémie, *Revue de théologie et de philosophie* 12 (1962), 81-92. Parmi les travaux récents, signalons : B. W. Anderson, The New Covenant and the Old, in *The Old Testament and Christian*

que j'ai retenus présentent l'avantage d'aborder la déclaration de Jér. 31,31-34 de façon franchement différente et en un sens complémentaire ; ils révèlent également quelles sont les trois grandes questions que pose notre texte : qu'y a-t-il de particulier dans Jér. 31,31-34 ? Quels sont les rapports de ce passage avec la tradition deutéronomiste ? Quels liens offre-t-il avec les déclarations d'Ezéchiel et du Second Isaïe relatives à l'avenir de la *b^e^rit* ?

* * *

I. Mgr J. Coppens a écrit sur Jér. 31,31ss., une étude qu'on peut qualifier de classique ; elle contient la présentation d'une traduction, l'analyse du texte hébreu et le relevé des traits essentiels de l'oracle prophétique. De l'ensemble des remarques faites par le professeur de Louvain, je retiens des points suivants quitte à revenir sur d'autres éléments dans l'exégèse.

Pour Mgr J. Coppens, « l'affirmation centrale et capitale de notre péricope porte sur l'inscription de la loi sur le cœur de la maison d'Israël » [6]. Cette loi qui se réfère, selon lui, à l'événement du Sinaï, ne consiste pas nécessairement dans le décalogue, comme l'ont pensé M. Robert et P. Volz, ni même dans un code de lois déterminé, mais elle ne suppose pas davantage la suppression de toute promulgation externe de la volonté divine, comme ont tendance à l'affirmer les auteurs protestants [7]. Le don de la loi dans le sein des croyants n'exclut pas pour Mgr J. Coppens, le respect des lois externes, on pourrait dire plutôt qu'il le permet.

Faith, London, 1964, pp. 225-242 ; G. P. Couturier, *The Jerome Biblical Commentary*, 1968 ; J. Bright, Jeremiah (*The Anchor Bible*), 1968 et An Exercise in Hermeneutics, *Interpretation* 20 (1966), 188-210 ; Th. Ludwig, The Shape of Hope : Jeremiahs Book of Consolation, *Concordia Theological Monthly* 39 (1968), 526-541 ; J. Schreiner, Ein neuer Bund unverbrüchlichen Heils, *Bibel und Leben* 7 (1966), 242-255 (du même cf. aussi *Die Welt der Bibel*, 20, 1967) ; O. Garcia de la Fuente El complimiento de la ley en la nueva alianza según los profetas, *Estudios Biblicos*, 28 (1969), 293-311 ; M. H. Goshen-Gottstein signale qu'un de ses étudiants, Fr. Seilhamer, doit publier prochainement sa dissertation sur Jér. 31, dans *Wort, Lied und Gottesspruch. Beiträge zur Psalmen und Propheten*, Festschrift f. J. Ziegler, 2, 1972, p. 167, note 32 ; cf. encore l'article de L. Dequeker, 1972, signalé à la note 3.

6. *Op. cit.*, p. 17.

7. J. Steinmann exprime un point de vue différent dans « Le prophète Jérémie » (*Lectio Divina*, 9) 1952 en écrivant : « Jérémie annonce le remplacement de l'alliance légale et didactique par une alliance d'amour et de grâce... la loi, enseignement extrinsèque et formel, deviendra un penchant du cœur et une intuition de l'âme, éclairée du dedans par Dieu. La création nouvelle de la Palestine sera une création religieuse et mystique, une pentecôte des âmes » (p. 256). A mon avis il extrapole les données de Jér. 31,31ss.

Ce sur quoi notre auteur insiste le plus, c'est sur l'originalité du texte que nous lisons. Le v. 33, écrit-il « ne possède pas de parallèle rigoureusement exact ni en Jérémie ni ailleurs »[8]. D'autres passages certes parlent de purification du cœur, de sa circoncision, ou encore de la transformation d'un cœur de pierre en cœur de chair, ou enfin d'un cœur nouveau, mais ces expressions qu'on rencontre notamment chez Jérémie et chez Ezéchiel ne sont pas identiques à ce qui est dit ici. « La mention d'une telle donation est unique dans les Écritures de l'Ancien Testament » conclut Mgr J. Coppens[9].

Cette remarque, fondée sur le v. 33, peut être renouvelée à propos du v. 34 qui présente deux particularités : l'ère de la nouvelle alliance sera caractérisée par l'absence de tout besoin d'instruction — « nous affrontons là, remarque notre auteur, une notion de l'action divine qui, elle non plus, ne trouve ailleurs une correspondance parfaite »[10] —, et l'affirmation « de la rémission des péchés qui n'est pas non plus sans présenter des traits particuliers par rapport à d'autres passages du livre de Jérémie »[11].

De tous les parallèles évoqués à propos de Jér. 31,31ss., deux textes seulement méritent d'être pris en considération, estime Mgr Coppens, mais ici encore, ils ne sont pas identiques avec le contenu de notre oracle et présentent d'ailleurs un timbre jérémien plus accusé que la péricope que nous étudions.

Le professeur de Louvain en conclut que celle-ci ne saurait être l'œuvre du prophète lui-même, mais plutôt d'un de ses disciples ; elle doit être antérieure à plusieurs déclarations du Second ou du Troisième Esaïe avec lesquelles elle offre certaines affinités. Cet oracle post-jérémien, qui serait une anticipation d'affirmations comme celles d'Es. 54,13 ; 59,21 et de Jl. 3,1-4, semble finalement « avoir frayé la voie à ce que nous pourrions appeler une démocratisation du charisme prophétique, une promotion du peuple de Dieu à la grâce du prophétisme »[12].

On peut se demander si cette dernière remarque est justifiée : Mgr J. Coppens a beaucoup insisté sur l'importance de la loi dans Jér. 31,31ss., il parle maintenant de don prophétique, ce qui me semble relever d'une autre réalité. Mais on retiendra surtout de l'étude du professeur de Louvain qu'elle souligne l'unicité de notre péricope qui, écrit-il « est d'une originalité qui paraît avoir échappé à la plupart des commentateurs »[13].

* * *

8. *Op. cit.*, p. 17.
9. *Ibid.*
10. *Op. cit.*, p. 18.
11. *Op. cit.*, p. 19.
12. *Op. cit.*, p. 20s.
13. *Op. cit.*, p. 21.

Tout autre est la démarche du P. Buis qui traite de Jér. 31,31-34 conjointement avec neuf autres textes qui se réfèrent tous, selon lui, au thème de la nouvelle alliance [14]. Partant de Jér. 32,37-41, notre auteur pense en effet retrouver dans ces divers passages, en dépit de leur variété, un même schéma qu'il appelle « structure de l'annonce de la nouvelle alliance » et qui comporterait 5 thèmes : rassemblement du peuple et retour ; définition de l'alliance ; rénovation intérieure du peuple ; annonce d'une conclusion définitive ; bénédictions. Dans Jér. 31,31-36 (!) on compterait 4 de ces éléments [15].

Ce schéma de la nouvelle alliance ne se rapproche pas comme on pourrait s'y attendre de celui de la réparation d'alliance (Bundeserneuerung) — car dans ce dernier cas c'est la communauté qui prend l'initiative de réparer la *b*^{e}*rit* rompue par elle —, ni du schéma de l'alliance sinaïtique, de type bilatéral, puisque celui-ci comporte une engagement mutuel comme l'attestent les textes de E,D et du Dtr., mais bien plutôt des perspectives théologiques de la tradition sacerdotale qui insistent sur les dispositions prises par Dieu en faveur des hommes.

Plus exactement, la nouvelle *b*^{e}*rit* serait une sorte de synthèse entre l'ancienne alliance, car elle maintient les obligations des deux partenaires, et le point de vue sacerdotal, puisqu'elle repose sur la décision unilatérale de Yahvé [16]. Le P. Buis écrit à ce propos : « En face de l'échec constaté de l'alliance du Sinaï, Jérémie, Ezéchiel, l'école sacerdotale se reportent à une alliance plus ancienne qui tient encore, sur laquelle on pourra s'appuyer pour rebâtir : celle d'Abraham. La nouvelle alliance n'en sera qu'une expression » [17].

Enfin le théologien catholique se pose la question de « l'initiateur » de cette forme littéraire ainsi définie et estime que Jér. 31,31ss. est à bien des égards le texte le plus ancien de la collection ; à côté de Dt. 30,1-10, qui en serait une ébauche, il est le témoin « où s'affirme définitivement la forme littéraire originale qui structure l'annonce de la nouvelle alliance », les autres passages cités par l'auteur montrant que celle-ci s'est développée durant et après l'exil [18].

Le P. Buis a parfaitement raison de rappeler que l'oracle de Jér. 31,31ss. dont Mgr J. Coppens a dit la spécificité, n'est d'une certaine manière pas seul de son genre. Il fait partie des déclarations prophétiques — ou recueillies dans les livres prophétiques —, qui tentent de

14. Ces textes sont Ez. 32,37-41 ; 37,21-28 ; Ba. 2,29-35 ; Jér. 31,31-36 ; Ez. 34,25-31 ; 36,22-35 ; Za. 7,7-8,17 ; Jér. 24,5-7 ; Ez. 16,53-63 ; Dt. 30,1-10.

15. Dans Jér. 31,31-34 (et non 36), je ne retrouve que 3 éléments de la structure de l'annonce de la nouvelle *b*^{e}*rit*, soit la définition de l'alliance, la rénovation intérieure du peuple et l'annonce d'une alliance définitive.

16. *Op. cit.*, pp. 7-12 et notamment p. 12.

17. *Ibid.*

18. *Op. cit.*, pp. 12ss.

répondre au lendemain de 587 à l'échec de la première *b^e^rit* et aux questions que le peuple élu se pose sur son avenir. Notre auteur insiste également à bon droit sur l'antériorité de notre péricope sur d'autres passages de l'époque exilique, en particulier sur certaines expressions d'Ezéchiel et du Second Esaïe.

Mais je me demande si on peut réellement parler à propos des textes qu'il étudie d'une structure de l'annonce de la nouvelle alliance. Admettre une structure à la base des dix témoins cités par le P. Buis implique, me semble-t-il, que l'on suppose l'existence d'un modèle dont se seraient inspirés les divers auteurs exiliques ou postexiliques ; autrement dit nous serions en présence d'un certain cadre qui s'imposerait avec plus ou moins de rigueur aux prophètes ou à leurs disciples ; on reconnaîtrait un certain ordre dans la présentation des thèmes, des articulations caractéristiques, ce qui ne me paraît pas être le cas ici. La variété des témoins cités par le P. Buis atteste plutôt l'absence d'un modèle au point de départ de la collection des oracles relatifs à la nouvelle *b^e^rit*.

Nous sommes plutôt en présence d'un phénomène assez courant avec et après l'exil que j'appellerai, à la suite de M. Robert, anthologique. Les textes de cette époque résultent d'un procédé d'accumulation, les divers éléments qui les composent ayant été ajoutés les uns aux autres, d'une façon assez libre, dans le souci évident qui caractérise l'esprit de la période qui fait suite à 587 de ne rien négliger de la tradition, de ne rien perdre du passé.

Il me semble donc difficile de parler, comme le propose le P. Buis dans un article qui ose s'aventurer sur des voies nouvelles et renferme bien des remarques intéressantes, d'un schéma de la nouvelle alliance comme il me paraît délicat de relier en quelque sorte directement, comme ses expressions le laissent supposer, la *b^e^rit* de Jér. 31 à l'alliance abrahamique.

* * *

Avec S. Herrmann nous changeons encore de perspective, puisque, pour le théologien allemand, la péricope de Jér. 31,31-34 appartient sans aucun doute à la tradition deutéronomiste. Il convient donc de l'examiner à partir de celle-ci.

Selon S. Herrmann en effet la langue comme le contenu de notre passage relèvent de l'école deutéronomiste : on retrouve ainsi dans Jér. 31,31ss. la formule d'alliance traditionnelle dans ce milieu : « Je serai leur Dieu et ils seront mon peuple » [19], de même que des notions

19. Cette formule se retrouve dans le livre de Jérémie notamment dans Jér. 7,23 ; 11,4 ; 13,11 ; 24,7 ; 30,22 ; 31,1,33 ; 32,38. P. Buis remarque à son propos que «la formule d'alliance se rencontre presque exclusivement chez des auteurs proches

typiquement deutéronomistes telles que celles de thora, de connaissance ou d'amour de Yahvé, de pardon des péchés, ou encore des allusions à des thèmes deutéronomistes comme ceux des pères ou de Baal en Jér. 31,32 [20].

Cette nouvelle *b^e^rit* ne se réfère pas avant tout, comme on le pense d'ordinaire, au pacte du Sinaï, mais à une série de conclusions d'alliance, qui, selon la tradition deutéronomiste, marquent les grandes étapes de la destinée d'Israël : l'alliance égyptienne — ou avec les pères — qui exige d'Israël qu'il ne reconnaisse qu'un Baal c.-à-d. Yahvé (cf. Jg. 2,1ss.), l'alliance sous Josué, qui fixe l'attitude du peuple de Yahvé au sein de la Terre promise (Jos. 24), l'alliance sous Josias qui est une réparation d'alliance après une époque d'égarement. (2 Rois, 23) [21].

La nouvelle alliance n'est donc pas le simple vis-à-vis de la *b^e^rit* sinaïtique, avec laquelle elle formerait un diptyque ; elle doit être vue de manière génétique et non statique, comme un épisode parmi d'autres des relations de Yahvé avec son peuple. Elle s'inscrit dans une histoire, écrite selon les vues deutéronomistes, et relève d'une réflexion théologique dont elle marque l'aboutissement [22]. Elle n'a pas en vue une réalité dernière, eschatologique, comme on le dit parfois, puisqu'elle vise à répondre à un problème immédiat posé aux théologiens deutéronomistes confrontés à la fin du royaume de Juda ; elle ne présente pas davantage ce caractère exceptionnel qu'on lui reconnaît souvent, car elle fait partie d'une tradition qui s'est exprimée déjà avec Osée et qu'elle a été longuement préparée par le courant deutéronomiste.

On ne s'étonnera donc pas de rencontrer dans ce texte des éléments attestés ailleurs [23] ; il n'inaugure que sur un point en intériorisant les relations de Yahvé avec Israël ou mieux en combinant audacieusement la notion de *b^e^rit* avec le thème deutéronomiste de l'intériorité de la religion yahviste [24]. Jér. 31,31-34 est en fait un fruit de la prédication deutéronomiste [25].

de l'exil et gravitant autour de Jérusalem et de la liturgie du temple... elle est particulièrement bien en situation entre la liquidation de l'alliance du Sinaï et l'instauration espérée d'une nouvelle alliance. » (*Op. cit.*, p. 4). Sur cette formule, cf. surtout R. SMEND, Die Bundesformel (*Theologische Studien*, 68), 1963.

20. *Op. cit.*, pp. 182ss.

21. *Op. cit.*, pp. 180-182.

22. *Op. cit.*, pp. 183, 204, etc. S. HERRMANN prend ici ses distances par rapport à diverses explications de Jér. 31,31-34, dont celles de H. ORTMANN, W. LEMPP, E. ROHLAND, M. NOTH, A. WEISER (pp. 195-204).

23. S. HERRMANN parle d'une combinaison nouvelle d'éléments déjà attestés par la tradition, il]estime qu'il n'y a pas une donnée de Jér. 31,31ss. qui n'ait déjà été exprimée avant cet oracle (*op. cit.*, p. 183).

24. *Op. cit.*, p. 183.

25. *Op. cit.*, p. 204.

Enfin S. Herrmann ne se contente pas de parler, comme E. Rohland [26], d'une péricope retravaillée par un disciple de l'école deutéronomiste, il voit dans l'oracle relatif à la nouvelle alliance un texte parfaitement intégré à la théologie deutéronomiste.

Sans doute a-t-il mis en évidence les liens existant entre notre passage et l'école deutéronomiste, mais il n'a pas assez souligné l'originalité de Jér. 31,31ss. par rapport à celle-ci. Il n'a pas vu la spécificité de la déclaration prophétique dont il a fait un simple prolongement de la tradition deutéronomiste.

Il existe en réalité un hyatus entre notre texte et le courant théologique auquel il est censé appartenir. Jér. 31,31-34 regarde hardiment vers l'avenir, alors que les écrits deutéronomistes apparaissent plutôt comme une méditation basée sur le passé ; il pose comme base à la nouvelle *b^erit* le pardon divin, tandis que l'école deutéronomiste voit en celui-ci la réponse de Yahvé à la repentance de son peuple [27] ; il ne se contente pas de réclamer, avec le Deutéronome, l'obéissance à la thora, il la rend possible ; il ne dit pas seulement qu'Israël doit aimer Yahvé, il révèle comment Dieu suscitera au sein des siens la connaissance qu'il attend d'eux.

En définitive S. Herrmann me semble avoir minimisé les particularités de Jér. 31,31ss. ; il n'a pas remarqué qu'il y avait entre l'oracle du prophète d'Anatot et les vues habituelles des Deutéronomistes une sorte de rupture, un renversement dans les perspectives, qui me paraît capital, et qui s'expliquerait mieux si nous admettons que notre passage est l'œuvre de Jérémie lui-même plutôt que celle d'un épigone.

Les rapprochements que notre auteur a notés entre Jér. 31,31ss. et la tradition deutéronomiste ne sauraient donc être niés mais ils mettent peut-être davantage en relief ce qu'il y a de nouveau dans la nouvelle alliance et il se pourrait bien que cette nouveauté soit le fait du prophète lui-même.

* * *

II. Il nous faut revenir dans une deuxième partie, au texte lui-même et élucider pour commencer la question de son auteur. Les critiques

26. E. ROHLAND, *Die Bedeutung der Erwählungstraditionen Israels für die Eschatologie der alttestamentlichen Propheten* (Diss. Heidelberg), 1956, pp. 66-73.

27. S. HERRMANN déclare bien que la notion de pardon des péchés fait partie de la théologie deutéronomiste, ce qui est exact, mais les textes qu'il cite (*op. cit.*, p. 183) (comme 1 Rois, 8,34,36,50 ou Dt. 29,19) ne présentent pas les mêmes perspectives que Jér. 31,31ss. Ils lient le pardon d'Israël à sa repentance, alors que la déclaration jérémienne fonde sur la grâce divine de nouvelles possibilités de relations entre Yahvé et son peuple. Même un passage comme Dt. 30,1ss. n'offre pas la même netteté à cet égard que Jér. 31,31-34 où l'avenir d'Israël repose tout entier sur l'initiative de son Dieu.

admettent généralement que Jérémie est responsable de cette déclaration et plusieurs saluent dans cet oracle le sommet de sa prédication ou son testament spirituel [28].

Mais il ne manque pas de commentateurs pour mettre en doute l'authenticité de cette péricope, attribuée dès lors à quelque scribe de l'époque postexilique dont l'idéal légaliste aurait été de connaître par cœur la thora, *dixit* B. Duhm, ou, comme nous venons de le voir, à l'école deutéronomiste, thèse que S. Herrmann a brillamment défendue, ou encore à un proche disciple du prophète, ainsi que le pense, après S. Mowinckel, Mgr J. Coppens [29].

E. Rohland estime que Jér. 31,31-34 relève de Jérémie, mais que cette déclaration a été récrite dans une perspective deutéronomiste ; G. von Rad déclare que ce passage ne représente probablement pas la rédaction originale de Jérémie [30], J. Bright conteste l'opinion de ceux qui s'appuient sur le fait que ce texte est en prose pour affirmer son inauthenticité, et admet que pour le fonds tout au moins, si non pour la forme, le thème de la nouvelle *b^e^rit* peut être attribué au prophète d'Anatot [31].

Ce point de vue me paraît prudent et nuancé. Jér. 31,31-34 ne nous offre peut-être pas les *ipsissima verba*, selon l'expression de J. Bright, de Jérémie, mais l'annonce que Yahvé conclura une nouvelle alliance avec Israël n'est en rien contredite par ce que nous savons de son message [32]. Ce qu'il y a même d'original dans cet oracle, n'infirme pas son caractère jérémien, comme le croit Mgr J. Coppens, car il n'est nullement incompatible avec la prédication de celui qui a vainement appelé son peuple à la repentance et a dénoncé finalement son incapacité à se convertir — « à changer de peau » (Jér. 13,23) — mais qui entrevoit aussi à l'heure du châtiment que Dieu est capable, lui, de donner à Israël une

28. Selon J. BRIGHT, *The Anchor Bible*, *ad loc.*, ce passage est le sommet de la théologie du prophète ; pour G. P. COUTURIER, *op. cit.*, *ad loc.*, il marque le testament spirituel de Jérémie ; Th. M. LUDWIG, *op. cit.*, pp. 538ss. rappelle le point de vue de B. DUHM et met en garde contre une idéalisation de ce texte.

29. S. MOWINCKEL (*RHPhR*, 22 (1942) 93ss.) voit dans Jér. 31,31ss. l'œuvre d'un disciple influencé par Ezéchiel, alors que Th. W. LUDWIG, *op. cit.*, pp. 540ss., rapproche cette déclaration de celles du Second Esaïe et voit en elle le dernier stade de l'évolution de l'espérance qui s'exprime dans « le livre de consolation de Jérémie ».

30. G. VON RAD, *Theologie des Alten Testaments*, 2, 1960, 226ss. ; éd. fr. (1967) 184s.

31. *Op. cit.*, 1965, *ad loc.*, et 1966, p. 183.

32. On s'accordera pour admettre que « le rôle du cœur, siège de la connaissance, l'appel à la repentance intérieure, la constatation de l'endurcissement d'Israël sont des thèmes familiers au prophète d'Anatot » (R. MARTIN-ACHARD, *op. cit.*, p. 87). A. GELIN, *Jérémie*, 1952, 160ss., écrit de son côté « La nouvelle alliance... n'est autre que la projection dans l'avenir de la propre expérience de Jérémie ».

nouvelle possibilité de vivre (Jér. 32,1ss.) en le transformant radicalement [33].

Jér. 31,31-34 confirme à la fois le jugement sévère porté par le prophète sur les siens « Eux ont rompu mon alliance » (v. 32) et le fait que Yahvé leur offre une nouvelle chance (v. 33-34) ; l'annonce de la culpabilité du peuple élu et la proclamation de son salut au moment de la chute de Juda ne forment-ils pas les deux axes de la prédication de Jérémie ?

J'estime ainsi, sans naturellement pouvoir le prouver de façon irréfutable, qu'on peut attribuer à Jérémie la paternité de notre oracle, du moins pour l'essentiel. Les points de contact que S. Herrmann a relevés entre Jér. 31,31ss. et la tradition deutéronomiste n'infirment pas cette conclusion, puisque sur un point capital — et décisif — le texte jérémien se distingue de la théologie deutéronomiste : il déclare que Yahvé instaurera de sa propre initiative un nouveau régime en faveur d'Israël, qui permettra à celui-ci d'être fidèle à ce que les théologiens deutéronomistes attendent de lui.

Il reste à préciser le moment où le prophète d'Anatot peut avoir annoncé que Dieu accorderait une nouvelle *b^e^rit* à son peuple. Avec la majorité des critiques j'estime que notre péricope date de l'époque qui a vu Juda succomber définitivement sous les coups des Babyloniens, elle ne suppose pas nécessairement les événements de 587, mais elle a été composée alors que la cause était entendue et Juda pratiquement perdu. Je ne puis suivre W. Rudolph quand il relie notre oracle à la prédication de Jérémie au temps de Josias, alors que ce souverain tente de reconstituer un état aux dimensions du royaume davidique en récupérant les territoires du nord. Sans doute le prophète s'est-il alors adressé à Ephraïm pour l'inviter à rentrer dans l'alliance de son Dieu et de son roi, comme l'attestent divers passages des chapitres 30 et 31 ; mais ce qu'on appelle « le livre de la consolation de Jérémie » [34] est constitué par un ensemble de déclarations d'âges et de perspectives différents et relève sans doute d'un travail rédactionnel. Autrement dit il faut lire Jér. 31,31-34, en tout cas dans un premier temps, sans tenir compte de son contexte actuel.

Dans ce passage Jérémie s'adresse à l'ensemble d'Israël et non aux seuls Ephraïmites [35] : la nouvelle *b^e^rit* concerne le peuple de Yahvé

33. J. SCHREINER, *op. cit.*, p. 251 remarque que Jér. 31,31ss. n'est pas totalement inédit et cite Jér. 24,5-7 comme un texte qui prépare à la déclaration sur la nouvelle alliance.

34. Parmi les auteurs récents, Th. M. LUDWIG (*op. cit.*, note 5) s'est particulièrement intéressé au livre de consolation de Jérémie et à l'histoire de sa composition.

35. La mention de Juda est sans doute due à un glossateur qui a pensé qu'Israël ne désignait que le royaume du nord, elle manque au v. 33 ; B. W. ANDERSON,

dans son entier et on imagine difficilement que le prophète ait réservé à un moment de sa carrière aux gens du nord la possibilité de recevoir le pardon divin et le privilège de connaître Yahvé et de vivre selon ses lois. Le contenu de Jér. 31,31ss. plaide en faveur de l'interprétation traditionnelle : à une des heures les plus sombres que connaît son peuple, Jérémie proclame à ses contemporains qu'il y a un avenir non seulement possible, mais certain pour Israël, puisqu'il repose sur la volonté de Yahvé de renouer avec lui en lui pardonnant ses fautes.

* * *

Quels sont les éléments essentiels de la déclaration prophétique dont je donne maintenant une traduction ?

(v. 31) « Voici des jours viennent, oracle de Yahvé, où je scellerai avec la maison d'Israël... une alliance nouvelle,

(v. 32) non comme l'alliance que j'ai scellée avec leurs pères, au jour où je les ai saisis par la main pour les faire sortir du pays d'Égypte, et eux rompirent mon alliance, quoique je fusse leur maître !

(v. 33) Car voici l'alliance que je scellerai avec la maison d'Israël après ces jours, oracle de Yahvé : Je mettrai ma loi en leur sein et sur leur cœur je l'écrirai, et je serai leur Dieu et ils seront mon peuple.

(v. 34) Ils n'auront plus à s'instruire, chacun son compagnon, ni chacun son frère en disant : « Connaissez Yahvé », car eux tous me connaîtront, du plus petit d'entre eux jusqu'au plus grand, oracle de Yahvé.
Car je pardonnerai leurs iniquités et de leurs péchés je ne me souviendrai plus. »

J'examinerai brièvement, de façon synthétique, ce texte en considérant d'abord les remarques de Jérémie sur ce qu'ont été jusqu'ici les relations de Yahvé et d'Israël et ensuite comment il envisage leur avenir.

En ce qui concerne le passé, Jérémie rappelle au v. 32 d'une part ce que Dieu a fait pour son peuple et de l'autre comment celui-ci a réagi à l'œuvre divine. La première partie du v. 32 est une sorte de « credo historique » de type particulier, où S. Hermann pense retrouver la marque deutéronomiste [36]. Le texte fait en effet mention de l'alliance

op. cit., p. 229 ; J. SCHREINER, *op. cit.*, p. 242 ; G. P. COUTURIER, *op. cit.*, *ad loc.*, etc. sont du même avis ; cf. déjà sur ce point : A. GELIN, *Le sens du mot « Israël » en Jérémie* XXX-XXXI, in *Memorial J. Chaine*, 1950, pp. 160ss.

36. S. HERRMANN, *op. cit.*, en particulier pp. 179ss. insiste sur la relation que Jér. 31,32 fait entre l'alliance et l'exode et également sur l'allusion aux pères et à

avec les pères plutôt que de la *b*^{e}*rit* sinaïtique et on sait combien la théologie deutéronomiste rapproche la conclusion d'un pacte entre Yahvé et Israël de la promesse faite aux patriarches ; ce même fragment relie directement l'alliance à l'intervention divine en Égypte, comme si celle-là devait achever et consacrer celle-ci. En un sens l'Exode est vu ici à travers la *b*^{e}*rit* [37].

En quelques mots Jérémie révèle le sort fait par Israël au lien établi ainsi par Yahvé. « Quant à eux ils rompirent mon alliance » (v. 32bα) et il ajoute « quoi que je fusse leur maître » (v. 32bβ) pour souligner l'énormité de la faute du peuple envers son Dieu. L'expression utilisée par le prophète évoque le message d'Osée, notamment les premiers chapitres, et une autre déclaration de Jérémie qui vise le royaume du nord [38], elle suggère que Yahvé est à la fois le maître et l'époux d'Israël, son seul Baal légitime [39].

Cette rétrospective du v. 32 révèle qu'au moment où Jérémie s'adresse à ses contemporains, l'histoire de Yahvé avec son peuple est comme suspendue, l'attitude d'Israël a provoqué une interruption dans les relations entre Dieu et les siens. L'œuvre divine est stoppée, mise en question apparemment anéantie. C'est cette situation qu'illustrent et confirment les événements de 587.

Baal. La mention du jour de la sortie d'Égypte se retrouve en Jér. 7,22 ; 11,4 ; 34,13.

37. On trouvera des indications bibliographiques sur la *b*^{e}*rit* et la théologie deutéronomiste dans E. Kutsch, *op. cit.* varia ; G. Fohrer, *Geschichte der israelitischen Religion*, Berlin, 1969, 301ss. et maintenant dans L. Perlitt, *Bundestheologie im Alten Testament* (*WMANT* 36) 1969.

38. On notera d'abord au v. 32b le contraste voulu entre « eux » et « moi », et ensuite, avec Mgr J. Coppens, *op. cit.*, p. 14 la difficulté de traduire ce fragment. Les versions suggèrent un autre verbe que בעלתי, peut être געלתי : Yahvé se serait désintéressé, dégoûté de son peuple. Si nous maintenons la version massorétique, on peut comprendre comme nous l'avons fait (cf. aussi BP « bien que je fusse leur maître ») ce qui indique qu'Israël a en quelque sorte rompu le lien conjugal qui l'unit à son maître et seigneur, plutôt que comme le veut Mgr J. Coppens « et, moi, j'ai dû sévir contre en époux » qui s'accorde avec BJ (« Alors, moi, je leur fis sentir ma maîtrise », qui ferait allusion aux mesures prises par Yahvé contre son peuple infidèle. H. Cazelles traduit en 3,14 une formule très proche par « car c'est moi qui ait été constitué votre maître » (*VT* 18 (1968) 158).

39. Il n'est pas nécessaire de voir avec S. Herrmann dans l'emploi de cette forme verbale un trait deutéronomiste ; par ailleurs on remarquera que l'auteur n'emploie pas les expressions « à main forte et à bras étendu » ou encore « à main forte » familières au milieu deutéronomiste (cf. Dt. 4,34 ; 5,15 ; 7,29 et 6,21 ; 7,8 ; 9,26 etc.) mais une formule moins stéréotypée « je les ai saisis par la main » qui indique l'acte libérateur de Yahvé, et non comme le veut A. Weiser un geste à connotation liturgique évoquant l'élection divine ; les textes signalés à ce sujet par A. Weiser, *ATD*, 1955, *ad loc.* (Ps. 73,23 ; Es. 41,10,13 ; 45,1 et 42,6) ne correspondent pas exactement à notre texte.

Le prophète envisage pour l'avenir une nouvelle intervention divine qu'il qualifie de *b^erît ḥadāshāh*. On notera d'abord, avec A. Weiser, le caractère théocentrique de la nouvelle alliance qui, due à une initiative unilatérale de Yahvé en faveur de son peuple, sera réalisée par lui et vise à unir définitivement Israël à son Dieu. Yahvé déclare en effet : « *Je* scellerai... *je* mettrai... *je* serai... *je* pardonnerai » ; il s'agit de *son* alliance et de *sa* loi, et le résultat de son action est ainsi défini : « Ils seront *mon* peuple... » et « Tous *me* connaîtront ». L'alliance jérémienne repose de bout en bout sur Dieu (v. 33-34).

La nouvelle *b^erit*, dans Jér. 31,31-34, forme un tout, elle est en même temps don d'une loi inscrite dans le cœur des fidèles, connaissance directe de Yahvé et pardon des péchés. Il faut commencer par prendre acte de cette dimension globale de l'œuvre accomplie par Dieu en faveur des siens sans en privilégier tel ou tel aspect. Dans un second moment certes, il est possible de discerner un certain enchaînement dans les dires du prophète : l'alliance à venir se fonde sur la rémission des fautes (v. 34b), elle continue par une transformation profonde des membres du peuple élu (v. 33) et débouche sur une connaissance authentique de Yahvé (v. 34a) [40].

La *b^erit* jérémienne est donc en premier lieu un acte de miséricorde de Dieu à l'égard des coupables, elle repose sur le pardon divin (v. 34b) [41]. Yahvé liquide d'un trait le passé sans attendre que son peuple manifeste son repentir en faisant un pas vers lui, comme le voudrait la tradition et notamment l'école deutéronomiste. Dieu commence par pardonner, il offre souverainement sa grâce qui crée une nouvelle possibilité de communion entre lui et Israël [42]. Yahvé peut dès lors intervenir à nouveau auprès de son peuple en imprimant sa loi en son sein.

Jér. 31,31ss. ne nous parle pas d'une simple réparation d'alliance comme on pourrait le penser ; le prophète n'envisage pas une pure restauration de la *b^erit* des pères. Il faut prendre au sérieux le terme *ḥadāshāh* qui dépeint l'alliance jérémienne : cet adjectif doit être compris

40. En général on attache une importance particulière au don de la loi intérieure annoncée au v. 33 comme étant l'élément le plus original de l'oracle de Jérémie, cependant il faut bien voir que ce point est lié aux deux autres avec lesquels il représente l'ensemble de la nouvelle démarche de Yahvé en faveur d'Israël. Il est d'ailleurs difficile, à propos de ce verset en particulier et du texte jérémien dans son ensemble, de faire abstraction de leurs relectures néotestamentaires et chrétiennes. Jérémie a envisagé ici autre chose que ce qu'un Juif de l'époque essénienne ou un théologien chrétien informé — et déformé — par plusieurs siècles de discussion sur la nouvelle alliance, peut entrevoir.

41. On notera avec L. KÖHLER (*KBL*, *ad loc.*) que le verbe employé ici a toujours Dieu comme sujet.

42. B. W. ANDERSON, *op. cit.*, p. 230 insiste sur le rôle important et différent des particules *Ki* dans cet oracle. Le dernier pourrait presque être traduit pour « Oui, je pardonnerai... »

dans un sens fort et ce n'est pas sans raison que la Septante a utilisé à son propos le qualificatif *kainos* plutôt que *neos* [43]. L'accent est mis ici sur la nouveauté de ce que Yahvé se propose de faire, dont il est déjà question dans un texte curieux et difficile du prophète (Jér. 31,22) et plus nettement encore dans le message du Second Esaïe [44].

Jérémie prend en effet ses distances par rapport à l'alliance du passé, comme le montre la double négation qui se trouve en tête des v. 32 et 34 (« Il n'en sera pas comme... » (v. 32), « Non, ils n'enseigneront plus... » (v. 34). La *b^erit* nouvelle est d'abord définie par opposition à celle des pères ; en premier lieu elle ne sera pas une alliance qu'on pourra rompre et qui donc échouera, et deuxièmement elle n'aura pas besoin comme la précédente de la médiation d'un enseignement. Positivement la déclaration de Jérémie signifie que la nouvelle alliance aboutira, puisque les Israélites auront en eux la loi divine et que tous, du plus petit au plus grand, connaîtront Yahvé pour le servir et s'attacher à lui.

La transformation opérée par Yahvé en faveur des siens concerne en effet l'ensemble du peuple élu ; l'aspect « individualiste » de la nouvelle alliance ne doit pas en masquer la face communautaire. Il s'agit pour Jérémie d'amener à l'obéissance non quelques individualités religieuses, mais Israël dans sa totalité (cf. v. 34 : « tous »).

La *b^erit* jérémienne est caractérisée par le fait que Dieu imprime sa volonté au sein d'Israël et le rend ainsi capable de suivre ses commandements ; il lui permet une fidélité en quelque sorte immédiate et spontanée. Cet élément de la déclaration prophétique a particulièrement retenu l'attention des commentateurs qui ont vu dans le geste de Yahvé gravant sa loi, non plus sur des tables de pierres comme au temps des pères (Ex. 24,12 ; 34,28s.) ou dans un « livre » comme aux jours de la réforme deutéronomiste, mais dans la réalité la plus intime des membres de son peuple, la grande nouveauté de la *b^erit* annoncée par Jérémie, son aspect quasi révolutionnaire [45].

Sans doute la décision divine à cet égard est-elle capitale ; elle change en un sens le statut de la loi, comme l'a remarqué P. Beauchamp, qui, de condition de la promesse, devient objet de la promesse ; elle fait de

43. Cf. à ce sujet les articles du ThWNT aux articles *καινός, νέος, παλαιός*. Il est vraiment curieux que l'expression *b^erīt hadāshāh* ne se rencontre qu'ici, dans ce texte de Jérémie, comme si le terme utilisé était trop fort et finalement incompatible avec la notion d'alliance. On s'est empressé d'accoler à celle-ci des qualificatifs moins dangereux comme *shālōm* ou *'ōlām*. Remarquons aussi que l'expression « ancienne alliance » ne se lit pas dans l'Ancien Testament, elle n'apparaît que dans 2 Cor. 3,14 (cf. cpdt. Héb. 8,13).

44. Th. M. Ludwig, *op. cit.*, 340s., insiste particulièrement sur les liens de Jér. 31,31 avec Jér. 31,22 et surtout avec le Second Esaïe.

45. Cf. par ex. Mgr J. Coppens, *op. cit.*, p. 17.

la thora un don [46]. Mais cet aspect de l'oracle de Jér. 31,31ss. qui bouleverse les conceptions habituelles d'Israël et notamment les vues deutéronomistes, ne doit pas être séparé de ce qui le précède, le pardon, et le suit, la pleine connaissance de Dieu.

Pour le reste Jérémie se montre beaucoup plus proche de la tradition. Son alliance met en présence les mêmes partenaires : Dieu et Israël ; elle se réfère à la même loi, déjà exposée au Sinaï ; elle poursuit le même but : unir Israël à Yahvé. « Les deux alliances sont identiques, sauf sur un point, à vrai dire décisif, celui des moyens utilisés par Dieu pour en assurer l'efficacité » [47]. Yahvé agit de telle sorte que son peuple infidèle lui devienne fidèle ; implantant sa loi dans le cœur des Israélites, il crée en eux l'amour qu'il réclame d'eux. La nouveauté de la *berit* jérémienne consiste donc dans la transformation profonde du vis-à-vis humain de Dieu, elle est donc d'ordre anthropologique, comme l'a noté G. von Rad [48], mais du même coup elle nous révèle jusqu'où Yahvé est capable d'aller dans sa *ḥesed* envers Israël. Elle a donc aussi un aspect théologique, puisqu'ici Jérémie rend compte de l'attachement de Dieu pour les siens en dépit de leur attitude passée et qu'il rejoint l'intuition fondamentale d'Osée que Yahvé ne manifeste jamais mieux sa sainteté que quand il fait grâce (Os. 11,9).

* * *

Il reste à dire quand Dieu scellera cette nouvelle alliance avec Israël. Les expressions utilisées dans Jér. 31,31ss. sont à la fois traditionnelles et vagues, elles peuvent être susceptibles de plusieurs interprétations.

L'une, « voici des jours viennent » (v. 31) se retrouve à plusieurs reprises dans le livre de Jérémie ; l'autre, « après ces jours » (v. 33) lui est sans doute équivalente bien qu'on les ait parfois opposées [49]. La déclaration prophétique vise une seule intervention divine qui se situe dans l'avenir.

46. Dans un cours donné à la faculté de théologie de Fourvière, Lyon, sur *Le Deutéroisaïe dans le cadre de l'alliance*, 1970, p. 39. On peut se demander si dans l'intention divine, la loi n'a pas toujours été comprise comme un don et que trop souvent le partenaire humain de Dieu en a fait une servitude.

47. R. Martin-Achard, *op. cit.*, p. 91.

48. *Op. cit.*, édit. all. p. 283, édit. fr., p. 232.

49. L'expression « Voici des jours viennent » se retrouvent en Jér. 7,32 ; 9,24 ; 16,14 ; 23,5,7 ; 30,3 ; 31,27,31,28 ; 33,14, etc. ; la formule « après ces jours-là » est curieuse, on s'attendrait plutôt à « en ces jours-là » ; peut-être le responsable du texte a-t-il consciemment ou non pensé à une autre tournure (dans la suite /la fin des jours באחרית הימים); W. Rudolph oppose dans son commentaire les jours mentionnés au v. 31 et ceux du v. 33 ; Mgr J. Coppens établit également une nuance entre les deux expressions ; les versions nous invitent cependant à estimer que l'auteur annonce de deux manières différentes qu'après la misère présente et dans un proche avenir Dieu interviendra en faveur d'Israël.

Ce futur ne saurait être lointain, eschatologique au sens étroit et étymologique du terme [50], puisque Jérémie entend répondre à un besoin immédiat ; il parle à et pour ses contemporains.

Puisque l'alliance avec les pères est rompue, et le temps comme suspendu pour Israël, vidé de sa substance, puisque l'existence du peuple élu ne repose plus sur rien, Jérémie lie le sort de ses frères non plus à un passé que l'attitude d'Israël a mis radicalement en question, mais à un lendemain qui est d'autant plus certain qu'il ne dépend pas d'une repentance aléatoire des Israélites, mais uniquement de la décision bienveillante que Yahvé a prise à leur égard. C'est donc pour sa génération que le prophète prononce la parole sur la nouvelle alliance, c'est à elle qu'il promet une *b^erit* fondée sur l'initiative unilatérale de Yahvé.

Telle est l'alliance dont il est question dans Jér. 31,31-34. En un sens elle demeure étroitement liée à la *b^erit* des pères, puisqu'elle la récupère et la confirme en la réalisant, mais elle ne peut se confondre avec elle, car elle réussit là où l'autre a échoué ; elle et elle seule permet au dessein divin de s'accomplir. Il faut donc distinguer les deux alliances dont parle Jérémie, mais non les opposer radicalement, car l'une ne se conçoit pas sans l'autre. On a souvent prononcé à propos de Jér. 31 les termes de continuité et de discontinuité, les commentateurs insistant selon leur tendance théologique sur l'un ou l'autre aspect de la déclaration du prophète. Il me semble que la discontinuité constatée sur le plan de l'histoire d'Israël (v. 32 : « eux ont rompu ») s'inscrit dans une volonté de continuité qui se trouve en Yahvé (v. 33s. : « je serai leur Dieu et ils seront mon peuple... tous me connaîtront »). Il va sans dire qu'au point de vue de la tradition biblique, celle-ci, la continuité, l'emporte sur celle-là, la discontinuité [51].

* * *

III. Il s'agit, dans une dernière partie, d'évoquer brièvement l'attitude des trois grands prophètes, qui ont vu la fin du royaume de Juda, envers l'avenir de la *b^erit* et de comparer leurs interventions sur ce point. C'est ici que les trois auteurs cités précédemment, Mgr J. Coppens, le P. Buis et le professeur S. Herrmann, vont encore nous rendre service.

50. E. ROHLAND parle d'eschatologie à propos de Jér. 31,31ss., ce que S. HERRMANN conteste, *op. cit,*. p. 202 ; de son côté B. W. ANDERSON approuve R. BULTMANN d'avoir souligné le caractère eschatologique de la nouvelle *b^erit* (*op. cit.*, p. 231). Il faudrait évidemment commencer par s'accorder sur une définition de l'eschatologie.

51. B. W. ANDERSON insiste également sur la continuité et la discontinuité de deux alliances, selon Jér. 31,31ss. (*op. cit.*, pp. 238s. et 242). Ne retrouve-t-on pas dans Rom. 9-11 la même problématique et la même solution à la question posée par l'attitude du peuple de Dieu vis-à-vis du plan divin ?

Il n'est pas aisé de situer respectivement les déclarations de Jérémie, d'Ezéchiel et du Second Esaïe sur les relations futures de Yahvé avec son peuple. En effet ceux-ci appartiennent sensiblement à la même époque et se trouvent placés devant des problèmes semblables. On ne s'étonnera donc pas de constater que leurs prises de position offrent plus d'un point commun. Mais surtout leurs oracles nous ont été transmis par leurs disciples qui les ont tout naturellement complétés en tenant compte d'une certaine tradition qui s'est constituée sur le sort futur d'Israël ; il est donc vraisemblable qu'il s'est produit plusieurs interférences durant ce travail de relectures de sorte qu'il n'est pas toujours possible de distinguer de qui revient à l'un ou à l'autre prophète. Le P. Buis a parfaitement noté que les oracles de ce temps s'accordent sur de nombreux points et plusieurs commentateurs parlent d'une façon très générale du thème de la nouvelle alliance attesté, selon eux, aussi bien chez Ezéchiel et le Second Esaïe que chez Jérémie [52].

Mais l'intervention des écoles prophétiques ne doit pas empêcher de relever les traits principaux et caractéristiques du message de chacun d'entre eux relatif au régime du peuple élu au lendemain de 587. C'est du moins ce que je vais tenter de faire en reconnaissant qu'il reste dans cette comparaison une part d'hypothèse, puisque nos sources sont composites [53].

* * *

Ezéchiel ne me paraît pas avoir accordé une place centrale à l'alliance dans ses vues prospectives. Certes le terme de *b^erit* se rencontre 18 fois dans son livre, mais trois textes seulement méritent d'être pris en considération pour cette enquête, et il n'est pas certain qu'ils soient l'œuvre du prophète lui-même.

Dans Ez. 16, Ezéchiel médite sur les relations de Yahvé avec Sion, il reprend à cette occasion le symbolisme conjugal déjà utilisé par Osée, puis par Jérémie. Un paragraphe final, et complémentaire, annonce au terme de ce long chapitre le rétablissement de l'alliance entre Yahvé et Jérusalem, ce qui aura pour résultat de conduire la coupable à prendre

52. A côté du travail du P. Buis, rappelons l'étude extrêmement fouillée et documentée de O. Garcia de la Fuente OSA, signalée à la note 5. Remarquons que si ce dernier souligne les points de contact entre Jérémie et Ezéchiel, Th. M. Ludwig, *op. cit.*, note 5 rapproche notre passage des déclarations du Second Esaïe. S'il est juste d'indiquer les vues communes des prophètes du temps de l'exil sur l'avenir du peuple de Yahvé, il est aussi nécessaire de relever la spécificité de chacun de leurs messages.

53. Dans cette brève enquête il ne peut être question d'examiner tous les problèmes exégétiques soulevés par les textes mentionnés ; on se reportera aux commentaires.

conscience de ses fautes et à reconnaître enfin la seigneurie de Yahvé (v. 59-63).

La *b^erit* n'apparaît pas vraiment nouvelle ici (v. 60,62). Le prophète envisage plutôt le rétablissement de l'ancien et unique lien qui unit la cité à son Dieu, et son existence future repose sur le souvenir que Yahvé garde de la première et définitive décision qu'il a prise en faveur de Jérusalem. La *b^erit* est donc qualifiée de *'ōlām* pour souligner son caractère infrangible ; elle ne peut être remise en question [54].

Nous lisons dans Ez. 34 une péricope (v. 25-30) qui offre des analogies souvent relevées avec Lv. 26, et peut être détachée de son contexte. Le prophète annonce ici la conclusion d'une alliance particulière avec les animaux sauvages au bénéfice d'Israël. Il ne s'agit pas d'une *b^erit* entre Yahvé et son peuple, mais d'une intervention divine destinée à assurer la sécurité des Israélites. La même idée est déjà exprimée par Osée (Os. 2,20) et il n'est pas étonnant de constater que l'alliance est appelée dans ce texte *b^erīt shālōm*, alliance de paix (v. 25). Le péricope indique que Dieu se révèle d'abord comme le garant de l'existence d'Israël avant de combler celui-ci de ses bénédictions.

Un fragment du chapitre 37 contient une sorte de compendium des promesses d'avenir pour Israël (v. 24b-28). Il y est question d'obéissance aux lois divines, de réinstallation en Terre promise, du renouveau de la dynastie davidique, etc. Le mot *b^erit* apparaît ici à deux reprises, accompagné des qualificatifs de *shālōm* et de *'ōlām* déjà rencontrés précédemment (v. 26, cf. 16,60 et 34,25). Le terme de *'ōlām* n'est pas moins utilisé de cinq fois dans ce court passage, il révèle la préoccupation majeure de son auteur. Il s'agit qu'Israël puisse compter sur un statut sûr, définitif, irrévocable.

Or ce souci de la permanence, de la continuité, de l'indéfectibilité est particulièrement attesté dans la tradition sacerdotale, et notamment dans les passages où l'auteur de P insiste sur le caractère décisif et éternel des dispositions prises par Dieu envers l'humanité (par ex. Gn., 9,16 à propos de la *b^erit* noachique) ou vis-à-vis d'Abraham et de sa descendance (ainsi Gn. 17,7,19 à propos de l'alliance abrahamique). Ezéchiel partage avec le clergé le désir de voir Yahvé accorder à son peuple un statut que rien ne puisse remettre en question.

De ce rapide tour d'horizon sur les perspectives d'Ezéchiel relatives à l'avenir de la *b^erit*, on conclura que le prophète n'attache pas une importance spécifique à une initiative divine concernant une nouvelle alliance ; ses vues sur la *b^erit* appartiennent à la tradition et notamment

54. On notera l'emploi des verbes *zākar* et *qūm*, qui, comme P. A. H. de Boer l'a montré dans une étude qui précède à propos de Gn. 9, impliquent qu'il ne s'agit pas tant d'instaurer un statut nouveau que de maintenir en vigueur une réalité déjà existante.

à la tradition sacerdotale. Il n'est pas surprenant dans ce cas qu'Ezéchiel n'emploie pas, à notre connaissance tout au moins, l'expression *b^e^rīt ḥadāsāh.*

Sur un point le prophète est plus original et bien qu'il ait pu connaître les déclarations de Jérémie — G. von Rad pense qu'Ezéchiel a dû lire le texte de son prédécesseur ! — il va plus loin dans la précision quand il évoque la transformation intérieure que Dieu opérera au sein des Israélites (cf. notamment Ez. 36,24ss.) [55]. Ezéchiel semble s'être surtout préoccupé de l'action interne et profonde que Yahvé doit accomplir, il revient selon le témoignage de son livre à plusieurs reprises sur ce point dans Ez. 11,19 ; 18,31 et surtout dans Ez. 36,26s. Dans ce dernier passage, qui n'est pas sans rappeler le psaume 51, le prophète parle du don d'un cœur nouveau et d'un esprit nouveau, et il précise que le cœur de pierre deviendra un cœur de chair c.-à-d. que l'homme rebelle et obstiné sera désormais souple et docile, ou encore que Yahvé animera de son souffle son peuple pour lui permettre de vivre selon ses lois. Ce que Dieu attend encore des siens, selon Ez. 18, il l'accorde aux exilés de 597 d'après Ez. 11, il le confère aux rescapés de 587 dans Ez. 36.

La nouveauté de l'œuvre divine consiste ici non dans la conclusion d'une alliance, mais dans la transformation intérieure et profonde du partenaire humain de Yahvé. Ezéchiel s'intéresse particulièrement à l'aspect anthropologique de l'action future de Dieu, et la minutie avec laquelle il en parle dérive probablement de sa formation sacerdotale. Il importe en effet au prêtre que ceux qui se présentent devant Yahvé pour lui rendre un culte soient non seulement purifiés de leurs fautes passées, mais encore rendus totalement aptes, par le don d'un cœur nouveau et d'un esprit nouveau, à rencontrer le Dieu saint.

Des remarques que je viens de faire, on peut conclure que si Ezéchiel est à certains égards proche de son prédécesseur, on ne retrouve pas chez lui une déclaration sur la nouvelle alliance dans le style de Jér. 31,31ss.

* * *

Le Second Esaïe a peu parlé de la *b^e^rit*. Il en est question quatre fois dans les chapitres 40-55, et ces mentions présentent des traits particuliers.

En Es. 54,10, le prophète de l'exil rapproche l'alliance de paix qui unit Yahvé à Israël de la tradition noachique ; il veut assurer ses contemporains que Dieu leur porte un amour inébranlable. Sa préoccupation n'est pas sans rappeler celle d'Ezéchiel et il est significatif que nous lisions dans la péricope d'Es. 54,1-10 les termes de *'ōlām* (v. 8) et de *shālōm* (v. 10) comme dans certaines déclarations d'Ezéchiel. Pour

55. G. von Rad, *op. cit.*, édit. all. p. 249 (227) ; édit. fr. p. 203 (185).

persuader ses frères que la décision divine en leur faveur est définitive, le prophète évoque l'époque de Noé et le serment que Yahvé a alors prononcé. Dieu ne s'irritera plus jamais contre les siens de même qu'il a promis de ne plus permettre aux eaux de ravager la terre (v. 9). Israël peut donc compter absolument sur la bienveillance de Yahvé à son égard : les événements qui ont signifié une mise en question radicale du cosmos (le déluge) et d'Israël (la chute de Jérusalem) ne se reproduiront pas.

C'est à l'alliance noachique, avec le serment qui l'accompagne (Gn. 9,8ss., cf. aussi Gn. 8,20ss.) que le Deutéroésaïe se réfère quand il se porte garant devant son peuple de l'avenir des relations de celui-ci avec Dieu.

Selon Es. 55,3, Yahvé a l'intention de conclure pour les siens une alliance « éternelle ». Le prophète ne fait pas cette fois allusion à la *b^e^rit* noachique, il ne se rapporte pas davantage à l'alliance sinaïtique, mais il établit un lien étroit entre l'intervention future de Dieu et David (v. 3). L'expression utilisée par le Second Esaïe a été l'objet d'interprétations divergentes, mais il ne fait pas de doute que le prophète applique ici à son peuple ce qui est dit généralement du grand roi [56]. On assiste à une sorte de démocratisation de la *b^e^rit* davidique : Israël hérite de ses privilèges (v. 3) et de sa mission (v. 4-5). Le fait que le Deutéroésaïe qualifie l'alliance de *'ōlām* est une manière de rappeler l'ancienneté du lien qui unit la maison de David à Yahvé et la promesse faite au roi (cf. avec 2 Sam. 7, 2 Sam., 23,5 ; Ps. 89,27ss.), qui sont autant de gages donnés maintenant aux rescapés de 587.

On notera que dans ce passage le prophète fonde ses vues sur l'avenir d'Israël sur la tradition davidique ; l'alliance dont il est ici question n'est pas à proprement parler nouvelle, elle consiste plutôt dans une extension de la *b^e^rit* davidique.

Enfin nous lisons dans Es. 42,6 et 49,8 une expression curieuse *b^e^rīt 'ām* qui a donné lieu à de multiples discussions parmi les exégètes, comme le souligne un récent article de J. J. Stamm [57]. Je ne puis ici aborder tous les problèmes soulevés par ces deux textes qui appartiennent, selon l'opinion la plus courante, aux cantiques du Serviteur ; je signale que *b^e^rīt 'ām* est mis en relations avec une autre formule *'ōr gōyim* (cf. Es. 42,6 dont la tradition textuelle est incertaine, et Es.

56. On comparera les diverses traductions de ce verset (Es. 55,3) qui a donné lieu à des interprétations contradictoires, comme l'attestent par ex. l'étude de O. EISSFELDT, The Promises of Grace to David in Isaiah 55,1-5, dans *Israel's Prophetic Heritage, Essays in honor of J. Muilenburg*, New York, 1962, pp. 196-207 et celle de A. CAQUOT, Les « grâces de David ». A propos d'Isaïe 55,3b, *Semitica*, 15 (1965) 45-59.

57. J. J. STAMM, B^e^rît 'am bei Deuterojesaja, dans *Probleme biblischer Theologie, G. von Rad zum 70. Geburtstag*, München, 1971, pp. 510-524.

49,6,8). Certains pensent que ces deux tournures concernent la même vocation du Serviteur à l'égard du monde païen ; d'autres estiment, et je pense qu'ils ont raison, que *b^erīt ʿām* vise un aspect de l'activité de l'Ebed, et *ʾōr gōyim* un autre, car il semble, d'après d'autres passages, que la vocation du Serviteur soit double : elle intéresse aussi bien Israël que les nations. Dans ce cas un des rôles de l'Ebed est d'éclairer l'humanité et sa raison d'être vis-à-vis des exilés est définie par *b^erit ʾām*. Le Serviteur permettrait aux siens de se reconstituer comme peuple en assumant une fonction médiatrice ; en quelque sorte il assurerait une sorte de *b^erīt* avec Israël pour permettre à celui-ci d'être à nouveau le peuple de l'alliance ! Il y aurait peut-être ici une allusion à la *b^erit* sinaïtique et à la fonction de type mosaïque dévolue au Serviteur [58]. Il reste que cette interprétation demeure hypothétique compte tenu des multiples difficultés que nous offrent ces textes du Deutéroésaïe.

Mais on remarquera de toutes façons la liberté avec laquelle le Second Esaïe reprend le thème de l'alliance et le peu de place qu'il paraît accorder au problème de l'avenir du lien sinaïtique. Ses perspectives de salut se réfèrent plutôt aux données relatives à l'élection d'Israël qu'à celle de la *b^erit* des pères ; par contre le prophète n'hésite pas à faire appel aux traditions noachique et davidique pour assurer ses contemporains qu'Israël peut compter sur un statut futur qui peut être qualifié de *shālōm* et de *ʿōlām*.

Le prophète anonyme dit à sa manière ce que ses prédécesseurs Jérémie et Ezéchiel ont jugé important de proclamer, encore qu'il se différencie d'eux sur un point essentiel : il ne se préoccupe guère de l'aspect anthropologique de la *b^erit* ; son attention est tout entière dirigée vers ce que Yahvé fera, directement ou par l'intermédiaire de son Serviteur, en faveur des exilés. On ne trouve pas chez lui d'allusion à l'impression de la loi divine au sein des Israélites, ni d'annonce de la transformation des cœurs : l'essentiel, pour le Second Esaïe, demeure l'activité divine accomplie en un sens en dehors d'Israël, mais finalement pour lui.

On conclura de cette enquête que chez le Second Esaïe également, comme chez Ezéchiel, le thème de la nouvelle alliance n'a pas la signification que lui reconnaît Jérémie.

* * *

Des textes où Jérémie annonce à son peuple une possibilité de vivre au-delà du jugement, Jér. 31,31-34 me paraît le plus particulier et le plus percutant. Même une péricope comme celle qu'a étudiée le P. Buis,

58. Sur la relation entre le Serviteur et Moïse, cf. par ex. G. von Rad, *op. cit.*, édit. all. pp. 273s. ; édit. fr. pp. 224s.

Jér. 32,37-41, ne présente ni la même netteté, ni la même originalité que notre passage et pourrait être l'œuvre d'un disciple influencé à la fois par Jérémie et par Ezéchiel.

Mgr J. Coppens a dit la spécificité de la déclaration jérémienne sur la nouvelle alliance et S. Herrmann a montré les liens de ce texte avec la tradition deutéronomiste. Je crois que ces deux remarques doivent être retenues pour comprendre les particularités de Jér. 31,31-34. Je vois en effet dans cet oracle sur le *b^{e}rīt ḥadāshāh* une réponse du prophète aux vues deutéronomistes.

On sait qu'il est difficile de situer exactement l'attitude de Jérémie envers la réforme deutéronomiste. Le prophète ne s'est guère prononcé à son sujet. On pense parfois qu'il a d'abord salué favorablement le mouvement réformateur dont il se serait ensuite distancé.

Il a pu en tous les cas constater son échec. Ce qui a été tenté au temps de Josias n'a pas abouti et a peut-être même bercé le peuple dans l'illusion qu'il était en règle avec son Dieu (cf. Jér. 7). La réforme loin de contribuer à rapprocher Israël de Yahvé l'a plutôt endurci contre lui. Jérémie sait qu'il peut compter de moins en moins sur une repentance de ses contemporains ; le salut ne viendra pas d'une conversion de Jérusalem que la théologie officielle réclame encore. Israël est incapable de faire le geste qui le sauverait, comme un Éthiopien de changer sa peau et un léopard d'enlever ses tâches (Jér. 13,23). Il ne reste au prophète qu'à dénoncer les péchés de Juda et à le préparer au jugement qui l'attend. Jérémie prêche la catastrophe et invite Jérusalem à reconnaître dans Nébucadnetsar l'instrument de la colère de Yahvé contre elle.

Au milieu du désastre, à un moment qu'il n'est pas possible de préciser, Jérémie découvre dans une intuition bouleversante, comme jadis Osée au milieu de son drame personnel, et plus tard Ezéchiel, mais dans un style tout différent, que Dieu fera ce que son peuple n'a pas pu faire, ou mieux que Yahvé interviendra de telle sorte qu'Israël devienne enfin ce que depuis toujours il a été appelé à être.

La nouvelle alliance de Jérémie est la réponse du prophète à l'échec de la réforme deutéronomiste.

Alors s'expliquent à la fois l'accent théocentrique de notre oracle, le contraste que Jérémie souligne entre la *b^{e}rit* qu'il annonce et l'alliance des pères que le mouvement deutéronomiste a vainement essayé de sauver, la proclamation presque révolutionnaire que la thora, au lieu d'être présentée au peuple sur des pierres ou dans un document écrit, mais toujours comme une réalité extérieure, sera imprimée dans le cœur des Israélites (v. 33) et encore l'affirmation qu'Israël n'aura plus besoin d'être enseigné, alors que la réformiste suppose un intense effort de propagande dont le Deutéronome est le reflet, lui qui insiste précisément sur la nécessité que, génération après génération, Israël soit instruit dans la tradition (cf. par ex. Dt. 6) (v. 34).

Jérémie répond ici à la tentative avortée des deutéronomistes de faire marcher le peuple élu dans la voie que Yahvé lui a prescrite. Il présente une solution tout autre d'un problème qui, après l'échec de la réforme, devient insoluble ; il fait appel à Dieu pour le résoudre. Sans doute le prophète d'Anatot suit-il ici l'exemple d'Osée et on a souvent dit les rapports entre celui-ci et Jérémie. Mais ce dernier ne peut se contenter de répéter ce qu'a dit son prédécesseur, il vit à une autre époque et la situation qui est la sienne est différente ; il doit en particulier tenir compte de la théologie deutéronomiste ; il lui faut donc en un sens inventer une nouvelle solution à la question de l'avenir des relations entre Yahvé et Israël. C'est alors qu'il opère un renversement dans les perspectives traditionnelles en laissant à Dieu le soin de faire le salut de son peuple, et tandis qu'à vues humaines il ne reste aucun espoir à Juda, il proclame que Yahvé lui-même créera les conditions nécessaires au sein d'Israël pour que celui-ci vive de sa communion.

Jérémie agit ici de la même manière que le fera plus tard l'apôtre Paul quand, au lendemain de la mort du Christ, il bouleversera les données habituelles des théologiens de son temps sur les rapports entre Dieu et sa créature.

Contre ceux qui ont tendance à gommer la spécificité de Jér. 31,31-34, il faut souligner, avec Mgr J. Coppens, l'originalité de l'oracle que nous devons au prophète d'Anatot, dont l'actualité, confirmée par l'Évangile, me paraît évidente.

R. MARTIN-ACHARD

See *Supplementary note*, p. 218.

10

ALTTESTAMENTLICHE WEISHEIT IN CHRISTLICHER THEOLOGIE?

I

Innerhalb der fortschreitenden Erarbeitung des Werkes von Dietrich Bonhoeffer ist die Frage, was er mit der nicht-religiösen Interpretation biblischer Begriffe wirklich gemeint habe, nach wie vor umstritten. [1] In die Diskussion um die Entchifferung dieser von Bonhoeffer nicht mehr ausgeführten Formel hat sich kürzlich Martin Kuske eingeschaltet. In einer Rostocker Dissertation handelt er über „*Das Alte Testament als Buch von Christus. Dietrich Bonhoeffers Wertung und Auslegung des Alten Testaments*“. [2] Im letzten Teil dieses Buchs fragt Kuske unter der Überschrift „Der Beitrag des Alten Testaments für ein Verstehen der Aussagen Bonhoeffers über die ‚Mündige Welt‘“ nach dem, was aus Bonhoeffers Umgang mit dem Alten Testament nicht zeitgebunden war, sondern auch für uns heute übernehmbar ist. Hierbei möchte Kuske untersuchen, ob die Aussagen Bonhoeffers in seinen berühmten letzten Briefen zum Thema „Welt“ durch die Schrift gedeckt sind. Nachdem mehrere Erwägungen zu Bonhoeffers Sicht des Alten Testaments angestellt worden sind, kommt Kuske schließlich (S. 119) — hierbei Hans Schmidt folgend [3] — bei der Erörterung des Begriffs „Mündige Welt“ zu der überraschenden Frage, ob Bonhoeffers Gedanken über diese „Mündige Welt“ unter anderem nicht von der alttestamentlichen Weisheitsliteratur her zu verstehen seien. Wegen und bei dieser Sicht der Dinge hat nun Hans Schmidt Bonhoeffer eine Verleugnung der Geschichte vorgeworfen und geschrieben: „Bei seinem Versuch, eine

1. Zu dieser Diskussion vgl. die bei KUSKE (s. die folgende Anm.) auf S. 111ff. verarbeitete und auf S. 137 zusammengestellte Lit.; dazu neuerdings E. FEIL, *Die Theologie Dietrich Bonhoeffers*, ²München, 1971, 223ff., dort auch weitere Lit.

2. Berlin und Göttingen, 1971.

3. H. SCHMIDT, *Das Kreuz der Wirklichkeit? Einige Fragen zur Bonhoeffer-Interpretation*, in: *Mündige Welt* IV, München, 1963, 79-108; die Zitate dort S. 100 und 107, bei KUSKE S. 120. — Zu SCHMIDT auch R. SCHULZE, *Hauptlinien der Bonhoeffer-Interpretation*, EvTh 25 (1965) 681-700 (besonders 696-698) und FEIL, a.a.O., 206f. und 372; vgl. weiter auch *Glaube und Weltlichkeit bei Dietrich Bonhoeffer* (ed. P. A. H. NEUMANN), Stuttgart 1969.

religionslose Welt für das Gottesreich in Anspruch zu nehmen, kam Bonhoeffer auf den ‚heilsgeschichtslosen universalen Jahweglauben' der israelitischen Weisheit und auf deren ‚Pathos des Erkennens' zurück", wobei Schmidt bei dieser Charakterisierung der Weisheit Worte Gerhard von Rad's aufnimmt [4] und betreffs Bonhoeffer meint, er entdecke nun „das in sich selbst bereits ungeschichtliche Weltbewußtsein spätjüdischer Weisheit, nicht aber das von Jesus vollendete Geschichtsverständnis der Landverheißung des Alten Bundes und der prophetischen Geschichtszeugnisse."

An diesem hier kurz skizzierten Sachverhalt ist einerseits erstens interessant, daß man die Weisheitsliteratur wieder einmal glaubt heranziehen zu können, um einen Trend heutiger Theologie — wenn auch hier gegenüber Bonhoeffer kritisch — unterbauen zu können. Auch Götz Harbsmeier meinte, daß Bonhoeffer bei der nicht-religiösen Interpretation letztlich „eine Sache der Weisheit" im Blick gehabt habe. [5] Andererseits ist bemerkenswert, was Kuske zu diesem Interpretationsversuch Bonhoeffers durch H. Schmidt sagt [6]: „Dem Versuch... ist jedoch zu widersprechen. Das Heranziehen der spätisraelitischen Weisheit zur Erläuterung von Bonhoeffers Aussagen über die ‚Mündige Welt' ist von vornherein suspekt, weil hier das Alte Testament in einer Bonhoeffer nicht gemäßen Weise benutzt wird... Das heißt vor allem: Man kann nicht an Jesus Christus vorbei ins Alte Testament greifen... Durch Jesus Christus hindurch müssen wir den entsprechenden alttestamentlichen Gesprächspartner suchen..." Das Alte Testament ist vom Menschgewordenen, Gekreuzigten und Auferstandenen her zu lesen. Hier aber sind es dann die Propheten, nicht die Weisheit, und die Propheten sonderlich mit ihrer Gerichtsbotschaft, die einen Partner abgeben können im Gespräch zwischen Jesus Christus und der Welt, „den Bonhoeffers Wertung und Auslegung des Alten Testaments im Blick auf die ‚mündige Welt' allein zuläßt." [7]

Den Streit um eine rechte Bonhoeffer-Interpretation hier beiseite lassend, bleibt als zweites festzuhalten, daß nach der Argumentation von Kuske das Geschichtsverständnis der Propheten und das der Weisheit nicht deckungsgleich sind und eines gegen das andere abgewertet wird, daß außerdem Weisheit des Alten Testaments und Christusgeschehen des Neuen Testaments nicht zusammenzubringen sind. [8]

Die Weisheitsliteratur wird hier entdeckt, um bestimmte Probleme heutiger theologischer Existenz und heutigen theologischen Denkens

4. Vgl. ders., *Theologie des A.T.*, Bd. I, 444; II 319. — SCHMIDT verweist auch (99f.) auf I, 321,415,432,438,447ff.
5. *Mündige Welt* II, München, 1956, 89ff. (vgl. bei KUSKE, 120).
6. A.a.O., 121.
7. A.a.O., 122.
8. Vgl. a.a.O., 128ff.

beleuchten oder gar lösen zu helfen. Sie wird aber auch kritisiert, da sie zur Christusoffenbarung in Spannung steht. Schauen wir in diese Probleme noch an anderer Stelle hinein.

Friedemann Merkel hat 1966 über „*Die Predigt weisheitlicher Texte als hermeneutisches Problem*" gehandelt [9] und dabei in *der* Weise auf die Weisheitsliteratur zurückgegriffen und hingewiesen, daß sie als Lebenshilfe, als christliche Kunst das Leben zu meistern anzusehen und zu predigen sei. Auch Erhard Gerstenberger fordert [10] „theologische Gleichberechtigung" für die Weisheitsliteratur, zumal die „Flut der Offenbarungs- und Geschichtstheologie verebbe", was er offensichtlich begrüßt und für notwendig hält. Auch Hans Heinrich Schmid möchte [11] vom heilsgeschichtlich-linearen Verständnis von Geschichte, wie es außerhalb der Weisheit im Alten Testament vorliege, wegkommen, um hinzuführen zur Geschichte als Geschichtlichkeit, wie sie sich in der Weisheit als Welt und Sprachlichkeit der Wirklichkeit zeige und erneut geschichtlich werden wolle. [12] Die Weisheit gibt zwar die Möglichkeit, durch ihre Herausstellung des Tun-Ergehen-Zusammenhangs ‚a-theistisch' von Gott zu reden, da sie Gott als Schöpfer und Erhalter zeige, ohne ihn stets zu nennen oder nennen zu müssen. Hier wird die Vernunft ins Werk gebracht und in Funktion gesetzt, da Gott hier ohne Offenbarung erkennbar sei, was besonders für die Ethik von Bedeutung ist. Allgemein-Menschliches begegnet in der Weisheit als Wort Gottes, und dieses sei Erfahrung aus der Empirie, sei die Verstehensbewegung, welche die Wirklichkeit als Sprachlichkeit erfaßt und so hermeneutische Funktion im Verstehen von Welt habe. Als Weiterführung dieser Problematik vergleiche man Schmid's Aufsatz über „Amos. Zur Frage nach seiner ‚geistigen Heimat'", wo die Folgerungen und Folgen dieser Sicht noch deutlicher werden. [13]

So häufen sich in neuerer Zeit die Bemühungen, der alttestamentlichen Weisheitsliteratur einen nicht nur legitimen, sondern auch notwendigen und wesentlichen Ort innerhalb der alttestamentlichen und sogar auch der christlichen Theologie anzuweisen [14]. Gerhard von Rad stellte direkt die Frage, „warum denn der christliche Glaube nicht in ähnlicher

9. ThViat 10 (1965/66) Berlin 1966, 196-212. — Zum folgenden vgl. meinen Aufsatz „*Erwägungen zum theologischen Ort alttestamentlicher Weisheitsliteratur*", EvTh 30 (1970) 393-417; dort auch weitere Lit.

10. *Zur alttestamentlichen Weisheit*, VuF 14 (1969), 28-44; vgl. schon ders., *Wesen und Herkunft des „apodiktischen Rechts" im Alten Testament* (WMANT 20), Neukirchen 1965, 147f.

11. *Wesen und Geschichte der Weisheit* (BZAW 101), Berlin 1966, 80-82.

12. Vgl. a.a.O., 199f.

13. WuD NF 10, Bethel 1969, 85-103; sehe auch ZThK 70 (1973) 1-19.

14. Vgl. weiter dazu (mit Lit.) EvTh 30, 1970, 412-417.

Weise solche Lebenshilfe anzubieten hat " [15], zumal hier auf theologische Begründungen, die der Empfänger auch nicht erwarte, ganz verzichtet werden könnte. Welchen Stellenwert soll dieser Verzicht wohl haben ? Man wird — wenn auch nicht sofort bei von Rad, so doch bei anderen der zitierten Äußerungen — den Verdacht nicht los, daß hier auf etwas verzichtet werden soll, was man der heutigen Zeit und Welt (und damit sich selbst) nicht mehr ‚ zumuten ' möchte. Christus und sein Kreuz scheinen dem viel zitierten Menschen von heute erspart werden zu sollen. Die Theologie wird weltförmig, will modern und vernunftgemäß sein und werden. James L. Crenshaw hat darauf hingewiesen, daß hier עֵצָה über דָּבָר oder gar an seine Stelle gerückt werden soll. [16] Da man nicht mehr sagen könne und wolle ,, So spricht der Herr ", ziehe man sich aus der zu anspruchvollen prophetischen Vollmacht auf das weisheitliche ,, Höre mein Sohn die Weisung deines Vaters " zurück. [17] Wird hier nun damit die Autorität des göttlichen Anspruchs im Wort nur verlagert oder preisgegeben ? Oder ist Gottes Wort hier wie dort nichts anderes als Menschenwort ?

Wenn hier Klarheit geschaffen werden soll, ist nach dem Selbstverständnis der israelitischen Weisheit zu fragen und zu untersuchen, wie dieses in der heutigen alttestamentlichen Wissenschaft gesehen und aufgenommen wird.

II

Verzichtet die altisraelitische Weisheitsliteraur bei ihren Lebensratschlägen wirklich auf theologische Begründung in Mahnung und Sentenz ? Meint man, dies nicht bejahen zu können, ist die der Weisheit zu Grunde liegende theologische Anschauung aufzuspüren und nach deren Verhältnis zur Christusoffenbarung zu fragen, wenn anders der Alttestamentler sich als christlicher Theologe versteht. [18]

a) Die altisraelitische Weisheitsliteratur ist in ihren ältesten Texten (d.h. in Spr. 10-31, wobei auf eine genauere Differenzierung in der Datierung einzelner Untersammlungen hier verzichtet werden kann) durch ihr Verhaftetsein an das Denken im Tun-Ergehen-Zusammenhang

15. *Christliche Weisheit ?* in *125 Jahre Christian Kaiser Verlag*, München, 1970, 60-65 (dort S. 60) ; jetzt auch in : *Ges. Studien* II, 1973, 267ff.

16. *Prophetic Conflict* (BZAW 124), Berlin, New York, 1971, 116ff., besonders 122.

17. ZAW 82, 1970, 395 ; vgl. ders., *Prophetic Conflict*, 116. — Vgl. auch R. B. Y. Scott, *The Way of Wisdom in the O.T.*, New York, 1971, Kap. 1.

18. Vgl. dazu : *Das Alte Testament im Rahmen der Theologie als kirchlicher Wissenschaft*, DPfrBl 72 (1972, Nr. 11) 356-360.

als dem Prinzip der Weltordnung geprägt. [19] Selbst wenn Einzelsprüche aus diesen Sammlungen als allgemeine Lebensweisheit verstanden werden können, so geht es insgesamt doch stets letztlich darum, diese Welt auf ihre „ Weltordnung " abzutasten, diese zu erkennen, zu formulieren und zu tradieren. Kosmische wie ethische Lebensordnungen werden gesucht, und wenn die Einzelsprüche deren verschiedene Aspekte zu fixieren suchen, so wollen sie jeweils einen Teilbereich dieser Welt, damit aber ein Stück ihrer Gesamtordnung erfassen, somit aber zugleich die Welt als Ordnung insgesamt verstehen lernen bzw. lehren. Weisheit hat damit per se den Drang zum System in sich, zum Dogma, und der Zug zur Systematisierung ist keineswegs in ihr erst ein zweiter oder gar ein die ursprüngliche Weisheit entstellender Schritt. [20] Dem Guten wird es gut ergehen, dem Bösen ebenso folgerichtig schlecht. Diese Weltordnung glaubt die Weisheit erkennen, ihr gemäß leben und damit erfolgreich sein zu können. Sie ist ihrem Ansatz und Ziel entsprechend optimistisch und sieht diese Welt als eine prinzipiell heile an. [21] Es sind nicht wenige Texte innerhalb der Proverbien, die diese Weltschau expressis verbis ausdrücken [22], und die Vielzahl der einschlägigen Belege macht hierbei offenkundig, daß es sich bei dem Tun-Ergehen-Zusammenhang, bei der These von der „ Gerechtigkeit als Weltordnung " [23] nicht um ein Randphänomen in der israelitischen Weisheit handelt, zumal auch die Weisheitsliteratur der Umwelt Israels, aus der Israel nachweislich Texte entlehnt hat, diesem Denken und Glauben verhaftet war. Dieses allgemeine Prinzip hinter und in den Weisheitstexten nicht sehen zu wollen bzw. auf diese aufdeckende Hinterfragung glauben verzichten zu können [24], verkennt die Weisheit in ihrer Grundstruktur. Sie will keineswegs nur eine Zusammenstellung freundlicher Lebensregeln und Alltagshilfen sein und bieten, sondern versucht die Welt als Ordnung zu verstehen, zu vermitteln und wieder neu zu gestalten, in der ein Zusammenhang von Tun und Ergehen waltet.

Nun könnte man natürlich schon hier einwenden, ob nicht ein solches Denken, das ja nicht untheologisch sein will und mit Säkularisierung nichts zu tun hat, als eine Art „ horizontale Offenbarung " verstehbar ist [25], womit diese Erfahrungen der Weisheit zur Offenbarung gemacht

19. Dazu genauer EvTh 30 (1970) 396ff. (mit Lit.).

20. Gegen H. H. SCHMID, *Wesen und Geschichte der Weisheit*, 196 und öfter.

21. Vgl. G. FOHRER, ThZ 26 (1970) 15.

22. Spr. 10,2.4.6.9.16.17.24.30 ; 11,2.3.6.8.17.18.19.21.23.30 ; 12,7.11.19.26.28; 13,6.18.21.25 ; 14,11.22.34 ; 15,19.24.32 ; 16,17 ; 17,20 ; 19,5.9.29 ; 20,7.13 ; 21,5.11. 21.25 ; 22,22f. ; 23,19-21 ; 24,3f.15f.19f. ; 25,21f.23 ; 26,2 ; 27,12 ; 28,1.2.18.19 ; 29,23 ; 30,17.

23. Vgl. dazu H. H. SCHMID, *Gerechtigkeit als Weltordnung*, Tübingen, 1968.

24. So MERKEL, a.a.O., 197.

25. So B. GEMSER, HAT I 16, S. 11 (mit RYLAARSDAM) ; G. ZIENER, in : *Wort*

und als solche gewertet würden. Jedoch wird hierbei — und bei vielen positiv empfehlenden Voten zur Weisheitsliteratur — etwas sehr Wesentliches übersehen, nämlich die Tatsache, daß dieses Denken der Weisheit bereits innerhalb des Alten Testaments (wie des Alten Orients !) selber in eine Grundsatzkrise geraten ist, was nun ebenfalls noch kurz [26] erörtert werden soll.

b) Die Krise der alttestamentlichen (wie altorientalischen) Weisheit besteht nun schlicht vor allem darin, daß ihr Zentraldogma vom Tun-Ergehen-Zusammenhang der Empirie nicht mehr standhielt und nicht standhalten konnte. Qohelet macht das mehr grundsätzlich deutlich [27], wenn er scharf beobachtend und mit harter Konsequenz reflektiert und darlegt, daß und wie diese weisheitliche Grundüberzeugung nicht stimmt. Weisheit bringt keinen Erfolg [28], das hat Qohelet „ gesehen " bei seiner empirisch-kritischen Durchleuchtung der Welt wie der Weisheitstheologie, die diese Welt meint erkenntnismäßig bewältigen zu können. Gottesfurcht [30] bleibt als letzter Halt, was an Hiobs Unterwerfung erinnern mag.

Im Hiobbuch ist das „ Dogma " vom Tun-Ergehen-Zusammenhang sowohl für die Freunde [31] als auch für Hiob feststehend [32], nur ziehen die Gesprächspartner daraus verschiedene Folgerungen. Für die Freunde kann Hiob wegen seines Ergehens kein Gerechter sein, für Hiob ist Gott (!) wegen seines Tuns an einem gerechten Menschen ungerecht. Der Zweifel an Gott geht dem an diesem „ Dogma " des Tun-Ergehen Zusammenhanges weit voraus. Erst eine neue Begegnung mit Gott läßt Hiob die Andersartigkeit Gottes erkennen und führt dadurch dann zum Bruch mit dem Dogma, das diesen Gott nicht beschreiben, nicht umschreiben, nicht einfangen kann. [33] Die in Hiob und Qohelet sich artikulierende Krise der Weisheit in Israel ist aber nun eine wesenhafte, keine akzidentielle, eine sich mit Notwendigkeit, nicht aber nur zufällig einstellende oder vermeidbare. Dies kann zuerst durch den Hinweis auf die analoge Lage innerhalb der Weisheitsliteraturen der Umwelt des

und Botschaft (ed. J. Schreiner), Würzburg 1963, 263. — „ Vertikale Offenbarung " meint dann das Gesetz und die Propheten.

26. Ausführlicher in EvTh 30 (1970) 400-406 (mit Lit.).

27. Pred. 1,3 ; 2,26 ; 3,14 ; 5,9f. ; 6,7ff. ; 7,15 ; 8,10.14 ; 9,1-10.11f. — 8,12f. sind Glosse.

28. Pred. 7,23f. ; 8,17 ; 10,1 und öfter.

29. Pred. 5,17 ; vgl. 1,13 ; 2,14 ; 4,13-16 ; 7,11f.19f. ; 9,13-18.

30. Pred. 5,6 ; 7,15-18 ; 12,1ff.

31. Hi 4,8f. ; 5,1-7 ; 8,20 ; 11,20 ; 15,17-38 ; 27,7-23 ; auch 34,10-12 ; 36,5-7.12-15.

32. Hi 12,5 ; 16,16f. ; 21,7-34 ; 29,2-20.

33. Vgl. auch Hi. 27,7-23 als Parodie auf die Weisheit und Hi. 28 als späterer Zusatz, der aber genau diesen Aspekt unterstreichen will.

alten Israel unterstrichen werden. Auch dort war man mit der optimistischen Anschauung des funktionierenden Tun-Ergehen-Zusammenhanges angetreten [34], wobei der Zwang zum System auch hier diesem Denken sofort eingestiftet war, nicht aber als sekundäre, vielleicht noch sogar als vermeidbar anzusehende Entwicklung zu werten ist. Wer so antritt, wie die Weisheit es tat, wird folglich immer wieder in diese Krise des Denkens und Glaubens geraten, wird immer wieder das Scheitern dieser Weltschau und Lebenspraxis erleben müssen, sei es mehr intellektuell wie Qohelet oder stärker existentiell wie Hiob. So ist denjenigen, welche weisheitliche Texte predigen wollen, nicht nur die Frage nach ihrer Christologie zu stellen, sondern schon die viel vordergründigere, wie sie verhindern wollen, daß der Hörer heute diesen Weg des Scheiterns eben durch diese Verkündigung ebenfalls geführt wird, ohne daß ihm mehr gesagt werden kann oder anderes gesagt werden soll, da dieses „andere" in der Weisheit nicht nur nicht mitangelegt ist, sondern in krassem Widerspruch zu ihr steht.

III

Diesen Gedanken wird nun immer wieder entgegengehalten, daß man die Weisheitsliteratur doch nicht in dieser Weise *neben* das Alte Testament stellen könne, wo sie doch nun einmal ein Teil desselben sei. Wird nicht auch viel zu sehr übersehen, daß die Weisheitsliteratur eben doch auch von Jahwe rede, damit aber von seiner Art geprägt sei? Wird das Gewicht des Namens (und damit doch wohl des Wesens?!) Jahwes nicht übersehen oder zumindest zu gering veranschlagt? Kann, wo Jahwe genannt wird, von all dem völlig abgesehen werden, was das Alte Testament sonst von ihm sagt, da doch sehr wahrscheinlich der Israelit, der als „Weiser" von Jahwe sprach, dessen Handeln mit im Gedächtnis hatte und sozusagen von Glauben, Kult, Geschichte Israels, wie das Gesetz und die Propheten diese bezeugen, herlebte und alles irgendwie im Rücken hatte? Ist dies aber wahrscheinlich, wo doch davon aber auch gar nichts in der älteren Weisheit zu entdecken ist? Liegt es nicht doch näher, hier an eine andere Art von Frömmigkeit zu denken, an den Versuch eines israelitischen Humanismus nach der Art der Umwelt des alten Israel?

Weil nun die These einer „Jahwesierung" der israelitischen Weisheit oder die von einem grundlegenden und oft auch verändernden Einfluß des Jahweglaubens mir aufgrund früherer Ausführungen oft kritisch entgegengehalten wurde, bin ich kürzlich in einer eigenen Studie über

34. Ausführlicher dazu und mit Textbelegen wie Literaturverweisen wieder in EvTh 30 (1970) 403f.

Das Gottesbild der älteren Weisheit Israels diesen Fragen ausführlicher nachgegangen. [35] Hier seien jetzt nur die Ergebnisse kurz referiert.

Die ältere Weisheit nennt Jahwe vor allem in sechs Zusammenhängen. Vornehmlich ist er — und das wird nach dem bisher Ausgeführten nicht überraschen — der Stifter und Garant der kosmisch-sittlichen Weltordnung, d.h. des Tun-Ergehen-Zusammenhanges. [36] Dieser Zusammenhang von Tat und Tatfolge ist dem richtenden Walten Jahwes eingeordnet. Jahwe setzt diese Ordnung [37], wirkt in ihr und durch sie, ist ihr Garant und hält sie und dadurch die Welt in Gang. [38] Er ,, vergilt " innerhalb ihrer. [39] Wer Gutes tut, dem läßt die Ordnung bzw. Jahwe es gut gehen [40], wobei stets der einzelne, nicht aber das Bundesvolk im Blick ist.

Nun wird niemand behaupten wollen, daß *diese* Art von Jahwe zu reden auch dem sonstigen Alten Testament eigen ist. Daß Jahwe der Gott der Gerechtigkeit als Weltordnung sei, die einzelnen Frommen zu dem ihnen gebührenden Glück verhilft, ist außerdem eine Art von Gott zu reden, die analog auch der übrigen altorientalischen Weisheitsliteratur absolut geläufig ist. Von typisch Jahwistischem ist hier keine Spur. [41] Auch wenn in den Proverbien mehrmals betont wird, daß Jahwes Handeln trotz aller Fixierung an die Weltordnung letztlich nicht immer ganz dem Menschen einsichtig ist, so ist auch diese Einschränkung nicht in den letzten Grundüberzeugungen des Jahweglaubens verwurzelt [42], sondern findet sich vielfach ähnlich in Texten der Weisheitsliteratur des Alten vorderen Orients.

Diesem Ordnungsdenken zugeordnet sind (zweitens) die Aussagen über Jahwe als dem Schöpfer [43], eben weil er *als* Schöpfer auch und vornehmlich Schöpfer dieser Weltordnung ist, nach der es z.B. Arme und Reiche, Gerechte und Frevler gibt ; und daß Jahwe als Schöpfer sich besonders der Witwen und Waisen sowie der Armen annimmt [44], ist ebenfalls — wie die Aussagen von der Gottheit als Schöpfer — hier

35. In : VT Suppl. XXII, 1972, 117-145.

36. Vgl. etwa Spr. 10,6.9.24.30 ; 11,8.11.17.18.19.21.25.31 ; 12,2 ; 25,23 ; 26,20.

37. Spr. 12,2.

38. Spr. 10,3.22 ; 15,25 ; 16.1.9 ; 20,24 ; 21,1.31.

39. Spr. 22,23 ; 23,11 ; 24,12.18.22 ; 25,22. — Vgl. den Gebrauch von שלם und dann 10,29 ; 11,31 ; 12,2 ; 14,27 ; 15,25 ; 16,3.5 ; 18,10 ; 19,17 ; 20,22 ; 22,4.23 ; 24,12 ; 25,21f. ; 29,25.

40. Spr. 10,2.4.15.30 ; 11,11.21 ; 12,11.14.21 ; 13,21.25 ; 14,14.22 ; 15,6.32 ; 18,7 ; 26,20 ; 29,6.18 u.ö.

41. Die Belege aus den Texten der altorientalischen Weisheitsliteratur sind jeweils in der in Anm. 35 genannten Studie zusammengestellt.

42. So G. von Rad, *Weisheit in Israel*, Neukirchen 1970, 138 ; vgl. 141 (und andere).

43. Spr. 14,31 ; 16,4 ; 17,15 ; 19,17 ; 20,12 ; vgl. 16,11 ; 22,2 ; 19,13.

44. Spr. 14,31 ; 15,25 ; 22,22ff. ; 23,10f. ; 28,8.

nichts spezifisch Jahwistisches, wie überhaupt *diese* Art von Jahwe als dem Schöpfer zu reden in vielen analogen Aussagen altorientalischer Weisheitstexte ihre Parallele hat. Daher kann man m.E. auch den theologischen Ort der Weisheit des Alten Testaments nicht im Rahmen der Schöpfungsaussagen bestimmen [45], da diese Art von „ Schöpfungstheologie " gerade nicht spezifisch jahwistisch ist und innerhalb des Alten Testaments auch eine isolierte Theologie der Schöpfung (abgesehen von den ursprünglich nicht israelitischen Psalmen 8,19a,29 und 104), eine sozusagen von ihrer „ Fortsetzung " losgelöste Theologie der Urgeschichte, sich nicht findet.

Als Schöpfer und Erhalter der Weltordnung ist Jahwe dann selbstverständlich (drittens) auch derjenige, welcher alles vorherbestimmt und vorherbestimmt hat. Er lenkt darin nämlich alles der Ordnung gemäß [46]. Göttliche Führung und Allmacht stehen erneut und auch hier im Dienst des Tun-Ergehen-Zusammenhanges. [47] Auch die Aussagen darüber, daß Jahwe alles sieht [48], stehen im Dienst des Weltordnungsdenkens. Jahwe weiß alles, folglich entgeht z.B. niemand seiner Strafe. [49] Besonders in Texten der altägyptischen Weisheit (z.B. Mahnworte des Ipu-wer) ist das Problem der Prädestination durch den Schöpfergott ein ausführlich erörtertes. [50] Auch in diesem Bereich gehen folglich die Aussagen über Jahwe in der älteren israelitischen Weisheit nicht über analoge aus Texten der Umwelt des alten Israel hinaus.

Diese Feststellung trifft (viertens) ebenfalls zu betreffs der Texte, die von Jahwes „ Wohlgefallen " oder „ Abscheu " reden, da es auch hier wörtliche Parallelen in gleichen semantischen Zusammenhängen in Israels Umwelt gibt. [51]

Schließlich pflegt man, wenn vom prägenden oder sogar umprägenden Einfluß des Jahweglaubens auf die — wahrscheinlich sogar zuerst aus der Umwelt übernommene — Weisheit Israels die Rede ist, besonders gern und intensiv [52] auf die Rede von der Furcht Jahwes (so fünftens innerhalb dieser Zusammenhänge) [53] bzw. (sechstens) vom Vertrauen

45. Dazu (mit Lit.) wieder EvTh 30 (1970) 413 (zu ZIMMERLI, GEMSER, BAUER-KAYATZ, PRIEST und MERKEL).

46. Spr. 18,22 ; 19,14 ; 21,31 ; vgl. weiter 19,21 ; 16,1.9 ; 20,24.27 ; 21,1.

47. Spr. 16,4.7.9.33.

48. Spr. 15,3.11 ; 20,27.

49. Spr. 24,12 ; vgl. 24,17f.

50. Vgl. dazu jetzt G. FECHT, *Der Vorwurf an Gott in den „ Mahnworten des Ipu-wer "*, Heidelberg 1972, 128ff. ; früher auch S. MORENZ, *Untersuchungen zur Rolle des Schicksals in der ägyptischen Religion*, Berlin, 1960.

51. Vgl. wieder die Belege in der in Anm. 35 genannten Studie.

52. Vgl. nur G. VON RAD, *Weisheit in Israel*, 91ff.

53. Spr. 10,27 ; 14,26f. ; 15,16.23 ; 16,6 ; 19,23 ; 22,4 ; 23,17f. ; 24,21f. ; 28,14 ; 31,30 ; vgl. 14,2. — Immer „ Furcht Jahwes ", nie „ Furcht Gottes " !

auf Jahwe [54] hinzuweisen. Aber auch hier gibt es ähnlich lautende Texte aus der Weisheitsliteratur der Umwelt Israels. Und betreffs der ,, Furcht Jahwes " hat kürzlich J. Derrousseaux [55] reichhaltiges Material aus dieser Umwelt beigebracht, das auch hier analoge Aussagen belegt, wenn einerseits auch eine instruktive Häufung der Belege in den Proverbien sowie eine deutlich erkennbare Steigerung ihrer Anzahl, die mit abnehmendem Alter der Untersammlungen des Proverbienbuchs fortschreitend zunimmt, erkennbar ist, andererseits eine deutlich weisheitliche Prägung dieser ,, Furcht Jahwes " in Koppelung auch hier mit dem Tun-Ergehen-Zusammenhang nicht übersehen werden darf. Jahwefurcht ist hier Weisheit und bringt wie sie gute Frucht ; sie lohnt sich, schenkt Zukunft und Erfolg, verbürgt Sicherheit und hat positive Folgen.

Wer nicht bereits hier merkt, daß es mit einem Verstehen der Weisheitstexte des Alten Testaments allein nicht getan ist, sondern daß sich laut und vernehmlich die Frage nach der Wertung und Geltung dieser Textaussagen im Bereich der Geltung des Kreuzes Christi erhebt, sei auf zwei weitere Beobachtungen verwiesen. Das Denken und Glauben im Tun-Ergehen-Zusammenhang ist ein Stück natürlicher Theologie, wobei das Wort ,, natürlich " hier nicht den Bereich des ersten Artikels meint, sondern die Art, wie der sog. natürliche Mensch sich Gott denkt und wünscht. Es ist die (z.B. jedem Krankenseelsorger bekannte) Art, die stets fragt, ,, warum mir dieses oder jenes widerfährt ", ,, womit ich dieses oder jenes verdient habe ", und die glaubt, Gott auf diese Weise aufrechnen zu können, die meint, daß sein Wirken einsichtig sei und zu sein habe. Leid wird als Strafe interpretiert und läßt nach dem Grund des Leidens als der Strafe fragen. Hier aber scheint mir das Neue Testament ein besonders deutliches Plus gegenüber dem Alten Testament zu bieten, wo Kreuz Christi doch *auch* heißt, daß Gott auch im Negativen als nah und gütig geglaubt werden darf. Diese Sicht ist eine klare Alternative zu jeder Theologie eines Tun-Ergehen-Zusammenhanges, nicht aber eine Glaubensart, die sich mit dieser noch irgendwie verträgt. Das wird auch anderenorts innerhalb des Neuen Testaments ausdrücklich festgestellt, wenn nämlich von Jesus ausgesagt wird, daß er es abgelehnt habe, die Warum-Frage als eine legitime aufzunehmen, sie vielmehr sofort auf die

54. 22,19 (als Plus gegenüber dem Quellentext Amenemope !) ; weiter 16,20 ; 20,22 ; 28,25 ; 29,25 ; 30,5 ; vgl. 16,3 ; 18,10. — Zum sonstigen Gebrauch von בטח innerhalb der Hoffnungsaussagen des A.T. siehe J. van der Ploeg, RB 61 (1954), 481-507 ; C. Westermann, in : *Forschung am A.T.*, München, 1964 (TB 24), 219-265 ; A. Deissler, in : *FS Schlier (Die Zeit Jesu)*, 1970, 15-37 ; W. Zimmerli, *Der Mensch und seine Hoffnung im A.T.*, Göttingen, 1968 ; dann A. Jepsen, ThWAT I, Sp. 608-615 und E. Gerstenberger, THAT I, Sp. 300-305.

55. *La crainte de Dieu dans l'A.T.*, Paris, 1970, 301-357 ; zur Weiterführung und Auseinandersetzung mit ihm siehe die in Anm. 35 genannte Studie in ihrem Abschnitt VI.

Existenz des Fragers zurückgebogen habe, — so in der Szene mit der Frage nach der Schuld des Blindgeborenen bzw. der seiner Eltern (Joh. 9,1ff.) wie in der nach dem Turm von Siloah, der auf Menschen fiel (Luk 13,1-5). Jedes Fragen nach einem Tun-Ergehen-Zusammenhang wird angesichts des Wortes und Werkes Christi durchgestrichen und abgelehnt.

Folglich gehen die Aussagen über Jahwe in Spr. 10-31 über entsprechende Aussagen über Gott oder Götter in der Weisheitsliteratur der Umwelt des alten Israel in keinem Punkt hinaus. ,, Jahwesiert " wurde die Weisheit noch nicht hier, sondern weithin erst später (vgl. Jes Sir ; Sap), wo sie jedoch manches aus ihrem Proprium aufzugeben genötigt wird bzw. wo auch der Jahweglaube wiederum manches aus seinem Spezifikum preisgibt oder uminpretiert (vgl. etwa die Rede vom Gesetz in Jes Sir).

Vom Einfluß des ,, echten " Jahweglaubens ist aber wohl angesichts der Art und Weise zu sprechen, wie die Gottesreden des Hiobbuchs [56] — auf die Erörterungen der Freunde und die Herausforderung Hiobs reagierend — Jahwe als über den Tun-Ergehen-Zusammenhang schlechthin erhaben (vgl. dagegen den Prosarahmen des Hiobbuchs), als nicht aufrechenbar, als totaliter aliter bezeugen. Was hier in Form einer Theophanie, welche sonst der Weisheit des Alten Testaments wie der ähnlichen ,, Hiobliteratur " des Alten Orients in dieser Form bezeichnenderweise fremd ist, aufbricht, ist die Krise, die Infragestellung des weisheitlichen Ansatzes überhaupt. *Hier* scheint mir der Einfluß des Jahweglaubens greifbar und zwar in typischer Weise, d.h. aber im Scheitern der Weisheit vor Jahwe. ,, Die Lösung der ganzen Frage (bei Hiob) liegt in der Erlösung von der Fragestellung. " [57] Jahwe meldet sich in völlig unweisheitlicher Weise zu Wort und sprengt damit die Weisheit in ihrem Denk- und Frageansatz des Tun-Ergehen-Zusammenhanges auf. Auch dieses inneralttestamentliche ,, Geschick " der Weisheit und ihrer Weltschau sollte uns davor bewahren, alttestamentliche Weisheit in christliche Theologie integrieren zu wollen. Jahwe und Jahwe sind innerhalb des so vielschichtigen Alten Testaments offenkundig nicht immer derselbe und dergleiche. Die These eines prägenden Einflusses des Jahweglaubens oder Jahwenamens auf die Weisheit allgemein ist ein Postulat, das sich nicht verifizieren läßt.

Selbst die jüngere Weisheit in Proverbien Kap. 1-9 ist nicht durchweg vom Jahweglauben durchdrungen [58]. Die Kapitel 1-9 sind in ihrer

56. Hi 38,1-42,6.

57. So Matthies SIMON, zitiert bei Jean LÉVÊQUE, *Job et son Dieu*, Tome II, Paris, 1970, 531, Anm. 3 ; siehe dort bei *L.* auch S. 499ff. zur Theophanie im Hiobbuch und S. 654ff. zur ,, *Weisheit im Schach* " betr. Hi und Qoh.

58. Vgl. Kap. 4-6 ; dann in 2,1-19 noch V. 9-11 mit V. 5-8 ; dazu N. C. HABEL,

Endformulierung natürlich nicht allein deswegen als jüngste, nachexilische Weisheit anzusehen, weil sie längere Texteinheiten, d.h. weisheitliche Lehrreden und nicht kurze Einzelsprüche enthalten. Wohl aber zeigen hier die Reden von der Weisheit [59] als Schöpfungs- und Offenbarungsmittlerin und dem darin angelegten Hinweis auf eine mögliche allgemeine Offenbarung, von der Weisheit als Erzieherin, als göttlicher Anruf an den Menschen [60], als Heil anbietende Person und anderes die gegenüber Proverbien Kap. 10ff. weiterführen wollende, spätere theologische Entwicklung an. Proverbien 1-9 wurden — ähnlich dem Psalm 1 beim Psalter, Genesis 1 beim Pentateuch — als jüngste Stücke dieser Art, die aber damit dem Denken der kanonbildenden und kanonabschließenden Kräfte nahestanden, den älteren absichtlich vorangestellt, weil man wollte, daß von ihnen her nun auch das ältere Gut tunlichst verstanden werden sollte. Jeder der meint, daß hierdurch die Weisheit nun wirklich ,,jahwesiert" sei und ihren Platz im Alten Testament erhalten habe, muß sich — abgesehen davon, ob durch ein später vorgesetztes gotisches Portal eine sonst romanische Kirche nun auch insgesamt als romanisch anzusehen sei — zwei Fragen stellen lassen: 1) Welcher Begriff vom biblischen Kanon liegt einer solchen These zugrunde? Anerkennung des Kanons kann m.E. nur heißen, daß ich bereit bin, mich dem Anspruch und dem Zeugnis der in ihm vereinten Schriften zu stellen und auszusetzen, nicht aber die damals oder überhaupt vollzogene inhaltliche Begründung für seine Existenz und Zusammensetzung zu akzeptieren. Diese muß vielmehr erst selbst bejaht werden können, kann jedoch nicht als Voraussetzung oder Vorleistung gefordert werden. 2) Geben die in Proverbien Kap. 1-9 (vgl. noch, wenn auch mit anderen Akzenten, Hiob 28) angebotenen theologischen Interpretationen der Weisheit wirklich eine theologisch vertretbare und helfende (!) Schau israelitischer Weisheit ab, die das im damals Gesagten Gemeinte auch heute noch klärend aussprechen könnte, ohne nur rezitiert zu werden? [61]

Somit bleibt — in weiterer Auseinandersetzung und Abgrenzung — nun noch zusammengefaßt und zusammenfassend die Frage zu bedenken, ob überhaupt es angesichts der altisraelitischen Weisheitsliteratur mit einem nachzeichnenden Verstehen sein Bewenden haben kann, oder ob nicht die Frage nach der *Geltung* dieser Texte ausdrücklich zu stellen

Interpretation 26 (1972), 146f. — Zur Problematik von 4,21-35 vgl. B. LANG, *Die weisheitliche Lehrrede*, (SBS 54) Stuttgart, 1972, 30f., Anm. 19.

59. Vgl. G. VON RAD, *Theologie I*[5], 454ff.

60. Ebd., 454.

61. Vgl. selbst VON RAD, a.a.O., 458 mit seiner Bemerkung, daß die Frage, wie nun diese Weisheit theologisch zu umschreiben wäre, doch nicht ganz leicht zu beantworten ist.

ist. Es wird auch an dieser Stelle nämlich wieder neu deutlich, daß der Alttestamentler ex officio seine Arbeit innerhalb christlicher Theologie (!) nur unter ständiger Einbeziehung systematisch-theologischer Fragestellungen verrichten und nur so assertorisch reden kann. [62]

IV

Einen erneuten Beweis seines Willens sowie seiner Fähigkeit zu kongenialem Hören, Lesen und Verstehen hat nun Gerhard von Rad in seinem Buch über die *Weisheit in Israel* [63] gegeben. Dieses Werk macht aber zugleich wie kaum ein anderes zum Thema offenkundig, daß und wie dieser Wille zum Verstehen hier angesichts des Zeugnisses der Weisheitsliteratur des Alten Testaments durch das Fragen nach Wertung und Geltung des so Erhobenen ergänzt werden muß. [64]

Gerhard von Rad's Werk verheimlicht nicht, daß es dem Leser die Weisheit Israels nicht nur möglichst einfühlend nahebringen, sondern ihn sozusagen selbst zu einem solchen Weisen machen, zu dieser Weltschau einladen möchte, zu einem Erfahrungswissen, das sich ,, so merkwürdig aufs Messers Schneide zwischen Wissen und Glauben bewegt " [65]. Immer wieder warnt von Rad davor, die einzelnen Sentenzen gleich von anderen her interpretieren oder gar in ein übergreifendes Verstehenssystem einfügen zu wollen [66], spricht dann aber doch selbst und mit Notwendigkeit von ,, dem " Wirklichkeitsverständnis des alten Israel und vom Ordnungsdenken der Weisheit, vom Tun-Ergehen-Zusammenhang, der hier konstitutiv ist und wirkt. [67] Die in dem genannten Buch gebotene Darstellung der Weisheit Israels soll hier nicht wiederholt werden; es sei vielmehr nur auf einige kritische Punkte aufmerksam gemacht.

Israel versuchte also Erfahrungen zu formulieren und auszuwerten. [68] Wir haben heute Schwierigkeiten, das Phänomen der Weisheit als eine bestimmte Form der menschlichen Erkenntnisbemühung sachgemäß zu bestimmen, da wir es uns nicht an einer Entsprechung in unserem

62. Vgl. dazu meinen in Anm. 18 genannten Aufsatz.

63. Neukirchen, 1970; vgl. auch ders., *Theol.* I[5], 430ff., dort aber ohne den werbenden Unterton.

64. Einige Fragen schon bei W. ZIMMERLI, *Die Weisheit Israels*, EvTh 31 (1971) 680-695 (hauptsächlich von Hiob und Qohelet her); vgl. ferner meine Besprechung des von Rad'schen Buchs in DPfrBl 71 (1971, Nr. 5) 161f.

65. *Weisheit in Israel*, 16.

66. Vgl. dort schon das Vorwort, dann etwa 16f., 19,394f. und öfter.

67. A.a.O., siehe das Stichwortregister; vor allem 384.

68. A.a.O., 271 und öfter.

Geistesleben verdeutlichen können. [69] Ist dieser Abstand aber nur Zufall, sozusagen geistesgeschichtlicher Verfall oder ein Stück notwendiger Erkenntnisfortschritt oder Glaubenskorrektur? Wir fragen heute z.B. außerdem, ob nicht in der Weisheit die gesamte Wirklichkeit rational vergewaltigt wurde. [70] Die Weisheit aber ist der Meinung, daß alle Widerfahrnisse gelenkt sind (Tun-Ergehen-Zusammenhang), daß auf dem Grund der Dinge eine Ordnung waltet [71], daß die Schöpfung eine Aussage für den Menschen hat [72], sogar Wahrheit entläßt [73] für die Kunst zu leben. [74] Der moderne Betrachter, der sich so entschieden zu den (nach von Rad damals einsamen) [75] Thesen des Predigers Salomo bekennt, sollte auch sehen und sich sagen lassen, daß die Weisheit den Mißton in der Welt nicht sucht, sondern die Welt als gute Schöpfung ansieht. [76] Kann man dies nun aber so einfach konstatieren? Könnte es nicht sein, daß dieser Prediger Salomo — trotz aller vermeintlichen Einsamkeit — genauer hingesehen und tiefer erkannt hat? Weisheit ist nach von Rad in Israel eine Antwort des mit bestimmten Welterfahrungen konfrontierten Jahweglaubens [77], wenn auch sehr verschieden von anderen Selbstdarstellungen dieses Glaubens. Weisheit war ein Versuch einer Humanität Israels. [78] Bei aller Überzeugung von der Ambivalenz der Phänomene und Widerfahrnisse [79] und dem Aufbrechen von Aporien [80] unternimmt der Weise doch die „heikle Aufgabe" [81], in einer Welt, die ganz auf Gott hin offen war, nach Regeln zu forschen. [82] Hier wird das Heil von den Urgegebenheiten der Schöpfung selbst abgeleitet. [83] Die Frage, ob dies alles ungebrochen auch heute gelten kann, wird nicht gestellt, ebenso nicht, ob hier wirklich der Jahweglaube zur Sprache kommt, zumal ein durchgängiger Vergleich mit Texten aus der Umwelt unterbleibt und Material von dort nur eklektisch herangezogen wird.

69. A.a.O., 375.
70. A.a.O., 382.
71. *Theol.* I⁵, 441.
72. *Weisheit in Israel*, 384.
73. A.a.O., 385.
74. *Theol.* I⁵, 433.
75. Wirklich? Die analogen Texte des Alten Orients werden souverän übergangen.
76. *Weisheit in Israel*, 388f.
77. A.a.O., 390.
78. A.a.O., 391.
79. A.a.O., 395.
80. A.a.O., 397.
81. A.a.O., 398.
82. Ebenda.
83. A.a.O., 399.

Was ist die letzte Absicht dieses Buchs ? Es dürfte jedem Leser bald klar werden, daß von Rad nicht nur distanziert schildert, sondern — von seiner Sache selbst ergriffen — den Leser möglichst in diese Denkbewegung der Weisheit hineinholen möchte. Er möchte hinführen zu diesem Wirklichkeitsverständnis, zu diesem Vertrauen in die Welt, zu ihrem Lebensmut aufgrund der erkennbaren Ordnung, die diese Welt durchwaltet.

Hierbei sieht von Rad als guter Exeget jedoch schon selber die hier waltende Problematik, die nicht nur darin besteht, daß sich keine Entsprechungen im heutigen Geistesleben finden, wenn auch von Rad merkwürdig kritiklos vorauszusetzen scheint, daß dies nur zu bedauern, nicht aber auf seine Gründe zu hinterfragen sei. Darüberhinaus ist schon der Gesamtversuch einer Ortung der Weisheit als solcher eine „heikle Aufgabe", da von Rad es ablehnt, gängige Antworten zu schnell zu übernehmen, ja betont neu fragen und verunsichern will. Es soll vermieden werden, daß man zu schnell mit dem Phänomen Weisheit fertig zu sein glaubt [84], — ein Vorwurf, den von Rad vielleicht auch dem Referenten machen würde.

So stehen nun bei von Rad Empfehlungen und positive Hinweise neben kritischen Einwänden und dem Aufweis von Aporien, wenn auch letzteren gern immer wieder etwas von ihrem Gewicht genommen wird. Die Weisheit packt eben viele Probleme an, läßt dann aber doch den, der es mit ihr versucht, in gewisser Ratlosigkeit und angesichts wichtiger, bald aufbrechender Fragen ohne Antwort.

Genau so aber verfährt und endet auch das hier angesprochene Buch, bei dessen Lektüre der Leser nicht selten gleichfalls in den Aporien, den Fragen, im Aufweis von Problemen belassen wird. Mag sein, daß für Israel z.B. Glaube und Einsicht in der Weisheit (auch sonst ?) zusammenhingen. Welchen Stellenwert aber haben Einsicht und Vernunft für den Glauben überhaupt ? Darf man hier das eine ansprechen, das andere aber nicht ? Kann man auf das in der Weisheit Israels sich kundtuende Angebot einer anderen Wirklichkeitsschau nun eingehen ? Gilt es auch uns ? Wie steht es mit dem Heimatgefühl des Menschen in dieser Welt, wie um die vertrauensvolle, die heile Welt selber ? Kann hier alles so schwebend belassen werden ? Gibt es auch für uns die unbeirrbare Gewißheit, daß die Schöpfung dem, der sich auf sie einlässt, ihre Wahrheit selbst erweisen wird [85], und welche Wahrheit ist dann gemeint ? An anderer Stelle hat von Rad dies noch weiter ausgeführt und bewußt unter die Frage nach der „Christliche(n) Weisheit ?" gestellt. [86] Auch dort heißt es, daß die Schöpfung sich selbst interpretiert

84. Vgl. auch *Theol.* I[5], 447 unten.
85. *Weisheit in Israel*, 403.
86. Vgl. den in Anm. 15 genannten Aufsatz.

und vertrauenswürdig ist.[87] Nur darf man dieser Erfahrung die Beantwortung der Heilsfrage nicht aufbürden.[88] Wie aber, wenn diese sich angesichts heutiger Welterfahrung stellt ? Oder soll hier Schöpfung von Welt unterschieden werden ?

Kurz : Kann man die Geltungsfrage für die Christen von heute beim Blick auf diese Texte derartig ausklammern, das Zeugnis des Neuen Testaments bei der Wertung des Gesamtphänomens wie der Schau der Welt so übergehen, vom anderen Weltverständnis zu schweigen ? Kann hier Exegese direkt zum Kerygma, kann alttestamentliche Textauslegung zum exegetischen Positivismus mit kerygmatischem Anspruch (G. Sauter) werden ? Was heißt es konkret, daß man das Warnsignal des Predigers Salomo zwar nicht übersehen soll, ihn als prinzipiellen Wächter gegenüber der Weisheit aber nicht anerkennen kann ?[89] Soll man trotz des Warnsignals in diese Sackgasse hineinfahren ? Ist die Krise der Weisheit bei Qohelet und Hiob nicht tiefer und wesenhafter, als von Rad wahrhaben will ?[90] Wie kann man die Geltungsfrage übergehen, wenn so gewichtige Themen wie die nach dem Verhältnis von Glaube und Denken, Erfahrung und Glaube, Schöpfung und Heil, Schöpfung und Offenbarung zur Debatte stehen ? Sind die hier selbst der Weisheit bewußt werdenden Grenzen nur unwesentliche, oder kommt nicht die Weisheit insgesamt an ihre Grenze ? Gibt es eine christliche Weisheitstheologie ?[91] Liegt dieses Offenbleiben vieler Fragen wirklich nur an der Weisheit, oder nicht vielleicht auch daran, daß ein Exeget hier nicht werten will, wo er werten muß ? Kann man zum Eingehen auf dieses Weisheitsdenken einladen, dann aber denjenigen allein lassen, der es damit versucht und dann mit Notwendigkeit vor die Fragen Hiobs und Qohelets sich gestellt sieht ? Kann es im Sinne christlicher Verkündigung sein, Menschen auf diesen Weg zu stellen ?

Aber es ist nicht allein die christliche Theologie, die der alttestamentlichen Weisheit einen Ort in ihrem Denken verweigern muß. Es ist schon der Traditionsweg, es ist die Geschichte dieser Weisheit innerhalb des Alten Testaments selber, welche die Weisheit in ihrem Grundanliegen scheitern ließ. Alle Versuche, weisheitliche Texte in heutige Theologie und Verkündigung aufzunehmen, müssen sich den hier aufgezeigten Problemen stellen.

Gerhard von Rad möchte die heutige Wirklichkeit nicht gottlos machen oder sehen, Gott nicht weltlos bezeugen.[92] In diesem Anliegen

87. Dort S. 61 und 63.

88. A.a.o., 63.

89. *Weisheit in Israel*, 401.

90. In dieser Richtung fragt besonders W. ZIMMERLI (vgl. Anm. 64).

91. Das Buch von H. WEGENER, *Beiträge zur Geschichte der Weisheitsreligion*, Graz, 1970, behandelt unter diesem Thema — Theosophie und Esoterik !

92. *Weisheit in Israel*, 403 ; vgl. 378.

ist ihm nur zuzustimmen. Ob es aber von einer neu entworfenen weisheitlichen Ordnungsschau her erreicht werden kann, bleibt zu bezweifeln. Der Glaube an Gott, den Vater Jesu Christi, als dem Schöpfer und Erhalter dieser Welt, meint etwas anderes als den Gott eines Tun-Ergehen-Zusammenhangs. Das sollte nicht vergessen werden in einer Zeit, in der das Thema „ Weisheit " en vogue ist.

H. D. PREUSS

See *Supplementary note*, p. 219.

11

LE CONTREPOINT THÉOLOGIQUE APPORTÉ PAR LA RÉFLEXION SAPIENTIELLE

On chercherait en vain dans les livres sapientiaux de la Bible, avant l'époque de Ben Sira, des développements sur l'alliance, sur la révélation du Sinaï, sur l'élection d'Israël ou ses espérances messianiques. De même, durant de longs siècles, les maîtres de sagesse, concentrant leur attention sur les expériences et le destin de l'individu, n'ont rien dit des relations de Yahweh avec son peuple ni de sa seigneurie sur l'ensemble des nations. Ces thèmes historiques ou prophétiques, que l'on retrouve si souvent dans toute étude sur la théologie de l'Ancien Testament, semblent tout à coup muets dès que l'on pénètre dans le domaine de la littérature sapientiale. Un tel silence a depuis longtemps intrigué les biblistes, et plusieurs se sont efforcés, avec raison, de relativiser l'isolement des écrits de sagesse, soit en soulignant certains points de contact entre les sages et les diverses traditions yahwistes [1], en particulier celles qui ont trait au droit [2] et à l'histoire [3], soit en relevant l'influence des sages sur

1. Cf. A. Robert, *Le yahwisme de Prov. X,1-XXII,16 ; XXV-XXIX*, dans *Mémorial Lagrange*, 1940, 163-182 ; H.-J. Hermisson, *Studien zur israelitischen Spruchsweisheit*, Leiden, 1968 ; J. R. Boston, *The Wisdom Influence upon the Song of Moses*, JBL 87 (1968) 198-202 ; voir également : G. Fohrer, *Die Weisheit im Alten Testament*, dans *Studien zur alttestamentlichen Theologie und Geschichte* (BZAW 115), Berlin, 1969, 242-274 (= TWNT VII, 476-496) ; H. Cazelles, *Les débuts de la sagesse en Israël*, dans *Les sagesses du Proche Orient ancien*, Paris, 1963, 27-40 ; H.-H. Schmid, *Wesen und Geschichte der Weisheit* (BZAW 101), Berlin, 1966 ; U. Skladny, *Die ältesten Spruchsammlungen in Israel*, Göttingen, 1962 ; L. Alonso Schökel, *Motivos sapienciales y de alianza en Gen. 2-3*, *Bibl.* 43 (1962) 295-346 ; A. Barucq, Art. *Proverbes (livre des)*, dans *DB Suppl.* VIII, fasc. 47 (1972), col. 1395-1476.

2. Cf. W. Richter, *Recht und Ethos, Versuch einer Ortung des weisheitlichen Mahnspruches*, München, 1966 ; J. Malfroy, *Sagesse et Loi dans le Deutéronome*, VT 15 (1965) 49-65 ; E. Gerstenberger, *Wesen und Herkunft des apodiktischen Rechtes im Alten Testament* (WMANT 20), Neukirchen, 1965 ; G. von Rad, *Das fünfte Buch Mose* (ATD 8), Göttingen, 1964, p. 12 ; W. Zimmerli, *Ort und Grenze der Weisheit im Rahmen der alttestamentlichen Theologie*, dans *S.P.O.A.*, 121-138 ; G. Heinemann, *Untersuchungen zum apodiktischen Recht Israels*, Diss. Hamburg 1958, dact.

3. Cf. J.-L. McKenzie, *Reflections on Wisdom*, JBL 86 (1967) 1-9 ; et l'attitude

les prophètes [4] ou des prophètes sur les sages [5]. Tous ces travaux, dans la mesure où ils remédient à un cloisonnement excessif des divers courants de pensée en Israël, vont dans le sens de la vraisemblance historique et ont contribué à assainir le climat de la recherche. En même temps, des analyses plus fines des parallèles égyptiens [6] et mésopotamiens [7] sont venues préciser ce qu'on pouvait espérer et ce qu'on ne devait pas attendre du comparatisme.

Ce regain d'intérêt pour l'étude scientifique de la littérature de sagesse a donc déjà porté des fruits. Nous nous heurtons cependant encore aujourd'hui à de grandes difficultés dès que nous cherchons à articuler l'apport des livres sapientiaux sur une théologie d'ensemble de l'Ancien Testament [8]. A cela, certes, nous avons bien des excuses : seul un choix de livres didactiques nous a été conservé par la Bible ; des chaînons peut-être importants nous manquent, en particulier aux quatrième et troisième siècles, pour pouvoir retracer objectivement l'histoire de la réflexion sapientielle israélite ; et nous sommes encore incapables de dire s'il s'agit à proprement parler d'un mouvement, avec la continuité

très réservée de J. L. CRENSHAW, *Method in Determining Wisdom Influence upon "Historical" Literature*, JBL 88 (1969) 129-142.

4. Cf. J. FICHTNER, *Jesaia unter den Weisen*, TLZ 74 (1949) 75-80 ; — *Jahwes Plan in der Botschaft des Jesaia*, ZAW 63 (1951) 16-33 ; J. A. SANDERS, *Suffering as Divine Discipline in the Old Testament and Post-biblical Judaism*, New York, 1955 ; H. CAZELLES, *Bible, Sagesse, Science*, RSR 48 (1960) 45 ; J. LINDBLOM, *Wisdom in the Old Testament Prophets*, dans VT Suppl. III, Leiden, ²1960, 192-204 ; S. TERRIEN, *Amos and Wisdom in Israel's Prophetic Heritage*, dans *Essays in Honor of J. Muilenburg*, New York, 1962 ; H. W. WOLFF, *Amos' geistige Heimat* (WMANT 18), Neukirchen, 1964, 24-30 ; W. MCKANE, *Prophets and Wise Men*, London, 1965, 65ss. ; R. J. ANDERSON, *Was Isaiah a Scribe ?*, JBL 79 (1960) 57s. ; M. DELCOR, *Le livre de Daniel*, Paris, 1971, 30s ; D. E. GOWAN, *Habakkuk and Wisdom*, dans *Perspective* 9 (1968) 157-166 ; J. L. CRENSHAW, *The Influence of the Wise upon Amos*, ZAW 79 (1967) 42-52.

5. Cf. A. ROBERT, *Les attaches littéraires de Prov. I-IX*, dans RB 43 (1934) 42-63, 172-204, 374-384 ; 44 (1935) 344-365, 502-525 ; H. BARDTKE, *Prophetische Züge im Buche Hiob*, dans BZAW 105, 1967, 1-10 ; C. LARCHER, *Études sur le livre de la Sagesse*, Paris, 1969, 90-93.

6. Voir la bibliographie rassemblée par J. LECLANT, dans *Les sagesses du Proche-Orient ancien*, Paris, 1964, 18-26 ; ajouter Christa KAYATZ, *Studien zu Proverbien 1-9. Eine form- und motivgeschichtliche Untersuchung unter Einbeziehung ägyptischen Vergleichsmaterials* (WMANT 22), Neukirchen, 1966.

7. Cf. J. J. A. VAN DIJK, *La sagesse suméro-akkadienne*, Leiden, 1953 ; E. I. GORDON, *Sumerian Proverbs, Glimpses of everyday Life in ancient Mesopotamia*, Philadelphie, 1959 ; W. G. LAMBERT, *Babylonian Wisdom Literature*, Oxford, 1960 ; P. GRELOT, *Les Proverbes araméens d'Ahiqar*, dans RB 68 (1961), 178ss. ; M. LAMBERT, *Recherches sur les Proverbes sumériens de la collection I*, dans *Rivista degli studi orientali*, 42 (1967) 75-79.

8. Cf. H.-H. SCHMID, *op. cit.*, p. 201 : „ Die Frage nach der „ Weisheit " muss in Exegese und Systematik neu überdacht werden ".

et l'infrastructure sociale que cela suppose, ou simplement d'un niveau de pensée, toujours présent, mais plus ou moins étoffé selon les époques. Une autre difficulté, et pas la moindre, tient à l'imprécision congénitale de la langue des sages d'Israël, beaucoup plus attentifs à silhouetter les choses qu'à définir des notions. Cette approche « stéréométrique » [9] des problèmes, qui est par ailleurs un des aspects les plus attachants de l'esthétique des anciens Sémites, défie les analyses trop rapides et renvoie sans cesse l'exégète à une écoute plus patiente et plus accueillante, autrement dit à une attitude plus sapientielle, et partant mieux accordée à l'objet de sa recherche.

La lecture en profondeur s'avère particulièrement nécessaire dès que l'on aborde la théologie des sapientiaux. Il va de soi, en effet, que de simples inventaires des thèmes clairement exprimés ne suffisent pas pour comparer utilement la pensée des sages à celle des prophètes, des psalmistes ou des hommes de la Torah : il faut au préalable explorer pour elle-même la théologie sous-jacente aux énoncés sapientiels et en discerner si possible les lignes de force. Alors seulement la confrontation a des chances d'amener un enrichissement réciproque des diverses traditions, et on peut espérer qu'à ce niveau plus profond le rattachement de la théologie sapientielle aux autres courants théologiques devienne possible. Encore faut-il ne pas préjuger trop rigidement du mode de ce rattachement. Instinctivement l'on s'attend à des emprunts, à des recouvrements partiels ou à des convergences plus ou moins frappantes ; et de fait il n'en manque pas [10]. Mais il convient de laisser place également à un autre type de rapport, analogue, toutes proportions gardées, à celui que réalise en musique le contrepoint.

Suivant la belle définition qu'en donne le compositeur H. Barraud, « le contrepoint est l'art de faire chanter en toute indépendance apparente des lignes mélodiques superposées, de telle manière que leur audition simultanée laisse percevoir, au sein d'un ensemble cohérent, la beauté linéaire et la signification plastique de chacune d'elles, tout en lui ajoutant une dimension supplémentaire, née de sa combinaison avec les autres » [11]. Transposée dans la théologie de l'Ancien Testament, cette notion de contrepoint permettrait, semble-t-il, d'apprécier équitablement la singularité des livres sapientiaux, qui paraissent à la fois

9. Voir B. Landsberger-W. von Soden, *Die Eigenbegrifflichkeit der babylonischen Welt*, 1965, 17.

10. Pour nous borner à un seul exemple : dans les discours de Job on retrouve à chaque pas le langage des psaumes de plainte ou des hymnes, des images venues des prophètes, et même, au ch. 19, une véritable anthologie des Lamentations. Voir l'index scripturaire de notre ouvrage *Job et son Dieu. Essai d'exégèse et de théologie biblique* (coll. *Études Bibliques*), Paris, Gabalda, 1970, 785-794 et 801-811. Nous renverrons désormais à ce livre par le signe JD.

11. Article *Contrepoint*, dans *Encyclopedia Universalis*, vol. 4, 972, Paris, 1968.

farouchement autonomes et remarquablement aptes au dialogue à l'intérieur de l'ensemble cohérent de la révélation vétéro-testamentaire.

Pour vérifier cette hypothèse de travail, nous tenterons ici de retrouver un contrepoint théologique dans la présentation sapientielle des relations de l'homme et de Dieu. Si l'on se réfère à la totalité du corpus sapientiel de la Bible, on s'aperçoit que le mystère de la rencontre du croyant et de Yahweh a été comme projeté horizontalement sur deux plans : celui de la création et celui de l'existence personnelle. Nous allons donc nous situer successivement à ces deux niveaux que les sages ont privilégiés, et nous nous demanderons d'abord comment le monde matériel médiatise la rencontre du Créateur et de l'homme créé, puis comment l'homme et Dieu se cherchent et se trouvent malgré les apories de l'existence.

I. Le sage d'Israël et le langage du cosmos

Israël n'a jamais séparé l'homme de son environnement cosmique, et les sages tout spécialement ont mis à profit l'idée très riche de l'homme comme être-au-monde, à la fois accueilli et accueillant au sein de l'univers créé. Avec une audace tranquille et une curiosité toujours en éveil, les maîtres ont exploré le domaine de l'homme et guetté ses réactions. Ils ont observé le monde, scruté la vie journalière et essayé de détecter, derrière l'apparente contradiction des phénomènes, une secrète ordonnance des choses et des vivants. Rapprochant le semblable du semblable, ils ont établi des catégories de faits, réguliers, alternants, cycliques, et même parfois franchement énigmatiques [12]. Puis ils ont relevé des analogies entre les faits de la nature et les données de leur expérience [13], et ils se sont appliqués à capter et à objectiver dans les jeux du langage les lois du monde et celles de l'homme-au-monde. Repoussant ainsi patiemment le chaos, ils ont humanisé l'espace où ils vivaient par l'éclairage rationnel qu'ils lui imposaient, par leur souci incessant de passer de la constatation à la norme et de l'extérieur des choses à l'intime qui donne sens. La poésie hébraïque, avec sa faculté surprenante de tout laisser inachevé et de juxtaposer presque à l'infini les fragments d'expérience comme autant de perceptions colorées, leur permettait de renouveler continuellement cette rencontre intense et esthétique [14] du réel.

12. Cf. Job 38-41 ; Sir 39,26-35 ; 43 ; Ps. 148.

13. Ex. : Pr. 25,14-23 ; 26,11-20 ; 27,17-20 ; Sir. 13,1s.

14. Sur l'importance de l'expérience esthétique du réel, voir H.-G. GADAMER, *Wahrheit und Methode*, Tübingen, 1965, spécialement, pp. 77-96, le chapitre : *Wiedergewinnung der Frage nach der Wahrheit der Kunst*, où l'auteur souligne la phrase suivante : „ alle Begegnung mit der Sprache der Kunst Begegnung mit einem unabgeschlossenem Geschehen und selbst ein Teil dieses Geschehens ist " (p. 94).

Cette recherche de l'ordre immanent au monde s'est développée dans un climat de grande liberté intellectuelle, mais jamais en dehors ni surtout au détriment de la foi yahwiste. Même les plus anciens livrets des Proverbes [15] mentionnent très souvent Yahweh [16]. Partout son pouvoir créateur et sa seigneurie universelle sont présupposés : « ses yeux sont en tout lieu », « même le Sheol et l'Abaddon sont devant lui », et « il a fait toute chose en vue de sa fin » (Pr. 15,3.11 ; 16,4) ; et le fait que, dans les sentences les plus anciennes, les phrases qui expriment une expérience de Dieu s'entremêlent librement avec des textes qui traduisent l'expérience du monde (ex. Pr. 16,7-12) montre bien que les sages d'Israël n'ont jamais ressenti l'antinomie moderne entre discours séculier et discours théologique [17]. Pour eux les conquêtes de la raison n'ont jamais impliqué des défaites de la foi. Toute la réalité empirique était le domaine de Yahweh en même temps que le royaume de l'homme, et « ce qu'Israël percevait de ce qui l'entourait était en fin de compte un ensemble de lois perçues par la foi » [18].

Libre au cœur d'un monde circonscrit et pénétré par le mystère de Dieu, la science d'Israël n'a jamais éprouvé le besoin de s'émanciper. C'est pourquoi, si souvent, les maîtres insistent sur le rôle de la crainte de Dieu dans toute démarche sapientielle : « ceux qui recherchent Dieu comprennent tout » (Pr. 28,5). C'est dire que la crainte de Yahweh, entendue à la fois comme une connaissance, un attachement et une obéissance [19], conduit l'homme à la sagesse et le dispose à entrer dans un savoir efficace et sanctifiant (Pr. 1,7 ; 9,10 ; 15,33 ; Jb. 28,28 ; cf. Ps. 111,10). Seule une juste attitude devant Dieu permet une saine appréciation du réel. Comme l'écrit G. von Rad : « On sera compétent, on saura ce que sont les règles de la vie lorsqu'on partira de ce qu'on sait sur Dieu et pas avant » [20]. Cette présence discrète de la foi au creux même de l'acte de connaître explique que les thèmes de la création et de la seigneurie cosmique de Yahweh aient été développés de plus en plus largement dans les écrits sapientiaux à mesure que le cercle des expériences s'élargissait en Israël (Pr. 8 ; Job 28 ; 38-41 ; Sir. 24 ; 42,15-43,33).

15. Les deux collections « salomoniennes » : 10,1-22,16 et 25-29.

16. Respectivement 54 et 6 fois.

17. Cf. G. VON RAD, *Israël et la sagesse*, traduction E. DE PEYER, Genève, 1971, 72-79.

18. G. VON RAD, *Théologie de l'Ancien Testament*, vol. 1, trad. E. DE PEYER, Genève, 1963, 369-370.

19. Voir J. BECKER, *Gottesfurcht im Alten Testament (Analecta Biblica 25)*, Rome 1965 ; L. DEROUSSEAUX, *La crainte de Dieu dans l'Ancien Testament* (coll. *Lectio Divina* n° 63), Paris, 1970.

20. *Israël et la sagesse*, p. 83.

L'une des certitudes qui se sont imposées progressivement aux maîtres de sagesse est que le monde porte en lui un message destiné à l'homme. Le sens que Dieu a incorporé à l'univers lors de sa création se dévoile au croyant en quête de sa propre vérité. Partout il peut découvrir des constantes, des correspondances harmonieuses, des récurrences fidèles de phénomènes qui tous ont leur « temps » favorable. Par sa grandeur, son équilibre et sa variété, le monde provoque l'homme à l'admiration et le tourne vers Dieu : « le soleil, en se montrant, proclame à son lever : Créature admirable, œuvre du Très-Haut ! Grand est le Seigneur qui l'a fait ; par sa parole il a précipité sa marche ! » (Sir. 43,2.5).

En même temps le monde éduque l'homme au sens de ses limites. « Dans le grand intérêt de la sagesse pour l'homme et le monde, écrit H.-J. Hermisson [21], il n'y a pas pour base quelque idée que l'homme est la mesure de toute chose ; au contraire : c'est l'homme qui est mesuré en fonction du monde dans lequel il est placé ». De fait, au-delà de ce qu'ils peuvent maîtriser par leur science ou leur savoir-faire, les humains débouchent très vite sur des zones marginales pleines d'inconnu et d'imprévisible, où seules évoluent à l'aise l'intelligence et la liberté de Dieu.

Cette perception aiguë du caractère insondable des œuvres de Dieu marque particulièrement les doxologies disséminées dans le livre de Job [22]. Ainsi Sophar demande à Job révolté :

> « Trouveras-tu le mystère (*ḥēqer*) d'Eloah ?
> Jusqu'à la limite (*taklīt*) de Shadday parviendras-tu ?
> Elle est plus haute que les Cieux : que feras-tu ?
> plus profonde que le Sheol : que sauras-tu ?
> Plus longue que la Terre est sa dimension,
> et plus large que la Mer ! » (Job 11,7-9).

La « limite » de Dieu n'est situable nulle part dans l'univers de l'homme : ce tour concret de la pensée sémitique souligne admirablement que toute imagination spatiale est dépassée, comme est vaincue d'avance devant Eloah toute prétention à un savoir et à un pouvoir autonomes : « que sauras-tu ? que feras-tu ? ». Plus loin Bildad, après avoir décrit l'empire du Créateur sur le monde souterrain et les confins du monde, rappelle, en reprenant des images mythiques, sa victoire primordiale sur Yām et Rahab, les monstres du chaos, et il ajoute :

21. *Op. cit.*, 150s. ; cité par G. von Rad, *Israël...*, p. 361.

22. Dans les discours des amis de Job : 5,9-18 ; 11,7-11 ; 22,12.29s. ; 25,1-6 ; 26,5-14 ; pour Job, uniquement dans le premier cycle de discours (4-14), en 7,12.17.20 ; 9,4-13 ; 10,8-12 ; 12,7-10.11-25.

« Ce sont là (seulement) les contours de ses œuvres ;
quel murmure [23] de parole nous en percevons !
Mais le tonnerre de sa puissance, qui le comprendra ? » (Job 26,14).

Face aux limites de leur savoir, les sages ont réagi de plusieurs manières. En général leur saisie intuitive du *ḥēqer* de Dieu stimule leur recherche et redouble leur louange : « Qui sera rassasié de voir sa gloire ? » (Sir. 42,25). Le Siracide développe même sur ce thème toute une parénèse :

« Nous pourrions dire encore bien des choses, mais nous n'arriverions pas !
L'achèvement de nos paroles, c'est qu'Il est le tout.
Pour le glorifier, où trouverions-nous la force ?
Car lui, il est le Grand, supérieur à toutes ses œuvres.
Le Seigneur est redoutable et terriblement grand,
merveilleuse est sa puissance.
En glorifiant le Seigneur, exaltez-le
autant que vous pourrez, car il sera toujours au-dessus !
En l'exaltant, multipliez votre force,
ne vous épuisez pas, car vous n'arriverez pas au bout.
Qui donc l'a vu et pourrait le raconter ?
Qui l'exaltera selon ce qu'il est ?
Bien des choses cachées sont plus grandes que celles-là ;
peu nombreuses sont celles de ses œuvres que nous avons vues »
(Sir. 43,27-33).

D'une manière moins sereine, l'auteur du poème de Job 28 sur la sagesse introuvable tire argument des limites du savoir humain pour tempérer l'enthousiasme de l'homme grisé par la technique :

« L'argent a un lieu d'origine
et l'or un endroit où on l'épure,
le fer est extrait du sol
et une pierre fondue devient du cuivre...
On a bouleversé les montagnes par la base,
on a exploré les sources des fleuves...
Mais la Sagesse, d'où sort-elle,
et quel est le lieu de l'intelligence ?
L'homme n'en connaît pas le chemin
et elle ne se trouve pas sur la terre des vivants » (Job 28,1.2.9-13)

23. Pour ce sens donné au mot *šemeṣ*, voir J. LÉVÊQUE, JD, 305s. Le Siracide dira de même (42,22) que l'homme ne peut contempler qu'une « étincelle » des œuvres de Dieu.

Avec ce chapitre 28 de Job, que la plupart des auteurs considèrent comme un ajout, nous avons affaire à un stade déjà tardif de la réflexion sapientielle. Pour le poète de la partie dialoguée (Ve siècle), la voix de la création joue un rôle autrement positif : en rappelant l'homme au sens de ses limites, elle l'invite à la conversion. C'est le thème développé tout au long de la théophanie (38,1-42,6) où Dieu répond enfin à Job du sein de la tempête. Si l'on restaure ce chef-d'œuvre dans sa logique primitive, avec un seul discours de Yahweh et une seule réponse de Job [24], on saisit aisément le but visé par l'auteur : au sommet théologique de toute son œuvre, il a voulu que la critique de la suffisance humaine entre dans le champ d'un dialogue direct entre Dieu et l'homme. Le discours de Dieu ne fait qu'expliciter le message de la création, mais si Dieu donne ainsi la parole à ses œuvres, c'est pour qu'elles conduisent Job de leur mystère à Son mystère. En dévoilant à Job les limites de son savoir et de son pouvoir, Yahweh cherche beaucoup moins à le condamner et à l'humilier qu'à lui révéler des richesses auxquelles il n'accédait pas. Semblant oublier le drame que vit son partenaire, Yahweh, sans hâte, feuillette l'album de l'univers, retrouvant dans chaque merveille de la nature des reflets de sa pensée créatrice et de sa providence. En réalité, Dieu n'oublie pas qu'il parle à un homme révolté par la souffrance ; mais il pense que la création a son mot à dire lorsque l'homme s'interroge sur son destin, parce que les œuvres déjà réussies par Dieu répondent de celles qu'il se réserve encore. La création, appelée comme témoin, retrouve alors toute sa dignité. En 30,22s., Job voyait en elle l'alliée de Dieu pour un dessein de cruauté :

> « Tu m'emportes sur le vent, tu me fais chevaucher,
> tu me liquéfies dans le fracas (de l'orage).
> Je sais que tu m'emmènes à la mort,
> et au rendez-vous de tout vivant. »

Maintenant la création redevient un langage de Dieu qui interpelle l'homme. En se situant à sa vraie place dans la nature, Job apprend à se situer par rapport à Dieu ; en accueillant le message du créé, il retrouve les mots de l'humilité et de la louange. Ainsi le monde œuvre pour sa part dans la rédemption du cœur de l'homme et, paradoxalement, dans cette dynamique du salut, l'indigence du savoir humain ouvre l'accès à une sagesse reçue de Dieu.

Ces réflexions sur le langage du cosmos vont nous permettre d'entendre et d'isoler à un premier niveau quelques thèmes du contrepoint sapientiel.

24. Nous avons proposé dans *Job et son Dieu*, 499-508, la reconstitution suivante : discours de Yahweh : 38,1.2s. ; 38,4-39,30 ; 40,2.8-14 ; réponse de Job : 40,3-5 ; 42,2-3.5-6.

Redisons, tout d'abord, que la conception sapientielle du monde et de ses valeurs suppose toujours, en arrière-fond, sinon une théologie vraiment élaborée de la création, — ce qui serait anachronique pour les recueils les plus anciens —, du moins une attitude foncièrement croyante. Les maîtres de sagesse savent que les choses ou les êtres doivent leur perfection originelle et leur permanence uniquement à l'acte libre de Yahweh qui les a voulus. Ils sont convaincus que la hardiesse de leurs enquêtes rationnelles ne peut aucunement porter ombrage à la seigneurie universelle de Dieu. Ils occupent sans crainte, et souvent avec une sorte d'aisance tranquille, la place de choix que Yahweh assigne à l'homme dans l'univers [25]. La présence du mal dans le monde les désarçonne parfois, mais jamais ils ne sont tentés de l'attribuer à un pouvoir étranger à celui de Dieu, à des forces mythiques vraiment capables de contrecarrer son dessein. A leur manière, tantôt réaliste, tantôt lyrique, rarement amère, ils développent, en contrepoint du thème de la création, une théologie de l'homme-au-monde. En un sens, l'optimisme des maîtres touchant la cohérence de l'œuvre de Dieu ou les affinités électives de l'homme et de l'univers rappelle l'allégresse des deux récits bibliques de la création (Gen. 1-2). Quand le sage, patiemment, met de l'ordre dans son univers et lui redonne sens, il prolonge le discernement primordial de la lumière et des ténèbres ; quand il inventorie les créatures, découvrant à chaque pas combien chacune est « bonne », quand il « nomme » les êtres et les phénomènes, il accomplit, à sa place et en son temps, la tâche de l'Adam de toujours, explorant et pacifiant son domaine.

Cette familiarité des sages avec l'univers comme lieu de l'efficacité divine explique en grande partie les convergences si fréquentes que l'on relève entre les écrits sapientiaux et la tradition hymnique d'Israël. Il importe toutefois de souligner l'optique particulière de certains passages hymniques des livres de sagesse. Si nous nous reportons, par exemple, aux doxologies du livre de Job [26], nous nous apercevons qu'elles ne se laissent pas réduire sans plus au genre littéraire des hymnes du psautier. Certes, dans leurs louanges de la majesté de Dieu, les trois visiteurs de Job — pour commencer par eux — associent toujours au thème de la création celui de l'homme-devant-Dieu, au souvenir de l'omniprésence active de Yahweh, celui du non-savoir, de l'impuissance ou de l'indignité de l'homme. Tout cela suit les lois du genre hymnique. Mais nulle part chez les amis de Job la louange n'est vraiment gratuite, car une visée

25. „Während die heidnischen und philosophischen Schöpfungstheorien meist schon den Keim des Pessimismus in sich tragen, vermag Israel kraft seines Schöpfungsglaubens zu kraftvoller Weltbejahung zu gelangen" (W. Eichrodt, *Theologie des Alten Testaments*, II, 68).

26. Cf. plus haut, note 22.

parénétique, voire polémique, reste partout présente et partout première. Et ce trait suffit à singulariser leurs doxologies, car dans les hymnes du psautier, qu'ils soient de type pur ou mixte, le glissement vers la parénèse n'apparaît que de façon tout à fait occasionnelle et marginale [27], tandis qu'aux yeux des amis de Job, l'essentiel est de réduire l'homme au silence. Les doxologies de Job lui-même sont sollicitées, elles aussi, mais dans une direction toute différente : en retenant quasi uniquement les thèmes qui exaltent la puissance de Dieu, Job, au fond, poursuit sa plainte [28] ; il habille ses griefs d'images hymniques pour les rendre en quelque sorte plus mordants et mettre plus efficacement la force de Dieu en opposition avec son *ḥesed*. Il reste cependant que les doxologies de Job révolté veulent porter à Dieu ses doutes et son désarroi ; elles sont encore prises dans une structure de dialogue, et par là rejoignent bien la ferveur qui anime les hymnes d'Israël.

Ainsi, sur la basse continue de l'idée de création, la voix des psalmistes et celle des sages savent rester distinctes, même lorsqu'il leur arrive de se retrouver à l'unisson. Ce contrepoint très souple se manifeste également à propos du message que l'univers adresse au croyant (Job 12,7-9 ; 28 ; Sir. 42,15-43,33). C'est un message sur Dieu et sur l'homme, et bien qu'il vienne de Dieu, la voix qui parle n'est pas celle de Yahweh ni celle d'un ministre du culte ou d'un prophète charismatique. Pour les sages, il ne fait aucun doute que cette voix demande à être entendue, parce qu'elle révèle à l'homme, de la part de Dieu, sa dépendance créaturale et sa place, à la fois royale et dérisoire, au sein du monde créé.

En Job 26,14 affleure l'idée d'un double témoignage de Yahweh, celui qu'il attend de la création et celui qu'il apporte lui-même par ses interventions personnelles. Les œuvres de Yahweh ne nous laissent percevoir qu'un « murmure », mais, ajoute Bildad, « le tonnerre (*ra'am*) de sa puissance, qui le comprendra ? » Le substantif *ra'am* et le verbe correspondant [29] renvoient toujours, dans l'A.T., aux théophanies du Dieu d'Israël, qu'il s'agisse de théophanies de révélation (Sinaï) [30], de libération (Exode, David, Ariel) [31] ou simplement de puissance [32]. Bildad compare donc le témoignage rendu par les créatures au témoignage que Dieu se rend à lui-même dans ses théophanies. Le second témoignage est au premier ce que le tonnerre est au murmure. Si donc, en admirant l'œuvre cosmique de Dieu, l'homme n'atteint, au mieux, que les « con-

27. Voir JD, 310s.
28. JD, 312-328.
29. Au *hif'il* : *hir'im*.
30. Ps. 81,8.
31. I Sam. 2,10 ; 7,10 ; 2 Sam. 22,14 ; Is. 29,5 (Yahweh vient sauver Ariel) ; Ps. 18,14 et 77,19. En Job 40,9 on trouve une allusion limpide aux théophanies de châtiment (cf. les versets 10-13).
32. Ps. 104 ; Ps. 29,3, avec historicisation du thème au v. 10.

tours » ou les franges du mystère divin, à plus forte raison sera-t-il toujours incapable de saisir la plénitude de puissance et de vie qui fait irruption dans le monde dès que Dieu parle aux hommes ou intervient dans leur histoire.

L'interprétation du Ps. 19, pris dans son ensemble, est à chercher dans la même ligne, mais un souci de plus grande précision théologique s'y fait jour. La première partie (v. 1-7), préexilique, recueille pour ainsi dire le kérygme du firmament et en rappelle la légitimité : les jours et les nuits se le transmettent sans faute ni répit depuis la création ; toutefois ce que « les cieux racontent de la gloire de Dieu » « n'est point récit ni langage, n'est point une voix qu'on puisse entendre » (v. 4), et l'écriture des cieux, tout universelle qu'elle soit (v. 5), reste muette. C'est pourquoi sans doute, beaucoup plus tard (pas avant l'époque d'Esdras), le psaume a reçu un long appendice : la louange de la Torah « parfaite » et du « témoignage véridique » de Yahweh (v. 8ss.). On a senti le besoin d'associer le kérygme in-ouï proclamé par le cosmos et la révélation toujours audible de Dieu dans sa Torah ; on s'est soucié de hiérarchiser l'un par rapport à l'autre les deux témoignages.

Les différences d'accents entre ces deux textes sont instructives. Des deux côtés on se heurte à une limite ; mais pour Bildad la limite est chez l'homme, incapable de comprendre le langage des théophanies, tandis que pour le psalmiste, c'est le cosmos qui est limité, ne possédant pas vraiment de langage. Pour Bildad l'excès de puissance déployé dans les théophanies étouffe le murmure audible de la création ; pour le psalmiste, au contraire, seule la Torah est assez puissante et douce pour atteindre le cœur de l'homme et devenir « lumière des yeux » (v. 9).

Le Ps. 19 représente, à vrai dire, un cas un peu particulier. D'autres psaumes, anciens (89,6) ou postexiliques (97,6 ; 145,10), ne marquent pas la même réserve et parlent sans ambages du témoignage spécifique et de la louange qui émanent de la création, en plein accord sur ce point avec la sagesse théologienne. Le monde créé et son message semblent donc avoir fourni à la tradition hymnique et à la réflexion sapientielle à la fois un terrain d'entente et la base d'un dialogue fructueux.

II. Les sages devant le mystère de l'homme

Si nous abordons maintenant le deuxième niveau de notre enquête : la conception sapientielle du destin de l'homme, nous allons voir la personnalité théologique des sages s'affirmer encore plus nettement.

Dans l'analyse de l'existence humaine une certaine évolution est perceptible lorsqu'on suit les différents stades de la réflexion sapientielle israélite. A l'époque royale, la sagesse reste marquée d'une relative euphorie. Les maîtres, ressaisissant l'héritage du vieux bon sens et de l'humour populaire, poursuivent et affinent leurs observations. Ils essaient d'embrasser l'ensemble des données de la condition humaine, cherchent des normes d'efficacité pour le travail et des conditions de stabilité pour la famille et les relations sociales. L'idéal de vie qu'ils proposent est censé mener à la fois à la sagesse et au bonheur. L'échec et le malheur sont imputables non à des anomalies de l'existence, mais aux fautes ou à la maladresse de l'homme : à lui d'entendre les sentences des sages et d'en faire son profit. Après l'exil, à l'époque où les prêtres et les scribes éditent le corpus prophétique, un maître de sagesse compose Pr. 1-9 pour en faire le prologue du corpus didactique des Proverbes. Il tente en même temps une première synthèse théologique en intégrant à sa réflexion sapientielle les thèmes alors dominants de Yahweh créateur et de sa providence. Plus consciemment théologienne, la sagesse se fait désormais un peu moins encyclopédique et restreint le champ de ses recherches. Mais ce qu'elle perd en envergure, elle le regagne en profondeur [33]. On s'interroge désormais non plus seulement sur les lois de l'épanouissement humain, mais, surtout avec Job et Qohelet, sur le mystère de l'homme et sur le sens de la conduite de Dieu. Enfin, beaucoup plus tard, le Siracide, bien qu'il se présente modestement comme « le dernier venu », comme un grappilleur après la vendange (33,16), réalisera en fait une tâche assez délicate en juxtaposant — sans trop le dire — dans ses larges strophes des éléments hérités de la tradition (8,9) et des interrogations étrangement proches des soucis de Qohelet (ex. Sir 11,2-4, 11-12 ; 15,16 ; 16,1-3 ; 33,13-15), et « en interprétant de nouvelle façon la notion de crainte de Dieu, à une époque où la volonté de Dieu s'exprime par la Torah écrite » [34].

En dépit des variations et des déplacements d'accent que l'on constate nécessairement au cours d'une si longue histoire, un élément essentiel demeure constant, c'est que la réflexion sur l'homme constitue une démarche de la foi. Jamais les sages n'ont été contraints de raccorder vaille que vaille la foi d'Israël à une psychologie ou une sociologie qui se seraient développées dans un premier temps de manière totalement neutre et indépendante. Les maîtres ne connaissent et n'étudient que l'homme intégral, dans sa triple relation au monde, à ses semblables et à Dieu. Pour eux, même l'expérience de Dieu fait partie du réel de l'homme, et c'est pourquoi elle a fait l'objet de plus en plus privilégié de la phénoménologie sapientielle.

Cet approfondissement théologique ne s'est d'ailleurs pas réalisé sans difficultés ni sans souffrances, car en explorant le destin de l'homme, en affrontant le problème de la mort et du malheur immérité, en soulevant l'énigme de la rétribution, les sages se sont heurtés plus que jamais aux

33. Cf. G. VON RAD, *Israël et la sagesse*, 86.
34. *Ib.*, p. 285.

limites de leur savoir, et parfois se sont sentis retenus par une sorte de scandale intérieur.

Déjà le grand recueil « salomonien » soulignait que Yahweh tient dans sa main les rênes de toute existence, et que lui seul est maître de l'irréversible :

« A l'homme sont les projets du cœur,
mais de Yahweh (vient) la réponse de la langue.
Toutes les voies de l'homme sont pures à ses yeux,
mais c'est Yahweh qui pèse les esprits. (Pr. 16,1s.)
Le cœur de l'homme médite sa voie,
mais c'est Yahweh qui affermit ses pas. (16,9)
Nombreuses sont les pensées dans le cœur de l'homme,
mais c'est le dessein de Yahweh qui se réalisera. (19,21)
Le cheval est préparé pour le jour du combat,
mais à Yahweh appartient la victoire. » (21,31)

Ainsi l'homme ne passe pas à volonté de l'intention à la réalisation effective. Une faille apparaît parfois qui arrête le projet humain, et « dans cette intervalle échappant au calcul, les maîtres ont discerné le domaine particulier de Yahweh » [35].

De même « il y a un temps pour tout, un temps pour tout faire sous le ciel » (Qoh. 3,1-8), et c'est tout un art que de savoir discerner ou attendre le moment favorable (cf. Sir. 1,23s. ; 4,20) ; mais Qohelet se plaindra que Dieu, trop souvent, en garde le secret : « J'ai vu le tracas que Dieu a donné aux fils d'homme pour qu'ils s'en tracassent. Il a fait toute chose convenable en son temps ; il a mis aussi la durée dans leur cœur, malgré quoi l'homme ne découvre pas l'œuvre que Dieu a faite du commencement à la fin » (Qoh. 3,10s.).

Autre limite imposée à l'entreprise sapientielle : la contingence des faits analysés. Comme le note G. von Rad : « Les phénomènes ne sont jamais objectivés ; ils sont toujours perçus dans leurs rapports avec l'homme mis en cause. Ces rapports étaient cependant toujours des plus variables et surtout on ne pouvait les évaluer de manière absolument claire. Sous la doctrine des sages, il y a donc une profonde conviction de l'ambivalence des phénomènes et des événements. (...) Il est certain que la richesse est une bonne chose ; mais elle peut aussi être préjudiciable ; il est certain que la pauvreté est quelque chose de mauvais, mais elle peut aussi être bonne. Toute sentence restait fondamentalement ouverte à un complément quelconque » [36].

35. *Ib.*, p. 126.
36. *Ib.*, pp. 360s.

Enfin, limite plus fondamentale encore ; les sages se voyaient dans l'impossibilité de clarifier philosophiquement le rapport entre les lois immanentes au monde humain et les libres interventions de Yahweh. Cette tension, à la fois théologique et existentielle, se reflète dans la manière dialectique dont ils proposent leur enseignement, juxtaposant de manière souvent imprévisible les certitudes et les apories, l'amertume et les cris de louange, l'héritage du passé et les interrogations nouvelles de leur temps.

Les maîtres n'ont pas tous fait face de la même manière aux limites qu'ils percevaient dans leur maîtrise de l'existence humaine. Tantôt ils s'en sont accommodés, pensant que Dieu, en prenant le relais, protégeait l'homme contre ses propres erreurs ou le faisait réussir au-delà même de ses projets : « c'est du Seigneur que vient la victoire ». Tantôt le sage, comme Qohelet, se laisse déprimer et paralyser en songeant d'avance à la vanité de ses efforts. Tantôt enfin, comme dans le livre de Job, l'homme se révolte contre ses limites parce qu'il y voit le signe d'une hostilité de Dieu :

> « Puisque les jours de l'homme sont décrétés,
> puisque le nombre de ses mois est connu de toi,
> *puisque tu as fixé sa limite et qu'il ne la franchira pas,*
> détourne de lui ton regard et laisse-le,
> jusqu'à ce que, comme un mercenaire,
> il s'acquitte de sa journée ! » (Job 14,5-6)

Cette image de la limite (*ḥoq*) à ne pas franchir renvoie directement au thème de la puissance cosmique de Dieu. C'est en effet au moment de la création que Dieu a « imposé à la pluie une limite (*ḥoq*) » (Job 28,26) ; de même il a « établi les astres à jamais, rendu un arrêt (*ḥoq*) qu'on ne transgresse pas ». Mais c'est surtout à Yam, la Mer démontée, que Dieu a fixé un *ḥoq* pour contenir ses révoltes (Jer. 5,22 ; Job 38,8-11 ; Pr. 8,29). Job, par une distorsion audacieuse du thème, utilise comme reproche à Dieu l'image de la « limite » qui ailleurs évoque la prévenance de Yahweh pour l'humanité. A mots couverts, il fait grief à Dieu de soumettre l'homme à la même loi d'airain que l'univers matériel ; et la limite temporelle imposée à la vie des humains rejoint dans son esprit la limite spatiale qui jusqu'à la fin bridera le mouvement des astres et de la mer. C'est la généralisation d'une autre plainte de Job : « Eloah a muré ma route pour que je ne passe pas » (19,8).

Ces premiers sondages dans l'enseignement sapientiel sur l'existence laissent déjà pressentir à quelle profondeur les questions y sont posées, tour à tour à l'homme et à Dieu. Nous sommes par là-même invités à poursuivre notre enquête sur l'homme et son destin, et à nous demander à ce sujet où se situe l'apport spécifique des maîtres de sagesse.

Il semble qu'on puisse percevoir leur contrepoint en suivant trois thèmes : *les bases de l'éthique, l'historicité de l'homme, la reconnaissance de Dieu* quand son action le rend méconnaissable.

Par l'attention toute spéciale qu'ils portent aux expériences heureuses ou malheureuses de l'homme et aux normes constatables de l'efficacité et du bonheur, les sages élargissent le champ de la réflexion éthique. En effet, alors que les prophètes rattachaient la morale yahwiste à une histoire de salut, les maîtres, tout aussi yahwistes par ailleurs, tirent volontiers leurs règles de conduite d'une induction patiente à partir de multiples comportements observés. Il y a, pour eux, une manière authentiquement humaine de se situer par rapport aux choses et aux événements, et cet art de vivre n'est pas étranger à la volonté de Dieu ; il y a une cohérence interne de l'agir humain qui s'accorde à la cohérence de l'œuvre cosmique du Créateur ; bref : il y a une soumission au réel qui est une manière de se soumettre à Yahweh. Cette osmose entre la morale yahwiste et la théologie de la création s'est intensifiée, évidemment, à partir du retour de l'exil [37], comme nous le constatons dans le poème de Pr. 8, qui rappelle le Deutéro-Isaïe (40,9.12 ; 45,19.21 ; cf. Dt 32,18) et annonce l'optimisme de Gen. 1 (cf. encore Ps. 90,2 ; 104).

Un problème théologique redoutable s'est dès lors posé aux sages d'Israël : comment concilier ces lois inscrites en l'homme avec la voix de Yahweh répercutée historiquement par les prophètes et dans la Torah ? L'harmonisation a été réalisée peu à peu, et comme indirectement, à mesure que s'affinait la théologie de la Sagesse de Dieu. Les sages ont pu établir un lien entre la Sagesse comme ouvrière cosmique et la Sagesse comme éducatrice des hommes par le truchement de la notion d'ordre. Principe de l'ordre universel, la Sagesse de Dieu fut reconnue sans peine comme principe de l'ordre moral. Cela allait de soi dès que l'on voyait dans la création une œuvre de Yahweh consonante à tous les niveaux. Après avoir assisté Dieu lorsqu'il créait le monde « très bon », il était naturel que la Sagesse intervînt, comme une mère aimante ou une épouse attentive, pour rendre l'homme heureux, efficace, équilibré [38].

Dès Pr. 1-9 la Sagesse de Dieu gagne pour ainsi dire en autonomie personnelle, et elle agit en éducatrice non plus seulement de loin, mais sur la terre et parmi les hommes (Pr. 1,20s.). Sa prédication devient, en somme, prophétique. De plus son aide est offerte libéralement à tous les hommes de bonne volonté (Pr. 8,4.17). Mais tout en s'adressant à l'ensemble des hommes sans aucune discrimination, la Sagesse ambitionne, au nom de Dieu, des relations personnelles avec chacun (Pr. 4,6 ; 7,4 ;

37. Cf. R. Tournay, *Proverbes 1-9 : première synthèse théologique de la tradition des Sages*, dans *Concilium* n° 20 (1966²) 49-56.

38. Cf. I Rois 3,12.28 ; 5,9.26 ; 10,24 ; Dt. 34,9 ; Is. 11,2 ; Jer. 9,11 ; ou encore Gen. (E) 41,16.38 ; Ex. (P) 28,3 ; 31,3.6 ; 35,31 ; 36,1.

8,32.34s.). Les accents parénétiques de Pr. 1-9 rappellent le Deutéronome et sa doctrine des « deux voies » (Dt, 30,15-20), mais la Sagesse qui parle en ces chapitres innove en adressant directement à l'individu ses conseils et ses promesses. Cette interpellation personnelle invite chaque croyant à sortir de l'anonymat du peuple : chacun, s'il le veut et s'il s'en rend digne par son comportement moral, peut entrer dans l'amitié de la Sagesse divine (cf. plus tard Sir 51,13-22). Dès l'époque du livret I des Proverbes, par conséquent, « la sagesse est la forme sous laquelle se présente aux hommes la volonté de Yahweh, de même que sa conduite des événements, autrement dit, son salut : elle est la substance de ce qui est nécessaire à l'homme pour vivre justement et ce que Dieu lui accorde. Mais l'essentiel est que cette sagesse n'est pas une chose, une doctrine, une direction, un salut, mais une personne, un Moi qui adresse un appel. Elle est ainsi la figure sous laquelle Yahweh se présente et sous laquelle il veut que l'homme le cherche » [39]. Cette idée de la Sagesse comme appel de Dieu adressé à l'homme mûrira en Israël et aboutira, chez le Siracide et dans le parallèle sapientiel de Bar. 3,9-4,4, à une identification explicite de la Sagesse avec la Torah donnée par Dieu.

L'approfondissement de l'éthique yahwiste favorisa également l'osmose entre le thème de la sagesse et celui de la crainte de Yahweh. A ce sujet, il faut remarquer tout de suite que les deux couples théologiques Sagesse-Torah et sagesse-crainte de Dieu n'envisagent pas le même aspect de la *ḥokmāh* ni le même mode de la relation de l'homme à Yahweh. C'est la Sagesse *de Dieu* qui est identifiée à la Torah, mais c'est la sagesse de l'homme qui se condense dans une attitude de crainte révérencielle. Le rapprochement de la *ḥokmāh* et de la *yir'at yhwh* avait été amorcé en Dt 32,6, où déjà la *ḥokmāh* désigne la conduite pieuse du peuple, en Os. 14,10 (ajout sapientiel), Ps. 107,43 et 90,12, où le sage est celui qui comprend les voies droites de Yahweh, les manifestations de sa grâce et le caractère éphémère de toute existence d'homme. Parallèlement, l'idée de *yir'at yhwh* s'était enrichie jusqu'à s'identifier à celle de religion intérieure. Associée par le Deutéronome à l'amour (*'hb*) pour Dieu et à l'accomplissement enthousiaste de sa volonté (Dt. 6,2.5.13), la crainte de Dieu est considérée en Is. 11,2 comme un fruit de l'Esprit à l'égal de la sagesse, et les Psaumes 112,1 et 128,1 font d'elle une béatitude. Aussi bien le très ancien livret II des Proverbes employait-il déjà *ḥokmāh* et *yir'at yhwh* dans des phrases étroitement parallèles (13,14 ; 14,27 ; 15,33a). Le livret I, après l'exil, souligne encore davantage le fondement religieux de la sagesse qui informe la vie de l'homme : la crainte de Yahweh est le commencement de la sagesse (Pr. 1,7 ; 9,10 ; cf. Ps. 111,10 ; Job 28,28). La Septante de Pr. 22,4 appellera même la crainte du Seigneur : *γενεὰ σοφίας*, « la naissance de la sagesse ». C'est

39. G. von Rad, *Théologie de l'A.T.*, I, 384s.

un thème que le Siracide affectionne particulièrement. Pour lui la crainte du Seigneur, entendue avec toutes ses résonances spirituelles, est à la fois le commencement, la racine, la couronne et la plénitude de la sagesse (Sir 1,14.16.18.20 ; cf. 1,27). En Sir 25,10, la crainte de Yahweh semble même prendre le pas sur toute sagesse de l'homme. Enfin Sir 19,20 et 21,11 mêlent étroitement les thèmes du *φόβος*, du *νόμος* et de la *σοφία*.

Sur l'historicité de l'homme, également, les sages ont apporté des lumières et surtout des questions toutes nouvelles. Non pas qu'ils se soient beaucoup souciés d'articuler leur doctrine sur les traditions de l'histoire du salut : il faudra attendre l'époque très tardive de Ben Sira pour voir un maître de sagesse brosser une fresque d'histoire (Sir 44-50, « éloge des ancêtres », d'Enok au grand prêtre Simon) [40]. Et cela ne peut étonner si l'on se rappelle tout ce qui séparait les sages et les chroniqueurs dans leur approche des faits. Les sages recherchaient des règles fermes, des constantes qui puissent s'exprimer dans des lois ; ils étaient en quête d'une maîtrise de l'existence par l'homme ; tandis que les historiens brassaient des événements déjà irréversibles, advenus sous le signe de l'*éphapax* et de l'initiative absolue de Yahweh. De plus les sages restaient conscients que le champ de leur investigation, aussi largement qu'ils l'étendissent, serait toujours cerné par l'indicible, par le mystère de Dieu (Pr. 25,2), alors que les narrateurs, ayant déjà pris la mesure de tous les événements, ne laissaient pas pressentir l'inexplicable.

Il ne faut donc pas attendre des sages qu'ils redisent le passé d'Israël ni à la manière des historiens, ni à la manière des prophètes. L'axe de leur recherche est ailleurs : ils préfèrent observer les réactions de l'homme-dans-le-temps, étudier le sens et les conséquences de sa temporalité.

Pour Job, porte-parole de l'humanité souffrante, le temps ne fait que hâter l'échéance inexorable de la mort (Job 7,7 ; 10,18-22 ; 17,1). Ne voyant pas le sens de sa propre vie ni de celle des malheureux, il maudit le jour de sa naissance (Job 3,3-10, démarquant probablement Jer. 20,14-18). Pour Qohelet, le temps n'est que le support des « vanités ». Toute chose a son rythme (1,5) et souvent obéit à une loi d'alternance (3,1-8) ou d'implacable succession (1,4). Les promesses des choses sont toujours un leurre (1,7s. ; 4,7s. ; 5,9 ; 6,7 ; 11,10). Tout passe ; et le temps qui fuit n'apportera jamais rien de nouveau sous le soleil, car ce temps se referme sur lui-même pour ramener demain ce qui fut hier (3,15 ; 1,6-11). Si bien que l'homme se lasse d'essayer de penser ce monde clos où « tout ce que Dieu fait sera à perpétuité », où « il n'y a rien à ajouter et rien à retrancher » (Qoh. 3,14).

Certes, les sages ne présentent pas tous la vie sous un jour aussi sombre : le temps imparti à l'homme peut être aussi rempli des bénédictions que

40. Cf. également les allusions très claires de Sir. 16,8s. ; 17,12 ; 24,7-11.

Yahweh réserve aux justes. Mais de toute façon, optimistes ou non, les sages se sont préoccupés de l'existence concrète de l'individu. Ils ont valorisé le *quotidien*, et non l'événementiel. C'est là sans doute l'une de leurs intuitions les plus originales, et la théologie biblique est encore loin d'avoir intégré cette richesse. Non pas qu'il faille le moins du monde minimiser l'importance des événements qui ont fondé le peuple de Dieu et ponctué l'histoire du salut ; mais on gagnerait à entendre ici encore le contrepoint des sages, et à étoffer comme eux la théologie de l'Alliance par la théologie des réalités quotidiennes au sein desquelles cette Alliance est vécue. Qui est, en effet, le sujet de l'Alliance, le partenaire de Dieu, sinon l'homme immergé dans l'ordinaire, qui retrouve chaque jour les mêmes liens avec les choses, les mêmes compagnonnages, la même ambivalence des sentiments, les mêmes joies, bien sûr, mais aussi le même voisinage avec la souffrance et la mort ? Qui est l'homme appelé au salut, sinon l'homme de tous les jours ?

L'homme concret se retrouve également chaque jour avec les mêmes certitudes de foi, mais aussi, parfois, avec les mêmes hésitations devant un visage de Dieu qu'il ne reconnaît plus.

Le grand mérite du livre de Job, au moins dans la partie dialoguée, est d'avoir accepté jusque dans ses dernières conséquences la problématique d'un double visage de Dieu, le visage d'Eloah « qui était avec lui aux jours de son automne » (Job 29,4) et celui de Dieu qui « déracine son espérance » (19,10). Bien d'autres témoins de Dieu ont dû porter le poids de son silence ou accepter l'apparente incohérence de son dessein : Abraham s'est heurté au mystère d'une double parole de Dieu, la parole de la promesse et l'ordre de sacrifier son fils ; Jacob a dû lutter toute une nuit contre l'Ange de Yahweh ; Moïse est dépeint par la théologie deutéronomiste comme un médiateur souffrant, écrasé sous le poids de sa mission ; David a dû monter « en pleurant, la tête voilée et nu-pieds, par la montée des Oliviers », abandonnant son palais et l'Arche de Dieu, sans savoir si Yahweh lui rendrait sa faveur (2 Sam. 15,17-30) ; Osée, Jérémie, Ezéchiel sont devenus signes pour Israël par leurs épreuves et par leur silence aussi bien que par leur parole. Mais la plainte que ces hommes de Dieu font entendre n'égale jamais en audace la triple contestation de Job, qui s'en prend à la fois à la bonté, à la sainteté et à la sagesse de Dieu. Est-ce, en effet, de la part de Yahweh une marque de *bonté* que d'offrir à l'homme une vie éphémère, douloureuse, vouée au Sheol ? Dès que s'installe chez un homme « l'amertume de l'âme et l'angoisse de l'esprit » (Job 10,1), l'existence n'est plus que leurre et déception, et le juste souffrant devient le mašal qui fait rire (17,4-6), la parabole vivante du non-sens de la vie. Mieux vaudrait, selon Job, « n'avoir pas été » ou « être passé du ventre à la tombe » (10,19), puisque la vie ne sera jamais qu'une gestation manquée, l'avortement d'un projet de l'homme-devant-Dieu (cf. 3,16). De plus, Dieu sait et veut les souffrances de Job, et cet acharnement irrationnel révèle « ce qu'il cache en son cœur » (10,13) depuis toujours : l'intention première et dernière de Shadday est de « mener à la mort » (30,23). Où est, par ailleurs, la *sainteté* de Dieu, s'il invente de toutes pièces la culpabilité de Job, s'il crée le péché pour pouvoir l'imputer ? Job ne trouve d'explication à sa souffrance que dans l'agression de Dieu et dans sa « cruauté » (30,21). C'est donc la faute de Dieu ; la faute est en Dieu. Puisque c'est Dieu qui a rompu le pacte, c'est à lui de revenir à l'homme, et la reprise du dialogue exige au préalable une conversion de Dieu. Où est, enfin, la *sagesse* de Dieu, puisque Eloah, en « méprisant l'œuvre de ses mains » (10,3), désavoue son travail de créateur et rend vaines ses « fatigues » (10,3 ; cf. 9,29), puisque, après avoir aimé, il va détruire ?

Pour Job, à l'heure du désespoir, l'image de Dieu se dédouble : derrière le Dieu ami se profile le Dieu de l'épouvante ; derrière le Dieu sage, le Dieu aux choix incohérents ; derrière le Dieu de l'Alliance, un Dieu étrangement allergique à la présence et au bonheur de l'homme. Souvent, las d'hésiter entre deux visages de Dieu, Job ne veut plus retenir que les traits du Dieu hostile. C'est alors qu'il laisse libre cours à son agressivité. Mais en substituant au portrait révélé de Dieu les images sécrétées par son angoisse, Job s'aventure seul loin des appuis de sa foi, et sa parole d'homme prend le pas sur la parole de Dieu.

Nulle part ailleurs, sinon peut-être chez Qohelet, la réflexion sapientielle n'a atteint un tel degré de hardiesse en contrepoint des thèmes de l'Alliance. A longueur de discours ce contrepoint crée la dissonance. Plus Job clame sa révolte devant une existence faussée jusqu'à l'absurde, et plus son cri semble se perdre au loin, comme pour reculer d'autant les limites de la transcendance de Dieu.

Mais l'audace finalement s'avère libératrice, parce que Job n'a jamais cessé d'attendre et de réclamer une rencontre, pour sauver coûte que coûte la *ṣ^e^dāqāh* de Dieu. L'excès même de la souffrance a creusé ainsi un espace nouveau pour l'adoration. C'est ce que Yahweh en personne vient révéler à Job du sein de l'orage théophanique : l'homme ne peut rejoindre sa liberté s'il ne laisse pas de place à la liberté de Dieu, et il faut qu'il se reçoive lui-même de Dieu pour que son univers prenne sens. Mais, inversement, l'univers a son rôle à jouer dans le cheminement de l'homme, et tout le discours de Yahweh tend à rappeler cette médiation du cosmos que Job avait dédaignée. Après les négations de Job, Yahweh se devait de défendre son œuvre, et il le fait en réintégrant la création dans l'univers spirituel de Job : le monde devra désormais rester pour lui un chemin vers Dieu, sur lequel il découvrira sans cesse la prévenance du Créateur et le sens de ses propres limites.

* * *

Monde créé, existence humaine : nous retrouvons là, réunis, les deux thèmes qui ont structuré notre enquête. Ils n'épuisent certes pas l'apport des sages, mais ils nous ont permis de situer l'entreprise sapientielle au carrefour de la culture et de la foi, à l'endroit précis et pourtant insaisissable où l'initiative de l'homme rencontre l'initiative de Dieu, où la créativité de l'homme trouve en Dieu créateur à la fois sa source et sa limite. Nous avons vu ces penseurs-poètes ramener, patiemment ou impatiemment, dans le champ de leur regard de foi [41] tout le réel de l'homme, tout ce qui fait chaque jour sa tâche, sa joie ou son scandale. En contrepoint de l'histoire du salut, ils ont sans cesse réaffirmé la permanence de l'alliance de l'Arc entre Yahweh et la terre, et par là ils ont maintenu et favorisé l'ouverture œcuménique [42] du peuple de Dieu. Transposant à leur manière l'idée centrale de l'Alliance historique, ils nous ont rappelé que toute question sur l'homme est en définitive une question posée à Dieu ; et sans doute irons-nous au-devant de bien d'autres richesses en suivant sans réticences cette aile marchante humaniste de la théologie d'Israël.

J. Lévêque

See *Supplementary note*, p. 220.

41. Cf. R. Gordis, *Biblical Wisdom and Modern Existentialism*, dans *Conservative Judaism* 21 (1966/67) 1-10.
42. Cf. A. Barucq, *Israele e Umanesimo*, dans *Bibbia e Oriente* 11 (1969) 97-107.

SUPPLEMENTARY NOTES (1989)

1

M. Dahood, *Northwest Semitic Texts and Textual Criticism of the Hebrew Bible*, 11-37.

Mitchell Dahood died on 8 March 1982 in Rome: cf. D.J. McCarthy, *Mitchell Dahood, S.J. (1922-1982): In Memoriam*, in *Biblica* 63 (1982) 298-299, and also J.-L. Cunchillos, in *Estudios Bíblicos* 41 (1983) 169-171.

Dahood urged the relevance of Northwest Semitic languages, especially Ugaritic, Phoenician (cf. *Phoenician-Punic Philology*, in *Orientalia* 46, 1977, pp. 462-475) and Eblaite, for the understanding of the Old Testament. This main interest, which is evident in his contribution to the present volume, continued in many other articles. For a general chronological overview, see: E.R. Martinez, *Hebrew-Ugaritic Index II, with an Eblaite Index to the Writings of Mitchell J. Dahood. A Bibliography with Indices of Scriptural Passages, Hebrew, Ugaritic and Eblaite Words, and Grammatical Observations. Critical Reviews, Doctoral Dissertations and Related Writings* (Subsidia Biblica, 4), Rome, 1981. The first part appeared in 1967: E.R. Martinez, *Hebrew-Ugaritic Index to the Writings of Mitchell J. Dahood. A Bibliography with Indices of Scriptural Passages, Hebrew and Ugaritic Words, and Grammatical Observations* (Scripta Pontificii Instituti Biblici, 116), Rome, 1967. Volume II can be supplemented with Dahood's bibliography as listed in W.L. Michel, *Job in the Light of Northwest Semitic I*, Rome, 1987, pp. 338-344.

Besides his *Ugaritic-Hebrew Lexicography*, printed in instalments in *Biblica* from 1963 to 1974, Dahood contributed to the three volumes of *Ras Shamra Parallels*: *Ugaritic-Hebrew Parallel Pairs*, in L. Fisher (ed.), *Ras Shamra Parallels. The Texts from Ugarit and the Hebrew Bible.* Volume I (Analecta Orientalia, 49), Rome, 1972, pp. 71-382 (cf. *supra* p. 18, n. 19); *Ugaritic-Hebrew Parallel Pairs*; *Ugaritic-Hebrew Parallel Pairs Supplement*, in L. Fisher (ed.), *Ras Shamra Parallels. The Texts from Ugarit and the Hebrew Bible.* Volume II (Analecta Orientalia, 50), Rome, 1975, pp. 1-33, 34-39; *Ugaritic-Hebrew Parallel Pairs*; *Ugaritic-Hebrew Parallel Pairs Supplement*, in S. Rummel (ed.), *Ras Shamra Parallels. The Texts from Ugarit and the Hebrew Bible.* Volume III (Analecta Orientalia, 51), Rome, 1981, pp. 1-178, 178-206.

Regarding the biblical books of Job and Isaiah, of which several texts are discussed in *Northwest Semitic Texts and Textual Criticism of the Hebrew Bible* (*supra*, pp. 11-37), mention should be made of articles published by Dahood after the Leuven Colloquium of 1972:
Is the Emendation of yādîn *to* yāzîn *Necessary in Job 36,31?*, in *Biblica* 53 (1972) 539-541.

Some Rare Parallel Word Pairs in Job and in Ugaritic, in R.J. Clifford & G.W. McRae (eds.), *The Word in the World: Essays in Honor of Frederick L. Moriarty, S.J.*, Cambridge (Mass.), 1973, pp. 19-34.
Ḥôl *«Phoenix» in Job 29:18 and in Ugaritic*, in *CBQ* 36 (1974) 85-88.
Chiasmus in Job: A Text-Critical and Philological Criterion, in H.N. Bream, R.D. Heim, C.A. Moore (eds.), *A Light unto my Path: Old Testament Studies in Honor of Jacob M. Myers* (Gettysburg Theological Studies, 4), Philadelphia, 1974, pp. 119-130.
Four Ugaritic Personal Names and Job 39,5.26-27, in *ZAW* 87 (1975) 220-221.
Ugaritic-Phoenician Forms in Job 34,36, in *Biblica* 62 (1981) 548-550.
The Dative Suffix in Job 33,13, in *Biblica* 63 (1982) 258-259.
The Breakup of Two Composite Phrases in Isaiah 40,13, in *Biblica* 54 (1973) 537-538.
Isaiah 51,19 and Seffîre III,22, in *Biblica* 56 (1975) 94-95.
Isaiah 19,11 ḥkmy *and 1QIs*[a] ḥkmyh, in *Biblica* 56 (1975) 420.
UT, 128 IV 6-7, 17-18 and Isaiah 23,8-9, in *Orientalia* 44 (1975) 439-441.
The Ugaritic Parallel Pair qra/qba *in Isaiah 62,2*, in *Biblica* 58 (1977) 527-528.
UT, 'nt:III:25-26 and Isaiah 21,12, in *Orientalia* 50 (1981) 194-196.
Isaiah 53,8-12 and Massoretic Misconstructions, in *Biblica* 63 (1982) 566-570.
See moreover *Hebrew-Ugaritic Index II* nrs. 251, 252, 269, 275.

With respect to the book of Isaiah, Dahood directed a doctoral dissertation: W.H. Irwin, *Isaiah 28-33. Translation with Philological Notes* (Biblica et Orientalia, 30), Rome, 1977. Surprisingly, Irwin does not make reference to Dahood's article in *Questions disputées* when dealing with Is 30,27 (pp. 96ff.) and 33,2-3 (pp. 136ff.).

Concerning the book of Job another dissertation (cf. *supra*, p. 24: A. Blommerde) was written within the 'Dahood school': A. Ceresko, *Job 29-31 in the Light of Northwest Semitic. A Translation and Philological Commentary* (Biblica et Orientalia, 36), Rome, 1980. This study must be supplemented with the first volume of a philological commentary on Job, very similar to the work of Dahood: W.L. Michel, *Job in the Light of Northwest Semitic. Volume I: Prologue and First Cycle of Speeches (Job 1:1 — 14:22)* (Biblica et Orientalia, 42), Rome, 1987 (*Questions disputées* is throughout the book wrongly refered to as *ETL* instead of *BETL*: see e.g. pp. 33-78).

Since 1977 Dahood became engaged with the mid-third millennium culture and language of Ebla (Tell Mardikh), e.g.:
& G. Pettinato, *Ugaritic* ršp gn *and Eblaite* rasap gunu(m)^{ki}, in *Orientalia* 46 (1977) 230-232.

Ebla, Ugarit and the Old Testament, in *VTS* 29 (1978) 81-112.
Ebla Discoveries and Biblical Research, in *Month* 13 (1980) 275-281.
Le scoperte archeologiche di Ebla e la ricerca biblica, in *Civiltà Cattolica* 131 (1980) 319-333.
Eblaite ḫa-rí *and Genesis 40,16* ḥōrî, in *Biblische Notizen* 13 (1980) 14-16.
Eblaite ì-du *and Hebrew* 'ēd, *«rain cloud», in CBQ* 43 (1981) 534-538.
Eblaite and Biblical Hebrew, in *CBQ* 44 (1982) 1-24.
Hebrew hapax legomena in Eblaite, in L. CAGNI (ed.), *Il bilinguismo a Ebla* (Studi Asiatici min., 22), Naples, 1984, pp. 439-470.
See moreover *Hebrew-Ugaritic Index II* nrs. 283, 284, *285, *286, 288, *289, *290, *305, 306, 313, *314, 315, *316, 317, [319-B], [319-C], [319-D], [319-F], [319-G], [319-H], [319-I], [319-J], [319-K], [319-O], [319-Y], [320-B], [320-C], [320-F].

Applying the method and work of Dahood, lexical material from Ebla is used in: E. ZURRO, *Procedimientos iterativos en la poesía ugarítica y hebrea* (Biblica et Orientalia, 43), Rome, 1987.

Dahood's remark concerning the Northwest Semitic prepositions (*supra*, p. 11 and esp. n. 4) should be supplemented by:
Z. ZEVIT, *The So-Called Interchangeability of the Prepositions* b, l *and* m(n) *in Northwest Semitic*, in *JANES* 7 (1975) 103-112.
M.D. FUTATO, *The Preposition 'Beth' in the Hebrew Psalter*, in *Westminster Theological Journal* 41 (1978s) 63-83 (the author criticizes Dahood's opinion that the Hebrew *b* can mean 'from').
M. DAHOOD, in *Orientalia* 46 (1977) 330 (*b* = 'after', Qoh 11,1); *Biblica* 59 (1978) 174-175 (*b* = 'throughout', Thren 1,2).
R. MEYER, *Gegensinn und Mehrdeutigkeit in der althebräischen Wort- und Begriffsbildung* (Sitzungsberichte der Sächsischen Akademie der Wissenschaften zu Leipzig, Phil.-hist. Klasse, 120/5), Berlin, 1979.

The reference to C. van Leeuwen as one of the scholars who have acknowledged the presence of Phoenician and Hebrew verb forms with suffix *-y* in the third person singular (*supra*, p. 16 and n. 15) rests upon a misreading. Van Leeuwen states: «Als het juist is [= If it were correct] met Dahood aan te nemen dat in het hebreeuws evenals in het fenicisch de *j* als suffix voor de 3e pers. moet hebben bestaan (zo Nelis op p. 22)...» (*Nederlands Theologisch Tijdschrift* 24, 1969-1970, pp. 139-140).
To n. 15 we should now add:
L. BOADT, *A Re-examination of the Third-Yod Suffix in Job*, in *UF* 7 (1975) 59-72.
Z. ZEVIT, *The Linguistic and Contextual Arguments in Support of a Hebrew 3 m.s. Suffix* -y, in *UF* 9 (1977) 315-328.

Of the revision of Gesenius' lexicon, «scheduled to appear in 1975» (*supra*, p. 23), R. Meyer prepared a first draft in Jena, which is now revised by H. Donner and U. Rüterswörden in Kiel. The first part recently appeared: W. GESENIUS, *Hebräisches und Aramäisches Handwörterbuch über das Alte Testament.* Unter verantwortlicher Mitarbeit von U. RÜTERSWÖRDEN bearbeitet und herausgegeben von R. MEYER und H. DONNER, 18. Auflage, 1 Lieferung (*'-g*), Berlin — Heidelberg — New York, 1987. See a critical review by J.A. EMERTON in *VT* 39 (1989) 104-110.

Of the *Dictionnaire des inscriptions sémitiques de l'ouest*, edited by C.F. JEAN and J. HOFTIJZER in 1965 (see *supra*, p. 28), a new completely revised edition is prepared by J. Hoftijzer and will shortly appear. Moreover, a linguistic data base of Hebrew epigraphic texts is set up by G.I. DAVIES at Cambridge University in view of the making of a concordance of the epigraphic materials.

For the study of the Ugaritic texts and the related Hebrew literature we refer to the annual volume of *Ugarit-Forschungen*, which has appeared since 1969 under the direction of O. Loretz. The last issue (no. 19, 1987) contains a good deal of lexicographical material. We should moreover mention G. DEL OLMO LETE's authoritative textbook *Mitos y leyendas de Canaán según la tradición de Ugarit. Textos, versión y estudio* (Fuentes de la Ciencia Bíblica, 1), Madrid, 1981, as well as his collected studies *Interpretación de la mitología cananea. Estudios de semántica ugarítica* (Fuentes de la Ciencia Bíblica, 2), Valencia, 1984.

Many disagree with the method and the results of Dahood's labor. In regard to the discussion, in the present volume, between Dahood and Barr on the basis of the text of Job 3, see: O. LORETZ, *Ugaritisch-Hebräisch in Job 3,3-26. Zum Disput von M. Dahood und J. Barr*, in *Ugarit-Forschungen* 8 (1976) 123-127. L.L. GRABBE, *Comparative Philology and the Text of Job: A Study in Methodology* (SBL Dissertation Series, 34), Missoula, MT, 1977, examines the methodology of Hebrew comparative philology; this work reflects the influence of the thorough research of J. Barr and the insights of modern linguists.

The broader scholarly debate is dealt with in W.D. BARRICK, *Current Trends and Tensions in Old Testament Textual Criticism*, in *The Bible Translator* 35 (1984) 301-308. See also M.S. MOORE, *A Short Note on Mitchell Dahood's Exegetical Methodology*, in *Hebrew Studies* 22 (1981) 35-38, as well as the bibliographical supplement listed by J. Barr (*infra*, p. 209).

M.V.

2

J. Barr, *Philology and Exegesis. Some General Remarks, with Illustrations from Job*, 39-61.

The subsequent death of Professor Dahood makes it sad to look back on the debate here recorded. Nevertheless the issues remain and he would not have wished them to be forgotten.

The writer's *Comparative Philology and the Text of the Old Testament*, which was the starting point of the discussion, continues in print, and an enlarged edition was recently published in the United States (Winona Lake, Indiana: Eisenbrauns, 1987). The text of the original was unchanged apart from minor typographical corrections, but a *Postscript* was added (pp. 355-361) and three other essays by the writer were also reprinted in the same volume, this one and two others: *Ugaritic and Hebrew* 'šbm'?, in *Journal of Semitic Studies* 18 (1973) 17-39 and *Limitations of Etymology as a Lexicographical Instrument in Biblical Hebrew*, in *Transactions of the Philological Society*, Oxford: Blackwell, 1983, 41-65. Both of these contain references to texts in Job.

On the book of Job in particular, I published some other articles, e.g.: *The Book of Job and its Modern Interpreters*, in *Bulletin of the John Rylands Library* 54 (1971) 28-46; *Hebrew* עַד, especially at Job i.18 and Neh. vii.3, in *Journal of Semitic Studies* 27 (1982) 177-192; *Hebrew Orthography and the Book of Job*, in *Journal of Semitic Studies* 30 (1985) 1-33.

On the entire question of the application of comparative philology to the Book of Job, see the comprehensive study of Lester L. Grabbe, *Comparative Philology and the Text of Job: a Study in Methodology* (Society of Biblical Literature Dissertation Series, 34), Missoula, Montana: Scholars Press, 1977.

On the relation between comparative philology and modern translations of the Bible see my *After five Years: a Retrospect on two major Translations of the Bible*, in *Heythrop Journal* 15 (1974) 381-405. All the signs are that, after the luxuriant blooming of new semantic identifications on the basis of comparative philology («semantic emendations» as they might be called) in the work of Dahood and in versions like the *New English Bible*, much greater reserve will be used in the next generation of Bible translations. A survey by an international group of scholars (see D. Barthélemy, *Critique textuelle de l'Ancien Testament I*, 1982, p. xiv, and my review in *Journal of Theological Studies* 37, 1986, 445-50) uses new philological identifications very sparingly, and it is widely expected that the forthcoming revision of the *New English Bible* will remove from its Old Testament many of the novel identifications of words which marked the original.

The last word in the matter has not yet been spoken and no doubt discussion will long continue. Professor Dahood set one model of approach before us, and other new models are likely to be proposed in time to come.

University of Oxford J. BARR
The Oriental Institute
Pusey Lane
Oxford OX1 2LE

3

J.F.A. SAWYER, *The «Original Meaning of the Text» and Other Legitimate Subjects for Semantic Description*, 63-70.

There have been various developments since 1972 which have encouraged biblical scholarship to move still further away from an exclusive quest for the «original meaning of the text», in the narrowest 'archaeological' sense of the term. Childs' «canonical criticism» is one obvious and influential example, motivated by theological concerns. Subsequent interest in the «final form of the text», not always in an explicitly theological context, is evident in essays on *Rhetorical Criticism, Canon and Authority*, and the like.

More recently Robert Alter's equally influential literary approach represents another development that shifts the emphasis from how things were in ancient Israel to what the text is about. As a measure of the traditional bias towards the «original» among modern readers of the Bible, he cited the vast readership of the *Biblical Archaeologist*, among both specialists and lay people, in contrast to that of more literary and religious publications. Alter and the increasing number of writers adopting various «literary approaches» have reminded us that there are still many questions to be asked about the meaning of the Biblical stories, as autonomous pieces of literature, without constant reference to questions of authorship, original intention, historicity, ancient near eastern parallels and the like.

An important biproduct of the work of Alter and other Jewish scholars, is that not infrequently conclusions about the meaning of the

Hebrew text reached by modern critical techniques, turn out to be the same as those reached in the Midrash, Rashi, Ibn Ezra and other precritical Jewish commentators. This is simply because both approaches are concerned with the same kind of question: Why did the author use this word or phrase here and not another? What are the special associations or nuances of this or that image? Critical scholars have often tended to dismiss the rabbinic and mediaeval Jewish sources as «late» (i.e. unreliable) or «unscientific». Yet these early Hebraists sometimes achieve a higher degree of semantic subtlety than many modern commentators. Since mishnaic, mediaeval and even modern Hebrew is closer to biblical Hebrew, both historically and semantically, than many of the ancient Ugaritic or Akkadian sources frequently quoted in our standard commentaries and dictionaries, then, unless we continue with the exclusive quest for originals — emending, reconstructing, hypothesizing — Eliezer ben Yehuda's *Thesaurus totius hebraitatis* or Even Shoshan's מילון חדש should be at least as familiar to the biblical hebraist as Aistleitner or von Soden.

A new scholarly interest in the history of interpretation is another indication of the shift in emphasis away from «originals». Much is published on the later stages of biblical tradition (e.g. post-exilic prophecy, Chronicles) and the apocrypha and pseudepigrapha. The ancient versions are increasingly being studied as literature in their own right, as evidence for Hellenistic Jewish thought (LXX), or the history of Eastern Christianity and the origins of Islam (Peshitta), rather than merely as witnesses to the Hebrew text. There are *Alttestamentler* who devote as much energy to mediaeval Jewish exegesis or Christian hebraists as to Canaanite myths and legends.

The same can be said of the most recent developments in the history of interpretation, namely, feminist hermeneutics and liberation theology. Some of the brilliant interpretations of the Bible by Trible, Fiorenza and Ruether, on the one hand, and Miranda, Gutierrez and Croatto on the other, have broken new ground in biblical research, and the widely published interpretations coming from the «base communities» of the Church in parts of Latin America, South Africa, Korea, the Philippines and elsewhere, are taken seriously by a growing number of critical scholars. Like the precritical Jewish commentators just referred to, such interpreters grapple with the text as it stands, and find within it truth and hope, which may or may not have been in the mind of the original author, but which, provided no-one pretends that they were, are nonetheless important and valuable as part of the history of interpretation.

Faced with the vast array of interpretations from the earliest stages in the ancient world down to the present, we have to distinguish those that are convincing, inspiring and morally acceptable from those that are contrived, demoralizing and evil, whatever their date and historical context. In a discipline where surely chronological priority cannot be the only criterion of truth, is the admitted bias of the feminists and liberation theologians in favour of justice and peace in their selection and interpretation of biblical texts, any less justified than the traditional academic bias in favour of «the original meaning of the text»?

Select Bibliography:

R. ALTER, *The Art of Biblical Narrative*, New York, 1981.
—, *The Art of Biblical Poetry*, New York, 1985.
R. ALTER & F. KERMODE (eds.), *The Literary Guide to the Bible*, New York, 1987.
J. BARTON, *Reading the Old Testament. Method in Biblical Study*, Philadelphia, 1984.
—, *Oracles of God, Perceptions of Ancient Prophecy after the Exile*, London, 1986.
J.H. CHARLESWORTH (ed.), *The Old Testament Pseudepigrapha*, 2 vols., London, 1983-85.
B.S. CHILDS, *Introduction to the Old Testament as Scripture*, Philadelphia, 1979.
S. CROATTO, *Biblical Hermeneutics*, Maryknoll (N.Y.), 1987.
G.W. COATS & B.O. LONG (eds.), *Canon and Authority*, Philadelphia, 1977.
E.S. FIORENZA, *Bread Not Stone. The Challenge of Feminist Biblical Hermeneutics*, Boston, 1984.
—, *The Ethics of Biblical Interpretation: De-centering Biblical Scholarship*, in *JBL* 107 (1988) 3-17.
M. FISHBANE, *Biblical Interpretation in Ancient Israel*, Oxford, 1985.
H.N. FRYE, *The Great Code: The Bible and Literature*, London, 1982.
N.K. GOTTWALD, *The Bible and Liberation: Political and Social Hermeneutics*, Maryknoll (N.Y.), 1983.
G. GUTIERREZ, *On Job*, Maryknoll (N.Y.), 1987.
J.J. JACKSON & M. KESSLER (eds.), *Rhetorical Criticism: Essays in Honour of James Muilenberg*, Pittsburgh, 1974.
D. JOBLING, *The Sense of Biblical Narrative*, Sheffield, 1978.
W. MCKANE, *Selected Christian Hebraists*, 1988.
J.P. MIRANDA, *Marx and the Bible*, London, 1983.
D. PATTE, *What is Structuralist Exegesis?*, Philadelphia, 1976.
R.M. POLZIN & E. ROTHMAN, *The Biblical Mosaic: Changing Perspectives*, Philadelphia & Chico, California, 1982.
P. RICŒUR, *Essays on Biblical Interpretation*, Philadelphia, 1980.
J. ROGERSON *et al.* (eds.), *The History of Christian Theology, Vol.2. The Study and Use of the Bible*, 1988.
L.M. RUSSELL (ed.), *Feminist Interpretation of the Bible*, Oxford, 1985.

J.F.A. SAWYER, *A Change of Emphasis in the Study of the Prophets*, in *Israel's Prophetic Tradition* (eds. R.J. COGGINS *et al.*), Cambridge, 1982, pp. 233-249.
—, *The role of Jewish Studies in Biblical Semantics*, in *Scripta signa vocis* (ed. H.L.J. VANSTIPHOUT), Groningen, 1986, pp. 201-208.
P. TRIBLE, *God and the Rhetoric of Sexuality*, Philadelphia, 1978.
—, *Texts of Terror: Literary Feminist Readings of Biblical Narratives*, Philadelphia, 1984.

University of Newcastle upon Tyne
Newcastle upon Tyne NE1 7RU

J.F.A. SAWYER

4

E. KUTSCH, *Gottes Zuspruch und Anspruch*, 71-90.

Das hier gewonnene Bild — dass *b^{e}rît* nicht «Bund» bedeutet, sondern die einseitige «Setzung» («Bestimmung», «Verpflichtung») meint — wird bestätigt durch den Sachverhalt, daß an einer Reihe von Stellen — nämlich *2 Kön.*, 11,17 mit *2 Chron.*, 23,16; *2 Kön.*, 23,3a.b; *Jer.*, 34,15 bα. 18aß.b; 50,5; *2 Chron.*, 15,12; *Esra*, 10,3, dazu *Ex.*, 34,10 — *b^{e}rît* lediglich die Selbstverpflichtung des Subjekts der *b^{e}rît* bezeichnet, ohne daß ein als «Bundespartner» denkbares Gegenüber genannt wird. Nach *2 Kön.*, 11,17a hat der Oberpriester Jojada zwischen Jahwe, dem König (Joas) und dem Volk die *b^{e}rît* festgesetzt, «das Volk Jahwes zu sein». Es ist erkennbar: allein der König und das Volk übernehmen bei dieser *b^{e}rît* eine Verpflichtung[1]. In ähnlicher Weise setzt in *2 Kön.*, 23,3 der König Josia — hier nun ausdrücklich «*vor* Jahwe» — die *b^{e}rît* fest, «Jahwe nachzufolgen und seine Gebote, Verordnungen und Satzungen mit ganzem Herzen und mit ganzer Seele zu halten»; und nach V. 3b tritt das Volk[2] in diese *b^{e}rît* ein. Nach *Jer.* 34,13.14a hat Jahwe den Vätern der Judäer für jedes siebte Jahr die Freilassung der «hebräischen» Sklaven durch eine *b^{e}rît* (= ein Gebot) angeordnet. Die Durchführung dieses Gebotes haben die Judäer nunmehr übernommen, indem sie eine *b^{e}rît* (= Selbstverpflichtung) *vor* Jahwe festsetzten (V. 15aß.b; vgl. V. 18aß.b). In *Jer.* 50,5 erscheint in der Rede der (nach Jahwes Ankündigung) heimkehrenden Israeliten als Inhalt einer «ewigen *b^{e}rît*, die nicht vergessen wird», daß sie Jahwe anhangen wollen[3]. Nach *2 Chron.*, 15,12 «treten» die Judäer und Israeliten in die *b^{e}rît* ein, Jahwe zu suchen, und in *Esra*, 10,3 erklärt Schechanja ben Jehiel im Anschluß an ein Schuldbekenntnis: «Wir wollen eine *b^{e}rît* festsetzen für unseren Gott, daß wir unsere (fremden) Frauen und die von ihnen Geborenen verstoßen;» und dies zu tun beschwören anschließend Priester und Volk ausdrücklich (V.

5b). In diesen Zusammenhang gehört dann auch die *b^erît* (= Zusage) Jahwes, unerhörte Wunder zu tun[4].

Bei diesem reichlichen Material handelt es sich nicht um ein «sekundäres und zufälliges Nebengleis der Begriffsgeschichte» von *b^erît*[5]; hier ist ganz offensichtlich die ursprüngliche Bedeutung von *b^erît* — die eben *nicht* «Bund» ist, sondern «Setzung, Selbst- oder Fremdverpflichtung» — vorausgesetzt[6].

1. Die Parellele in *2 Chron.*, 23,16 verdeutlicht diesen Sachverhalt noch, indem sie «zwischen Jahwe» durch «zwischen ihm (d.h. dem Oberpriester)» ersetzt hat.
2. *2 Chron.*, 34,33a vermerkt: «auf Veranlassung des Königs».
3. In Fortsetzung des Imperativs *bo'û* «kommt» lies *w^enillawäh* (mit BHK, BHS und Kommentaren).
4. S. oben S. 81.
5. So Chr. LEVIN, *Die Verheißung des neuen Bundes in ihrem theologiegeschichtlichen Zusammenhang ausgelegt* (FRLANT, 137), Göttingen, 1985, S. 122. Levin führt hier nur drei Belege an.
6. Levin hält zwar die Bedeutung «Bund» fur *b^erît* fest. Immerhin aber beobachtet er zum Beispiel, daß in *Gen.*, 15,18 der «Bund... alles Gegenseitige verloren hat» (a.a.O. S. 250), daß in *2 Kön.*, 23,3 «Joschijas Bundesschluß nichts als die Selbstverpflichtung, dem aufgefundenen Gesetz zu gehorchen,» bedeutet (a.a.O. S. 122 Anm. 179), und muß sogar feststellen, daß die «entschiedene Einseitigkeit» der *b^erît* «im theologischen Gebrauch von *brjt* von Anfang an angelegt ist» (a.a.O. S. 250). Daß mit eben *dieser* Erkenntnis der Begriff *b^erît* richtig verstanden ist, lehrt bereits die Septuaginta: Sie hat *b^erît* konsequent mit διαθήκη (einseitige «Setzung»; von da aus «Testament») — und nicht mit συνθήκη («Bund») — wiedergegeben. — [Der Hilfsannahme, daß diese Einseitigkeit von *b^erît* die «Gleichsetzung von Verheißung und Bund» voraussetze (Levin a.a.O. S.250), bedarf es nicht: *b^erît* ist — bis auf vereinzelte Ausnahmen im profanen Bereich, wo eine Mehrzahl Subjekt einer *b^erît* ist — nicht «Bund». Vgl. dazu weiter: *Neues Testament — Neuer Bund?*, Neukirchen-Vluyn, 1978, und den Artikel *Bund: I-III*, in *TRE* VII, S. 397-410.]

Ina-Seidel-Straße 10
D-8520 Erlangen-Frauenaurach

E. KUTSCH

5

D.J. MCCARTHY, *Covenant-Relationships*, 91-103.

Dennis J. McCarthy died on 29 August 1983 at Salamanca, Spain: cf. J. WELCH, *Dennis J. McCarthy, S.J. (1924-1983): In Memoriam*, in *Biblica* 64 (1983) 591-592 and R.F. COLLINS in *ETL* 60 (1984) 207.

His article on *Convenant-Relationships* has been reprinted in:
D.J. MCCARTHY, *Institution and Narrative. Collected Essays* (Analecta Biblica, 108), Rome, 1985, pp. 54-66, with some (partly wrong) *Errata corrigenda* on p. 416.

This volume also contains seven other covenant studies, which McCarthy has published between 1964 and 1982:
pp. 3-13: *Three Covenants in Genesis* [in *CBQ* 26 (1964) 179-189] (see *supra* p. 95, n. 10);
pp. 14-20: *Hosea XII 2: Covenant by Oil* [in *VT* 14 (1964) 215-221];
pp. 21-41: B^e^rît *and Covenant in the Deuteronomistic History* [in P.A.H. DE BOER (ed.), *Studies in the Religion of Ancient Israel* (VTS, 23), Leiden, 1972, pp. 65-85] (see *supra* p. 91, n. 1);
pp. 42-53: b^e^rît *in Old Testament History and Theology*. Review article on Lothar Perlitt's *Bundestheologie im Alten Testament* [in *Biblica* 53 (1972) 110-121];
pp. 67-73: *Ebla,* ὅρκια τέμνειν, ṭb, šlm*: Addenda to* Treaty and Covenant[2] [in *Biblica* 60 (1979) 247-253];
pp. 74-91: *Compact and Kingship: Stimuli for Hebrew Covenant Thinking* [in T. ISHIDA (ed.), *Studies in the Period of David and Solomon and Other Essays*. Papers Read at the International Symposium for Biblical Studies, Tokyo 5-7 December 1979, Tokyo, 1982, pp. 75-92];
pp. 92-111: *Covenant and Law in Chronicles-Nehemiah* [in *CBQ* 44 (1982) 25-44].

To this list we may add: *Covenant in Narratives from Late OT Times*, in H.B. HUFFMON, F.A. SPINA, A.R.W. GREEN (eds.), *The Quest for the Kingdom of God: Studies in Honor of George E. Mendenhall*, Winona Lake, Indiana, 1983, pp. 77-94.

In 1976, D.J. McCarthy finished a revised edition of his well-known thoroughgoing study on *Treaty and Covenant* (1963): *Treaty and Covenant. A Study in Form in the Ancient Oriental Documents and in the Old Testament*. New Edition Completely Rewritten (Analecta Biblica, 21A), Rome, 1978 (with an extensive bibliography on pp. 309-342). A survey of the concern with Old Testament ideas and forms of covenant that has developed since about 1960 from comparisons with secular vassal treaties is given in *Old Testament Covenant. A Survey of Current Opinions* (Growing Points in Theology), Oxford, 1972. The body of this book is a version of a German form, which McCarthy published in 1966 (*Der Gottesbund im Alten Testament*, SBS 13, Stuttgart, [2]1967). A Postcript in the English edition treats the relevant material to covenant which has appeared since.

The bibliographical references in McCarthy's contribution to the present volume should be supplemented by two general surveys, the one dealing with the lexeme *b^e^rît: TWAT I*, cols. 781-808 (M. Weinfeld; 1973), the other concerning the covenant theme: E.W. NICHOLSON, *God and his People. Covenant and Theology in the Old Testament*, Oxford, 1986 (*supra*, n. 1, p. 91 and n. 22, pp. 102-103). See moreover the studies of P. Buis (1976) and J. Vermeylen (1986), listed by L. Dequeker (*infra*,

p. 217). For a study of the literary growth of Gn 21,22-34; 26,23-33 and 31,25-32,3 (*supra*, p. 92-100 and nn. 4-5) see recently E. Blum, *Die Komposition der Vätergeschichte* (WMANT, 57), Neukirchen-Vluyn, 1984.

M.V.

6

P.A.H. de Boer, *Quelques remarques sur l'arc dans la nuée*, 105-114.

The thesis defended in de Boer's contribution on Gn 9,8-17 is taken up and rectified by C.J.L. Kloos, *The Flood on Speaking Terms with God*, in *ZAW* 94 (1982) 639-642. It is Kloos's opinion that the Priestly writer accorded the concept of the 'flood' (*mabbûl*) as an instrument of God with the concept of the 'sea' (*yam*) as the defeated arch-enemy of God, by conceiving of the flood as an independent power, which was temporarily released to punish mankind and to force them to renewed obedience. Compare also L. Dequeker, *L'alliance avec Noé (Gen 9,1-17)*, in J. Chopineau (ed.), *Noé, l'homme universel* (Publications de l'Institutum Iudaicum Bruxelles, 3), Brussels, 1978, pp. 1-19.

A study of the structure and theme of the pericope is done by A. Bonora, *La promessa-impegno di dio con il mondo (Gen. 9,8-17); Proposta di struttura letteraria*, in *TItSett* 7 (1982) 37-45.
See moreover:
G.J. Wenham, *The Coherence of the Flood Narrative*, in *VT* 28 (1978) 336-348, and comp. the critical examination of this and other attempts to defend the unity of Gn 6-9 by J.A. Emerton in *VT* 37 (1987) 401-420 and 38 (1988) 1-21.
L. Neveu, *Entrelacs bibliques sur le déluge. Recherches sur la structure littéraire de Gn 6,5-9,17*, Angers, 1981.
For a 'new approach': see R. Couffignal, *La geste de Noé. Approches nouvelles de Genèse, vi-ix*, in *Revue Thomiste* 85 (1985) 607-619.

In regard to the *b*ᵉ*rît* terminology, reference should be made to the bibliographical supplements to the contributions of E. Kutsch (p. 213), D.J. McCarthy (p. 214) and L. Dequeker (p. 217). For the *b*ᵉ*rît ḥădāšāh* in Jeremiah, see the supplementary note by R. Martin-Achard (p. 218).

The *tôledôt* formulae (*supra*, p. 105) are discussed by S. Tengström, *Die Toledotformel und die literarische Struktur der priesterlichen Erweiterungsschicht im Pentateuch* (Coniectanea Biblica; Old Testament Series, 17), Gleerup, 1982, as well as P. Weimar, *Struktur und Komposition der priesterschriftlichen Geschichtsdarstellung*, in *Biblische Notizen* 23 (1984) 81-134, pp. 88-98.

M.V.

7

L. DEQUEKER, *Noah and Israel. The Everlasting Divine Covenant with Mankind*, 115-129.

Although C. WESTERMANN (*Genesis*, BKAT I/8, 1973) stresses the notion of *b^erît* as an interpretament in the Flood Story of P, and while he underlines the complementarity of Creation and Flood, even now almost no attention is paid by biblical scholars to the meaning of the Israel-Covenant for all mankind.

E.W. NICHOLSON (*God and his People. Covenant and Theology in the Old Testament*, Oxford, 1986) totally neglects P's theological interpretation of the Flood with relation to Israel.

P. BUIS (*La notion d'alliance dans l'Ancien Testament*, Lectio divina 88, Paris, 1976), while referring to the present study, considers the covenants in the Bible as successive events in sacred history, developing from the universal to the particular.

J. VERMEYLEN (*Le Dieu de la promesse et le Dieu de l'alliance*, Lectio divina 126, Paris, 1986) takes into account the divine guarantees for Israel's redemption given by the covenant with Noah, in the version of P. Still, the universal scope for all mankind of both the covenant with Noah and the covenant with Abraham is not dealt with.

K.U. Leuven
Faculteit Letteren en Wijsbegeerte
Blijde Inkomststraat 21
B-3000 Leuven

L. DEQUEKER

8

P. BUIS, *Comment au septième siècle envisageait-on l'avenir de l'Alliance? Étude de Lv. 26,3-45*, 131-140.

L'auteur a donné une nouvelle analyse de ce texte dans: P. BUIS, *La notion d'alliance dans l'ancien testament* (Lectio divina, 88) Paris: Cerf, 1976, pp. 86-91.

La structure dominante du texte est une proposition de contrat: «si vous marchez selon mes lois... si vous n'écoutez pas...». Mais elle recouvre un récit des relations entre YHWH et son peuple depuis les origines jusqu'au coeur de l'exil. Après un temps de fidélité et de bénédiction, le peuple a refusé d'obéir aux lois et on n'envisage pas qu'il revienne à l'obéissance. Ce qu'on attend de lui au long des 25 versets c'est qu'il reconnaisse sa faute, autre manière de reconnaître l'autorité de YHWH et de renouer une relation avec Lui. Mais ce ne sera possible qu'une fois le peuple séparé de sa terre, qu'il avait entrainée dans l'infidélité.

La terre était un intermédiaire entre YHWH et Israël: c'est par elle que venaient les bénédictions, par elle que s'exerçaient les répresailles destinées à «venger l'alliance». Cette médiation disparait, ainsi que les sanctuaires (v. 31) qui concrétisaient la présence du Seigneur. Les lois elles-mêmes ne sont plus mentionnées, comme moyen d'entrer en relation. Au terme de ce chapitre, toutes les médiations ont disparu, ce qui rejoint plusieurs oracles de Jérémie (29; 31,33-34).

Grand séminaire spiritain
BP 3933 Libreville
Gabon

P. Buis

9

R. Martin-Achard, *Quelques remarques sur la nouvelle alliance chez Jérémie (Jérémie 31,31-34),* 141-164.

D'une manière générale et en accord avec la tendance actuelle de l'exégèse biblique, qui insiste sur le rôle du Deutéronome et de son école dans l'épanouissement, voire même l'éclosion de la littérature vétéro-testamentaire, les spécialistes attribuent une date tardive (6ème siècle, ou même 5ème siècle) à la péricope de Jér. 31,31-34 (ainsi R.P. Caroll, 1981; C. Levin, 1985; etc.); certains auteurs défendent cependant l'authenticité, de fond tout au moins, sinon de forme, de l'oracle jérémien (ainsi H. Weippert, 1979; H.D. Potter, 1983; J. Briend, 1983; etc.).

Malgré les savantes études consacrées récemment à contester un lien direct entre le prophète d'Anatot et la promesse de «la nouvelle alliance», ma position fondamentale n'a pas changé: Jér. 31,31-34 relève, du fait de son originalité, voire de son unicité, d'un prophète; ces versets s'intègrent au message de Jérémie; ils constituent sa réponse à l'échec de la réforme deutéronomiste. Ce point de vue mérite d'être pris en considération.

Parmi les travaux parus ces dernières années, citons:

J. BRIEND, *L'espérance d'une nouvelle alliance*, dans *Lumière et Vie* 32/165 (1983) 31-43.

R.P. CAROLL, *From Chaos to Covenant. Uses of Prophecy in the Book of Jeremiah*, New York, 1981.

G. FOHRER, *Der Israel-Prophet in Jeremia 30-31*, dans *Mélanges bibliques et orientaux H. Cazelles* (AOAT, 212), Neukirchen-Vluyn, 1981, pp. 135-148.

W.E. LEMKE, *Jeremiah 31:31-34*, dans *Interpretation* 37 (1983) 183-187.

C. LEVIN, *Die Verheißung des neuen Bundes in ihrem theologiegeschichtlichen Zusammenhang ausgelegt* (FRLANT, 137), Göttingen, 1985 (lit.).

N. LOHFINK, *Der junge Jeremia als Propagandist und Poet. Zum Grundstock von Jer 30-31*, dans *Le Livre de Jérémie* (ed. P.-M. BOGAERT; BETL, 54), Leuven, 1981, pp. 351-368.

J. MEJIA, *La problématique de l'ancienne et de la nouvelle alliance dans Jérémie XXXI 31-34 et quelques autres textes*, dans *Congress Volume Vienna 1980* (VT.Suppl., 32), Leiden, 1981, pp. 263-277.

H.D. POTTER, *The New Covenant in Jeremiah XXXI 31-34*, dans *VT* 33 (1983) 347-357.

J. SWETNAM, *Why was Jeremiah's New Covenant New?*, dans *Studies on Prophecy* (VT.Suppl., 26), Leiden, 1974, pp. 111-115.

W. THIEL, *Die deuteronomistische Redaktion von Jeremia 26-45* (WMANT, 52), Neukirchen-Vluyn, 1981, notamment pp. 20-28.

H. WEIPPERT, *Das Wort vom neuen Bund in Jeremia XXXI 31-34*, dans *VT* 29 (1979) 336-351.

106, route de Ferney
CH-1202 Genève

R. MARTIN-ACHARD

10

H.D. PREUSS, *Alttestamentliche Weisheit in christlicher Theologie?*, 165-181.

Zu Anm. 3, S. 165:

Zum Thema «Das Alte Testament bei D. Bonhoeffer» vgl. jetzt auch F.I. ANDERSEN, in *RTR* 34 (1975) 33-34; I. BALDERMANN, in *Jahrb. für Bibl. Theol.* 1 (1987) 182ff.

Zu Anm. 9, S. 167:

Vgl. dazu jetzt mein Buch *Einführung in die alttestamentliche Weisheitsliteratur* (Urban-Taschenbuch, 383), Stuttgart/Berlin/Köln/Mainz, 1987, dort besonders § 7 (Zum theol. Ort der atl. Weisheitsliteratur) mit ausführlicherer Diskussion auch neuerer Thesen und genauerer Begründung, jedoch auch Differenzierung und Modifizierung der eigenen Position.

Zu Anm. 35, S. 172:

Daß außerdem das AT nicht auf einerlei Weise von JHWH redet, wird in der neueren Forschung zur Sache immer wieder unterstrichen; vgl. dazu die Diskussion in dem zu Anm. 3 nachgetragenen Buch; dort auch Hinweise auf neuere Textausgaben und Literatur zu Weisheitstexten aus der Umwelt des alten Israel.

Kreuzlach 20c
D-8806 Neuendettelsau

H.D. PREUSS

11

J. LÉVÊQUE, *Le contrepoint théologique apporté par la réflexion sapientielle*, 183-202.

Parmi les nombreux travaux consacrés depuis 1972 aux livres de sagesse et à la théologie sapientielle (cf. James L. CRENSHAW, *Old Testament Wisdom. An Introduction*, London, 1982), nous relèverons ici uniquement ceux qui ont trait plus directement aux thèmes de notre enquête.

Nous utiliserons, entre autres, le sigle suivant:
IW: *Israelite Wisdom. Theological and Literary Essays in Honor of Samuel Terrien* (ed. John G. GAMMIE), New York, 1978.

A propos des sagesses du Proche-Orient Ancient, on peut lire maintenant:
H. BRUNNER, *Zentralbegriffe ägyptischer und israelitischer Weisheitslehre*, dans *Saeculum* 35 (1985) 185-199.
G.L. BRYCE, *A Legacy of Wisdom. The Egyptian Contribution to the Wisdom of Israel*, Lewisburg Pa., 1979.
A. CAQUOT, *Israelite Perceptions of Wisdom and Strength in the Light of the Ras Shamra Texts*, dans *IW*, 25-33.
J. KHANJIAN, *Wisdom in Ugarit and in the Ancient Near East with Particular Emphasis on OT Wisdom Literature*, Diss. Claremont, 1974.
—, *Wisdom*, dans *Ras Shamra Parallels* 2 (ed. L.R. FISHER), Roma, 1975, pp. 371-400.
M. LICHTHEIM, *Late Egyptian Wisdom Literature in the International Context. A Study of Demotic Instructions*, Göttingen, 1983.
A. MARZAL, *Gleanings from the Wisdom of Mari*, Roma, 1976.
J.T. SANDERS, *Ben Sira and Demotic Wisdom*, Chico/California, 1983.

Touchant les relations de la sagesse et de l'histoire:
H.J. HERMISSON, *Weisheit und Geschichte*, dans *Festschrift für G. von Rad*, München, 1971, pp. 136-154.
D.F. MORGAN, *Wisdom in the OT Traditions*, Oxford, 1981.
R. RENDTORFF, *Geschichtliches und weisheitliches Denken im AT*, dans *Festschrift für W. Zimmerli*, Göttingen, 1977, pp. 341-353.

Les points de contact du courant de sagesse avec le prophétisme ont fait l'objet de recherches assez neuves:
W.A. BRUEGGEMANN, *The Epistemological Crisis of Israel's two Histories (Jer 9,22-23)*, dans *IW*, pp. 85-105.
J. JENSEN, *The Use of tôrâ by Isaiah: the Debate with the Wisdom Tradition* (CBQ Monograph Series, 3), Washington, 1973.
G.M. LANDES, *Jonah: A Masal?*, dans *IW*, pp. 137-158.
W. MCKANE, *Jeremiah 13,12-14: A Problematic Proverb*, dans *IW*, pp. 107-120.
J. VERMEYLEN, *Le Proto-Isaïe et la Sagesse d'Israël*, dans *La Sagesse de l'Ancien Testament* (ed. M. GILBERT; BETL, 51), Leuven/Gembloux, 1979, pp. 39-58.
J.M. WARD, *The Servant's Knowledge in Isaiah 40-55*, dans *IW*, pp. 121-136.
W. WHEDBEE, *Isaiah and Wisdom*, N.York, Abington, 1971.
H.W. WOLFF, *Micah the Moreshite — The Prophet and his Background*, dans *IW*, pp. 77-84.

Sous l'angle plus directement théologique, on peut consulter:
A. DE PURY, *Sagesse et Révélation dans l'Ancien Testament*, dans *RTP* III/27 (1977) 1-70.
H.J. HERMISSON, *Observations on the Creation Theology in Wisdom*, dans *IW*, pp. 43-57.
R.E. MURPHY, *Wisdom and Creation*, dans *JBL* 104 (1985) 3-11.
K.G. HOGLUND et al. (eds.), *The Listening Heart. Essays in Wisdom and the Psalms in Honor of R.E. Murphy*, Sheffield, 1987.
J. LÉVÊQUE, *L'argument de la création dans le livre de Job*, dans *La création dans l'Orient Ancien*, Congrès ACFEB (Lille 1985), Paris, 1987, pp. 261-299.
H.P. MÜLLER, *Die weisheitliche Lehrerzählung im Alten Testament und seiner Umwelt*, dans *Die Welt des Orients* 9 (1977) 77-98.
—, *Neige der althebräischen «Weisheit». Zum Denken Qohelets*, dans *ZAW* 90 (1978) 238-264.
—, *Die alttestamentliche Weisheitsliteratur*, dans *Der evangelische Erzieher* 37 (1985) 244-256.
A. NICCACI, *La theologia sapienziale nel quadro dell'Antico Testamento*, dans *Studii Biblici Franciscani*, Liber Annuus 34 (1984) 7-24.

Mais, c'est la dimension éthique des livres de sagesse qui a le plus retenu l'attention des chercheurs:

J.G. GAMMIE, *Spatial and Ethical Dualism in Jewish Wisdom and Apocalyptic Literature*, dans *JBL* 93 (1974) 356-385.
J. KENNETH KUNTZ, *The Retribution Motif in Psalmic Wisdom*, dans *ZAW* 89 (1977) 223-233.
B.W. KOVACS, *Is there a Class-Ethic in Proverbs?*, dans *Essays in OT Ethics* (eds. J. CRENSHAW et J.T. WILLIS), N.York, Ktav, 1974, pp. 173-189.
J. LÉVÊQUE, *Les motivations de l'acte moral dans le livre des Proverbes*, dans *Éthique, religion et foi* (Le point théologique, 43), Paris, 1985, pp. 105-121.
—, *Anamnèse et disculpation: la conscience du juste en Job 29-31*, dans *La Sagesse de l'Ancien Testament* (ed. M. GILBERT; BETL, 51), Leuven/Gembloux, 1979, pp. 231-248.
B. MALCHOW, *Wisdom Contibution to Dialogue*, dans *Biblical Theology Bulletin* 13 (1983) 111-115.
J. MARBÖCK, *Im Horizont der Gottesfurcht. Stellungnahmen zu Welt und Leben in der alttestamentlichen Weisheit*, dans *Biblische Notizen* 26 (1985) 47-70.
F. MICHAÉLI, *La sagesse et la crainte de Dieu*, dans *Hokhma* 2 (1976) 35-44.
J.F. PRIEST, *Humanism, Skepticism, and Pessimism in Israel*, dans *JAAR* 36 (1968) 311-326.
E. RUPRECHT, *Leiden und Gerechtigkeit bei Hiob*, dans *ZTK* 73 (1976) 424-445.

Institut Catholique de Paris
21 rue d'Assas
F-75006 Paris

J. LÉVÊQUE

LIST OF ABBREVIATIONS

ACFEB	Association catholique française pour l'étude de la Bible
AOAT	Alter Orient und Altes Testament
ATD	Das Alte Testament Deutsch
BETL	Bibliotheca Ephemeridum Theologicarum Lovaniensium
BHK	*Biblia Hebraica* (ed. R. KITTEL), Stuttgart, 1951
BHS	*Biblia Hebraica Stuttgartensia* (ed. K. ELLIGER & W. RUDOLPH), Stuttgart, 1968ff.
BHTh	Beiträge zur Historische Theologie
BJ	La bible de Jérusalem
BJRL	The Bulletin of the John Rylands University Library of Manchester
BKAT	Biblischer Kommentar AT
BP	Bibliothèque de la Pléiade (*La Bible: l'Ancien Testament*)
BWANT	Beiträge zur Wissenschaft vom Alten und Neuen Testament
BZAW	Beihefte zur Zeitschrift für die alttestamentliche Wissenschaft
CBQ	The Catholic Biblical Quarterly
CCD	Confraternity of Christian Doctrine
CML	G.R. DRIVER, *Canaanite Myths and Legends*, Edinburgh, 1956 (J.C.L. GIBSON, ²1978)
CTA	A. HERDNER, *Corpus des tablettes en cunéiformes alphabétiques découvertes à Ras Shamra-Ugarit de 1929 à 1939*, Paris, 1963
DPfrBl	Deutsches Pfarrerblatt
EvTh	Evangelische Theologie
FRLANT	Forschungen zur Religion und Literatur des Alten und Neuen Testaments
GB	W. GESENIUS, *Hebräisches und aramäisches Handwörterbuch über das Alte Testament*; Revised by F. BUHL, Berlin, ¹⁷1915
GK	W. GESENIUS & E. KAUTZSCH, *Gesenius Hebrew Grammar*; Revised by A.E. COWLEY, Oxford, ²1910
HAT	Handbuch zum Alten Testament
HUCA	Hebrew Union College Annual
ICC	International Critical Commentary of the Holy Scriptures
IW	*Israelite Wisdom. Theological and Literary Essays in Honor of Samuel Terrien* (ed. John G. GAMMIE), New York, 1978.
JAAR	Journal of the American Academy of Religion
JANES	Journal of the Ancient Near Eastern Society (of Columbia University, New York)
JBL	Journal of Biblical Literature
JD	J. LÉVÊQUE, *Job et son Dieu*, Paris, 1970
JSS	Journal of Semitic Studies
JThS	The Journal of Theological Studies
KAI	H. DONNER & W. RÖLLIG, *Kanaanäische und aramäische Inschriften*, Wiesbaden, 1962-1964
KBL	L. KOEHLER & W. BAUMGARTNER, *Lexicon in Veteris Testamenti Libros*, Leiden, 1958

KuD	Kerygma und Dogma
KTU	M. DIETRICH, O. LORETZ, J. SANMARTÍN, *Die keilalphabetischen Texte aus Ugarit* (AOAT, 24), Neukirchen-Vluyn, 1976
NEB	The New English Bible
OTS	Oudtestamentische Studiën
PEQ	Palestine Exploration Quarterly
RB	Revue biblique
RHPhR	Revue d'histoire et de philosophie religieuses
RTP	Revue de théologie et de philosophie
RTR	Reformed Theological Review
RSV	Revised Standard Version
SBS	Stuttgarter Bibelstudien
SPOA	*Les sagesses du Proche-Orient ancien.* Colloque de Strasbourg, mai 1962, Paris, 1963
TB	Theologische Bücherei
THAT	Theologisches Handwörterbuch zum Alten Testament
ThQ	Theologische Quartalschrift
ThSt	Theologische Studien
ThViat	Theologia Viatorum
ThZ	Theologische Zeitschrift
TItSett	Teologia. Revista della facoltà teologica dell'Italia settentrionale
TLZ	Theologische Literaturzeitung
TRE	Theologische Realenzyklopädie
TWAT	Theologisches Wörterbuch zum Alten Testament
TWNT	Theologisches Wörterbuch zum Neuen Testament
UT	C.H. GORDON, *Ugaritic Textbook*, Rome, 1965
VT	Vetus Testamentum
VTS/Suppl	Vetus Testamentum Supplement
VuF	Verkündigung und Forschung
WMANT	Wissenschaftliche Monographien zum Alten und Neuen Testament
ZAW	Zeitschrift für die alttestamentliche Wissenschaft
ZThK	Zeitschrift für Theologie und Kirche

INDEX OF AUTHORS

The exponent indicates full bibliographical references: the numbers refer to the notes and the asterisk to the text.

INDEX OF TEXTS

KTU order:

5. Other texts

Akkadian

Phoenician-Punic

Greek

SELECT INDEX OF SUBJECTS

WORDS AND PHRASES

BIBLIOTHECA EPHEMERIDUM THEOLOGICARUM LOVANIENSIUM

LEUVEN UNIVERSITY PRESS / UITGEVERIJ PEETERS LEUVEN

SERIES I

* = Out of print

*1. *Miscellanea dogmatica in honorem Eximii Domini J. Bittremieux*, 1947.
*2-3. *Miscellanea moralia in honorem Eximii Domini A. Janssen*, 1948.
*4. G. PHILIPS, *La grâce des justes de l'Ancien Testament*, 1948.
*5. G. PHILIPS, *De ratione instituendi tractatum de gratia nostrae sanctificationis*, 1953.
6-7. *Recueil Lucien Cerfaux*, 1954. 504 et 577 p. FB 1000 par tome. Cf. *infra*, n°s 18 et 71.
8. G. THILS, *Histoire doctrinale du mouvement œcuménique*, 1955. Nouvelle édition, 1963. 338 p. FB 135.
*9. J. COPPENS et al., *Études sur l'Immaculée Conception*, 1955.
*10. J.A. O'DONOHOE, *Tridentine Seminary Legislation. Its Sources and its Formation*, 1957.
*11. G. THILS, *Orientations de la théologie*, 1958.
*12-13. J. COPPENS, A. DESCAMPS, É. MASSAUX (éd.), *Sacra Pagina. Miscellanea Biblica Congressus Internationalis Catholici de Re Biblica*, 1959.
*14. *Adrien VI, le premier Pape de la contre-réforme*, 1959.
*15. F. CLAEYS BOUUAERT, *Les déclarations et serments imposés par la loi civile aux membres du clergé belge sous le Directoire (1795-1801)*, 1960.
*16. G. THILS, *La «Théologie Œcuménique». Notion-Formes-Démarches*, 1960.
17. G. THILS, *Primauté pontificale et prérogatives épiscopales. «Potestas ordinaria» au Concile du Vatican*, 1961. 103 p. FB 50.
*18. *Recueil Lucien Cerfaux*, t. III, 1962. Cf. *infra*, n° 71.
*19. *Foi et réflexion philosophique. Mélanges F. Grégoire*, 1961.
*20. *Mélanges G. Ryckmans*, 1963.
21. G. THILS, *L'infaillibilité du peuple chrétien «in credendo»*, 1963. 67 p. FB 50.
*22. J. FÉRIN & L. JANSSENS, *Progestogènes et morale conjugale*, 1963.
*23. *Collectanea Moralia in honorem Eximii Domini A. Janssen*, 1964.
24. H. CAZELLES (éd.), *De Mari à Qumrân. L'Ancien Testament. Son milieu. Ses Écrits. Ses relectures juives* (Hommage J. Coppens, I), 1969. 158*-370 p. FB 900.
25. I. DE LA POTTERIE (éd.). *De Jésus aux évangiles. Tradition et rédaction dans les évangiles synoptiques* (Hommage J. Coppens, II), 1967. 272 p. FB 700.
26. G. THILS & R.E. BROWN (éd.), *Exégèse et théologie* (Hommage J. Coppens, III), 1968. 328 p. FB 700.
27. J. COPPENS (éd.), *Ecclesia a Spiritu sancto edocta. Hommage à Mgr G. Philips*, 1970. 640 p. FB 1000.

28. J. Coppens (éd.), *Sacerdoce et célibat. Études historiques et théologiques*, 1971. 740 p. FB 700.
29. M. Didier (éd.), *L'évangile selon Matthieu. Rédaction et théologie*, 1971. 432 p. FB 1000.
*30. J. Kempeneers, *Le Cardinal van Roey en son temps*, 1971.

Series II

31. F. Neirynck, *Duality in Mark. Contributions to the Study of the Markan Redaction*, 1972. Revised Edition with Supplementary Notes, 1988. 252 p. FB 1200.
32. F. Neirynck (éd.), *L'évangile de Luc. Problèmes littéraires et théologiques*, 1973. Nouvelle édition augmentée, 1989.
33. C. Brekelmans (éd.), *Questions disputées d'Ancien Testament. Méthode et théologie*, 1974. *Continuing Questions in Old Testament Method and Theology*. Revised and Enlarged Edition by M. Vervenne, 1989. 246 p. FB 1200.
34. M. Sabbe (éd.), *L'évangile selon Marc. Tradition et rédaction*, 1974. Nouvelle édition augmentée, 1988. 601 p. FB 2400.
35. B. Willaert (éd.), *Philosophie de la religion – Godsdienstfilosofie. Miscellanea Albert Dondeyne*, 1974. Nouvelle édition, 1987. 458 p. FB 1600.
36. G. Philips, *L'union personnelle avec le Dieu vivant. Essai sur l'origine et le sens de la grâce créée*, 1974. Édition révisée, 1989. 299 p. FB 1000.
37. F. Neirynck, in collaboration with T. Hansen and F. Van Segbroeck, *The Minor Agreements of Matthew and Luke against Mark with a Cumulative List*, 1974. 330 p. FB 900.
38. J. Coppens, *Le Messianisme et sa relève prophétique. Les anticipations vétérotestamentaires. Leur accomplissement en Jésus*, 1974. Édition révisée, 1989. xiii-265 p. FB 1000.
39. D. Senior, *The Passion Narrative according to Matthew. A Redactional Study*, 1975. New impression, 1982. 440 p. FB 1000.
40. J. Dupont (éd.), *Jésus aux origines de la christologie*, 1975. Nouvelle édition augmentée, 1989. 458 p. FB 1500.
41. J. Coppens (éd.), *La notion biblique de Dieu*, 1976. Réimpression, 1985. 519 p. FB 1600.
42. J. Lindemans & H. Demeester (éd.), *Liber Amicorum Monseigneur W. Onclin*, 1976. 396 p. FB 1000.
43. R.E. Hoeckman (éd.), *Pluralisme et œcuménisme en recherches théologiques. Mélanges offerts au R.P. Dockx, O.P.*, 1976. 316 p. FB 1000.
44. M. de Jonge (éd.), *L'Évangile de Jean. Sources, rédaction, théologie*, 1977. Réimpression, 1987. 416 p. FB 1500.
45. E.J.M. van Eijl (éd.), *Facultas S. Theologiae Lovaniensis 1432-1797. Bijdragen tot haar geschiedenis. Contributions to its History. Contributions à son histoire*, 1977. 570 p. FB 1700.
46. M. Delcor (éd.), *Qumrân. Sa piété, sa théologie et son milieu*, 1978. 432 p. FB 1700.
47. M. Caudron (éd.), *Faith and Society. Foi et Société. Geloof en maatschappij. Acta Congressus Internationalis Theologici Lovaniensis 1976*, 1978. 304 p. FB 1150.
48. J. Kremer (éd.), *Les Actes des Apôtres. Traditions, rédaction, théologie*, 1979. 590 p. FB 1700.

49. F. NEIRYNCK, avec la collaboration de J. DELOBEL, T. SNOY, G. VAN BELLE, F. VAN SEGBROECK, *Jean et les Synoptiques. Examen critique de l'exégèse de M.-É. Boismard*, 1979. XII-428 p. FB 1400.
50. J. COPPENS, *La relève apocalyptique du messianisme royal*. I. *La royauté – Le règne – Le royaume de Dieu. Cadre de la relève apocalyptique*, 1979. 325 p. FB 1000.
51. M. GILBERT (éd.), *La Sagesse de l'Ancien Testament*, 1979. 420 p. FB 1700.
52. B. DEHANDSCHUTTER, *Martyrium Polycarpi. Een literair-kritische studie*, 1979. 296 p. FB 1000.
53. J. LAMBRECHT (éd.), *L'Apocalypse johannique et l'Apocalyptique dans le Nouveau Testament*, 1980. 458 p. FB 1400.
54. P.-M. BOGAERT (éd.), *Le Livre de Jérémie. Le prophète et son milieu. Les oracles et leur transmission*, 1981. 408 p. FB 1500.
55. J. COPPENS, *La relève apocalyptique du messianisme royal*. III. *Le Fils de l'homme néotestamentaire*, 1981. XIV-192 p. FB 800.
56. J. VAN BAVEL & M. SCHRAMA (éd.), *Jansénius et le Jansénisme dans les Pays-Bas. Mélanges Lucien Ceyssens*, 1982. 247 p. FB 1000.
57. J.H. WALGRAVE, *Selected Writings – Thematische geschriften. Thomas Aquinas, J.H. Newman, Theologia Fundamentalis*. Edited by G. DE SCHRIJVER & J.J. KELLY, 1982. XLIII-425 p. FB 1400.
58. F. NEIRYNCK & F. VAN SEGBROECK, avec la collaboration de E. MANNING, *Ephemerides Theologicae Lovanienses 1924-1981. Tables générales. (Bibliotheca Ephemeridum Theologicarum Lovaniensium 1947-1981)*, 1982. 400 p. FB 1600.
59. J. DELOBEL (éd.), *Logia. Les paroles de Jésus – The Sayings of Jesus. Mémorial Joseph Coppens*, 1982. 647 p. FB 2000.
60. F. NEIRYNCK, *Evangelica. Gospel Studies – Études d'évangile. Collected Essays*. Edited by F. VAN SEGBROECK, 1982. XIX-1036 p. FB 2000.
61. J. COPPENS, *La relève apocalyptique du messianisme royal*. II. *Le Fils d'homme vétéro- et intertestamentaire*. Édition posthume par J. LUST, 1983. XVII-272 p. FB 1000.
62. J.J. KELLY, *Baron Friedrich von Hügel's Philosophy of Religion*, 1983. 232 p. FB 1500.
63. G. DE SCHRIJVER, *Le merveilleux accord de l'homme et de Dieu. Étude de l'analogie de l'être chez Hans Urs von Balthasar*, 1983. 344 p. FB 1500.
64. J. GROOTAERS & J.A. SELLING, *The 1980 Synod of Bishops: «On the Role of the Family». An Exposition of the Event and an Analysis of Its Texts*. Preface by Prof. emeritus L. JANSSENS, 1983. 375 p. FB 1500.
65. F. NEIRYNCK & F. VAN SEGBROECK, *New Testament Vocabulary. A Companion Volume to the Concordance*, 1984. XVI-494 p. FB 2000.
66. R.F. COLLINS, *Studies on the First Letter to the Thessalonians*, 1984. XI-415 p. FB 1500.
67. A. PLUMMER, *Conversations with Dr. Döllinger 1870-1890*. Edited with Introduction and Notes by R. BOUDENS, with the collaboration of L. KENIS, 1985. LIV-360 p. FB 1800.
68. N. LOHFINK (éd.), *Das Deuteronomium. Entstehung, Gestalt und Botschaft / Deuteronomy. Origin, Form and Message*, 1985. XI-382 p. FB 2000.

69. P.F. FRANSEN, *Hermeneutics of the Councils and Other Studies*. Collected by H.E. MERTENS & F. DE GRAEVE, 1985. 543 p. FB 1800.
70. J. DUPONT, *Études sur les Évangiles synoptiques*. Présentées par F. NEIRYNCK, 1985. 2 tomes, XXI-IX-1210 p. FB 2800.
71. *Recueil Lucien Cerfaux*, t. III, 1962. Nouvelle édition revue et complétée, 1985. LXXX-458 p. FB 1600.
72. J. GROOTAERS, *Primauté et collégialité. Le dossier de Gérard Philips sur la Nota Explicativa Praevia (Lumen gentium, Chap. III)*. Présenté avec introduction historique, annotations et annexes. Préface de G. THILS, 1986. 222 p. FB 1000.
73. A. VANHOYE (éd.), *L'apôtre Paul. Personnalité, style et conception du ministère*, 1986. XIII-470 p. FB 2600.
74. J. LUST (éd.), *Ezekiel and His Book. Textual and Literary Criticism and their Interrelation*, 1986. X-387 p. FB 2700.
75. É. MASSAUX, *Influence de l'Évangile de saint Matthieu sur la littérature chrétienne avant saint Irénée*. Réimpression anastatique présentée par F. NEIRYNCK. Supplément: *Bibliographie 1950-1985*, par B. DEHANDSCHUTTER, 1986. XXVII-850 p. FB 2500.
76. L. CEYSSENS & J.A.G. TANS, *Autour de l'Unigenitus. Recherches sur la genèse de la Constitution*, 1987. XXVI-845 p. FB 2500.
77. A. DESCAMPS, *Jésus et l'Église. Études d'exégèse et de théologie*. Préface de Mgr A. HOUSSIAU, 1987. XLV-641 p. FB 2500.
78. J. DUPLACY, *Études de critique textuelle du Nouveau Testament*. Présentées par J. DELOBEL, 1987. XXVII-431 p. FB 1800.
79. E.J.M. VAN EIJL (éd.), *L'image de C. Jansénius jusqu'à la fin du XVIIIe siècle*, 1987. 258 p. FB 1250.
80. E. BRITO, *La Création selon Schelling. Universum*, 1987. XXXV-646 p. FB 2980.
81. J. VERMEYLEN (ed.), *The Book of Isaiah – Le Livre d'Isaïe. Les oracles et leurs relectures. Unité et complexité de l'ouvrage*, 1989. X-472 p. FB 2700.
82. G. VAN BELLE, *Johannine Bibliography 1966-1985. A Cumulative Bibliography on the Fourth Gospel*, 1988. XVII-563 p. FB 2700.
83. J.A. SELLING (ed.), *Personalist Morals. Essays in Honor of Professor Louis Janssens*, 1988. VIII-344 p. FB 1200.
84. M.-É. BOISMARD, *Moïse ou Jésus. Essai de christologie johannique*, 1988. XVI-241 p. FB 1000.
85. J.A. DICK, *The Malines Conversations Revisited*, 1989. 278 p. FB 1500.
86. J.-M. SEVRIN (ed.), *The New Testament in Early Christianity – La réception des écrits néotestamentaires dans le christianisme primitif*, 1989. XVI-406 p. FB 2500.
87. R.F. COLLINS (ed.), *The Thessalonian Correspondence*, 1989.
88. F. VAN SEGBROECK, *The Gospel of Luke. A Cumulative Bibliography 1973-1988*, 1989. 241 p. FB 1200.
89. G. THILS, *Primauté et Infaillibilité du Pape à Vatican I. Études d'ecclésiologie*, 1989.
90. A. VERGOTE, *Explorations de l'espace théologique. Études de théologie et de philosophie de la religon*, 1989.

ORIENTALISTE, P.B. 41, B-3000 Leuven